Gender, Culture, and Ethnicity

Gender, Culture, and Ethnicity
Current Research About Women and Men

Letitia Anne Peplau

Sheri Chapman DeBro

Rosemary C. Veniegas

Pamela L. Taylor

University of California, Los Angeles

Mayfield Publishing Company
Mountain View, California
London • Toronto

Library of Congress Cataloging-in-Publication Data

Gender, culture, and ethnicity : current research about women and men /
    [edited by] Letitia Ann Peplau . . . [et al.].
        p.   cm.
     ISBN 0-7674-0521-8
       1. Women—Research—United States.   2. Women—United States—
Psychology.   3. Men—Research—United States.   4. Sex Role—
Research—United States.   5. Ethnicity—Research—United States.
     I. Peplau, Letitia Anne.
HQ1181.U5G45   1998
305.3′07′073—dc21   98-19788
                                                 CIP

Mayfield Publishing Company
1280 Villa Street
Mountain View, CA 94041

Manufactured in the United States of America
10 9 8 7 6 5 4 3 2 1

Sponsoring editor, Franklin Graham; production editor, Melissa Kreischer; manuscript editor, Elizabeth von Radics; design manager, Susan Breitbard; text and cover designer, Detta Penna; cover art, *Heat Wave*, © 1993 by Gloria Hansen, Highstown, NJ; manufacturing manager, Randy Hurst. The text was set in 10/12 Berkeley by G & S Typesetters, Inc. and printed on acid-free 45# Baycoat Velvet by Banta Book Group.

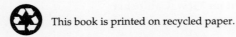 This book is printed on recycled paper.

Contents

Part VI: Sexuality and Childbirth

Part VII: Violence

Part VIII: Physical and Mental Health

Part IX: Toward More Inclusive Research Methods

Preface

This anthology brings together the best available research on the joint effects of gender, culture, and ethnicity in people's lives. This unique volume presents work by leading social science scholars and includes studies of ethnic minority populations in the United States as well as cross-cultural comparisons. The book is designed for use by undergraduate and graduate students enrolled in courses in the psychology of women; sex and gender; women's studies; and related topics. The readings present students with primary source materials that can serve as a companion to a standard textbook, or they can be used as the core readings in a course focusing on gender, culture, and ethnicity. The articles included in this volume were selected with several criteria in mind.

First, we made every effort to chose articles that students will find interesting, readable, and informative. Articles included in this collection were read and critiqued by undergraduates and by college instructors before final selections were made.

Second, we selected a set of articles that is comprehensive and balanced in content. The articles cover the range of standard topics addressed in courses in the psychology of women or gender. The volume includes both conceptual papers that review a body of literature and empirical research studies. The articles present important work by prominent researchers and consequently acquaint readers with outstanding research using diverse methods. For example, the collection includes both quantitative and qualitative methods. Instructors who use anthologies to provide their students with primary sources that illustrate different research approaches will find that the reader serves this purpose well.

Third, this collection represents a broad spectrum of cultural and ethnic populations. Major emphasis is given to African American, Asian American, and Latino/Hispanic groups in the United States. In addition, several articles present cross-cultural research from Mexico, Israel, Korea, New Guinea, and the Philippines. Several articles address issues of social class. Although some of the selections focus specifically on women of color, many of the articles address issues affecting both women and men.

Format and Pedagogical Features

This collection comprises 24 reprinted articles plus an introductory chapter and resource guide written by the editors. The articles are organized into nine thematic sections.

The book includes several pedagogical features:

- Most important, the articles themselves have been selected with student readers in mind, and were "pretested" and approved by undergraduates at UCLA.

- The book begins with two introductory chapters that explain key concepts such as culture and ethnicity, outline the nature of sociocultural analyses of gender, and set the stage for the articles that follow.

- Each article is preceded by a brief introduction. The purpose of these introductions is to alert students to the main issues in the article, to explain terms that may be unfamiliar, and to raise questions for students to consider while reading the article.

- Each article is followed by a set of "Questions for Thought," designed to stimulate critical thinking about the material. Students are asked to examine the arguments and evidence presented by the authors, to consider directions for future research, and to think about the practical implications of the work. These questions can be used to stimulate class discussion or as the basis for written assignments.

- The book includes a "Guide to Resources About Gender, Culture, and Ethnicity" that contains suggestions for instructors and students about additional materials. These include resources in the professional research literature as well as Internet Web sites, videos, films, literature, and other materials that can be used to enrich understanding of gender, culture, and ethnicity.

Acknowledgments

We are grateful to the many UCLA undergraduates who provided valuable comments about the articles included in this collection. Jennifer Frank provided much-needed assistance with library research. Erica Mimran and Kristin Beals also provided helpful comments. We thank the following reviewers for their time and insightful suggestions: Patricia L. N. Donat, Mississippi University for Women; Susan H. Franzblau, Fayetteville State University; M. Paz Galupo, Towson State University, and Paulette J. Leonard, University of Central Arkansas. We appreciate the support and encouragement of our partners: Steve Gordon, Richard DeBro, Cora Gamulo and Victor Mc-Frazier. Anne Peplau's participation in a faculty seminar sonsored by the Ford Foundation Ethnic Women's Curriculum Transformation Project at UCLA in 1989 provided a valuable introduction to scholarship on gender, culture, and ethnicity.

About the Editors

Letitia Anne Peplau is professor of psychology at the University of California, Los Angeles. Anne received her BA in psychology from Brown University and her PhD in social psychology from Harvard University. In 1973 she began teaching at UCLA, where she has developed both undergraduate and graduate courses on the psychology of gender. Long active in women's studies, Anne has served as co-director of the UCLA Center for the Study of Women and as director of the graduate program in social psychology. A past president of the International Society for the Study of Personal Relationships, Anne is the 1997 recipient of the Distinguished Scientific Achievement Award of the Society for the Scientific Study of Sexuality. Anne has published numerous articles and book chapters on such topics as friendship, heterosexual dating, homosexual relationships, social power, loneliness, and social support. Her other books include *Sociocultural Perspectives in Social Psychology* (with Shelley E. Taylor), *Social Psychology* (with Shelley E. Taylor and David O. Sears), *Loneliness: A Sourcebook of Current Theory, Research, and Therapy* (with Daniel Perlman), *Close Relationships* (with Harold H. Kelley, et al.), and an introductory text in *Psychology* (with Zick Rubin and Peter Salovey).

Sheri Chapman DeBro received her BA with departmental honors in psychology from UCLA. Her honors thesis earned the Outstanding Paper Award for Undergraduate Research given by the Western Psychological Association. Sheri received her PhD in social psychology from Claremont Graduate University, where she studied the sexual relationships of heterosexual women and men. She has published research articles and book chapters on heterosexual dating and the use of condoms to promote safer sex. Currently a visiting scholar at UCLA, Sheri has taught courses on the psychology of gender through UCLA Extension and participated in several "Teaching of the Psychology of Women" Workshops sponsored by Division 35 of the American Psychological Association (APA).

Rosemary C. Veniegas received her BA in psychology with a minor in women's studies from the University of Hawai'i. She is currently a PhD student in social psychology at UCLA, conducting doctoral research on the joint influence of ethnic identity and gender identity on women's reactions to perceived discrimination. Her dissertation research is funded by a grant from the UCLA Institute of American Cultures. Rosemary's research interests include discrimination related to gender, ethnicity, and sexual orientation. In 1997 Rosemary received the Student Research Award given by the Association for Women in Psychology and the Division on the Psychology of Women of the APA for her journal article "Power and the Quality of Same-Sex Friendships." A past recipient of an APA Minority Research Training Fellowship, Rosemary is currently the graduate student mentor for underrepresented students participating in the UCLA Psychology Department's undergraduate research training program.

Pamela L. Taylor received her BA in psychology in 1993 from Johnson C. Smith University, a historically Black university located in Charlotte, North Carolina. She received her Ph.D. in social psychology at UCLA in June 1998. Pamela's research has examined the combined influence of gender and ethnicity on group identity, group consciousness, perceived discrimination, and political attitudes. Previously, she received a minority fellowship award from the National Science Foundation. Pamela received a dissertation fellowship from UCLA's Center for African American Studies to complete her study of the impact of gender roles on the marital attitudes of single African Americans.

Guide to Resources About Gender, Culture, and Ethnicity

Rosemary C. Veniegas

Pamela L. Taylor

Letitia Anne Peplau

We hope that the articles in this anthology will promote interest in the interrelationships among gender, ethnicity, and culture. This guide presents a variety of resources that can enrich understanding of the lives of women and men from diverse cultural backgrounds. The guide begins with online computer resources offering information about ethnic minority and feminist topics. Next we provide brief descriptions of instructional films and videos that explore important aspects of women's and men's lives both in the United States and in other countries. The subsequent section describes fiction and biographies that offer vivid examples of the life experiences of women and men from diverse ethnic and cultural backgrounds. Next we list currently available bibliographies about research on gender and ethnic minority populations in the United States. The concluding sections offer many suggestions about professional books and journals relevant to the study of gender, culture, and ethnicity.

Computer and Online Resources

The Web sites and online resources listed in this section were located using Netscape Navigator in April 1998. As with many electronic sources, these addresses may change. The Web sites are listed alphabetically by topic.

African American Male Research   This Web site provides summaries of the latest social science research on African American men. The site also includes information on economic, legislative, and political developments relevant to African American men's lives. Web site

    http://www.tomco.net/~afrimale/

American Indian Institute   This organization manages the Native American Research Information Service, a computerized database listing published and unpublished research from 1969 to the present on American Indians. For information contact the University of Oklahoma College of Continuing Education, 555 Constitution Street, Suite 237, Norman, OK 73072-7820; phone (405) 325-4127; fax (405) 325-7757; e-mail aii@cce.occe.ou.edu. This Web site charges a fee for searches. Web site
http://www.occe.ou.edu/aii/

Asian American Studies Resources   This site provides numerous links to information on Asian American articles and to research institutes and relevant organizations. Web site
http://www.lib.uci.edu/home/collect/interdis/asamer.html

Chicano/Latino Network   This site provides information on Chicano/Latino issues including health, sexuality, literature, and events. A separate Web site provides information on issues relevant to Chicanas/Latinas. Web sites
http://latino.sscnet.ucla.edu *and* http://clnet.ucr.edu/

Resources for African American Women   This site provides links to sites offering information about African American women from both feminist sources and African American sources. Web site
http://www.uic.edu/~vjpitch/

South Asian Women's Network   This site has information relevant to south Asian women, including news, events, organizations, books, films, and health. Web site
http://www.umiacs.umd.edu/users/sawweb/sawnet/

Womanist Studies Consortium   This Web site provides links to sites by and for women of color. Topics covered include activism, media, and health. Web site
http://ash.cc.swarthmore.edu/capstone/w.color.html

Womanist Theory and Research   This Web site is a forum for exchanging feminist research, theory, and ideas among women-of-color scholars and students in the humanities, social sciences, education, theology, law, medicine, politics, journalism, art, information technologies, and telecommunications. Web site
http://www.uga.edu/~womanist

Films and Audiovisual Material

A growing number of films address issues of gender, culture, and ethnicity. Several successful wide-release movies are available in local video-rental stores. These include *Boyz 'n the Hood; Eat, Drink, Man, Woman; Mi Familia (My Family); Selena;* and *Waiting to Exhale.* This section provides a sampling of the many instructional videos available for rental or purchase. The catalogs and brochures of many film distributors now categorize their offerings by gender and by ethnicity.

Anderson, M. (Director). (1970). *I am somebody.* 28 minutes. This video chronicles a 1969 strike by 400 Black women hospital workers in South Carolina seeking union recognition and wage increases. After 113 days and several confrontations with the National Guard and the U.S. government, the hospital met the striking women's requests. This is useful for discussions about employment and the influence of socioeconomic status on women's lives. (Available from First Run/Icarus Films, 153 Waverly Place, Sixth Floor, New York, NY 10014; phone [212] 727-1711)

Bread and Roses Cultural Project (Producer). (1997). *Women of hope: Latinas abriendo camino.* 28 minutes. Twelve Latinas in the U.S. are profiled, including Miriam Colon, founder of the Puerto Rican Traveling Theater, and Sandra Cisneros, the noted writer. The women share their life stories and the challenges they faced in pursuing their goals. A study guide is available for purchase. (Available from Films for the Humanities and Sciences, P.O. Box 2053, Princeton, NJ 08543-2053; phone [800] 257-5126; fax [609] 275-3767)

Choy, C. (Producer/Director), Kim, E. (Producer), & Kim-Gibson, D. S. (Producer/ Director). (1993). *Sa-I-Gu: From Korean women's perspectives.* 36 minutes. This video includes interviews with Korean American women whose family businesses were destroyed in the 1992 Los Angeles riots. This video is relevant to discussions of ethnic relations and racism in the U.S. (Available from Crosscurrent Media, 346 9th Street, San Francisco, CA 94103; phone [415] 552-9550)

Cross-cultural comparison: Gender roles. (1994). 120 minutes. This two-part video discusses women's roles in Hindu and Islamic cultures and compares institutionalized attempts to shape gender roles across several cultures, including China, the former Soviet Union, and Sweden. (Available from Insight Media, 2162 Broadway, New York, NY 10024; phone [212] 721-6316; fax [212] 799-5309)

Egansteiner, E. (1996). *The dream becomes a reality(?).* 43 minutes. This video documents the experiences of six young women who fought in the 30-year struggle for Eritrean independence from Ethiopia. They discuss gender equality in the Eritrean People's Liberation Front, their combat experiences, and their views on women's roles. This video is relevant to discussions of women in combat and gender behavior across cultures. (Available from University of California Extension Center for Media and Independent Learning, 2000 Center Street, 4th Floor, Berkeley, CA 94704; phone [510] 642-0460)

Geddes, C. (Director). (1989). *Doctor, lawyer, Indian chief.* 29 minutes. Five Native American women talk about their careers: a band leader, an employment counselor, a government official, a deck hand on a fishing boat, and a lawyer. The women discuss the importance for their careers of Native spiritual beliefs, rituals, and art. (Available from Women Make Movies, Inc., 462 Broadway, Suite 500 D, New York, NY 10013; phone [212] 925-0606)

Genasci, S., & Velasco, D. (Directors). (1990). *Troubled harvest.* 30 minutes. This award-winning video depicts the lives of Mexican and Central American women who harvest crops in the United States. They are separated from their families by U.S. immigration policies and are often exposed to dangerous pesticides. This video is relevant to discussions of immigrant women and work. (Available from Women Make Movies, Inc., 462 Broadway, Suite 500 D, New York, NY 10013; phone [212] 925-0606)

Great Black women. (1997). 52 minutes. Black women leaders, including Coretta Scott King, Shirley Chisolm, and Oprah Winfrey are featured in this video about how Black women have achieved success in spite of adversity. (Available from Films for the Humanities and Sciences, P.O. Box 2053, Princeton, NJ 08543-2053; phone [800] 257-5126; fax [609] 275-3767)

Johnson, A. L. (Director). (1996). ***Evelyn Williams.*** 29 minutes. This documentary chronicles the life of a woman who struggled against race and class oppression. She describes her experiences with the Ku Klux Klan, the U.S. military, and aggressive land developers. (Available from Appalshop Video, 360EV Madison Street, Whitesburg, KY 41858; phone [606] 633-0108)

Latina women. (1992). 26 minutes. This video explores the diversity of experiences of Latina women. Topics include work, child rearing, dual-earner families, machismo, Latina feminism, and Latina professionals. (Available from Films for the Humanities and Sciences, P.O. Box 2053, Princeton, NJ 08543-2053; phone [800] 257-5126; fax [609] 275-3767)

Marriage and the Chinese family. 30 minutes. This video introduces viewers to marriage and child-rearing practices in mainland China. Topics include the high valuation of male children and changes in gender roles since the Communist takeover of 1949. (Available from Insight Media, 2162 Broadway, New York, NY 10024; phone [212] 721-6316; fax [212] 799-5309)

Nakasako, S. (1984). ***Talking history.*** 30 minutes. This video uses oral histories and film footage to describe the experiences of Chinese, Filipino, Japanese, Korean, and Laotian women who immigrated to America. (Available from Crosscurrent Media, 346 9th Street, San Francisco, CA 94103; phone [415] 552-9550)

Not a job for a nice Jewish girl: On becoming a woman rabbi. (1997). 60 minutes. This video portrays a young woman who became one of only three female rabbis in Australia. Her experiences in Judaism are relevant to discussions of women and organized religion. (Available from Films for the Humanities and Sciences, P.O. Box 2053, Princeton, NJ 08543-2053; phone [800] 257-5126; fax [609] 275-3767)

Ong, S. (Producer). (1992). ***Because this is about love: A portrait of gay and lesbian marriage.*** 28 minutes. This video depicts the lives of five gay and lesbian couples from various ethnic backgrounds. (Available from Filmakers Library, 124 E. 40th Street, Suite 901, New York, NY 10016; phone [212] 808-4980; fax [212] 808-4983)

Onwurah, N. (Director). (1993). **And I still rise.** 30 minutes. This video examines stereotypes of Black women's sexuality as depicted in popular culture. (Available from Women Make Movies, Inc., 462 Broadway, Suite 500 D, New York, NY 10013; phone [212] 925-0606)

Queer son. (1995). 48 minutes. The parents of gay and lesbian children from different ethnic backgrounds react to their children's sexual orientations. (Available from Frameline, 346 Ninth Street, San Francisco, CA 94103-3809; phone [415] 703-8654)

The politics of love: In Black and White. 33 minutes. American college-student couples talk about the trials and joys of being in interethnic relationships. Also included are interviews with Black and White students who oppose interracial dating. (Available from Insight Media, 2162 Broadway, New York, NY 10024; phone [212] 721-6316; fax [212] 799-5309)

Pozzan, C. (Director). (1990). **As the mirror burns.** 30 minutes. This video shows Vietnamese women who participated in guerrilla activities during the war in Vietnam. It can be used to discuss the impact of war on women's roles. (Available from Women Make Movies, Inc., 462 Broadway, Suite 500 D, New York, NY 10013; phone [212] 925-0606)

Quaregna, P., & Souleymane, M. (Directors). (1995). **Women of the Sahel.** 52 minutes. In the Sahel region of Nigeria, women have major responsibility for the economic and physical survival of their families. Their husbands frequently leave for seasonal work in other regions. Women manufacture goods, establish cooperative organizations, and support one another. (Available from First Run/Icarus Films, 153 Waverly Place, Sixth Floor, New York, NY 10014; phone [212] 727-1711)

Saeed-Vafa, M. (Director). (1994). **A Tajik woman.** 20 minutes. This video explores the experiences of Muslim women from Afghanistan and Iran who now live in the United States. The women talk about war, revolution, the loss of their homeland, and the challenges of following fundamentalist Islamic values. (Available from Women Make Movies, Inc., 462 Broadway, Suite 500 D, New York, NY 10013; phone [212] 925-0606)

Sanchez-Padilla, B. (Director). (1993). **De mujer a mujer (From woman to woman).** 46 minutes. Latinas discuss their experiences and views on sexuality, male-female relationships, teen pregnancy, and gay identity. (Available from Women Make Movies, Inc., 462 Broadway, Suite 500 D, New York, NY 10013; phone [212] 925-0606)

Sex and marriage. (1994). 30 minutes. This video examines customs and rituals related to sex and marriage in several Western and non-Western cultures. It also explores cultural and economic explanations about the structure of marriage and sexuality. (Available from Insight Media, 2162 Broadway, New York, NY 10024; phone [212] 721-6316; fax [212] 799-5309)

Taghioff, M. (1992). **Home.** 37 minutes. This is a video about gender roles in India. Two women share their lives with the videographer: one an Indian American journalist returning to India for the first time since she was teenager, and the other a student who disagrees with her father's ideas about women's roles. (Available from Crosscurrent Media, 346 9th Street, San Francisco, CA 94103; phone [415] 552-9550)

Wah, L. M., & Hunter, M. (Directors). (1994). **The color of fear.** 90 minutes. A discussion among eight men of Anglo, African, Asian, and Latino descent about the effects of racism on their lives. (Available from Stir-Fry Productions, 470 Third Street, Oakland, CA 94607; phone [510] 419-3930)

Women: A true story. (1997). 47 minutes each tape. This six-part series profiles women from Brazil, Kenya, the Philippines, Russia, and the United States. Their backgrounds range from beauty queens to political leaders. (Available from Films for the Humanities and Sciences, P.O. Box 2053, Princeton, NJ 08543-2053; phone [800] 257-5126; fax [609] 275-3767)

Zaman, N. (Director). (1994). **Beyond Black and White.** 28 minutes. Six women of biracial backgrounds discuss racism, media images of women of color, and whether the U.S. Census Bureau should add the category of "mixed ethnicity." (Available from Women Make Movies, Inc., 462 Broadway, Suite 500 D, New York, NY 10013; phone [212] 925-0606)

Fiction and Biographies

Personal essays and biographies provide vivid illustrations of the reciprocal influences of gender, culture, and ethnicity. This list includes recently published fiction and biographies along with classic books portraying the lives of men and women from varied cultural backgrounds. Books available in paperback are noted.

Allen, P. G. (1986). **The sacred hoop: Recovering the feminine in American Indian traditions.** Boston: Beacon Press. This collection of poetry, essays, and literary analyses by the noted American Indian writer explores gender and identity among Native American women. Available in paperback.

Angelou, M. (1983). **I know why the caged bird sings.** New York: Bantam. The autobiography of Maya Angelou describes the hardships faced by many African Americans during the first half of this century. It is a rich and detailed look into the lifestyle, thoughts, and feelings of a great writer. Available in paperback.

Brisco, C. (1996). **Big girls don't cry.** New York: Ballantine Books. Naomi Jefferson was raised in a nice Washington, D.C., neighborhood. As a teenager she worried more about being a virgin than about what it meant to be a Black woman in a racist society. After the death of her brother, who was on his way to a civil rights demonstration, she discovers more about herself and the world she had been protected from. Available in paperback.

Brooks, G. (1996). ***Nine parts desire: The hidden worlds of Islamic women.*** New York: Anchor Books. A woman examines how male power and privilege have shaped the political, cultural, and religious lives of women in Muslim society.

Cisneros, S. (1984). ***The house on Mango Street.*** New York: Vintage. A young Latina growing up in Chicago, Esperanza Cordero knows that neither her family nor society expect her to succeed. Rather than live down to their expectations, she struggles to define her own identity. Available in paperback.

Crow Dog, M. (1990). ***Lakota woman.*** New York: HarperPerennial. This is a story about a woman raised on an American Indian reservation who becomes active in the American Indian movement of the 1960s and 1970s. In fighting to end the cycle of alcoholism and institutionalized racism on the reservation, she attempts to reconcile her identities as a woman and an American Indian. Available in paperback.

Divakaruni, C. B. (1996). ***Arranged marriage: Stories.*** New York: Anchor Books. This collection of fictional stories about women in arranged marriages in India explores such topics as the clash between traditional and modern values, sexuality, and family relationships. Available in paperback.

Engle, M. (1995). ***Skywriting.*** New York: Bantam Books. Carmen Peregrin and her mother await the arrival of her brother who escaped from Cuba on a raft. This novel depicts the hopes and fears of many women who immigrate to the United States. Available in paperback.

Erdrich, L. (1984). ***Love medicine.*** New York: HarperPerennial. This novel follows the lives of two American Indian families who left their ancestral lands. It also describes the experiences of families who chose never to leave ancestral lands. The story depicts the challenges of resolving conflicts between traditional culture and contemporary society. Available in paperback.

Featherston, E. (Ed.). (1994). ***Skin deep: Women writing on color, culture, and identity.*** Freedom, CA: Crossing Press. Essays by several authors address identity formation related to skin color, social class, regional affiliation, multiple ethnicity, and age. Available in paperback.

Giddings, P. (1985). ***When and where I enter: The impact of Black women on race and sex in America.*** New York: Bantam Books. This collection of portraits of Black women in U.S. history includes Ida Wells-Barnett, a famous anti-lynching journalist, and Shirley Chisolm, who was a former presidential candidate. Available in paperback.

Gorkin, M., & Othman, R. (Eds.). (1996). ***Three mothers, three daughters: Palestinian women's stories.*** Berkeley: University of California Press. Oral histories from six Palestinian women present their views on courtship, motherhood, sex, and religion. The narratives portray the lives of women in the midst of war in East Jerusalem, in a West Bank refugee camp, and in Arab villages within Israel.

Hayslip, L. L. (1993). ***Child of war: Woman of peace.*** New York: Anchor Books. This is the autobiography of Le Ly Hayslip, who journeyed from Vietnam to the United States to marry an American man. Her description of adjusting to a new culture raises issues about acculturation, interracial marriage, and women's experiences in war. Available in paperback.

Krause, C. A. (1991). ***Grandmothers, mothers, daughters: Oral histories of three generations of ethnic American women.*** Boston: Twayne Publishers. Italian, Jewish, and Slavic women discuss education, gender roles, immigration, and work. In each ethnic group, two women from different generations were interviewed.

Lee, H. (1997). ***Still life with rice: A young American woman discovers the life and legacy of her Korean grandmother.*** New York: Simon & Schuster. The author tells the story of her grandmother, who grew up in Korea and immigrated to California. The grandmother helped to bring her family to America while still trying to fulfill the traditional roles prescribed for Korean women. Available in paperback.

Lim-Hing, S. (Ed.). (1994). ***The very inside: An anthology of writing by Asian and Pacific Islander lesbian and bisexual women.*** Toronto, Canada: Sister Vision. Through interviews, poetry, and short stories, Asian and Pacific Islander women describe their experiences living in ethnic communities, working for civil rights, and maintaining families and close relationships. Available in paperback.

Marks, M. A. (1996). ***Nice Jewish girls: Growing up in America.*** New York: Plume. This collection of fiction and biographical sketches from Jewish women writers explores such topics as body image, family history, and aging. Available in paperback.

McBride, J. (1997). ***The color of water: A Black man's tribute to his White mother.*** New York: Riverhead Books. This true story details the author's personal search for his mother's history. His mother was the daughter of a rabbi who grew up in the American South and later ran away to Harlem. This book is relevant to discussions of ethnic identity and parent-child relationships. Available in paperback.

McCall, N. (1994). ***Makes me wanna holler.*** New York: Vintage Books. A respected journalist for the *Washington Post* describes his youth in a working-class Black neighborhood, his time in jail for armed robbery, and the hope that drew him away from a life of violence and despair. Available in paperback.

Milligan, B., Guerro, M., & de Hoyos, A. (Eds.). (1995). ***Daughters of the fifth sun: A collection of Latina fiction and poetry.*** New York: Riverhead Books. This anthology by Latina authors and poets covers such topics as machismo, women's roles in the community, and Latina sexuality. Available in paperback.

Rodriguez, R. (1992). ***Days of obligation: An argument with my Mexican father.*** New York: Viking Books. In this story about a Mexican American family living in California, the protagonist discusses his ongoing struggle to reconcile his dual identities as a Mexican and an American. Available in paperback.

Shigekuni, J. (1995). **A bridge between us.** New York: Anchor Books. A cross-generational view into the lives of several Japanese American women living in present-day San Francisco. The book addresses immigration, cultural obligations, mother-daughter relationships, and love. Available in paperback.

Silvera, M. (Ed.). (1992). **A piece of my heart: A lesbian of color anthology.** Toronto, Canada: Sister Vision. Through poetry, prose, and interviews, women writers reflect on what it means to be a lesbian woman of color. The issues considered include assimilation, coming out, coalitions among women of color, identity, and sexuality. Available in paperback.

Villarreal, J. A. (1959). **Pocho.** New York: Anchor Books. This classic story about *pochos,* Americans whose parents came from Mexico, is told through the eyes of a young boy named Richard. Themes include the tension between traditional cultural family values and a new culture, changes in marital relationships due to immigration, and immigrants' hopes for a better life. Available in paperback.

Villasenor, V. E. (1991). **Macho!** New York: Delta Books. Seventeen-year-old Roberto Garcia crosses the U.S.-Mexican border seeking work and success. Once in the United States, he becomes one of the many desperate laborers who follow the crop-picking seasons. Available in paperback.

Wade-Gayles, G. (Ed.). (1997). **Father songs.** Boston: Beacon Press. Well-known African American writers including Malcolm X, John Edgar Wideman, Audre Lorde, and Ntozake Shange pay tribute to their fathers. This anthology of prose, poetry, and fiction focuses on the relationships among Black fathers, sons, and daughters.

Washington, M. H. (1990). **Black-eyed Susans/Midnight birds: Stories by and about Black women.** New York: Anchor Books. This collection of fiction and writings from women including Gwendolyn Brooks, Toni Morrison, and Alice Walker features such themes as resisting oppression by the dominant culture, seeking female power, and having dual identities. Available in paperback.

Wyatt, G. E. (1997). **Stolen women: Reclaiming our sexuality, taking back our lives.** New York: J. Wiley. First-person accounts and the author's psychological research are used to illustrate key issues in Black women's sexuality. Topics covered include health, relationships, sexual behavior, and sexual orientation.

Yamanaka, L. (1996). **Wild meat and the bully burgers.** New York: Farrar Straus Giroux. This critically acclaimed story about a Japanese American girl growing up in rural Hawaii deals with cultural norms concerning beauty and intelligence. A useful book for discussions about gender and ethnic stereotypes. Available in paperback.

Research Bibliographies

Several bibliographies provide valuable information about social science research on gender, ethnicity, and culture.

Amaro, H., Russo, N. F., & Pares-Avila, J. A. (1987). Contemporary research on Hispanic women: A selected bibliography of the social science literature. *Psychology of Women Quarterly, 11,* 523–532.

Evans, B. J., & Whitfield, J. R. (Eds.). (1988). *Black males in the United States: An annotated bibliography from 1967–1987.* Washington, DC: American Psychological Association.

Iijima-Hall, C., Evans, B. J., & Selice, S. (Eds.). (1989). *Black females in the United States: A bibliography from 1967–1987.* Washington, DC: American Psychological Association.

Feminist periodicals: A current listing of contents. (Available from University of Wisconsin, Women's Studies Librarian, 430 Memorial Library, 728 State Street, Madison, WI 53706; e-mail: wiswsl@macc.wisc.edu) This list includes the tables of contents of journals covering feminist research and theory. Index terms allow the reader to search by topic. There is a fee for copies of this publication.

Leong, F. T., & Whitfield, J. R. (1992). *Asians in the United States: Abstracts of the psychological and behavioral literature, 1967–1991.* Washington, DC: American Psychological Association.

Olmedo, E. L., & Walker, V. R. (1990). *Hispanics in the United States: Abstracts of the psychological and behavioral literature, 1980–1989.* Washington, DC: American Psychological Association.

Searing, S., & Shult, L. (Project directors). (1991). *Women, race, and ethnicity: A bibliography.* Madison, WI: University of Wisconsin Women's Studies Librarian's Office. (Available from University of Wisconsin, Women's Studies Librarian, 430 Memorial Library, 728 State Street, Madison, WI 53706; e-mail: wiswsl@macc.wisc.edu) This annotated bibliography includes work on women of various ethnicities. A fee is charged for copies of this publication.

Trimble, J. E., & Bagwell, W. M. (Eds.). (1995). *North American Indians and Alaska Natives: Abstracts of the psychological and behavioral literature, 1967–1994.* Washington, DC: American Psychological Association.

Academic Books

The growing importance of research on gender, ethnicity, and culture is reflected in the many scholarly books being published in these areas. This list includes a diverse sample of the many books currently available.

Adams, D. L. (1995). *Health issues for women of color: A cultural diversity perspective.* Thousand Oaks, CA: Sage Publications.

Adleman, J., & Enguidanos, G. (Eds.). (1995). *Racism in the lives of women: Testimony, theory and guides to antiracist practice.* New York: Haworth Press.

Bair, B., & Cayliff, S. E. (Eds.). (1993). *Wings of gauze: Women of color and the experience of health and illness.* Detroit, MI: Wayne State University Press.

Bayne-Smith, M. (Ed.). (1995). *Race, gender, and health.* Thousand Oaks, CA: Sage Publications.

Brislin, R. (1993). *Understanding culture's influence on behavior.* San Diego, CA: Harcourt Brace College Publishers.

Brown, L. B. (Ed.). (1997). *Two spirit people: American Indian lesbian women and gay men.* Binghampton, NY: Haworth Press.

Burlew, A. K. H., Banks, W. C., McAdoo, H. P., & ya Azibo, D. A. (Eds.). (1992). *African American psychology: Theory, research, and practice.* Thousand Oaks, CA: Sage Publications.

Chow, E. N., Wilkinson, D., & Zinn, M. B. (Eds.). (1996). *Race, class, and gender.* Thousand Oaks, CA: Sage Publications.

De Anda, R. (Ed.). (1996). *Chicanas and Chicanos in contemporary society.* Boston: Allyn and Bacon.

Dickerson, B. J. (Ed.). (1995). *African American single mothers: Understanding their lives and families.* Thousand Oaks, CA: Sage Publications.

Espin, O. M. (1997). *Latina realities: Essays on healing, migration, and sexuality.* Boulder, CO: Westview Press.

Espiritu, Y. L. (1997). *Asian American women and men: Labor, laws, and love.* Thousand Oaks, CA: Sage Publications.

Facio, E. (1996). *Understanding older Chicanas: Sociological and policy perspectives.* Thousand Oaks, CA: Sage Publications.

Fine, M., Weis, L., Powell, L. C., & Wong, L. M. (Eds.). (1997). *Off white: Readings on race, power, and society.* New York: Routledge.

Fujimura-Fanselow, K., & Kameda, A. (Eds.). (1995). *Japanese women: New feminist perspectives on the past, present, and future.* New York: Feminist University Press.

Gonzalez, R. (Ed.). (1996). *Muy macho: Latino men confront their manhood.* New York: Anchor Books.

Greene, B. (Ed.). 1994. ***Ethnic and cultural diversity among lesbians and gay men.*** Thousand Oaks, CA: Sage Publications.

Greene, B., & Comas-Diaz, L. (Eds.). (1994). ***Women of color: Integrating ethnic and gender identities in psychotherapy.*** New York: Guilford Press.

Hatfield, E., & Rapson, R. L. (1996). ***Love and sex: Cross-cultural perspectives.*** Boston: Allyn & Bacon.

Hull, G., Bell-Scott, P., & Smith, B. (Eds.). (1982). ***All the women are White, all Blacks are men, but some of us are brave.*** Old Westbury, NY: Feminist Press.

Irvine, J. M. (Ed.). (1994). ***Sexual cultures and the construction of adolescent identities.*** Philadelphia, PA: Temple University Press.

Kagitcibasi, C. (1996). ***Family and human development across culture.*** Hillsdale, NJ: Lawrence Erlbaum Associates.

Kimmel, M. S., & Messner, M. A. (1995). ***Men's lives*** (3rd ed.). Boston: Allyn & Bacon.

Landrine, H. (Ed.). (1995). ***Bringing cultural diversity to feminist psychology: Theory, research, and practice.*** Washington, DC: American Psychological Association.

Leadbeater, B. J. R., & Way, N. (Eds.). (1996). ***Urban girls: Resisting stereotypes and creating identities.*** New York: New York University Press.

Lonner, W. J., & Malpass, R. S. (Eds.). (1993). ***Readings in psychology and culture.*** Boston: Allyn and Bacon.

Marsiglio, W. (Ed.). (1995). ***Fatherhood.*** Thousand Oaks, CA: Sage Publications.

McAdoo, H. P. (Ed.). (1997). ***Black families.*** Thousand Oaks, CA: Sage Publications.

Min, P. G. (Ed.). (1995). ***Asian Americans.*** Thousand Oaks, CA: Sage Publications.

Mirande, A. (1997). ***Hombres y machos: Masculinity and Latino culture.*** Boulder, CO: Westview Press.

Padilla, A. M. (Ed.). (1995). ***Hispanic psychology: Critical issues in theory and research.*** Thousand Oaks, CA: Sage Publications.

Peplau, L. A., & Taylor, S. E. (Eds.). (1996). ***Sociocultural perspectives in social psychology.*** Englewood Cliffs, NJ: Prentice-Hall.

Root, M. P. P. (Ed.). (1997). ***Filipino Americans.*** Thousand Oaks, CA: Sage Publications.

Rosenblatt, P., Karis, T., & Powell, R. (1995). ***Multicultural couples: Black and White voices.*** Thousand Oaks, CA: Sage Publications.

Segall, M. H., Dasen, P. R., Berry, J. W., & Poortinga, Y. H. (Eds.). (1990). ***Human behavior in global perspective: An introduction to cross-cultural psychology.*** New York: Pergamon Press.

Stricker, G., Davis-Russell, E., Bourg, E., Duran, E., Hammond, W. R., McHolland, J., Pollie, K., & Vaughn, B. C. (Eds.). (1990). ***Toward ethnic diversification in psychology education and training.*** Washington, DC: American Psychological Association.

Trickett, E. J., Watts, R. J., & Birman, D. (Eds.). (1994). ***Human diversity: Perspectives on people in context.*** San Francisco: Jossey-Bass.

Tucker, M. B., & Mitchell-Kernan, C. (Eds.). (1995). ***The decline in marriage among African-Americans.*** New York: Russell Sage Foundation.

Vaz, K. M. (1995). ***Black women in America.*** Thousand Oaks, CA: Sage Publications.

Wyche, K. F., & Crosby, F. J. (Eds.). (1996). ***Women's ethnicities: Journeys through psychology.*** Boulder, CO: Westview Press.

Zambrana, R. E. (Ed.). (1995). ***Understanding Latino families: Scholarship, policy, and practice.*** Thousand Oaks, CA: Sage Publications.

Zinn, M. B., & Dill, B. T. (1994). ***Women of color in U.S. society.*** Philadelphia: Temple University Press.

Journals

These professional journals publish articles dealing with gender, ethnicity, and culture. The first year of publication for each journal is indicated in parentheses.

Feminism & Psychology. (1991–). Thousand Oaks, CA: Sage Publications.

Gender & Society. (1987–). Thousand Oaks, CA: Sage Publications.

Hispanic Journal of Behavioral Sciences. (1979–). Thousand Oaks, CA: Sage Periodicals Press.

Journal of Black Psychology. (1974–). Thousand Oaks, CA: Sage Periodicals Press.

Journal of Black Studies. (1970–). Thousand Oaks, CA: Sage Periodicals Press.

Journal of Cross-Cultural Psychology. (1970–). Thousand Oaks, CA: Sage Periodicals Press.

Journal of Family Issues. (1980–). Thousand Oaks, CA: Sage Periodicals Press.

Journal of Gender, Culture and Health. (1998–). New York: Plenum.

Journal of Marriage and the Family. (1964–). Minneapolis, MN: National Council on Family Relations.

Journal of Social Issues. (1945–). Malden, MA: Blackwell Publishers.

Psychology of Women Quarterly. (1976–). New York: Cambridge University Press.

Sex Roles. (1975–). New York: Plenum.

SIGNS: Journal of Women in Culture and Society. (1975). Chicago, IL: University of Chicago Press.

Teaching of Psychology. (1974). Columbia, MO: Division of the Teaching of Psychology, American Psychological Association.

Gender and Culture

Carole Wade

Carol Tavris

This introductory essay by Wade and Tavris provides an overview of some of the many ways in which the lives of women and men differ from one culture to another. The anatomy of sex is universal, but the behaviors, rights, and responsibilities considered appropriate for males and females are social inventions that vary enormously around the globe. These gender arrangements are not arbitrary, but rather depend on the economic realities and other practical conditions of life.

A young boy notices, at an early age, that he seems different from other boys. He prefers playing with girls. He is attracted to the work adult women do, such as cooking and sewing. He often dreams at night of being a girl, and he even likes to put on the clothes of girls. As the boy enters adolescence, people begin to whisper that he's "different," that he seems feminine in his movements, posture, and language. One day the boy can hide his secret feelings no longer, and reveals them to his parents.

The question: How do they respond?
The answer: It depends on their culture.

In twentieth-century North America and Europe, most parents would react with tears, anger, or guilt ("Where did we go wrong?"). After the initial shock, they might haul their son off to a psychiatrist, who would diagnose him as having a "gender identity disorder" and begin intensive treatment. In contrast, if their daughter wanted to be "more like a man," the parents' response would probably be far milder. They might view a girl's desire to play hockey or become a construction worker as a bit unusual, but they probably wouldn't think she had a mental disorder.

These reactions are not universal. Until the late 1800s, in a number of Plains Indians and western Indian tribes, parents and other elders reacted with sympathy and understanding when a young person wanted to live the life of the other sex. The young man or woman was often given an honored status as a shaman, a person with the power to cure illness and act as an intermediary between the natural and spiritual worlds. A boy was permitted to dress as and perform the duties of a woman, and a girl might become a warrior. In some Native American cultures, the young man would be allowed to marry another man, the young woman to marry another woman.

. . .

What these diverse reactions tell us is that although anatomical *sex* is universal and unchangeable (unless extraordinary surgical procedures are used), *gender,* which encompasses all the duties, rights, and behaviors a culture considers appropriate for males and females, is a social invention. It is gender, not anatomical sex, that gives us a sense of personal identity as male or female. Cultures have different notions about what gender roles should entail, how flexible these roles ought to be, and how much leeway males and females have to cross the gender divide.

Perhaps, however, there is something essential about the sexes, something lying *beneath* the veneer of culture, immutable and eternal. That assumption is certainly widespread, and it has guided the research of social scientists as well as the beliefs of laypersons. Let us examine this assumption more closely. Are there some aspects of masculinity and feminity that occur at all times and in all places? If certain characteristics are common, why is that so? What determines how men and women should act toward each other, what their rights and obligations should be, and what it means, in psychological terms, to be female or male?

Searching for the Essential Man and Woman

By comparing and contrasting different cultures around the world, social scientists have tried to identify those aspects of gender that are universally male or female. Their efforts may sound pretty straightforward. However, because researchers, like everyone else, are influenced by their own deeply felt perceptions and convictions about gender, the topic has been one of the most complex to study cross-culturally.

For many years American and European researchers looked for and found evidence that primate males (human and ape) were "by nature" competitive, dominant, and promiscuous, whereas primate females were "by nature" cooperative, submissive, and monogamous (Tavris, 1992). Because of their own preconceptions about male and female roles, based on their own cultural experiences, these observers often overlooked the evidence that contradicted their assumptions, even when the evidence was in front of their noses.

For example, many years ago the famous anthropologist Bronislaw Malinowski wrote a book on the Trobriand Islanders, in which he concluded that males controlled the economic and political life of the community. (Another of his biases is glaringly apparent in the title he gave his book: *The Sexual Life of Savages.*) But when Annette Weiner went to live among the Trobrianders many years later, she learned, by talking to the women, what Malinowski had not: that there was an important economic underground controlled by the labor and exchanges of women.

Similarly, in 1951, another famous anthropologist, E. E. Evans-Pritchard, reported that among the Nuer, a tribe living in the Sudan, husbands had unchallenged authority over their wives. Yet he himself described incidents in Nuer family life that contradicted his conclusion:

> [Should a Nuer wife] in a quarrel with her husband disfigure him—knock a tooth out, for example—her father must pay him compensation. I have myself on two occasions seen a father pay a heifer to his son-in-law to atone for insults hurled at the husband's head by his wife when irritated by accusations of adultery.

We don't approve of domestic violence, nor do we think the wife's actions cancel out men's political power over women in Nuer culture. However, as anthropologist Micaela di Leonardo observes, a husband's authority in the home is not absolute if his wife can insult him and knock his teeth out, and all he can do is demand that his father-in-law fork over a cow!

Many early researchers not only assumed that male dominance and aggression were universally the province of men; they also assumed that female nurturance was universally the province of women. Because of this assumption, Western researchers often overlooked the nurturing activities of men, or even *defined* nurturance in a way that excluded the altruistic, caring actions of men. When anthropologist David Gilmore (1991) examined how cultures around the world define manhood, he expected to find masculinity equated with selfishness and hardness. Instead he found that it often entails selfless generosity and sacrifice. "Women nurture others directly," notes Gilmore. "They do this with their bodies, with their milk and their love. This is very sacrificial and generous. But surprisingly, 'real' men nurture, too, although they would perhaps not be pleased to hear it put this way." Men nurture their families and society, he observes, by "bringing home food for both child and mother . . . and by dying if necessary in faraway places to provide a safe haven for their people." (pp. 229–230)

Our own cultural stereotypes, then, affect what we see in other cultures and how we interpret what we see. Still, a few common themes—not universal, mind you, but common—do emerge from the cross-cultural study of gender. Generally speaking, men have had, and continue to have, more status and more power than women, especially in public affairs. Generally speaking, men have fought the wars and brought home the meat. If a society's economy includes hunting large game, traveling a long way from home, or making weapons, men typically handle these activities. Women have had the primary responsibility for cooking, cleaning, and taking care of small children.

Corresponding with this division of jobs, in many cultures around the world people regard masculinity as something that boys must achieve through strenuous effort. Males must pass physical tests, must endure pain, must confront danger, and must separate psychologically and even physically from their mothers and the world of women. Sometimes they have to prove their self-reliance and courage in bloodcurdling initiation rites. Femininity, in contrast, tends to be associated with responsibility, obedience, and childcare, and it is seen as something that develops naturally, without any special intervention from others.

The Invention of Gender

From these commonalities, some theorists have concluded that certain fundamental aspects of gender must be built into our genes. Biological factors—the fact that women are (so far) the only sex that gets pregnant and that men, on the average, have greater upper body strength—undoubtedly play some role in the sexual division of labor in many societies. But biology takes us only so far, because, when we remove our own cultural blinders and look at the full cross-cultural picture, the range of variation among men and women, in what they do and in how they regard one another, is simply astonishing.

For instance, in some places women are and have been completely under the rule of men, an experience reflected in the haunting words of the Chinese poet Fu Hsuan: "How sad it is to be a woman! Nothing on earth is held so cheap." Women in Saudi Arabia today are not allowed to drive a car; many girls in India submit to arranged marriages as early as age nine; girls and women in the Sudan and other parts of Africa are subjected to infibulation (the practice of cutting off the clitoris and much of the labia, and stitching together the vaginal opening), allegedly to assure their virginity at marriage. Yet elsewhere women have achieved considerable power, influence, and sexual independence. Among the Iroquois, some of the older wives played an important role in village politics. Although they could not become members of the Council of Elders, the ruling body, they had a major say in its decisions. In this century, women have been heads of state in England, Israel, India, Sri Lanka, Iceland, and elsewhere.

Thus it is an oversimplification to say that men are the dominant sex, women the subordinate one. The status of women has been assessed by measures of economic security, educational opportunities, access to birth control and medical care, degree of self-determination, participation in public and political life, power to make decisions in the family, and physical safety. According to these indexes, the status of women worldwide is highest in Scandinavian countries and lowest in Bangladesh, with tremendous variation in between.

Similarly, cultures vary in many other aspects of male-female relations:

- The *content* of what is considered "men's work" and "women's work" differs from culture to culture. In some cultures, men weave and women do not; in others, it's the opposite. In many cultures women do the shopping and marketing, but in others marketing is men's work.

- In many cultures, women are considered the "emotional" sex and are permitted to express their emotions more freely than men. But in cultures throughout the Middle East and South America, men are permitted (and expected) to be as emotionally expressive as women, or even more so, whereas many Asian cultures expect *both* sexes to control their emotions. Moreover, the rules about which sex gets to display which emotion are quite variable. In one major international study, Israeli and Italian men were more likely than women to control feelings of sadness, but British, Spanish, Swiss, and German men were *less* likely than women to inhibit this emotion.

- Cultures differ in the degree of daily contact that is permitted between the sexes. In many farm communities and in most modern occupations in North America and Europe, men and women work together in close proximity. At the other end of the continuum, some Middle Eastern societies have a tradition of *purdah,* the veiling of women and the seclusion of wives from all eyes except those of their relatives.

- In some cultures, as in Iran or the Sudan, women are expected to suppress all sexual feeling (and certainly behavior) until marriage, and premarital or ex- tramarital sex is cause for the woman's ostracism from the community or even death. In others, such as Polynesia, women are expected to have sex before mar- riage. In still others, such as the Toda of India, women were allowed to have ex- tramarital affairs (as long as they told their husbands and didn't sneak around).

Perhaps no society challenges our usual assumptions about the universal nature of psychological maleness and femaleness as profoundly as Tahiti. For over two cen- turies, Western visitors to Tahiti have marveled at the lack of sexual differentiation among its peaceful inhabitants. Early European sailors who arrived on the island reported that Tahitian women were free to do just about everything the men did. Women could be chiefs, they could take part in all sports, including wrestling, and they enjoyed casual sex with many different partners.

In the 1960s, anthropologist Robert Levy lived among the Tahitians and con- firmed that they didn't share Westerners' ideas about gender. Men in Tahiti were no more aggressive than women, nor were women gentler or more maternal than men. Men felt no obligation to appear "manly" or defend "male honor," and women felt no pressure to be demure and "womanly." The Tahitians seemed to lack what psy- chologist Sandra Bem has called a "gender schema," a network of assumptions about the personalities and moral qualities of the two sexes. To Tahitians, Levy found, gen- der was just no big deal. Even the Tahitian language ignores gender: Pronouns are not different for males and females, and most traditional Tahitian names are used for both sexes.

The existence of cultures such as Tahiti, together with the wide variations in gender roles that exist around the world, suggest that the qualities that cultures link with masculinity and femininity are not innately male or female. Instead, they are, in the language of social science, *socially constructed.* As David Gilmore puts it, "gender ideologies are social facts, collective representations that pressure people into acting in certain ways."

Where Do the Rules of Gender Come From?

When most people read about the customs of other cultures, they are inclined to say, "Oh, boy, I like the sexual attitudes of the Gorks but I hate the nasty habits of the Dorks." The point to keep in mind is that a culture's practices cannot easily be exported elsewhere, like cheese, or surgically removed, like a tumor. *A culture's atti-tudes and practices regarding gender are deeply embedded in its history, environment, economy, and survival needs.*

To understand how a society invents its notions of gender, we need to under-stand its political system and its economy, and how that economy is affected by ge-ography, natural resources, and even the weather. We need to know who controls and distributes the resources, and how safe a society is from interlopers. We need to know the kind of work that people do, and how they structure that work. And we need to know whether there is environmental pressure on a group to produce more children, or to have fewer of them. In short, we need to know about *production* and *reproduction*.

For example, David Gilmore found that rigid concepts of manhood tend to exist wherever there is a great deal of competition for resources—which is to say, in most places. For the human species, life has usually been harsh. Consider a tribe trying to survive in the wilds of a South American forest; or in the dry and unforgiving land-scape of the desert; or in an icy Arctic terrain that imposes limits on the number of people who can survive by fishing. When conditions like these exist, men are the sex that is taught to hunt for large game, compete with each other for work, and fight off enemies. (As we've noted, this division of labor may originally have occurred because of men's relatively greater upper-body muscular strength and the fact that they do not become pregnant or nurse children.) Men will be socialized to resist the impulse to avoid confrontation and retreat from danger. They will be "toughened up" and pushed to take risks, even with their lives.

How do you get men to do all this? To persuade men to wage war and risk death, argues anthropologist Marvin Harris (1974), societies have to give them something—and the something is prestige, power, and women. That in turn means you have to raise obedient women; if the King is going to offer his daughter in marriage to the bravest warrior, she has to go when given. In contrast, David Gilmore finds, in cul-tures such as Tahiti, where resources are abundant and there are no serious hazards or enemies to worry about, men don't feel they have to prove themselves or set them-selves apart from women.

The economic realities of life also affect how men and women regard each other. Ernestine Friedl has described the remarkable differences between two tribes in New Guinea. One tribe, living in the highlands, believes that intercourse weakens men, that women are dangerous and unclean, and that menstrual blood can do all sorts of terrifying things. Sex is considered powerful and mysterious; if it is performed in a garden, the act will blight the crops. Antagonism between the sexes runs high; men often delay marriage and many remain single. Not far away, another tribe has an opposite view of women and sex. People in this tribe think sexual intercourse is fun and that it revitalizes men. Sex, they say, *should* take place in gardens, as it will foster the growth of plants. Men and women do not live in segregated quarters, as they do in the highlands, and they get along pretty well.

One possible explanation for these differences is that the highland people have been settled a long time and have little new land or resources. If the population increased, food would become scarce. Sexual antagonism and a fear of sexual inter-course help keep the birth rate low. The sexy tribe, however, lives in uncultivated areas and needs more members to work the land and help defend the group. Encouraging positive attitudes toward sex and early marriage is one way to increase the birth rate.

Cross-cultural studies find that when the sexes are mutually dependent and work cooperatively, as in husband-wife teams, sexual antagonism is much lower than when work is organized along sex-segregated lines. Among the Machiguenga Indians of Peru, where the sexes cooperate in growing vegetables, fishing, and recreation, husbands and wives feel more solidarity with each other than with their same-sex friends. Among the Mundurucu, however, women and men work in same-sex groups, and friendships rarely cross sexual lines; women therefore feel a sense of solidarity with other women, men with men.

In our own culture, changing conditions have profoundly influenced our ideas about gender as well as our family relationships. According to Francesca Cancian (1987), before the nineteenth century, the typical household was a cooperative rural community in which both spouses shared responsibility for the material and emotional well-being of the family. Men didn't "go to work"; work was right there, and so was the family. Women raised both chickens and children. This is not to say that the two sexes had equal rights in the public domain, but in psychological terms they were not seen as opposites.

But with the onset of the industrial revolution, shops and factories began to replace farming, and many men began to work apart from their families. This major economic change, argues Cancian, created a rift between "women's sphere," at home, and "men's sphere," at work. The masculine ideal adjusted to fit the new economic realities, which now required male competitiveness and the suppression of any signs of emotional "weakness." The feminine ideal became its opposite: Women were now seen as being "naturally" nurturant, emotional, and fragile.

What's Ahead?

In the twentieth century, two profound changes in production and reproduction are occurring that have never before happened in human history. Most jobs in industrial nations, including military jobs, now involve service skills and brainwork rather than physical strength. Reproduction, too, has been revolutionized; although women in many countries still lack access to safe and affordable contraceptives, it is now possible for women to limit reliably the number of children they will have and to plan when to have them. The "separate spheres" doctrine spawned by the industrial revolution is breaking down in this post-industrial age, which requires the labor of both sexes.

As these changes unfold, ideas about the "natural" qualities of men and women are also being transformed. It is no longer news that a woman can run a country, be a Supreme Court justice or a miner, or walk in space. It is no longer news that many men, whose own fathers would no more have diapered a baby than jumped into a vat of boiling oil, now want to be involved fathers.

What a cross-cultural, historical perspective teaches us, then, is that gender arrangements, and the qualities associated with being male and female, are not arbitrary. Our ideas about gender are affected by the practical conditions of our lives. These conditions are far more influential than our hormones in determining whether men are expected to be fierce or gentle, and whether women are expected to be financially helpless or Wall Street whizzes.

The cross-cultural perspective reminds us too that no matter how entrenched our own notions of masculinity and femininity are, they can be expected to change— as the kind of work we do changes, as technology changes, and as our customs change. Yet many intriguing questions remain. Do men and women need to feel that they are psychologically different from one another in some way? Will masculinity always rest on male achievements and actions, and femininity on merely being female? Since most of us cannot move to Tahiti, but must live in a world in which wars and violence persist, is it wise or necessary to make sure that at least one sex—or only one sex—is willing to do the dangerous work?

Marvin Harris has argued that male supremacy was "just a phase in the evolution of culture," a phase that depended on the ancient division of labor that put men in charge of war and women in charge of babies. Harris predicts that by the 21st century, male supremacy will fade and gender equality will become, for the first time in history, a real possibility.

Is he right? How will gender be constructed by our own culture in the next century? What do you think?

References

Cancian, Francesca (1987). *Love in America: Gender and self-development.* Cambridge, England: Cambridge University Press.

Gilmore, David (1991). *Manhood in the making.* New Haven, CT: Yale University Press.

Harris, Marvin (1974). *Cows, pigs, wars, and witches: The riddles of culture.* New York: Random House.

Tavris, Carol (1992). *The mismeasure of woman.* New York: Simon & Schuster.

Sociocultural Perspectives on the Lives of Women and Men

Letitia Anne Peplau

Rosemary C. Veniegas

Pamela L. Taylor

Sheri C. DeBro

This chapter explains the basic ingredients in a sociocultural analysis of gender. A major goal of this perspective is to identify ways in which specific features of a culture influence specific aspects of the lives of women and men. Key elements of culture are described and illustrated. These include norms, roles, social status, stereotypes, ideology, and values. We also discuss the experiences of American ethnic groups; three important components of ethnicity are culture, identity, and social status. A central message is that the meaning of being a woman (or a man) depends on the person's sociocultural context.

The lives of women and men are shaped in crucial ways by the social and cultural worlds they inhabit. Consider the behavior of women in two very different environments in Los Angeles.

At the University of California, Los Angeles (UCLA), women constitute about half the student body. UCLA students come from ethnically and culturally diverse backgrounds, but they share a belief in the value of education and a commitment to academic achievement. Although UCLA women may argue a point vigorously in class or yell angrily at a friend, physical fights between women on campus are rare.

Just a few miles from UCLA in an economically depressed section of the city, other young women live in a very different social world. In the culture of urban gangs, "gang girls" must be tough, fearless, and willing to fight (Sikes, 1997). According to research by Mary Harris (1994), gang girls often come from troubled families, drop out of school, and turn to gang membership for a sense of identity and belonging. Violence is a way of life. Gang girls get into fights and use weapons to hurt or even kill their enemies. As one gang girl, Maryann, explained, "It's not that you like to fight. You have to fight. But I like fighting" (p. 296). Girls living in dangerous neighborhoods gain a sense of support, knowing that other gang members will "back you up" in case of trouble. According to another gang member, Cindy, "We had to hurt others to take care of ourselves. Mostly I carried a switchblade in my sock" (p. 297). Being "bad," "crazy," or "wild" enhances a gang girl's status. The fiercest fighter is usually the leader of the girls' group. It is estimated that there are more than 7,000 female gang members in Los Angeles (Sikes, 1997).

Are women aggressive? Women on college campuses seldom use physical violence, but in urban ghettos, gang girls are prepared to fight for their lives. As this example indicates, there is no generic or typical woman whose life reflects the essential experiences of all women. Spelman (1988) correctly observed that "all women are women, but there is no being who is only a woman" (p. 102). All people are simultaneously affected by their gender and their sociocultural context.

The Spanish language conveys the inseparability of gender and culture more clearly than English: a *Chicana* is simultaneously a female and a person of Mexican American heritage; a *Chicano* is a Mexican American male. What it means to be a woman (or a man) depends on the person's *sociocultural context,* which includes the person's cultural, ethnic, and social class experiences and environment. In this reading we identify key elements in a sociocultural analysis of gender.

Toward a More Inclusive Understanding of Women and Men

In the past decade, social scientists and feminist scholars have grown increasingly aware of the importance of expanding their analyses of gender to incorporate culture, ethnicity, and social class. One reason is the increasing diversity of the American population. As shown in Table 1, White Americans of European heritage currently constitute 73% of the population, but the U.S. Census Bureau estimates that by 2050, European Americans will be barely half the population. To date, however, progress toward integrating the study of gender and culture has been slow.

American researchers continue to focus largely on the experiences of White, middle-class individuals, often college students. In a review of research in social psychology, David Sears (1986) showed that nearly 75% of published articles were based on college students, and 78% of studies were conducted in laboratories rather than in naturalistic settings. Sears argued persuasively that this heavy reliance on a very

Table 1 ▨ Background Characteristics of the United States Population*

	1997	*2050 (estimate)*
White/European	73%	53%
African/Caribbean	12	14
Hispanic/Latino	11	25
Asian/Pacific Islander	3	8
Native American	1	1

*Numbers are percentages of the total population. 8/10
Source: U.S. Bureau of the Census (1997).

narrow database can distort the view of human nature that emerges from psychological research. In an article titled "Most of the subjects were white and middle class," Sandra Graham (1992) reviewed articles published in six leading psychology journals during the 1970s and 1980s. The percentage of articles that included African Americans was low and actually declined over time. Although African Americans constitute 12% of the American population, they were included in only 3.6% of published studies in major journals. Also absent from mainstream psychology is cross-cultural research about the experiences of women and men from non-Western cultures (Lonner & Malpass, 1993).

Gender researchers have not avoided these problems. Feminist psychologists have repeatedly lamented that the existing "psychology of women" is, in reality, a psychology of White-middle-class American women (e.g., Espin, 1997, p. 35; Hyde, 1996, p. 212). In a review of psychological studies published between 1987 and 1994, Reid and Kelly (1994) demonstrated that empirical research continues to neglect women of color. For example, they found more than 1,600 journal articles on the topic of women and work, but only 4% considered African American women and less than 1% included Hispanic women. Ethnic minority women were similarly underrepresented in articles on women and therapy (1.2% African American, 0.2% Hispanic), rape (2.5% African American, 1.8% Hispanic), and body image (3.2% African American, 0.8% Hispanic).

Feminist publications may do a somewhat better job of including women of color than mainstream publications. Reid and Kelly (1994) found that about 15% of the empirical papers published in the journals *Psychology of Women Quarterly* and *Sex Roles* analyzed the impact of race or ethnicity. Nonetheless, Reid and Kelly concluded that research purportedly studying the "universal woman" usually focuses on White, middle-class populations.

Finally, it is also important to note that the growing research literature on race and ethnicity typically ignores gender. This trend is vividly illustrated in a publication of the American Psychological Association: *Psychological Perspectives on Human Diversity in America* (Goodchilds, 1991). This volume includes two comprehensive reviews, one about race and a second about ethnicity and culture. Neither mentions gender. Also included is a chapter on gender that does not address ethnicity or culture. As these chapters by leading scholars demonstrate, research on gender and research on ethnicity/race have developed largely in isolation from each other. Reid and Comas-Diaz (1990, p. 400) warn that "As in gender studies which ignore race, ethnic studies which overlook gender present us with an incomplete and, possibly, distorted view of the behaviors we attempt to investigate."

Many factors contribute to the neglect of culture and ethnicity in research on gender (cf. Albert, 1988; Graham, 1992). Researchers tend to study topics that are relevant to their personal experiences or concerns. The dramatic increase in research on women and gender in the past three decades has resulted in part from the influx of women into professional disciplines such as psychology and sociology, and the creation of women's studies as an academic field of inquiry. Most researchers, however, remain White and middle class, and lack familiarity with people from other cultural or ethnic backgrounds. Most researchers would feel more at home studying college students than gang members.

Another reason for the lack of research incorporating culture and ethnicity is that researchers often try to simplify the phenomena they study, to reduce the great complexity of human life to more manageable proportions. Focusing on a single familiar ethnic or cultural group makes the researcher's work easier. Third, few researchers have received training about ethnic or cultural issues and may lack the expertise to study unfamiliar populations. Fourth, some researchers may find it difficult to recruit ethnically diverse samples of participants. Fifth, researchers may be wary of conducting research with socially sensitive populations or studying controversial topics. Investigators may worry that reporting ethnic differences will contribute to stereotypes about ethnic minority groups or be used to justify discrimination against group members. Together these explanations suggest that many researchers may lack the motivation, training, or resources to conduct research that simultaneously addresses both gender and culture/ethnicity.

Equally important, researchers often lack an analytic framework for conceptualizing cultural variation. As Hope Landrine (1995, p. 2) noted, "reporting ethnic differences without theoretical explanation belittles culture." Consider these recent findings from social science research:

- Virtually all Korean American men (93%) marry Korean American women. In contrast, less than half of Korean American women (49%) marry Korean American men (Hwang, Saenz, & Aguirre, 1997, p. 766).

- According to U.S. census data, the gender gap in wages for full-time workers varies by ethnicity. Among Whites, women earn about 70% of what men earn; among Blacks, women earn about 89% of what men earn (Spain & Bianchi, 1996, p. 132).

- There are ethnic differences in the age when girls begin to menstruate, with puberty typically beginning earlier for African American girls, later for White girls, and later still for Asian American girls (Matlin, 1996, p. 132).

Without explanation, these findings are bits of cultural trivia that tell us little about the ways in which culture and gender are intertwined. To make sense of findings such as these, we need an understanding of the sociocultural context—an account that helps us to interpret the patterns observed. We agree with Landrine (1995) that

> the challenge for psychology . . . is to develop an explicit, theoretical framework through which sociocultural variables and differences will be rendered coherent. . . . Psychology as a whole and feminist psychology in particular need a model for understanding cultural variables, a theory of the relationship between culture and behavior that neither romanticizes cultures nor renders difference deviance (p. 2).

Sociocultural Analyses of Gender

The goal of a sociocultural analysis of gender is to identify ways in which specific features of a cultural context influence specific aspects of the lives of women and men. Consider the case of "man the hunter." In most hunting-and-gathering cultures, men hunt game animals, and women gather edible plants. This common sex difference has led some observers to suggest that men are natural-born hunters and that pregnancy and child care make women incapable of hunting. This view that "biology is destiny" was seriously challenged by a three-year study of the Agta hunter-gatherers of the Philippines (Goodman, Griffin, Estioko-Griffin & Grove, 1985). In Agta culture, women participate actively in hunting, providing almost half of the game animals killed. Hunting activities do not impair women's fertility or interfere with their maternal responsibilities. What factors enable these women to hunt successfully? The rich natural environment of the Agta permits hunting relatively close to living areas, which makes it easier for women to hunt. Women take nursing infants with them on the hunt, but are able to leave older children at home with relatives, who engage in cooperative child care. Further, although men often prefer to hunt alone, women tend to hunt in all-women or mixed-sex groups, which increases their efficiency. Together, the physical environment and the social customs of the Agta enable women to become highly effective hunters, even during their peak reproductive years. This research is informative because it provides a detailed analysis of cultural factors that make it possible for women to succeed at a task typically considered to be for men only.

Key Elements of Culture

In general terms, *culture* refers to the shared beliefs, values, traditions, and behavior patterns of a particular group. Material culture consists of those aspects of the environment made by people, everything from ceramic pots and woven baskets to flush toilets and personal computers. Culture is transmitted from one generation to the next by parents, teachers, religious leaders, and other respected members of the culture. In technological societies the mass media also convey cultural messages. This process of transmitting culture across generations is known as *socialization*. Because cultural beliefs are widely shared and can be taken for granted, they are seldom discussed by adults (Brislin, 1993). We may become most aware of our own culture when we interact with people from a different culture. Both the joys and frustrations of travel to other parts of the world are provided by exposure to new ways of life.

Because the goal of a sociocultural analysis of gender is to understand how specific features of a culture affect the lives of women and men, it is important to identify key elements of culture. In the following sections, we consider social norms, social roles, social status, ideology, stereotypes, and values.

Social Norms   Rules and expectations about how group members should behave are known technically as *social norms*. Americans tend to consider a friend late for a lunch meeting after 19 minutes; Brazilians give a friend nearly twice as long, not considering the friend late until 34 minutes after the arranged time (Levine, 1988). Americans talking to a stranger prefer to sit about 35 inches apart. In Venezuela the preferred distance is 32 inches, and in Japan it is 40 inches (Sussman & Rosenfeld, 1982). As these examples suggest, cultures develop norms about virtually all aspects of life. Gender norms define such things as the names considered appropriate for male versus female babies and the ways men and women dress or wear their hair.

Social Roles   This term refers to the set of social norms about how a person in a particular social position such as a mother or warrior is expected to act. *Social roles* define the rights and responsibilities of group members and prescribe which qualities and behaviors are appropriate or ideal and which are unacceptable. Cultures typically define distinctive roles for males and females. Traditionally, it has been assumed that women and men should perform different activities and possess different personality traits.

Consider an American example. When researchers asked midwestern college students about a typical first date, they found general agreement about what the man and woman are expected to do (Rose & Frieze, 1989). The man typically takes a leadership role on a first date. He initiates the date by asking the woman out and deciding what to do together. He meets his date at her home or dorm and chats briefly with parents or roommates. If going somewhere by car, the man opens the car door for the woman and drives. A first date might entail going to a movie or party and having something to eat. The man is expected to pay the couple's expenses. He is also the one to initiate physical contact—holding hands or kissing good-night. It is up to the man to ask for another date. The woman has a more responsive role on a first date, waiting for the man to pick her up, participating in the activities he proposes, allowing him to pay expenses, and accepting or rejecting his attempts at physical contact. These rules for a first date cast men and women in distinctive and complementary social roles based on their gender.

Status and Power   Cultures also define the social status of group members. *Social status* refers to a person's rank, privileges, or power in a group. Traditionally, age and gender have been important determinants of status, with greater power being accorded to elders and to men. In a system of patriarchy, the father or senior male is the acknowledged decision maker for the family. In some cultures male dominance is an accepted way of life. In the United States today, the balance of power between the sexes is harder to ascertain. In public life, laws denying women the vote and forbidding women to own property are a thing of the past. Women are increasingly visible in professional careers and government service. Nonetheless, the percentage of American women in positions of power as heads of government, CEOs of major corporations, and university presidents continues to be relatively small. In their personal lives, many heterosexual Americans describe their dating relationships and marriages as relatively egalitarian or equal in power (Peplau & Campbell, 1989). When relationships are perceived as unequal, male dominance is the most common pattern.

Ideology   Individuals' beliefs about proper or appropriate roles for women and men constitute their gender-role ideology. Traditionalists endorse a division of labor by gender and a pattern of male dominance. Egalitarians reject these beliefs, preferring to base social roles and power relations on factors other than gender. Gender-role ideology can be thought of as a continuum, ranging from traditional to egalitarian attitudes. In American society beliefs about women's and men's roles have changed considerably during this century. In 1936 only 18% of the American public approved of a married woman working for pay if her husband could support her. By

1976, 65% of men and 70% of women approved of wives working outside the home (Boer, 1977).

Cross-cultural research shows considerable variation in gender-role beliefs. Williams and Best (1990a) asked people in 14 countries to indicate their degree of agreement or disagreement with such statements as: "The husband should be regarded as the legal representative of the family group in matters of law" and "A woman should have exactly the same freedom of action as a man." Around the world, women tend to have less traditional attitudes about gender than men; these differences are fairly small, however, and pale in comparison to the larger differences found between cultures. In general, traditional attitudes are strongest in rural areas, in nonindustrialized societies, and in Muslim countries. Modern economic development, advances in women's education, and increases in the percentage of women working outside the home all tend to promote more egalitarian attitudes.

Stereotypes   Beliefs about the typical attributes of women and men are known as *gender stereotypes*. Researchers Williams and Best (1990b) described two imaginary people:

> One is said to be adventurous, autocratic, coarse, dominant, forceful, independent and strong. [The] other is described as affectionate, dependent, dreamy, emotional, sentimental, submissive, and weak. . . . Would it be easier to picture one of them as a male and one as a female? . . . Does it matter what nationality you are? (p. 15)

To answer these questions, Williams and Best (1990b) asked college students from 25 nations to indicate which of a long list of adjectives were more frequently associated with men or with women in their own culture.

The researchers found that core elements of gender stereotypes were quite similar among students from such diverse countries as Brazil, Canada, India, Japan, New Zealand, Nigeria, and Spain. In general, men were seen as stronger and more active than women. In all countries respondents identified being adventurous, aggressive, independent, capable, dominant, and strong as masculine qualities. They viewed being emotional, dependent, submissive, shy, and superstitious as female qualities. The researchers emphasized the cross-cultural consistency of their findings, but also noted some cross-cultural differences. For instance, in America men are seen as boastful, disorderly, and obnoxious; in Japan, these traits are linked to women (Williams & Best, 1990b).

The stereotype research we have discussed has explicitly focused on gender. A separate line of research has studied stereotypes about nationalities, assessing, for instance, beliefs about the typical attributes of Germans, Iranians, or Koreans. Research on national stereotypes asks about a group, such as "Italians," and does not specify the gender of the people in question. Eagly and Kite (1987) investigated whether stereotypes of nations reflect stereotypes of both women and men or, instead, are based largely on stereotypes of men. Their research demonstrated that stereotypes of nations are more similar to stereotypes of the men from these countries than of the women. Eagly and Kite suggested that this tendency to equate men and nationalities stems from men's higher status and greater participation in the political and social activities that shape public perceptions of nations.

Values   Beliefs about which behaviors and personal qualities are important and which are inconsequential—*values*—are another important component of culture. Consider the question of what people value in a marriage partner. David Buss and his collaborators (1990) asked more than 9,000 adults from 37 countries to evaluate the importance of 31 characteristics in choosing a mate. Universally, both men and women wanted a mate who was kind, understanding, intelligent, emotionally stable, dependable, and healthy. A few consistent sex differences also emerged:

> In all known cultures worldwide from the . . . tribal societies of . . . South America to the big cities of Madrid, London, and Paris, men place a premium on the physical appearance of a potential mate . . . [and] women place a premium on good earning capacity, financial prospects, ambition, industriousness, and social status (Buss, 1993, pp. 199–200).

Buss interpreted these sex differences in terms of evolutionary theory, proposing that men value attributes that signal a woman's reproductive capacity and women value attributes that signal a man's ability to provide resources for his mate and offspring. Other researchers interpret the same findings as reflecting differences in men's and women's traditional social roles (e.g., Hatfield & Sprecher, 1995). That is, as a result of socialization, people learn to value traits considered typical for each sex.

Buss also found important cross-cultural differences in mate preferences, most notably for such traditional values as premarital chastity, being a good cook and housekeeper, the desire for home and children, and being religious. For example, people from China, India, and Iran highly prize virginity prior to marriage, but people from Scandinavia and the Netherlands do not.

In sum, Buss and his colleagues found that both gender and culture affected people's values. Across the 31 mate characteristics that Buss et al. (1990) studied, the effects of gender were much smaller than those of culture. In technical terms, gender accounted for an average of only 2.4% of the variance in mate preferences, but culture accounted for 14% of the variance.

The Meaning of Behavior: Cultural Universals and Cultural Specifics

A particularly important aspect of culture concerns the *meaning* of behavior (Smith & Bond, 1993).

> Cultural differences are not primarily differences in behavior but differences in the meanings . . . attributed and attached to the "same" behavior. Culture can be regarded as the unwritten social and psychological dictionary that each person has memorized . . . and through which each person unwittingly interprets themselves and others (Landrine, Klonoff & Brown-Collins, 1992, p. 59).

Consider the sleeping arrangements that parents provide for babies (Morelli, Rogoff, Oppenheim & Goldsmith, 1992). In the United States, infants sleep alone in a crib, preferably in their own bedroom. Americans emphasize the importance of training babies to be self-reliant and independent. One mother commented about moving her infant son to his own bedroom: "It was time to give him his own room . . . his own territory. That's the American way" (Morelli et al., 1992, p. 604). In a world perspective, however, American sleeping patterns are atypical. In most cultures infants and young children sleep with other family members, often the mother or older siblings. For Mayan children and adults, sleeping alone is considered a hardship. Mayan mothers were shocked to learn from a researcher that American infants and toddlers sleep by themselves, and clearly disapproved of what they considered a heartless practice (Morelli et al., 1992). The point is that most behaviors are open to widely different interpretations, depending on one's cultural perspective.

A study by Landrine, Klonoff, and Brown-Collins (1992) illustrates the importance of meaning in understanding gender patterns. These researchers asked White, African American, Asian American, and Latina college women to use a seven-point scale to rate themselves on several gender-stereotypic phrases, including "I am assertive," "I am sensitive to the needs of others," and "I am feminine." The mean scores of the White women and the women of color were identical, suggesting that both groups of women viewed themselves similarly. In a second part of the study, however, the researchers demonstrated that these similarities in numerical ratings concealed differences in interpretation. Participants were given several definitions for each phrase and asked to circle the definition that best matched what she had in mind in making her numerical self-rating. An analysis of these interpretations identified several significant differences between White women and women of color. For instance, White women tended to define *passive* as "laid-back/easy-going"; women of color were more likely to define *passive* as "not saying what one really thinks." Although White women and women of color rated themselves similarly, they attributed different meanings to these ratings. The authors warn that social scientists cannot assume that their "standard" questions or experimental procedures (typically developed by middle-class White researchers) will be interpreted similarly by people from different cultural backgrounds. Recently, Landrine (1995) has advocated that researchers interested in gender and culture adopt an approach she calls *contextualism*. A contextualistic analysis requires that researchers determine the meaning of specific behaviors by analyzing the sociocultural context in which they occur.

As we have seen, the study of culture sometimes uncovers universals that appear to transcend national and ethnic boundaries and sometimes finds important differences among cultural groups. The effort to find cultural universals has been called *etic* analysis (Berry, 1989). In contrast, an *emic* analysis focuses on culture-specific features that differ among cultural groups. These terms are borrowed from a linguistic distinction between phon*etic*s (universal features of spoken sound) and phon*emic*s (sounds unique to a specific language).

Descriptions of cultural universals are invariably abstract. For instance, all cultures create a division of labor based on gender, but the specific tasks assigned to each sex are variable. Research on mate selection suggests that most people desire a dependable partner, but the meaning of dependability probably varies widely. In some cultures sexual fidelity is viewed as essential to dependability, whereas in other cultures it is not (Smith & Bond, 1993).

Finally, it is worth noting that cultural analysis can be applied to groups of varying sizes. In addition to analyses of nations and large cultural groups, we can also consider cultural differences among geographic regions. Richard Nisbett (1993) has argued that a "culture of honor" characterizes the southern United States and encourages White southern men to use violence to protect their homes and defend their honor. Culture can also be studied among relatively small groups, such as the girl gangs discussed earlier. Research into the social norms and customs of college fraternities provides another example. In a recent study, Boswell and Spade (1996) used the concept of "rape culture" to understand why some college fraternities are relatively dangerous places for women, with frequent incidents of rape, and other fraternities are safer environments. In the next section, we consider the application of a cultural analysis to ethnic groups within the United States.

American Ethnic Groups

The term *ethnicity* can refer to groupings of people based on their culture of origin (e.g., Korean Americans), religion (e.g., Jews), or language (e.g., French Canadians). The term *ethnicity* is also increasingly used to encompass race (Phinney, 1996). The concept of genetically determined and distinctive races has little scientific validity (e.g., Jones, 1997; Zuckerman, 1990). Rather, races are social categories determined by features such as skin color and facial characteristics. The United States Bureau of the Census currently uses five basic ethnic categories: Hispanic, non-Hispanic White, Black, Native American, and Asian/Pacific Islander.

Phinney (1996, p. 918) has argued persuasively that ethnicity is a multidimensional construct that, by itself, explains little. She urges researchers to "unpack the packaged variable of ethnicity . . . [to] identify and assess the variables associated with ethnicity that may explain its influence." Phinney identified three distinct components of ethnicity: culture, identity, and status.

The Cultural Component of Ethnicity

It is useful to analyze ethnic groups in terms of their distinctive cultural norms, values, attitudes, and behaviors. Some researchers have attempted to identify core characteristics of major American ethnic groups. Hispanic Americans, for example, have been characterized as a collectivistic culture that emphasizes the importance of the family, group loyalty, cooperation, and the avoidance of interpersonal conflict (e.g., Gaines, 1997; Marin & Marin, 1991). Broad cultural themes describing an entire ethnic group can be helpful, but they are not without problems. For instance, specific individuals may not possess the characteristics attributed to their ethnic group. A demonstration of this is provided in research about Chinese immigrant teenagers (Feldman, Mont-Reynaud & Rosenthal, 1992). In this study some American-born children of Chinese immigrants held values associated with Chinese culture, but others espoused values indistinguishable from European Americans.

Many Americans live in at least two social worlds—their own ethnic culture and mainstream American culture (LaFromboise, Coleman & Gerton, 1993). For example, African Americans are influenced both by their unique cultural heritage as African Americans and by their exposure to mainstream American culture (e.g., Jones, 1997). Recent immigrants to the United States face the challenge of adjusting to life in a new culture. In addition, the increase in interethnic marriages means that more children are of mixed cultural heritage. As a result, there is often much diversity within any particular ethnic group. Consequently, research about American ethnic groups should directly assess the attitudes, beliefs, and behaviors of research participants, rather than assuming that all members of a given group will necessarily be identical.

Finally, it is important to emphasize that all Americans have an ethnic heritage, including Whites. Cross-cultural researchers have described mainstream Euro-American culture as highly individualistic (e.g., Triandis, 1995). In an individualistic culture, a person's behavior is guided largely by personal goals, rather than the goals of collectives such as the family or workgroup. If a conflict arises between an individual's personal goals and the goals of the group, it is acceptable to put self-interest first. Feminist scholars have also begun to analyze the nature of "whiteness" (e.g., Hurtado & Stewart, 1997) and to raise concerns about the extent to which feminist scholarship is biased toward European American culture (Landrine, 1995).

The Identity Component of Ethnicity

Individuals vary in the strength and salience of their identification with their ethnic group, referred to as *ethnic identity* (Phinney, 1996). Teenagers from African American, Asian American, Native American, or Latino backgrounds sometimes struggle with the challenge of creating a personal identity that reconciles their ethnic heritage and their participation in mainstream American society. A Chinese girl who moved to the United States at age 12 described her feelings:

> I don't know who I am. Am I the good Chinese daughter? Am I an American teenager? I always feel I am letting my parents down when I am with my friends because I act so American, but I also feel that I will never really be an American (quoted in Olsen, 1988, p. 30).

Phinney (1990) suggests that there are four main ways in which this young woman might resolve the dilemma of identifying with Chinese and American cultures. She might largely give up her ethnic heritage, assimilate the culture of the dominant society, and develop a *mainstream identity* as an American. This is the traditional "melting pot" perspective on how new immigrants can best adjust to living in the United States. In contrast, the Chinese American teen might identify strongly with both cultures, forging a *bicultural identity*. Some researchers have suggested that the development of bicultural competence, the ability to navigate successfully in two cultural communities, may have important psychological benefits (LaFromboise et al., 1993). Third, the Chinese American girl might develop few ties to the majority culture and maintain a strong *ethnic identity* as Chinese. Finally, she might have weak ties to both groups and remain a socially marginal outsider.

Whereas ethnic identity is usually salient for members of cultural minority groups, it is not necessarily salient for the White majority. According to Hurtado and

Stewart (1997, p. 299), "a recurrent finding in the study of whiteness is the fact that white respondents do not consider their 'whiteness' as an identity or a marker of group membership." Some Whites identify with a particular heritage, such as being Amish or Irish American, but whiteness per se is not necessarily a relevant category.

The Status Component of Ethnicity

In American culture, ethnicity is often linked to social status. On average, White Americans tend to have higher status and power in the society and tend to be more affluent and better educated than ethnic minorities. There are, of course, exceptions—poor Whites and wealthy minorities, for example. Nonetheless, efforts to understand the life experiences of ethnic minority women and men must go beyond culture and identity to investigate issues of status, power, social class, and the related problems of prejudice and discrimination (Collins, 1997).

The association of ethnicity and status has important implications for sociocultural analyses of gender. Patterns observed among members of an ethnic group may reflect cultural factors, but may also reflect the group's economic, social, and political status in society. Brislin (1993) notes that Americans are reluctant to discuss social class. Yet the impact of class in determining a person's life circumstances and opportunities can be substantial. A careful sociocultural analysis of gender must disentangle the effects of culture, ethnicity, class, and privilege.

Final Thoughts

Sociocultural analyses of the lives of women and men offer the promise of new insights and increased understanding of important human experiences. A sociocultural perspective also poses challenges for feminist scholars.

Feminists have criticized traditional social science theory and research for generalizing about people based on the experiences of White, privileged men (Yoder & Kahn, 1993). This androcentric bias was reflected in the tendency to exclude women and other groups from study and to evaluate them against a White male standard. In correcting this male-centered bias, it is important that scholars not simply substitute a new and equally inaccurate female standard, based on the experiences of White, privileged women. Just as there is no essential or universal man, so there is no essential or universal woman (Spelman, 1988). At the same time, researchers also recognize that it would be "a tremendous mistake to conclude that 'all individuals are totally unique and different' and . . . therefore all generalizations about social groups are impossible and inherently oppressive" (Zinn, Hondagneu-Sotelo & Messner, 1997, p. 1). Analyses of women and men from diverse cultural groups provide one avenue for striking a balance between these two extremes.

Central to the sociocultural analysis of gender is the recognition that gender and culture are inseparable. Jeffries and Ransford (1980) used the term *unique social space* to refer to the distinctive social environment created when gender, ethnicity, class, and age intersect in particular combinations. Examples would be wealthy middle-aged White men, third-generation Japanese American women, or teenage African

American girls. The point is that we cannot understand the experiences of a Black teenage girl simply by adding together the categories to which she belongs, trying to sum the "effects" of being young, Black, and female (cf. Smith & Stewart, 1983). Rather, we need to understand the experiences of people who inhabit this particular social niche within American society. Of course, even groups such as Black teenage girls are heterogeneous, and we cannot assume that all African American adolescent girls are identical in their interests, values, or life experiences (cf. Morawski & Bayer, 1995). Nonetheless, efforts to study gender within specific sociocultural contexts will greatly enhance our understanding.

As researchers focus increasingly on the intersection of gender, culture, and ethnicity, we will become more skilled in our research methods and more sophisticated in our theory development. The readings in this volume present some of the very best available research and clearly demonstrate the value of sociocultural analyses of gender.

References

Albert, R. D. (1988). The place of culture in modern psychology. In P. A. Bronstein & K. Quina (Eds.), *Teaching a psychology of people*. Washington, DC: American Psychological Association.

Berry, J. (1989). Imposed etics-emics-derived etics: The operationalisation of a compelling idea. *International Journal of Psychology, 24,* 721–735.

Boer, C. de. (1977). The polls: Women at work. *Public Opinion Quarterly, 41,* 268–277.

Boswell, A. A., & Spade, J. Z. (1996). Fraternities and collegiate rape culture: Why are some fraternities more dangerous places for women? *Gender & Society, 2,* 133–147.

Brislin, R. (1993). *Understanding culture's influence on behavior*. Fort Worth, TX: Harcourt Brace College Publishers.

Buss, D. M., Abbott, M., Angleitner, A., et al. Asherian, A., (1990). International preferences in selecting mates: A study of 37 cultures. *Journal of Cross-Cultural Psychology, 21,* 5–47.

Buss, D. M. (1993). Mate preferences in 37 cultures. In W. J. Lonner & R. Malpass (Eds.), *Psychology and culture* (pp. 197–201). Boston: Allyn and Bacon.

Collins, P. H. (1997). On West and Fenstermaker's "Doing Difference." In M. R. Walsh (Ed.), *Women, men and gender: Ongoing debates* (pp. 73–75). New Haven, CT: Yale University Press.

Eagly, A. H., & Kite, M. E. (1987). Are stereotypes of nationalities applied to both women and men? *Journal of Personality and Social Psychology, 53,* 451–462.

Espin, O. M. (1997). *Latina realities: Essays on healing, migration, and sexuality*. Boulder, CO: Westview Press.

Feldman, S. S., Mont-Reynaud, R., & Rosenthal, D. A. (1992). When East moves West: The acculturation of values of Chinese adolescents in the U.S. and Australia. *Journal of Research on Adolescence, 2*(2), 147–173.

Gaines, S. O. (1997). *Culture, ethnicity, and personal relationship processes*. New York: Routledge.

Goodchilds, J. D. (Ed.). (1991). *Psychological perspectives on human diversity in America*. Washington, DC: American Psychological Association.

Goodman, M. J., Griffin, P. B., Estioko-Griffin, A. A., & Grove, J. S. (1985). The compatibility of hunting and mothering among the Agta hunter-gatherers of the Philippines. *Sex Roles, 12,* 1199–1209.

Graham, S. (1992). "Most of the subjects were white and middle class": Trends in published research on African Americans in selected APA Journals, 1970–1989. *American Psychologist, 47*(5), 629–639.

Harris, M. G. (1994). Cholas, Mexican-American girls, and gangs. *Sex Roles, 30,* 289–301.

Hatfield, E., & Sprecher, S. (1995). Men's and women's preferences in marital partners in the United States, Russia, and Japan. *Journal of Cross-Cultural Psychology, 26,* 728–750.

Hurtado, A., & Stewart, A. J. (1997). Through the looking glass: Implications of studying whiteness for feminist methods. In M. Fine, L. Weis, L. C. Powell & L. M. Wong (Eds.), *Off white: Readings on race, power, and society* (pp. 297–310). New York: Routledge.

Hwang, S., Saenz, R., & Aguirre, B. E. (1997). Structural and assimilationist explanations of Asian-American intermarriage. *Journal of Marriage and the Family, 59*(3), 758–772.

Hyde, J. S. (1996). *Half the human experience: The psychology of women,* 5th ed. Lexington, MA: D. C. Heath.

Jeffries, V., & Ransford, H. E. (1980). *Social stratification: A multiple hierarchy approach.* Boston: Allyn and Bacon.

Jones, J. M. (1997). *Prejudice and racism,* 2nd ed. New York: McGraw-Hill.

LaFromboise, T., Coleman, H. L. K., & Gerton, J. (1993). Psychological impact of biculturalism: Evidence and theory. *Psychological Bulletin, 114,* 395–412.

Landrine, H. (1995). Introduction: Cultural diversity, contextualism, and feminist psychology. In H. Landrine (Ed.), *Bringing cultural diversity to feminist psychology: Theory, research, and practice* (pp. 1–25). Washington, DC: American Psychological Association.

Landrine, H., Klonoff, E. A., & Brown-Collins, A. (1992). Cultural diversity and methodology in feminist psychology. *Psychology of Women Quarterly, 16,* 145–163.

Levine, R. V. (1988). The pace of life across cultures. In J. E. McGrath (Ed.), *The social psychology of time: New perspectives* (pp. 39–60). Newbury Park, CA: Sage.

Lonner, W. J., & Malpass, R. (Eds.). (1993). *Psychology and culture.* Boston: Allyn and Bacon.

Marin, G., & Marin, B. (1991). *Research with Hispanic populations.* Newbury Park, CA: Sage Publications.

Matlin, M. W. (1996). *The psychology of women,* 3rd ed. New York: Harcourt Brace College Publishers.

Morawski, J. G., & Bayer, B. M. (1995). Stirring trouble and making theory. In H. Landrine (Ed.), *Bringing cultural diversity to feminist psychology* (pp. 113–138). Washington, DC: American Psychological Association.

Morelli, G., Rogoff, B., Oppenheim, D., & Goldsmith, D. (1992). Cultural variations in infants' sleeping arrangements: Questions of independence. *Developmental Psychology, 28,* 604–613.

Nisbett, R. E. (1993). Violence and U.S. regional culture. *American Psychologist, 48,* 441–449.

Olsen, L. (1988). *Crossing the schoolhouse border: Immigrant students and the California Public Schools.* San Francisco: California Tomorrow.

Peplau, L. A., & Campbell, S. M. (1989). Power in dating and marriage. In J. Freeman (Ed.), *Women: A feminist perspective,* 4th ed. (pp. 121–137). Palo Alto, CA: Mayfield Publishing.

Phinney, J. S. (1990). Ethnic identity in adolescents and adults: A review of research. *Psychological Bulletin, 108,* 499–514.

Phinney, J. S. (1996). When we talk about American ethnic groups, what do we mean? *American Psychologist, 51,* 918–927.

Reid, P. T., & Comas-Diaz, L. (1990). Gender and ethnicity: Perspectives on dual status. *Sex Roles, 22,* 397–408.

Reid, P. T., & Kelly, E. (1994). Research on women of color: From ignorance to awareness. *Psychology of Women Quarterly, 18,* 477–486.

Rose, S., & Frieze, I. H. (1989). Young singles' scripts for a first date. *Gender and Society, 3,* 258–268.

Sears, D. O. (1986). College sophomores in the laboratory: Influences of a narrow data base on psychology's view of human nature. *Journal of Personality and Social Psychology, 51,* 515–530.

Sikes, G. (1997). *8 ball chicks: A year in the violent world of girl gangsters.* New York: Anchor Books.

Smith, P. B., & Bond, M. H. (1993). *Social psychology across cultures.* Boston: Allyn and Bacon.

Smith, A., & Stewart, A. J. (1983). Approaches to studying racism and sexism in Black women's lives. *Journal of Social Issues, 39*(3), 1–15.

Spain, D., & Bianchi, S. M. (1996). *Balancing act: Motherhood, marriage, and employment among American women.* New York: Russell Sage Foundation.

Spelman, E. V. (1988). *Inessential woman: Problems of exclusion in feminist thought.* Boston, MA: Beacon Press.

Sussman, N. M., & Rosenfeld, H. M. (1982). Influence of culture, language, and sex on conversational distance. *Journal of Personality and Social Psychology, 42,* 66–74.

Triandis, H. C. (1995). *Individualism and collectivism.* Boulder, CO: Westview Press.

social class, all were stereotypically feminine. In addition, the stereotypes of white women, and of middle-class women were most similar to traditional stereotypes of women. Thus, it was concluded that both race and social class are implicit variables in sex-role stereotypes.

In traditional investigations of stereotypes, participants are required to assign adjectives to status groups. Usually two status groups are presented, and they are described in terms of a single, isolated, status variable (i.e., men and women, or blacks and whites). In this fashion many investigators have empirically derived stereotypes by sex (Broverman, Vogel, Broverman, Clarkson, & Rosenkrantz, 1972; Cowen & Steward, 1977; Ellis & Bentler, 1973; Feinberger, 1948; Rosenkrantz, Vogel, Bee, Broverman, & Broverman, 1968; Spence, Helmreich, & Stapp, 1975). Others have derived stereotypes by either race, age, or national origin (Aaronson, 1966; Bayton, 1941; Brigham, 1969; Campbell, 1967; Child & Doob, 1943; Diab, 1963a, 1963b; Gardner, Kirby, Gorospe, & Villamin, 1972; Karlins, Coffman, & Walters, 1969; Katz & Braly, 1933; McCauley & Stitt, 1978; Tuckman & Lorge, 1956, 1958a, 1958b). The results of these investigations reveal that either different adjectives, or different values on the same adjectives, are attributed to the two status groups. From this investigators have concluded that the variance in the adjectives assigned to the groups is accounted for by the status variable chosen for the study. Bayton, McAlister, and Hamer (1956), however, demonstrated that such a conclusion may be erroneous.

In an investigation of Race × Class stereotypes Bayton et al. (1956) found that lower-class blacks and whites were described in the same negative terms and that upper-class blacks and whites were described in the same positive terms. That is, with both race and class varied systematically, Bayton et al. (1956) found that lower-class status accounted for the historically negative stereotypes of blacks and upper-class status accounted for the previously positive stereotypes of whites. Bayton et al. concluded that race stereotypes may actually be Race × Class stereotypes, and suggested that the variance in race stereotypes is accounted for not by race, but by the social-class status that participants assume correlates with race. These data were supported in a later investigation (Smedley & Bayton, 1978), and led Jones (1972) to suggest that any investigation of racial stereotypes that does not control for social class will yield results that are ambiguous at best. Nonetheless, stereotypes based on race, in isolation, continue to be derived.

On the whole these findings suggest that participants in stereotyping research do not necessarily assign adjectives to status groups on the basis of the status variable the investigator has chosen for study. Instead, they may attribute additional status variables to the stimulus person. Then they assign traits to this cognitive *multiple-status* stimulus, and as Bayton et al. (1956) suggested, those implicit status attributes may account for a greater proportion of the variance in the stereotypes than does the experimenter's (the explicit) variable. Such behavior may be understood as a result of the fact that status attributes never appear in isolation in the real world, but instead appear in organized Gestalts or constellations (because we occupy more than one status position at a time). Thus, perhaps our research participants cannot imagine a "black" without attributing a sex to that stimulus; similarly, perhaps we cannot imagine "a woman" without attributing a race, a social class, an age, and even a degree of physical attractiveness to the stimulus. In any event, the Bayton et al. (1956) results suggest that single-attribute stereotypes may in fact be multiple-status stereotypes, and thus raise the following questions about the meaning of the sex-role stereotypes we have derived: Are sex-role stereotypes actually sex-race stereotypes? That is, do our participants attribute white race when "women" is the stimulus? Are sex-role stereotypes really sex-class stereotypes, with our participants attributing middle-class status to the female stimulus? Is our stereotype of women a stereotype per se, or is it a stereotype of middle-class white women? Do female sex-role stereotypes exist, viz., is there a set of expectations for women that transcends both race and social class? Evidence which indicates that sex-role expectations differ significantly by race (Allen, 1978; Cox, 1976; Ladner, 1971; Wallace, 1979; Watkins & David, 1970) and by social class (Lynn, 1979; Weitzman, 1975) suggests affirmative answers to many of these questions. And indeed, the only study to date of Sex × Race stereotypes (Bayton & Muldrow, 1968) found that sex-role stereotypes differed significantly by race; the stereotypes of white women and men matched traditional sex-role stereotypes while those of black women and men did not. Although the Bayton et al. (1968) study suggests that race is implicit in sex-role stereotypes, the investigators did not control for social class (albeit Bayton et al., 1956, demonstrated that presumptions regarding class are enmeshed in perceptions of race). Thus, although the literature suggests that both race and social class are implicit variables in sex-role stereotypes, stereotypes by race, class, and sex have not been collected. The present study was undertaken to derive these race × class stereotypes of women. Given the Bayton et al. (1956) and Bayton and Muldrow (1968) results, it was hypothesized that the stereotypes of women would differ significantly by both social class and race and that the stereotypes of middle-class women, and of white women, would be most similar to our traditional stereotype of women.

Method

Subjects

The three men and 41 women undergraduate students in the sample ranged in age from 18 to 48 years, with a mean age of 22.3 years. Forty-two of the 44 participants were white, and two were black.

Procedure

Twenty-three adjectives, chosen for their frequency in all types of stereotyping investigations, were selected from Kirby and Gardner's (1972) list of adjectives. These were arranged alphabetically with Likert scales that ranged from 1 *(not at all)* to 9 *(extremely)* as indicated in the sample below.

■   **Society's stereotype of middle-class black women is:**

	Not at all								*Extremely*
Ambitious	1	2	3	4	5	6	7	8	9
Competent	1	2	3	4	5	6	7	8	9
Confused	1	2	3	4	5	6	7	8	9
Dependent	1	2	3	4	5	6	7	8	9

In order to reduce resistance to the task, a cover sheet of instructions required that the participant assign the adjectives to the groups in "the manner that best describes *society's* stereotype of the group." In addition, a space was provided (at the bottom of the questionnaire) where the participant could indicate that degree to which s/he personally agreed or disagreed (on a 9-point Likert scale) with the social stereotype. Given these instructions, no questionnaires were refused.

Four stimulus persons—middle-class black women, middle-class white women, lower-class black women, and lower-class white women—were used, each presented on a separate page. Each participant received all four stimulus persons (the order was random), a cover sheet of instructions, and a page on which to indicate his/her sex, race, and age.

Instructors (all white males) in two undergraduate psychology courses asked their students to participate in a research project. The faculty then distributed the anonymous questionnaires to those students who volunteered, requested that they read the instructions carefully, and then collected the questionnaires.

Results

A multivariate analysis of variance (MANOVA), with two independent group factors (class and race) and 24 dependent variables (23 adjectives and one degree-of-agreement rating), was run on the BMDP4V program. These MANOVA results are given in Table 1. As indicated in Table 1, main effects for social class and for race emerged, but no interaction effect was found. Thus, the stereotypes of middle-class and of lower-class women differed significantly on the best-weighted linear combination of the adjectives, and the stereotypes of black and of white women also differed significantly on the weighted composite of adjectives. The MANOVA was followed-up with a series of one-way ANOVAs by social class and race, respectively. The ANOVA results by social class are given in Table 2, along with the mean score for each group on each adjective (range: 1 = *not at all* to 9 = *extremely*).

As shown in Table 2, the stereotype of middle-class women received significantly higher ratings than the lower-class female stereotype on ambitious, competent, happy, intelligent, self-confident, vain, and warm. The stereotype of lower-class women was rated significantly higher than the middle-class female stereotype on confused, dirty, hostile, illogical, impulsive, incoherent, inconsiderate, irresponsible, and superstitious. The social-class stereotypes of women did not differ significantly on dependent, egocentric, emotional, passive, seductive, suggestible, or talkative.

Table 1   **MANOVA of Race × Class Stereotypes of Women**

Effect	*Hotelling's* T^2	*F*	*p*
Class	297.252	5.76	<.01
Race	208.073	4.03	<.01
Class × race	40.591	0.79	ns

p = level of statistical significance

Table 2 ▦ **Stereotypes by Social Class: Mean Scores on Each Adjective**

Variable	*Lower-class women*	*Middle-class women*	*p*
Ambitious	3.06	5.52	<.01
Competent	3.25	5.68	<.01
Confused	5.28	4.02	<.01
Dependent	6.63	4.99	ns
Dirty	4.77	2.79	ns
Egocentric	4.26	4.72	ns
Emotional	6.31	5.82	ns
Happy	3.56	5.86	<.01
Hostile	5.63	3.76	<.01
Illogical	5.49	4.02	<.01
Impulsive	5.59	4.86	<.05
Incoherent	5.55	3.58	<.01
Inconsiderate	5.25	3.59	<.01
Intelligent	3.25	5.72	<.01
Irresponsible	5.39	3.50	<.01
Passive	4.99	4.47	ns
Seductive	4.47	4.57	ns
Self-confident	3.23	5.69	<.01
Suggestible	4.39	4.74	ns
Superstitious	5.67	4.26	<.01
Talkative	6.61	6.46	ns
Vain	4.10	5.00	<.01
Warm	4.59	6.05	<.01
Ss agreement with stereotype	6.07	5.76	ns

ns = not significant
p = level of statistical significance

In addition, participants disagreed only slightly with the social-class stereotypes of women; on a personal endorsement scale from 1 = *strongly agree* to 9 = *strongly disagree* (such that a rating of 5 is the exact midpoint) participants' average disagreement with the stereotype of middle-class women was 5.76, and with the stereotype of lower-class women it was 6.07 (this difference was not significant). In summary of the above results, the stereotypes of women by social class differed significantly on the best-weighted linear composite of the adjectives. On the basis of the size of the *F*s, this difference was primarily the product of ratings on ambitious, competent,

Table 3 ▓ Stereotypes by Race: Mean Scores on Each Adjective

Variable	Black women ($\overline{X}$)	White women ($\overline{X}$)	p
Ambitious	4.13	4.46	ns
Competent	4.23	4.71	<.05
Confused	4.56	4.75	ns
Dependent	4.91	5.71	<.01
Dirty	4.16	3.41	<.01
Egocentric	4.36	4.61	ns
Emotional	5.71	6.42	<.01
Happy	4.60	4.82	ns
Hostile	5.10	4.28	<.01
Illogical	4.78	4.73	ns
Impulsive	5.14	5.32	ns
Incoherent	4.67	4.46	ns
Inconsiderate	4.60	4.24	ns
Intelligent	4.26	4.71	<.01
Irresponsible	4.66	4.24	ns
Passive	4.33	5.13	<.01
Seductive	4.25	4.49	ns
Self-confident	4.42	4.50	ns
Suggestible	4.59	5.03	<.05
Superstitious	5.36	4.57	<.01
Talkative	6.25	6.82	<.05
Vain	4.31	4.79	<.05
Warm	5.06	5.58	<.05
Ss agreement with stereotype	6.00	5.83	ns

ns = not significant

dirty, happy, hostile, illogical, incoherent, inconsiderate, intelligent, irresponsible, self-confident, superstitious, and warm (where the stereotype of lower-class women was rated significantly higher than that of middle-class women on the most unfavorable of these adjectives).

The ANOVAs by race, and the means on each adjective for the stereotypes of black and white women, are given in Table 3.

As indicated in Table 3, the stereotype of black women was rated significantly higher than that of white women on dirty, hostile, and superstitious. The white-female stereotype received significantly higher ratings than the black on competent, dependent, emotional, intelligent, passive, suggestible, talkative, vain, and warm. The stereotypes of women by race did not differ on ambitious, confused, egocentric, happy, illogical, impulsive, incoherent, inconsiderate, irresponsible, seductive, or self-confident. Again, participants' disagreement with the stereotypes was only slightly above the midpoint of the agreement scale: the average disagreement with the stereotype of black women was 6.00, and the average disagreement with the stereotype of white women was 5.83 (this difference was not significant). Thus the stereotypes of women by race differed significantly on the best-weighted linear adjective composite and, by the order of magnitude of the ANOVA Fs, hostile and passive were the most powerful adjectives (where the stereotype of black women was higher on hostile, and the stereotype of white women was high on passive). . . .

Discussion

As predicted the stereotypes of women differed significantly by race and social class. Given that the MANOVA F for race and that for class are of the same order of magnitude, neither variable was found to be more powerful than the other. The black-female stereotype was higher than the white on dirty, hostile, and superstitious, and the stereotype of white women was rated higher than the stereotype of black women on dependent, emotional, and passive (among other adjectives). Thus the stereotype of white women here is more similar to the traditional stereotype of women (as neat, nonaggressive, passive, dependent, and emotional) found by Broverman et al. (1972). Such a result raises the possibility that race is an implicit variable in sex-role stereotyping research (where our participants assume white race when asked to assign traits to women). The differences in the stereotypes of women by race did not, however, overshadow the similarities. That is, the stereotypes of black women and white women, in spite of differing significantly, were both stereotypically feminine: mean scores on ambitious, competent, intelligent, self-confident, and hostile, for example, irrespective of race, were in the range of the exact midpoint of the scale (5). Results of pilot investigations (Landrine, 1983), like those of Broverman et al. (1972), suggest that male stimulus persons receive much higher ratings on these adjectives. Given that the stereotype of black women had relatively low scores on these adjectives, no support for the "strong" black woman stereotype (suggested by Ladner, 1971; Lynn, 1979; Wallace, 1979) was found here.

The stereotype of lower-class women was rated higher than that of middle-class women on confused, dirty, hostile, illogical, impulsive, incoherent, inconsiderate, irresponsible, and superstitious. Such a result, like that for race, raises the possibility that social class may be an implicit variable in sex-role stereotypes (where our participants attribute middle-class status to the female stimulus). These differences in the stereotypes of women by social class did not, again, overshadow the similarities. The stereotypes of both lower- and middle-class women were stereotypically feminine, in spite of the differences between them, with neither rated much above the midpoint of the scale on attributes such as self-confident, ambitious, and competent. While the stereotypes of women by race differed on the most traditional of stereotypical terms (dependent, passive, and emotional), the stereotypes of women by social class did not differ on these adjectives. Thus the stereotype of lower-class women was both stereotypically feminine, and stereotypically lower-class. The stereotype of black women was less stereotypically feminine than that of white women, but stereotypically feminine nonetheless.

These results indicate that both race and social class have significant effects on stereotypes of women, and they are consistent with the findings of Bayton et al. (1968). Although the present sample was small and composed of primarily white middle-class women, Bayton, McAlister, and Hamer's (1956) and Bayton and Muldrow's (1968) studies employed relatively large, primarily black samples of lower- and middle-class women and men. Given that the present results are consistent with those of Bayton et al. (1968), it is unlikely that they are the product of the status attributes of the present sample. These findings, then, particularly when viewed in the context of the studies of the Bayton group, strongly suggest that race and social class are implicit in what we take to be sex-role stereotypes, and thereby have serious implications for the interpretation of previous sex-role stereotype research. In addition, these findings highlight the need for research on multiple-status stereotypes. Finally, to the extent that one may generalize from these results, the data here indicate that general endorsement of social stereotypes persists.

References

Aaronson, B. S. Personality stereotypes of aging. *Journal of Gerontology,* 1966, *21,* 458–462.

Allen, M. J. *Ethnic group differences in female sex roles.* Paper presented at the Western Psychological Association Convention, San Francisco, California, 1978.

Bayton, J. A. Racial stereotypes of Negro college students. *Journal of Abnormal and Social Psychology,* 1941, *36,* 97–102.

Bayton, J. A., McAlister, L. B., & Hamer, J. Race-class stereotypes. *Journal of Negro Education,* 1956, *25,* 75–78.

Bayton, J. A., & Muldrow, J. W. Interacting variables in the perception of racial personality traits. *Journal of Experimental Research in Personality,* 1968, *3*(1).

Brigham, J. C. *Ethnic stereotypes, attitudes, and treatment of ethnic group members.* Doctoral dissertation, University of Colorado, Ann Arbor, Michigan, 1969. (University Microfilms, No. 70-5822.)

Broverman, I., Vogel, S., Broverman, D., Clarkson, F. E., & Rosenkrantz, P. S. Sex-role stereotypes: A current appraisal. *Journal of Social Issues,* 1972, *28,* 59–78.

Campbell, D. T. Stereotypes and the perception of group differences. *American Psychologist,* 1967, *22,* 817–829.

Cox, S. Ethnic diversity of female experience. In S. Cox (Ed.), *Female psychology: The emerging self.* Chicago: SRA, 1976.

Child, I. L., & Doob, L. W. Factors determining national stereotypes. *Journal of Social Psychology,* 1943, *17,* 203–219.

Cowan, M. L., & Steward, B. J. A methodological study of sex stereotypes. *Sex Roles,* 1977, *3*(3), 205–216.

Diab, L. N. Factors affecting studies of national stereotypes. *Journal of Social Psychology,* 1663, *59,* 29–40.

Diab, L. N. Factors determining group stereotypes. *Journal of Social Psychology,* 1963b, *71,* 3–10.

Ellis, L. J., & Bentler, P. M. Traditional sex-determined role standards and sex stereotypes. *Journal of Personality and Social Psychology,* 1973, *25*(1), 28–34.

Feinberger, S. Persistence of stereotypes concerning sex differences. *Journal of Abnormal and Social Psychology,* 1948, *43,* 97–101.

Gardner, R. C., Kirby, D. M., Gorospe, F. H., & Villamin, A. C. Ethnic stereotypes: An alternative assessment technique, the stereotype differential. *Journal of Social Psychology,* 1972, 87, 259–267.

Jones, J. M. *Prejudice and racism.* Reading, MA: Addison-Wesley, 1972.

Karlins, M., Coffman, T. L., & Walters, C. On the fading of social stereotypes: Studies in three generations of college students. *Journal of Personality and Social Psychology,* 1969, 13, 1–16.

Katz, D., & Braly, K. Racial stereotypes of 100 college students. *Journal of Abnormal and Social Psychology,* 1933, 28, 280–290.

Kirby, D. M., & Gardner, R. C. Ethnic stereotypes: Norms on 208 words typically used in their assessment. *Canadian Journal of Psychology,* 1972, 26(2), 140–154.

Ladner, J. A. *Tomorrow's tomorrow: The black woman.* Garden City, NY: Doubleday, 1971.

Landrine, H. *The politics of madness.* Unpublished doctoral dissertation, University of Rhode Island, 1983.

Lynn, D. B. *Daughters and parents: Past, present and future.* Monterey, CA: Brooks/Cole, 1979.

McCauley, C., & Stitt, C. L. An individual and quantitative measure of stereotypes. *Journal of Personality and Social Psychology,* 1978, 36(9), 929–940.

Rosenkrantz, P., Vogel, S., Bee, H., Broverman, I., & Broverman, D. M. Sex-role stereotypes and self-concepts in college students. *Journal of Clinical and Consulting Psychology,* 1968, 32, 287–295.

Smedley, J. W., & Bayton, J. A. Evaluative race-class stereotypes by race and perceived class of subject. *Journal of Personality and Social Psychology,* 1978, 36(5), 530–535.

Spence, J. T., Helmreich, R., & Stapp, J. Ratings of self and peers on sex role attributes and their relation to self-esteem and concepts of masculinity and femininity. *Journal of Personality and Social Psychology,* 1975, 32(1), 29–39.

Tuckman, J., & Lorge, I. Perceptual stereotypes about life adjustments. *Journal of Social Psychology,* 1956, 43, 239–245.

Tuckman, J., & Lorge, I. Attitudes toward aging of individuals with experience with the aged. *Journal of Genetic Psychology,* 1958a, 92, 199–204.

Tuckman, J., & Lorge, I. The projection of personal symptoms into stereotypes about aging. *Journal of Gerontology,* 1958b, 13, 70–73.

Wallace, M. *Black macho and the myth of the superwoman.* New York: Dial Press, 1979.

Watkins, M., & David, J. (Eds.). *To be a black woman: Portraits in fact and fiction.* New York: Morrow, 1970.

Weitzman, L. J. Sex-role socialization. In J. Freeman (Ed.), *Women: A feminist perspective.* Palo Alto, CA: Mayfield, 1975.

Questions for Thought

1. Compare and contrast the stereotypes of Black versus White women and of middle-class versus lower-class women.

2. Landrine suggests that race is an "implicit variable" in research on gender stereotypes and that the stereotypes of "women" found by earlier researchers are really stereotypes of White women. What evidence from her own study and earlier research does Landrine use to support this point?

3. The sample for Landrine's study was small and comprised primarily of White women college students. Do you think she would have found similar or different results with a sample of Black women or with a sample of poor women? Explain your answer.

4. People have somewhat different stereotypes of specific subgroups of women, such as lower-class White women or middle-class Black women. In addition to race and class, what other personal or social factors might influence stereo-

types of women? Select one factor; then discuss and give examples of how this might affect college students' stereotypes of women.

5. Landrine studied stereotypes of women and considered the impact of two factors—race and social class. Design a study to investigate stereotypes of different types of *men*. Include two factors that you think are relevant to stereotypes of men. Describe at least two testable predictions about what your results would show.

6. Select a comedy, drama, or other fictional TV show or movie. Describe the different types of women and men presented. Do the main characters reflect stereotypes of women and men? Explain your answer.

Changing and Diverse Roles of Women in American Indian Cultures

Teresa D. LaFromboise

Anneliese M. Heyle

Emily J. Ozer

In traditional American Indian cultures, women were highly valued as caretakers and transmitters of cultural knowledge. Many tribes looked to women spirits for guidance. American Indian cultures also offered institutionalized alternatives to women's traditional roles, such as "manly-hearted woman" and "warrior woman." The Whites who ruled America attempted to replace Indian tribal culture with the values and practices of their dominant group. This process of acculturation decreased the status, power, and role flexibility once enjoyed by women in many Indian tribes. Today American Indian women, especially those who leave home to go to college or move to cities, live bicultural lifestyles. Although rooted in their tribal culture, these women are also exposed to the dominant culture's values of individual achievement and competition.

This article explores traditional and contemporary sex roles of Indian women. It emphasizes the renewing power of the feminine—a creative, healing balance that arises as traditional and contemporary strengths are brought together. The survival of the extended family throughout two hundred years of governmental policy attests to Indian women's resilience despite continuous role readjustment, value conflict, and economic pressure. Tribal diversity and predominantly egalitarian structural similarities are affirmed in this work through reviews of ethnographic studies addressing the roles of Indian women prior to European contact. The conventional and alternative roles of Indian women in traditional times are examined with an eye toward the spiritual source of Indian women's strength. Studies outlining the emotional and spiritual costs of contemporary

Indian women living bicultural lifestyles, especially those pursuing advanced educational training, highlight the continued use of traditional Indian coping mechanisms. Finally, the current movement toward retraditionalization of roles of Indian women as caretakers and transmitters of cultural knowledge is posited as an effective means of overcoming problems and achieving Indian self-determination.

A fundamental methodological issue in the study of sex roles of Indian women concerns the recognition of original diversity and eventual change in the social structures of American Indian societies (Allen, 1986; Medicine, 1980). Because traditional American Indian social systems and life patterns have been tremendously disrupted by White colonization and expansion, it is critical to consider gender roles over time and in several contexts: A study of American Indian women's activities and spheres of power must include an examination of their specific tribes' traditional structures, the varying direct and indirect effects of White culture on that tribe, the mediating factors affecting the magnitude and direction of White influence, and the personal and professional responses and adaptations of Indian women to cultural pressures and changes (Allen, 1986; Medicine, 1980).

There is a dearth of empirical research focused on American Indian women and written from an Indian cultural perspective. The extremely limited empirical research presented on contemporary Indian women provides more information regarding health and economic indicators than on sex roles and the status of women. In fact, there has been scant research on contemporary Indian women outside of a clinical or pathological perspective. While it is true that many current Indian practices and social structures now mirror Anglo culture as a result of forced acculturation, Christianization, and economic change (to name just a few significant forces), Indian women are a dynamic and diverse cultural group whose strength, contemporary lifestyles, and social structures merit increased empirical study and documentation (Hudson, 1980).

There is an increasing body of evidence to support the claim that the non-Indian, male-centered biases of traditional social science research has provided both inaccurate and incomplete depictions of American Indian social systems and behavior. Predominantly male, non-Indian ethnographers of American Indian cultures have selectively chosen to study and have had more access to male activities and male informants. This has led to indirect and distorted descriptions of Indian women's activities and beliefs (Leacock, 1986). The tendency to ignore fundamental female roles, blur tribal variations, and misunderstand the centrality of the Spirit World in Indian life suggests that the veracity of this body of work is questionable (Allen, 1981; Green, 1976; Medicine, 1980).

Ethnographic analysis has also been heavily influenced by stereotypical images, myths, and fantasies which limit Indian women to dichotomous princess/squaw roles (Green, 1976; Medicine, 1980; Powers, 1986; Terrell & Terrell, 1974; Welch, 1987). Koehler (1982) provides an excellent bibliography of the existing literature regarding Native American women. He points out that the inappropriate perspectives of previous custom studies which focused on isolated aspects of Indian women's lives without understanding their complexity and cultural contexts are finally being supplemented by Indian women's own reflections and research.

Theories and data generated by "outsider" observers regarding American Indian women not only reflect non-Indian expectations and stereotypes regarding Indian women (Christensen, 1975; Green, 1983; Lurie, 1972; Metoyer, 1979) but for the most part also represent the sex roles, status of women, and behavior only while the group conducted its external affairs or interacted with outsiders (Brady, Crome, & Reese, 1984). In some tribes, dealing with outsiders was a sex-differentiated activity fulfilled by men; non-Indians often overestimated male power within the tribe because they had little experience with women's spheres of power and activity (Parezo, 1982).

Furthermore, considering the widespread, long-term history of violence and oppression waged against Indian people by non-Indians, it would be hard to imagine why Indian women would trust outsiders with the knowledge of their intimate rituals, thoughts, or feelings. Many observer-researchers attempting to "study" American Indian women succeeded more in studying their useful defense mechanisms and coping strategies—such as passive resistance and secrecy—rather than their internal personalities or behavior patterns (Brady, Crome, & Reese, 1984). Male-centered assumptions—both Indian and non-Indian—have led to interpretations of Indian rituals and traditions now contested by American Indian women.

Roles of Women in Traditional Indian Life

A woman's identity in traditional Indian life was firmly rooted in her spirituality, extended family, and tribe (Allen, 1986; Green, 1980; Jaimes, 1982; LaFromboise, 1989; Welch, 1987; Witt, 1974). Women saw themselves as collective beings (Benally, 1988) fulfilling harmonious roles in the biological, spiritual, and social worlds: Biologically, they valued being mothers and raising healthy families; spiritually, they were considered extensions of the Spirit Mother and keys to the continuation of their people (Allen, 1986; Jenks, 1986); and socially they served as transmitters of cultural knowledge and caretakers of their children and relatives (Niethammer, 1977). Great value was ascribed to these traditional female roles.

Many western North American tribes—such as the Klamath—were based on egalitarian systems of reciprocity in which separate, complementary, and equally essential tasks were assigned to each sex (Blackwood, 1984). Contemporary Indian social scientists and writers argue that these social systems were misinterpreted by non-Indian observers socialized to equate difference with inequality and hierarchy (Albers & Medicine, 1983; Green, 1976). Tribal diversity must be stressed: The current claim is not that women in all tribes shared equal status and power with men, but that the high frequency of egalitarian relationships has been greatly underrepresented.

Allen (1981) and Beiswinger and Jeanotte (1985) emphasize the fundamentality of the Spirit World and tribal members' intensely personal relationships with particular spirits in the social structure and gender roles in traditional Indian life. In this traditional world view, everything in the universe, including a woman's (and man's) power and identity was derived from direct connections to the Spirit World (see Tanner, 1979, for a detailed account of the intertribal life and power of a Mohawk medicine woman). Many tribes looked to women spirits or mythological forebears of the people like Thought Woman of the Keres, Clay Lady of the Santa Clara Pueblo, Changing Woman of the Navajo, or White Buffalo Calf Woman of the Sioux for an understanding of life and guidance concerning how to behave (Jenks, 1986; Zak, 1988, 1989). Although tribes may have had conventional ideals of behavior for each gender group, nonconformity was identified and sanctioned through dreams or ceremonial connections with particular spirits.

Role and gender variations and sex-differentiated spheres of social and governing power differed according to the social structure and traditions of each tribal group (Medicine, 1978, 1980). Although in most tribes there were distinct areas of female and male production, this diversion was not entirely rigid and women's roles and tasks were often extremely variable. In some tribes, women enjoyed significant flexibility and latitude in their gender role and lifestyle preferences (Anderson, 1985; Blackwood, 1984; Hamamsy, 1957; Medicine, 1980; Metoyer, 1979; Parezo, 1982; Welch, 1987). In these societies, free expression of sexuality and nonconformist gender roles were permitted, with nontraditional males and females, gays, and lesbians accepted to varying degrees within the group (Allen, 1981, 1986; Blackwood, 1984; Jacobs, 1977).

Recent research demonstrates the existence of institutionalized alternative female roles alongside roles that have been interpreted as traditional. Women in Plains tribes, such as Canadian Blackfeet, have typically been pictured as chaste, submissive, and hard-working wives. There is evidence within this tribe for such institutionalized roles as: the independent and aggressive "manly-hearted women," the sexually promiscuous "crazy women," and chief or "sit-by" wife, and the important religious role of the Sun Dance woman. Other examples of alternative female roles in Plains tribes include daring Cheyenne women horse-riders and Lakota girls who were named "child beloved" and were honored by participation in the Buffalo Ceremony and Virgin Fire. There is also evidence from the Apache, Crow, Cheyenne, Blackfeet, and Pawnee tribes that the "warrior woman" role was widespread across the continent (Buchanan, 1986; Liberty, 1982; Medicine, 1983b).

As the "manly-hearted" and "warrior woman" names suggest, some of the Indian females' alternative roles specifically allowed them to express masculine traits or participate in male-associated occupations without dressing as men or assuming their social roles (Lewis, 1941). Other roles, however, such as the "berdache," which was socially sanctioned at various levels in at least 33 tribes, involved a woman's thorough shift to the male social and occupational role sometimes accompanied by homosexual marriage or sexual relationships (although the berdache's assumed lesbianism is a subject of debate) (Allen, 1981; Blackwood, 1984; Callender & Kochems, 1983; McCormack, 1976). The "berdache" role is also termed a "cross-gender" role (Blackwood, 1984).

Gender identification in pre-colonial Indian tribes, unlike that in Anglo culture, seemed to center on an individual's participation in gender-specific ceremonies and tasks rather than on her sexual anatomy or choice of sexual partners (Callender & Kochems, 1983). Transition to a male gender role could be prompted and validated by a girl's interest in traditionally male tasks or a refusal to perform female tasks; Kaska families that had all daughters yet desired a son would encourage the child with the most inclination to become "like a man" to participate in puberty initiation ceremonies and customs for boys instead of girls. Involvement in these activities publicly validated the role change. In the Cocopa tribe, cross-gender females followed the male custom of nose-piercing rather than getting their chins tattooed as did other women.

Although the socializing process differed from tribe to tribe, community recognition and validation of the women's new cross-gender role was acquired through acceptable channels. In the Southwest, for example, dream experience was very important in ritual life as an avenue to gain special powers and social sanction of the use of those powers. In such tribes, such as the Mohave, all cross-gender individuals reported dreaming about their role change.

Cross-gender women could not marry men because they could not perform traditional female-specific tasks; in order to gain the household and kinship benefits of marriage, they married women and fulfilled the household, community, and ritual obligations of a male. Cross-gender individuals were often unusually good providers and were valued for their economic contributions to the family and tribe; households with a cross-gender partner were often more wealthy than the norm, probably because they focused on work rather than on children (Callender & Kochems, 1983).

There is considerable anthropological debate regarding the defining characteristics, sexual behavior, degree of social acceptance, and prevalence of the cross-gender or "berdache" status; clarifications are often difficult due to confusion and disgust on the part of early non-Indian observers and social scientists. Callender and Kochems (1983) provide an excellent review of the contradictory "berdache" literature and highlight the methodological biases and limitations of the assessment of this alternative role. They indicate that outsider cultural biases against transvestitism, cross-gender roles, and cross-sexual behavior made for research that condemned rather than examined the existence of berdaches. Observer bias contributed to Indian reticence regarding berdache acceptance and prevalence, and perhaps led to within-tribe cultural sanctions against the berdache status (Callender & Kochems, 1983; Gatschet, 1891; McCoy, 1976; Swanton, 1911).

There is substantial support for the view that women were respected and rewarded for successful cross-gender role activity (Lewis, 1941); manly-hearted women and female berdaches earned high reputations (Niethammer, 1977) and were differentiated from other women by their wealth, status, boldness and efficiency. But although males in the berdache role could earn great respect for success and efficiency in traditionally feminine spheres of work, womanliness was certainly not the typical Indian male ideal.

The status of Indian woman, however, increased with their age (in contrast with Anglo culture's youth emphasis): A post-menopause woman, as the Winnebagos put it, was "just like a man" (Witt, 1974, p. 32). Older women's age and wisdom were revered and their opinions regarding tribal history, herbal medicines, and sacred matters were valued (Metoyer, 1979; Lurie, 1972). Thus, in some tribes it was possible for women to achieve status levels equal to men, but they earned equal status by accumulating years or success in cross-gender tasks.

Some Indian social systems, however, including the Cherokee, Montagnais-Naskapi, Navajo, Iroquois, Mandan, Hopi, Zuni, Northern Paiute and Eastern Pueblo tribes, provide clear evidence that women played critical economic, political, and spiritual roles in tribal life without the advantages of age or cross-gender task success (Allen, 1986; Anderson, 1985; Kidwell, 1979; Lynch, 1986; Witt, 1974). In these tribes, matrilineal patterns of inheritance were observed and in those with agricultural economies, the land, crops, houses, and tools were owned by the women while the men cultivated the gardens and were responsible for much of the labor. Even in non-agricultural economies women's close relationship to food and the supply of food conferred great power upon her (Seton & Seton, 1953).

Women sometimes exercised formal governing authority on the basis of their spiritual power, as was the case in pre-colonization Cherokee gynocracy, or "petticoat government," whose Women's Council had a significant influence on tribal decisions. The "Beloved Woman of the Nation," or head of the Women's Council of the Cherokee, was believed to speak the words of the Great Spirit (Allen, 1986).

Before the tribe's conversion to Catholicism, the Montagnais-Naskapi social system was striking in its women-centeredness and flexibility. Women exercised a great deal of control over family decisions (such as planning when to move) and other household affairs; in fact, missionaries reported, with dismay, that men followed their wives' advice and would not act against their wishes (Anderson, 1985). Women also enjoyed a tremendous amount of freedom regarding issues of sexuality, marriage, and divorce. In general, the Montagnais-Naskapi and Huron cultures were non-authoritarian and peaceful; children were not punished and women were encouraged to be independent and decisive (Allen, 1986; Anderson, 1985).

Although males might have monopolized public roles and positions of authority, important family and tribal decisions were also determined in the private sphere; therefore, the reality of power was often very different from its public manifestation (Friedl, 1967). Realizing the importance of private power is critical to understanding Indian cultural systems because—in general—Indian women exercised almost complete control over the home, the children, and belongings inside the home.

Impact of Acculturation on Gender Roles, Power, and Status

The effects of acculturation on American Indian gender roles of course depend on the original role and status of women before colonization and the nature of the acculturation strategies inflicted upon a woman's particular tribe. The overwhelming result of acculturation has been a breakdown of the complementary nature of male-female relations and a general increase in Indian male dominance and control over Indian women (Brady, Crome, & Reese, 1984; Welch, 1987). With the collapse of traditional religion and culture, women lost not only some very fundamental spiritual roles but also lost the significance and ritual power of the sex-specific activities and roles that they were allowed to maintain, such as puberty, menstruation, childbearing, and domestic responsibilities (Allen, 1986).

Colonizers considered tribal gender role flexibility, matrilocal and extended family patterns, complementarity in gender power relations, and sexual freedom on the part of women subversive to the intended European-style political, social, and religious order. Sometimes, as in the case of the Montagnais-Naskapi and the

Iroquois, Indian men collaborated with the colonizers and helped to subjugate Indian women by the establishment of male-dominated religious and social organizations within the tribe (Anderson, 1985; Livingston, 1974).

Anderson (1985) analyzes the relationship between the advent of commodity exchange and production systems and the subordination of women through an examination of the interactions between 17th-century French missionaries and the Montagnais-Naskapi and Huron tribes along the St. Lawrence River. The power of the missionaries to support the tribes' matriarchal and egalitarian social systems in which women were in no way subservient to men fundamentally lay in the colonizer's ability to capitalize on environmental conditions and then completely control the tribe's livelihood and society.

More recently, changes in the traditional economic system of the largest American Indian tribe, the Navajo, have also been identified as contributing to the decrease in women's status and power within the family and the transformation of the extended family pattern into independent households. Navajo women and men originally occupied complementary roles with a system of female inheritance; Navajo women made the family's financial decisions and had at least as much influence as their husbands in all spheres of life (Hamamsy, 1957).

With men's increased participation in off-reservation employment, there was a shift toward independent families. Some families moved to the outskirts of the reservation or to border towns. Women became more dependent on their husbands—characterized by Hamamsy (1957) as often erratic and irresponsible providers—for cash income. Men, however, began to claim that their wage labor earnings belonged to them and not to the family group. Complementary roles disintegrated. Women's troubles were compounded by the erosion of the extended family network because they no longer had extensive family help in raising their children. Sometimes Navajo girls were taken out of school to help at home, contributing to their limited education and outside job skills (Hamamsy, 1957). Recently, higher rates of hypertension were reported among elderly Navajo women than Navajo men due to acculturation, especially among the women who were most educated and isolated (Kunitz & Levy, 1986).

A major agent of acculturation started in the late 19th century in the practice of removing young Indian children from their homes to attend Bureau of Indian Affairs (BIA) boarding schools. Numerous studies in the past two decades attest to the psychological trauma and adjustment problems caused by experiences within these boarding schools (Attneave & Dill, 1980; Beiser, 1974; Dlugokinski & Kramer, 1974; Kleinfeld & Bloom, 1977). Recent research indicates that the stress associated with Indian women's forced attendance in schools away from home during adolescence has apparently been manifested in lowered self-esteem and inhibitions associated with maternal capabilities (Metcalf, 1976).

Many of the boarding schools were extremely regimented and Indian girls' education was eventually degraded into domestic labor for the school and for community homes and businesses. Indian girls were given less classroom instruction than Indian boys (Szasz, 1980) and were beaten if they resisted the work. Many tried to run away (Trennert, 1982). When female students returned to their reservations, they found that their domestic and cooking skills were not appropriate to the technology or culture of the reservation and they were often mocked or shunned for their "White ways." Some left the reservation to return to the cities to become maids, prostitutes, and dance hall girls (Trennert, 1982).

The establishment of both the boarding schools and the BIA field matron program represented only two efforts on the part of the U.S. government to teach Indian women how to behave (and work) like White women and thereby rescue them from the perceived drudgery and backwardness of their traditional lives (Bannan, 1984; Trennert, 1982). Even attempts to elevate Indian women to the status of White women through Indian New Deal policies seriously ignored the traditional, political roles Indian women played at that time (Bernstein, 1984). It was thought that if Indian women were shown the superiority of White lifestyles, they would then return to the reservation to "civilize" their own people.

Despite traumatic and confusing experiences such as the BIA boarding schools and other modes of forced acculturation, there is evidence that Indian women have been somewhat better able to adapt to acculturation than have Indian men (Attneave, 1982; Spindler & Spindler, 1958). Perhaps Indian women were seen as less threatening than Indian men. Their tradition of accepted role flexibility may have facilitated a readiness to take on work roles within the dominant society that Indian men would be unwilling or offended to pursue.

Women in some tribes, such as the Oglala Sioux and Northern Paiute, have been more effective than their male counterparts as landowners, political leaders, and liaisons with Whites, thereby increasing their relative power and status (Lynch, 1986; Mead, 1982; Powers, 1986). In the case of the Northern Paiute and Oglala Sioux, women received advanced training (primarily in the area of education and social welfare) under federal policies and were then able to better fulfill professional and governmental roles (Lynch, 1986; Powers, 1986). However, despite isolated accounts of positive advances resulting from acculturation (only relative to Indian men, of course, who have also suffered tremendous reductions in power and status), acculturation has been severely destructive to the status, power, and role flexibility that Indian women in many tribes once enjoyed. Acculturation brought about rigid, Christianized societies intolerant of religious freedom, traditional lifestyles, nonconformist gender and sex roles, and sexual freedom (Allen, 1986).

Bicultural Lifestyles

Living in two different cultural worlds, the Indian and the Anglo, can be "a feast of appreciation for human ingenuity, or it can be the bitterest trap" (Witt, 1981, p. 11). Regardless of an Indian woman's profession, lifestyle, or geographical base, she retains a sense of homeland and duty to her people (Witt, 1974). Adapting to the majority culture—by moving to cities, attending college or university, or seeking professional jobs and training—can provide greater economic and political opportunities for Indian women and the communities they represent but can also be a major source of conflict and stress (Barter & Barter, 1974; LaFromboise, 1988b) and can increase individuals' vulnerability to the development of psychological problems (Kemnitzer, 1973; Spindler & Spindler, 1958).

Although the high frequency of severe social and economic problems can make reservation life extremely bleak, an Indian woman within her own cultural context at least has the social support of her extended family network and a community of people who share her values and practices. Off the reservation, Indian women may become geographically and culturally isolated from their families and may find it extremely difficult to adjust—cognitively and socially—to "White" or majority culture.

In general, the majority culture espouses a work ethic centered around individual achievement, competitiveness, and the accumulation of property and titles; cultural traditions and family ties are often considered of secondary importance compared with personal social and professional mobility. Majority values and societal pressures clearly conflict with primary Indian communal concerns which emphasize observance of tradition, responsibility for extended family and friends, cooperation, and group identification.

Educational Issues

Studies of adolescent Indian females in academic and athletic competition reveal that they (like many women from other cultures) do not focus on their individual success when competing against males but rather will inhibit their own performance level, especially when the men are not performing well (Weisfeld, Weisfeld, & Callaghan, 1982; Weisfeld, Weisfeld, Warren, & Freeman, 1983). Indian girls' behavior is consistent with their cultural training which stresses cooperation and group cohesion but is clearly counterproductive in Anglo contexts in which individuals are rewarded through success in competition.

American Indian college students are clearly anomalies in communities characterized by illiteracy and tremendously high drop-out rates (Coladarci, 1983; Jacobson, 1973; Sanders, 1987). Nearly one-third of all Indian adults are classified as illiterate and only 31% of all Indians have a high school education (U.S. Bureau of the Census, 1983). American Indian women must work hard to break down powerful social and psychological barriers just to get into college (LaFromboise, 1984). Recent empirical research concerning American Indian college women provides evidence that they experience tremendous difficulties in adapting to the competitive culture of higher education institutions (Edgewater, 1981; LaFromboise, 1988b) and face a multitude of bicultural, conflicting pressures and expectations. Family and community members often discourage Indian women from pursuing post-secondary education and a survey of 61 Indian female undergraduates indicates that almost 90% of the students felt that they were going against their culture by attending college (Kidwell, 1976). Furthermore, attending college limits Indian women's chances for marrying within their culture because Indian men without college degrees will seldom marry a university graduate.

In light of the multitude of immediate and concrete pressures working against Indian college women's motivation and ability to lead a productive academic lifestyle, it is not surprising that their college completion rates—which unfortunately must be inferred from statistics for both Indian women and men—are extremely low: 18% for Indian undergraduates, 1% for masters' degree candidates, and .2% for doctoral degree candidates (National Research Council, 1986; Ryan, 1982). . . .

Retraditionalized Roles of Contemporary Indian Women

Retraditionalization—or the extension of traditional caretaking and cultural transmission roles to include activities vital to the continuity of Indian communities within a predominantly non-Indian society—represents a major current attempt on the part of Indian women to integrate traditional and contemporary demands in a positive, culturally-consistent manner (Green, 1983). The structure of the cultural system remains intact, but the specific jobs are modernized in accordance with social change.

Many Indian women are increasingly visible in professional roles such as social workers, psychologists, writers, artists, political leaders with the intent of serving their communities and tribes. Some noteworthy examples of Indian women leaders include: La Donna Harris (Comanche), president and director of American Indians for Opportunity; Wilma Mankiller, Chief of the Cherokee Nation; Jo Ann Sarracino (Laguna), developer of the Native American Mineral Engineering and Science Program; and Nancy Wallace (Comanche/Creek), manager of the Industrial Engineering Department at Digital, the third largest computer company in the world. These "retraditionalized" American Indian women have achieved success by exhibiting independence, leadership, confidence, competitiveness, and emotional control. Without ignoring their cultural heritage, losing acceptance among their people, or forfeiting the ability to behave appropriately within Indian cultures, Indian women leaders have increased respect and status for Indian people and gained professional recognition for themselves.

Women's political power in a substantial number of tribes is significant and on the rise. Their interest and position in the policy-making arena has stemmed from traditional concerns for the community and has often found a foundation in existing or vestigial female networks and power bases within the tribe. In a study of 10 tribal councils of Nevada reservations, Lynch (1986) reports that women constituted the vast majority of local committee and service clubs and that only one tribal council did not have women members.

On the Northern Paiute reservation, matrilocal marriage patterns still in effect—28 out of 32 households contained married men born and raised off of the reservation—facilitated women's ability to take active political roles within the tribe. Women's kinship connections and long-term concerns for community issues, along with the historical importance of women's contributions to the families' existence and their experience in coordinating people in social activities and common goals contributed to their effectiveness as leaders (Lynch, 1986).

Oglala Sioux women—who are steadily occupying more positions as tribal council members, judges, and decision-makers—also credit women's traditional family skills and experiences as important factors in their leadership ability; one Oglala Sioux woman judge explained that as a mother, she was accustomed to making unpopular decisions and making people "stick" to them (Powers, 1986). Although Oglala women of all ages have become politically active and many have led or participated in protests for treaty rights, few would consider themselves political activists but rather see themselves as people fulfilling vital tribal needs (Powers, 1986).

Thus, for many Indian women, positions of authority and prominence are natural evolutions of their caretaking role and they see their actions as personal rather than organizational. Their goal is to be productive yet humble leaders by virtue, not position (Campbell, 1988). It is important to recognize that retraditionalization efforts on the part of Indian women are often inconsistent with some goals of the current majority-culture women's movement. Non-Indian feminists emphasize middle-class themes of independence and androgyny whereas Indian women often see their work in the context of their families, their nations, and Sacred Mother Earth (Green, 1983; Medicine, 1983). Preservation and restoration of their race and culture is at least as important to Indian women as are their individual goals for professional achievement and success, although many Indian women clearly have made important professional commitments and value the role of work in their lives.

By maintaining their past traditions rather than shedding them, major social and political changes on the part of Indian women may take many years; however, these changes will be firmly based on a solid sense of identity and will involve lowered levels of psychological and interpersonal conflict. Indian women are in the process of redefining identities long-obscured by the stereotypes and misconceptions of others. Despite potential loss of their traditional spiritual base and traditional social and economic roles due to acculturation and the advent of male-centered cultural norms, Indian women have maintained their responsibilities to family and tribe and have continued to work to develop themselves and their communities. With a respect for the past and clear agendas for the future, Indian women remain as a strong force in their own land.

References

Albers, P., & Medicine, B. (1983). *The hidden half: Studies of Plains Indian women*. New York: University Press of America.

Allen, P. G. (1981). Lesbians in American Indian cultures. *Conditions, 7*, 67–87.

Allen, P. G. (1986). *The sacred hoop*. Boston: Beacon Press.

Anderson, K. (1985). Commodity exchange and subordination: Montagnais-Naskapi and Huron women, 1600–1650. *Signs: Journal of Women in Culture and Society, 11*(1), 48–62.

Attneave, C. L. (1982). American Indian and Alaska Native families: Emigrants in their own homeland. In M. McGoldrick, J. K. Pearce, & J. Giordano (Eds.), *Ethnicity and family therapy* (pp. 55–83). New York: Guilford Press.

Attneave, C., & Dill, A. (1980). Indian boarding schools and Indian women: Blessing or curse? In National Institute of Education (Ed.), *Conference on the Educational and Occupational Needs of American Indian Women* (pp. 211–230). Washington, DC: U.S. Department of Education.

Attneave, C. L., & Speck, R. V. (1974). Social network intervention in time and space. In A. Jacobs & W. Spradlin (Eds.), *The group as agent of change* (pp. 166–186). New York: Behavioral Publications.

Bannan, H. (1984). *True womanhood on the reservation: Field matrons in the United States Indian Service*. Tucson, AZ: Southwest Institute for Research on Women, University of Arizona.

Barter, E. R., & Barter, J. T. (1974). Urban Indians and mental health problems. *Psychiatric Annals, 4*, 37–43.

Beiser, M. (1974). A hazard to mental health: Indian boarding schools. *American Journal of Psychiatry, 131*, 305–306.

Beiswinger, J. N., & Jeanotte, H. (1985). *Medicine women*. Grand Forks, ND: University of North Dakota Press.

Benally, S. (1988, August). Guest editorial. *Winds of Change, 3*(3), 6.

Bernstein, A. (1984). A mixed record: The political enfranchisement of American Indian women during the Indian new deal. In W. Williams (Ed.), *Indian leadership* (pp. 13–20). Manhattan, KS: Sunflower University Press.

Blackwood, E. (1984). Sexuality and gender in certain Native American tribes: The case of the cross-gender females. *Signs: Journal of Women in Culture and Society, 10,* 27–42.

Brady, V., Crome, S., & Reese, L. (1984). Resist! Survival tactics of Indian women. *California History, 63,* 140–151.

Buchanan, K. M. (1986). *Apache women warriors.* El Paso, TX: Texas Western Press.

Campbell, L. (1988). The spirit need not die. A people in peril [Special issue]. *Anchorage Daily News.*

Callender, C., & Kochems, L. (1983). The North American berdache. *Current Anthropology, 24*(4), 443–470.

Christensen, R. (1975). Indian women: A historical and personal perspective. *Pupil and Personal Services Journal, 4,* 13–22.

Coladarci, T. (1983). High school dropout among Native Americans. *Journal of American Indian Education, 23,* 15–22.

Dlugokinski, E., & Kramer, L. (1974). A system of neglect: Indian boarding schools. *American Journal of Psychiatry, 131,* 670–673.

Edgewater, J. L. (1981). Stress and the Navajo university student. *Journal of American Indian Education, 20,* 25–31.

Friedl, E. (1967). The position of women: Appearance and reality. *Anthropological Quarterly, 40,* 97–108.

Gatschet, A. B. (1891). The Karankawa Indians, the coast people of Texas. *Papers of the Peabody Museum of Archaeology and Ethnology, 1*(2).

Green, R. (1976). The Pocahontas perplex: The image of Indian women in American culture. *Massachusetts Review, 14,* 698–714.

Green, R. (1980). Native American women. *Signs: Journal of Women in Culture and Society, 6*(2), 248–267.

Green, R. (1983). *Native American women: A contextual bibliography.* Bloomington, IN: Indiana University Press.

Hamamsy, L. (1957). The role of women in a changing Navaho society. *American Anthropologist, 59,* 101–111.

Hudson, G. (1980). Participatory research by Indian women in Northern Ontario remote communities. *Convergence: An International Journal of Adult Education, 13*(1–2), 24–33.

Jacobs, S. E. (1977). Berdache: A brief review of the literature. *Colorado Anthropology, 1,* 25–40.

Jacobson, D. (1973). *Alaskan Native high school dropouts. Report prepared for project ANNA.* Anchorage, AK: Alaska Federation of Natives. (ERIC Document Reproduction Service No. ED 088651).

Jaimes, M. A. (1982). Towards a new image of American Indian women. *Journal of American Indian Education, 22*(1), 18–32.

Jenks, K. (1986). "Changing women": The Navajo therapist goddess. *Psychological Perspectives, 17*(2), 202–221.

Kemnitzer, L. S. (1973). Adjustment and value conflict in urbanizing Dakota Indians measured by Q-sort techniques. *American Anthropologist, 75,* 687–707.

Kidwell, C. A. (1976, December). The status of American Indian women in higher education. In National Institute of Education, *Conference on the Educational and Occupational Needs of American Indian Women* (pp. 83–123). Washington, DC: U.S. Department of Education.

Kidwell, C. S. (1979). The power of women in three American Indian societies. *Journal of Ethnic Studies, 6,* 113–121.

Kleinfeld, J., & Bloom, J. (1977). Boarding schools: Effect on the mental health of Eskimo adolescents. *American Journal of Psychiatry, 134*(4), 411–417.

Koehler, L. (1982). Native women of the Americas: A bibliography. *Frontiers, 6*(3), 73–101.

Kunitz, S., & Levy, J. (1986). The prevalence of hypertension among elderly Navajos: A test of the acculturation hypothesis. *Culture, Medicine, and Psychiatry, 10,* 97–121.

LaFromboise, T. (1984). Professionalization of American Indian women in postsecondary education, *Journal of College Student Personnel, 25,* 470–472.

LaFromboise, T. (1988). *Cultural and cognitive considerations in the coping of American Indian women in higher education.* Unpublished manuscript, Stanford University, School of Education, Stanford.

LaFromboise, T. (1989). *Circles of women: Professionalization training for American Indian women.* Newton, MA: Women's Educational Equity Act Press.

Leacock, E. (1986). Women, power and authority. In L. Dube, E. Leacock, & S. Ardener (Eds.), *Visibility and power: Essays on women in society and development* (pp. 107–135). Delhi: Oxford University Press.

Lewis, O. (1941). Manly-hearted women among the Northern Piegan. *American Anthropologist, 43,* 173–187.

Liberty, M. (1982). Hell came with horses: Plains Indian women in the equestrian era. *Montana, 32,* 10–19.

Livingston, K. (1974). Contemporary Iroquois women and work: A study of consciousness of inequality. (Doctoral dissertation, Cornell Unviersity, 1974). *Dissertation Abstracts International, 35,* 3194A.

Lurie, N. O. (1972). Indian women: A legacy of freedom. In R. L. Iacopi & B. L. Fontana (Eds.), *Look to the mountaintop* (pp. 29–36). San Jose, CA: Gousha Publications.

Lynch, R. (1986). Women in Northern Paiute politics. *Signs: Journal of Women in Culture and Society, 11*(21), 352–366.

McCormack, P. (Ed.). (1976). Cross-sex relations and Native peoples [Special Issue]. *Western Canadian Journal of Anthropology, 6*(3).

McCoy, I. (1976). His presence was so disgusting. In J. Katz (Ed.), *Gay American history* (p. 300). New York: Crowell.

Mead, M. (1982). *The changing culture of an Indian tribe.* New York: Columbia University Press.

Medicine, B. (1978). *The Native American woman: A perspective.* Austin, TX: National Educational Laboratory Publishers, Inc.

Medicine, B. (1980). American Indian women: Spirituality and status. *Bread and Roses, 2*(1), 15–18.

Medicine, B. (1983). "Warrior woman"—Sex role alternatives for Plains Indian women. In P. Albers & B. Medicine (Eds.), *The hidden half: Studies of Plains Indian women* (pp. 267–280). Lanham, MD: University Press of America, Inc.

Metcalf, A. (1976). From schoolgirl to mother: The effects of education on Navajo women. *Social Problems, 23,* 535–544.

Metoyer, C. (1979). The Native American woman. In E. Snyder (Ed.), *The study of women: Enlarging perspectives on social reality* (pp. 329–335). New York: Harper and Row.

National Research Council. (1986). *Summary report 1988 doctoral recipient from United States universities.* Washington, DC: National Academy Press.

Niethammer, C. (1977). *Daughters of the earth.* New York: Macmillan.

Parezo, N. (1982). Navajo sandpaintings: The importance of sex roles in craft production. *American Indian Quarterly, 6*(1–2), 25–48.

Powers, M. (1986). *Oglala women: Myth, ritual, and reality.* Chicago, IL: University of Chicago Press.

Ryan, F. (1982). The federal role in American Indian education. *Harvard Educational Review, 52,* 423–430.

Sanders, D. (1987). Cultural conflicts: An important factor in the academic failures of American Indian students. *Journal of Multicultural Counseling and Development, 15,* 81–90.

Seton, E., & Seton, J. (1953). *The gospel of the redman: An Indian bible.* Sante Fe, NM: Seton Village.

Spindler, L., & Spindler, G. (1958). Male and female adaptations in culture change. *American Anthropologist, 60,* 217–233.

Swanton, J. R. (1911). Indian tribes of the Lower Mississippi Valley and adjacent coast of the Gulf of Mexico. *Bureau of American Ethnology Bulletin, 43.*

Szasz, M. (1980). "Poor Richard" meets the Native American: Schooling for young Indian women in eighteenth-century Connecticut. *Pacific Historical Review, 49*(2), 215–235.

Tanner, H. H. (1979). Coocoochee: Mohawk medicine women. *American Indian Culture and Research Journal, 3*(3), 23–41.

Terrell, J. N., & Terrell, D. M. (1974). *Indian women of the western morning: Their life in early America.* New York: Dial Press.

Thomas, R. K. (1981). The history of North American Indian alcohol use as a community-based phenomenon. *Journal of Studies on Alcohol, 9,* 29–39.

Trennert, R. (1982). Educating young girls at nonreservation boarding schools. *Western Historical Quarterly, 13,* 271–290.

U.S. Bureau of the Census. (1983). *1980 census of the population: Characteristics of the population.* U.S. Summary, PC80-1-B1. Washington, DC: U.S. Department of Commerce.

Weisfeld, C., Weisfeld, G., & Callaghan, J. (1982). Female inhibition in mixed-sex competition among young adolescents. *Ethology and Socialbiology, 3,* 29–42.

Weisfeld, C., Weisfeld, G., Warren, R., & Freeman, D. (1983). The spelling bee: A naturalistic study of female inhibition in mixed-sex competition. *Adolescence, 18*(71), 695–708.

Welch, D. (1987). American Indian women: Reaching beyond the myth. In C. Calloway (Ed.), *New directions in American Indian history* (pp. 31–48). Norman, OK: University of Oklahoma Press.

Witt, S. H. (1974). Native women today: Sexism and the Indian woman. *Civil Rights Digest, 6*(3), 29–35.

Witt, S. H. (1981). Past perspectives and present problems. In Ohoyo Resource Center Staff (Ed.), *Words of today's American Indian women: Ohoyo Makachi* (pp. 11–20). Wichita Falls, TX: OHOYO, Inc.

Zak, N. C. (1988). The earth mother figure of Native North America, *Revision, 10*(3), 27–36.

Zak, N. C. (1989). Sacred and legendary women of Native North America. In S. Nicholson (Ed.), *The goddess re-awakening: The feminine principle today* (232–245). Wheaton, IL: Theosophical Publishing House.

Questions for Thought

1. Compare and contrast "acculturation" and "bicultural lifestyle."

2. Use information presented by the authors to evaluate this proposition: "In traditional American Indian cultures, women often had considerable power and independence."

3. Traditional American Indian cultures often permitted biological females to participate in "cross-gender" roles. Discuss what this meant and give examples.

4. Explain the concept of "retraditionalization" as it applies to American Indian women.

5. Evaluate this statement: "Only American Indian researchers should study the lives of American Indians." Give arguments in *support* of this assertion. Give arguments *against* this assertion. What do you personally conclude?

6. Select an ethnic or cultural minority group other than American Indians. Discuss how the issues of acculturation and bicultural lifestyles may affect members of this group.

The Compatibility of Hunting and Mothering Among the Agta Hunter-Gatherers of the Philippines

Madeleine J. Goodman

P. Bion Griffin

Agnes A. Estioko-Griffin

John S. Grove

Those who hold that "biology is destiny" often assert that the burdens of reproduction and mothering necessarily prevent women from hunting wild animals and engaging in other traditionally "masculine" activities. This fascinating study of a hunting-and-gathering society in the Philippines challenges that view. Careful observations over a three-year period demonstrated the ability of mothers to hunt successfully. Hunting did not impair women's fertility. Situational factors that enable mothers to hunt included the possibility of hunting relatively close to home and assistance with child care by others in the group. The researchers conclude that women's ability to hunt depends on features of the social and physical environment rather than a basic biological incompatibility of hunting and mothering.

Women's hunting is widely held biologically impracticable in foraging societies, chiefly because hunting is presumed incompatible with maternal responsibilities. A three-year study of hunting practices among the Agta Negrito people of northern Luzon reveals women's active participation in hunting, singly and in groups, without detriment to normal fertility and child care.

It is a prevailing assumption of literature on hunter-gatherer societies that the burdens of reproduction prevent women from full participation in the hunting of large mammals (Brace, 1979; Quinn, 1977; Watanabe, 1968). Most studies of women's subsistence contributions in hunter-gatherer groups have therefore centered largely

Adapted from *Sex Roles*, 1985, *12*(11/12), 1199–1209. Copyright 1985 by Plenum Publishing Corporation. Used by permission.

on women's gathering activities (Dahlberg, 1981; Hiatt, 1970; Lee, 1979). Basing his argument on Watanabe's (1968) findings, Hayden (1981) argues that "men may be more innately predisposed to hunting, while women may be behaviorally predisposed to gathering" (p. 403)—psychologically or physiologically. Hayden associates women's nonparticipation in hunting with their "more sedentary and less aggressive" nature and with the needs of childcare: "Women would be handicapped in hunting excursions. Hunting forays would be seriously impaired by the need to nurse, care for and carry children." Further, gathering is said to require less mobility and involve "less risk to fertile females and their young" (p. 403). More speculatively, Hayden urges that "female body odors may at times constitute a major handicap under primitive hunting conditions that generally require approaches to within 25 m of the prey."[1]

Clearly, hunting is one of those activities which is susceptible through its symbolism to the projection of strongly marked gender roles. Anthropologists, as expositors and exegetes of cultural symbolisms, are as much participants in this process as are the members of the societies they study. Yet even in societies where women's hunting activity is deprecated, that activity can produce a valuable share of familial food supply. Romanoff (1983) writes of the Matases of the Peruvian rain forest,

> Men say that too many women can spoil a hunt, that excessive or inopportune intercourse can lessen a man's skill, and that women's presence at the tapir trap would leave an odor disgusting to the tapir. They say that women walk slowly, and that hunters can go farther in all-male groups (while a man thus complained to me, his wife, lagging a bit with a baby on her hip, located a paca; we all gave chase until she, correctly positioned, struck the animal with a machete). (p. 342)

Gender marking is expressed in the attitudes of Matse men toward women hunting but not sufficiently to rule out hunting activities from women's range of concerns: too many women are said to spoil a hunt but women do attend the hunt.

While it is true in most human foraging societies that men hunt and women gather, the rule is not strict. We now have evidence of several foraging societies in which women hunt. Among the Mbuti, the women are recognized as active hunters but their role is confined to assisting in driving the game into nets and helping in the portage of meat (Harako, 1981). Among the Tiwi and other groups women regularly hunt small animals but the hunting of large game is reserved for the men (Goodale, 1971). An early account by Landes (1938) recorded Ojibwa women hunting when there were no men present in the family. However, a later observer contested these observations as "grossly distorted" (Hickerson, 1962). Ainu women were occasionally observed to hunt large game using rope and dogs (Watanabe, 1968), and R. Gould (personal communication) observed women hunting with dogs among Western Australian Desert Aborigines. Among the Matses of the Peruvian Amazon rain forest, women are observed as active partners with their husbands in the hunt, taking part in the chase, driving game, encouraging dogs, and striking prey with sticks or machetes. But the rule that women do not hunt is not regarded as dis-

---

[1] Hayden, B. citing H. Dobkin de Rios, *Human Ecology*, 1976, *4*, 261.

counted by such evidence. After citing several such exceptional cases, Watanabe writes of the exclusion of women from hunting as "a universal phenomenon among modern food gatherers. It may be one of the ecological characteristics of man" (Watanabe, 1968, p. 75).

Among the hunter-gatherers of the Philippines reports of women hunting are longstanding. In 1952, Fox reported skillful women bow-and-arrow hunters among the Pinatubo Negritos of the Zambales mountains of western Luzon. More recently, Estioko-Griffin and Griffin (1975, 1981), studying the Agta of northeastern Luzon, and Cagayan provinces in the Philippines, have recorded extensive wild pig and deer hunting on the part of Agta women.

During 1980 and 1981, Griffin and Estioko-Griffin collected data on hunting activities and reproductive patterns among Agta in the Nanadukan valley of Cagayan province. The data they collected allow us now to reject the hypothesis that reproductive responsibilities entail women's inability to hunt. The outcome of their analysis has a significance beyond the immediate determination of the life patterns and strategies of the Agta, since evidence in favor of the compatibility of women's roles with activity as hunters will tend to disconfirm the widely held thesis that human evolution in the Plio-Pleistocene period took place in the context of radically differentiated gender roles necessitated by a presumed biological requirement that only males could engage in hunting (Estioko-Griffin & Griffin, 1985).

Our daily activity survey categorized time spent in various subsistence, domestic, and leisure activities, comprising 163 person-days of observations. Persons observed were randomly selected by the use of a table of random numbers. Among the 41 subjects observed, 10 men and 6 women were observed hunting, representing 29 man-days and 16 woman-days of hunting (Table 1). It is noteworthy in reference to the reproductive hypothesis that men's hunting participation did not drop below 40% in the years beyond puberty, but women's hunting activity peaked in the prime reproductive years. In every age group two to four times as many men as women engaged in hunting. No significant differences were found between the mean time per day women spent hunting (6.15 hours) and that of men (7.50 hours; $t = 1.54$). Multiple regression analysis revealed no significant linear age trend nor age-by-sex interaction in mean time spent hunting ($F_{3,41} = 1.03$).

From the complete reproductive histories assembled for Agta women living in the region it is possible to compare fertility patterns and anthropometric measures for women who hunt with those of women who never do (Table 2). Discriminant function analysis revealed no significant differences between Agta women hunters and nonhunters of comparable ages for age at menarche, age at first pregnancy, total parity or measures of height, weight, or skinfold triceps. Even age of youngest child

Table 1   **Hunting Days as a Ratio of Observation Days by Sex and Age**

Hunting	3–14	15–19	20–44	45–62	Total
			Age (years)		
Women	1/15 (6.7%)	1/9 (11.1%)	13/61 (21.3%)	1/10 (10.0%)	16/95 (16.8%)
Men	1/5 (20.0%)	2/5 (40.0%)	14/34 (41.2%)	12/26 (46.2%)	29/68 (42.6%)

Table 2 ■ **Characteristics of Agta Women Hunters vs. Nonhunters***

| | Hunters | | | Nonhunters | | | |
	N	Mean	SD	N	Mean	SD	t
Age	86	30.91	12.95	18	32.61	11.20	−0.52
Age at menarche	78	17.12	0.77	18	17.22	0.73	−0.53
Age at first pregnancy	73	19.58	2.68	16	20.25	3.73	−0.85
Age of youngest child	61	6.30	8.09	16	5.00	5.83	0.60
Total living children	70	2.69	2.23	16	2.75	2.18	−0.10
Height in cm	66	141.50	4.89	14	140.04	5.08	1.01
Weight in kg	66	36.36	5.39	14	38.40	6.20	−1.25
Skinfold triceps	59	9.25	3.35	13	12.62	7.64	−1.56

*The classification of "hunter" is assigned by self-report. However, 75 out of 86 hunters were observed to hunt during the fieldwork period.

did not seem to influence participation in hunting. The age of the youngest child was one year old or less for 23 out of 86 women hunters (27%). Among 18 nonhunters, a similar proportion of youngest children, 28%, were that age. It appears that hunting is entirely compatible with normal fertility patterns among the Agta.

Distinctive features of the Agta ecological setting may facilitate women's hunting activities. Foothills and forest where wild pig, deer, and monkey can be hunted are within 6 to 10 km of the coastal camp. In 450 observations of Agta subsistence activities (including hunting), 95.5% were conducted within 10 km of the base camp. A 20 to 30 minute walk up the bend of the river that flows by the camp will bring the hunters to the forested area. Thus women hunters can easily return home with game in less than an hour. The feasibility of hunts of less than a day's duration appears to be an important factor in the prevalence of hunting among Agta women.

There is no question that Agta women hunt successfully and effectively. As hunters, Agta women in single, all women, or women-and-children groups brought back some 30% of the large game animals captured during the period of our field observations (Table 3). If women's contributions in mixed groups are included, women seem to account for not much less than half of the total kill of major prey. In 185 days of observation, 22% by weight of game killed was accounted for by women. Mixed groups of women and men accounted for 35% of the kill by weight.

Several cultural and social factors contribute to Agta women's hunting proficiency. Hunting strategies adopted by the women differ from those most frequently employed by men. Where men generally hunt alone, stalking prey in the forest, women nearly always hunt in groups and with dogs (Table 4). Dogs offer both protection and assistance. Women are capable of hunting alone with their dogs but most of them choose, for social reasons and for the sake of increased efficiency, to hunt with others, whether sisters, children, father, or husband. Agta women are primary hunters, not assistants in male-organized hunting activities. Agta women were observed to hunt during menstruation without reluctance and to carry and nurse babies while on hunting forays.

Table 3 ▥ Agta Quarry by Composition of Hunting Party

	Wild pig	*Deer*	*Monkey*
Single male	5(27.8%)	4(25.0%)	4(44.4%)
Team male	1(5.6%)	—	—
Single female	—	2(12.5%)	—
Team female	6(33.3%)	3(18.8%)	—
Male and female	4(22.2%)	4(25.0%)	4(44.4%)
Male, female, and children	—	3(18.8%)	1(11.1%)
Female and children	2(11.1%)	—	—
Total kill	18(100.0%)	16(100.0%)	9(100.0%)

Table 4 ▥ Agta Hunting Strategies

	Forest stalk	*Tree ambush*	*Drive with dogs*	*Jack*	*Total*
Single male	49(74.2%)	4(6.1%)	2(3.0%)	11(16.7%)	66(100.0%)
Team male	4(33.3%)	2(16.7%)	3(25.0%)	3(25.0%)	12(100.0%)
Single female	—	—	6(100.0%)	—	6(100.0%)
Team female	—	—	20(100.0%)	—	20(100.0%)
Male and female pair	4(12.9%)	—	25(80.6%)	2(6.5%)	32(100.0%)
Male and children	1(50.0%)	—	1(50.0%)	—	2(100.0%)
Male, female, and children	—	—	7(100.0%)	—	7(100.0%)
Female and children	—	—	8(88.9%)	1(11.1%)	9(100.0%)
Children	—	—	—	1(100.0%)	1(100.0%)

The care of young children, which is traditionally supposed to be the chief restraint to women's hunting, poses little problem among the Agta. It cannot be assumed, however, that men take on major child care responsibilities in proportion to women's involvement in hunting. In our survey of child care covering 282 child-days for children under 11 years of age (Table 5), mothers consistently provided most of the child care given throughout the day. Grandmothers and the eldest female siblings were the next most frequent attendants. Men provided less child care, with fathers providing more than other male relatives, particularly on family foraging expeditions. Female attendants provide significantly more care to the youngest children, irrespective of sex of child. Male attendants tend to favor male children with more attention than female children, according to our observations, but the difference is not statistically significant.

The general pattern of Agta women hunters is to carry nursing infants with them

Table 5 ■ **Percent of Childcare Provided by Attendant over 8 Observations Spaced Out During the Day**

Relationship to child	Observations							
	5 a.m.	7 a.m.	9 a.m.	11 a.m.	1 p.m.	3 p.m.	5 p.m.	7 p.m.
Mother or stepmother	53.5%	47.9%	50.4%	50.4%	51.1%	49.6%	47.9%	63.1%
Father or stepfather	5.7%	3.5%	4.3%	3.5%	4.3%	3.5%	5.7%	5.0%
Grandmother	9.2%	8.5%	6.4%	5.3%	7.8%	6.4%	8.5%	8.5%
Grandfather	0.4%	1.4%	1.8%	2.1%	1.4%	1.1%	1.8%	1.4%
Elder sister	6.4%	13.5%	12.4%	12.1%	9.2%	11.0%	10.3%	6.4%
Elder brother	1.8%	1.4%	0.7%	1.4%	1.1%	1.1%	0.7%	0.7%
Elder female cousin	0.7%	1.8%	1.8%	1.4%	2.1%	1.4%	1.8%	0.4%
Elder male cousin	—	—	0.4%	0.4%	—	0.4%	—	—
Mother's sister	—	1.1%	1.1%	1.1%	1.1%	0.7%	—	—
Father's sister	0.4%	0.7%	0.4%	0.4%	0.7%	0.4%	—	0.4%

on the hunt, or to leave in the camp toddlers who are weaned, in the care of family members, usually females. Older children may accompany one or both parents on the hunt from an age when their presence would be deemed helpful. Thus, at no stage are mothers prevented from hunting by their child care responsibilities.

The Agta experience in the Nanadukan area gives clear evidence that hunting is well within the capabilities of women in a tropical foraging society. Proximity to the hunting grounds, use of dogs, and hunting in groups facilitate successful hunting records for Agta women. Cooperation in child care is a key facilitating factor. Indeed, the peak years of women's hunting activity coincide with the maximal childbearing years. No statistically significant differences were found in reproductive histories or anthropometric measures between women who participate in hunting and those who do not. Thus the Agta case seems clearly to disconfirm the hypothesis that women's widespread nonparticipation in subsistence hunting is an expression of biological necessity. Also disconfirmed is the thesis that women and men necessarily evolved under wholly divergent evolutionary constraints resulting from the exclusivity of hunting as a male domain.

As the disjunction between men's hunting and women's gathering recedes from acceptance as a scientific datum to the prehension as a structural symbolism the general rule by which foraging activities have been divided along gender lines becomes more a matter of relative emphases and less a matter of strict dichotomies. The relative contributions of men and women to group subsistence and the activities by which these contributions are produced would seem more a function of geographical situations and ecological possibility than biological limitations. Friedl suggested in 1975 that "the proportion of time and energy that men allocate to hunting and occasional gathering, and women to gathering, and the proportion of the total subsistence that each sex produces, vary as a result of the different geographical environments in the different regions of the world in which foragers live" (p. 18).

Our findings with regard to the Agta tend to confirm Friedl's hypothesis, especially when comparison is made, for example, with the situation of the !Kung San, whose environment is in many ways at an extreme remove from that of the Agta (Lee, 1979). The rich environment of the Agta facilitates brief hunting excursions, thus favoring women's hunting, just as the social organization of child care among the Agta facilitates the sort of absences from home that hunting in a tropical environment requires. A harsher environment or a more retentive or individualistic mode of child care and rearing might have discouraged women's hunting.

References

Brace, C. L. *The stage of human evolution: Human and cultural origins.* Englewood Cliffs, NJ: Prentice Hall, 1979.

Dahlberg, F. (Ed.). *Woman the gatherer.* New Haven, CT: Yale University Press, 1981.

Estioko, A. A., & Griffin, P. B. The Ebuked Agta of northeastern Luzon. *Philippine Quarterly of Culture and Society,* 1975, *3*(4), 237–244.

Estioko, A. A., & Griffin, P. B., Woman the hunter. In F. Dahlberg (Ed.), *Woman the Gatherer,* New Haven, CT: Yale University Press, 1981.

Estioko-Griffin, A. A., & Griffin, P. B. Women hunters: The implications for Pleistocene prehistory and contemporary ethnography. In M. J. Goodman (Ed.), *Women in Asia and the Pacific: Towards an East-West Dialogue,* Honolulu, Hawaii: University of Hawaii Press, 1985.

Fox, R. B. The Pinatubo Negritos, their useful plants and material culture. *Philippine Journal of Science,* 1952, *81,* 173–414.

Friedl, E. *Women and men: An anthropologist's view,* New York: Holt, Rinehart and Winston, 1975.

Goodale, J. *Twi wives: A study of the women of Melville Island, North Australia,* Seattle, Washington: University of Washington Press, 1971.

Harako, R. The cultural ecology of hunting behavior among Mbuti Pygmies in the Ituri Forest, Zaire. In R. S. O. Harding & G. Teleki (Eds.), *Omnivorous Primates: Gathering and Hunting in Human Evolution.* New York: Columbia University Press, 1981.

Hayden, B. Subsistence and ecological adaptations of modern hunter/gatherers. In R. S. O. Harding & G. Teleki (Eds.), *Omnivorous Primates: Gathering and Hunting in Human Evolution.* New York: Columbia University Press, 1981.

Hiatt, B. Woman the gatherer. In F. Gale (Ed.), *Woman's role in aboriginal society, Australian aboriginal studies.* Canberra: Australian Institute of Aboriginal Studies, 1970.

Hickerson, H. The Southwestern Chippewa: An ethnohistorical study. American Anthropological Association Memoir No. 92, *American Anthropologist,* 1962, 64.3, pt. 2.

Landes, R. *The Ojibwa woman,* New York: Columbia University Press, 1938.

Lee, R. B. *The Kung San: Man, women and work in a foraging society,* New York: Cambridge University Press, 1979.

Quinn, N. Anthropological Studies of Women's Status. *Annual Review of Anthropology,* 1977, *6,* 181–225.

Romanoff, A. Women as hunters among the Masters of the Peruvian Amazon. *Human Ecology,* 1983, *11,* 339–343.

Watanabe, H. Subsistence and ecology of northern food gatherers with special reference to the Ainu. In R. Lee & I. DeVore (Eds.), *Man the hunter,* Chicago: Aldine, 1968.

Questions for Thought

1. How do the hunting strategies used by Agta women differ from those used by Agta men? Why do men and women hunt in different ways?

2. The authors examine the hypothesis that women's reproductive responsibilities make it impossible for them to hunt. Summarize key findings that contradict this hypothesis.

3. Two factors that enable Agta women to hunt successfully are living in close proximity to hunting grounds and cooperation among group members in child care. Explain why these factors are important.

4. Both Agta women and contemporary American women confront the challenge of trying to coordinate child care responsibilities and work outside the home. Discuss the similarities and differences between the experiences of American and Agta women.

5. In what ways is a study of a small group of people in a remote region of the Philippines relevant to our general understanding of human capacities and limitations? Explain why the findings of this study challenge the idea that "biology is destiny."

Differences in Mothers' and Fathers' Behaviors Toward Children

A Cross-Cultural Comparison

Phyllis Bronstein

Cross-cultural research often identifies differences in the behaviors of people from different cultures. But sometimes, as in this study, cross-cultural research highlights similarities that transcend cultural boundaries. In the United States, fathers tend to act in a more playful way with their school-age children, and mothers tend to be more task-oriented. Would a similar gender difference in parental behavior be found in Mexico, a culture in which fathers are sometimes depicted as authoritarian disciplinarians? To find out, Bronstein observed the everyday interactions between parents and their children. Mexican mothers provided more physical nurturance than fathers, but fathers showed greater affection and playfulness and gave more information to their children than did mothers. In addition, fathers—but not mothers—differed in their behaviors toward their daughters versus their sons. Bronstein notes how closely these findings from Mexico match the results of observational studies in other cultures.

Systematic observations of 78 parent–child dyads in Mexican families revealed a number of differences between maternal and paternal behaviors. Some of the patterns observed run counter to the traditionally held views of Mexican parental roles—for example, that fathers are more aloof and authoritarian, whereas mothers are more warm and nurturant. Fathers, in fact, were found to be more playful and companionable with their children than mothers were, and mothers were more nurturant only in terms of providing immediate physical needs. In addition, fathers, but not mothers, differed significantly in their behavior toward girls and

Adapted from *Developmental Psychology,* 1984, 20, 995–1003. Copyright 1984 by the American Psychological Association, Inc. Used by permission.

boys: on reprimanding-restrictive and instrumental-directive behaviors they were substantially lower toward girls, whereas they directed more attention and cognitive involvement toward boys. The findings, when compared cross-culturally, proved to be similar to findings obtained in observational studies of parents' interactions with infants and young children in this country.

Until recently, little research had been done, both in this country and cross-culturally, on parent sex differences in the child-rearing process. The focus tended to be solely on mothers in relation to their children, with little attention paid to the father's role. Research that did include fathers was generally on children's *perceptions* of parental roles and behavior; fathers were perceived to be more restrictive and punitive, especially with sons, and mothers were perceived to be more nurturant, affectionate, and likely to use psychological rather than physical methods of control, especially with daughters (e.g., Armentrout & Burger, 1972; Bronfenbrenner, 1961; Droppelman & Schaeffer, 1963).

In the last 10 years, however, widespread changes in family roles and structures in this country and a growing interest in the sex role development of children have led researchers to focus increasingly on the role of the father in the family, particularly on the amount and kind of direct involvement he has with his children. The studies have generally been in two areas. The first has looked at fathers' interactions with infants in the first 2 years of life, comparing fathers' behaviors with mothers'. Beyond the fact that mothers consistently spent more time interacting with infants than fathers did (Kotelchuck, 1972; Pedersen & Robson, 1969; Rebelsky & Hanks, 1971), the most persistent findings were that fathers engaged in more active and stimulating interaction than mothers (e.g., Clarke-Stewart, 1978, 1980; Lamb, 1977a, 1977b; Power & Parke, 1981) and that mothers spent a greater proportion of their time with infants in caretaking functions (vs. play) than fathers did (e.g., Clarke-Stewart, 1978; Field, 1978; Kotelchuck, 1976; Lamb, 1980; Parke & Sawin, 1980). In addition, fathers were found to differ more than mothers in certain of their behaviors toward boys and girls; they interacted more with sons than with daughters (e.g., Kotelchuck, 1976; Lamb, 1977b, 1977c; Park & O'Leary, 1976; Rendina & Dickerscheid, 1976), were more negative toward sons' play with dolls and soft toys, and more encouraging of daughters' proximity (Fagot, 1978).

The second area of father–child research has focused on fathers' interactions with preschool-aged children, generally in a structured play, task, or teaching situation. Fathers again were found to be more active and physical than mothers (DiPietro, Jacklin, & Maccoby, 1981; Osofsky & O'Connell, 1972), to interrupt and talk simultaneously with children more than mothers did (Greif, 1979), to give more directives than mothers (Bellinger, 1980), and to give more functional information and encourage children's task performance more than mothers (Mazur, 1980). In addition, fathers were again found to differ more than mothers in their behaviors toward girls and boys. They interacted more positively and socially with daughters than with sons (Block, Block, & Harrington, 1974; Tauber, 1979), encouraged play with same-sex toys and discouraged play with cross-sex toys with both sexes, but particularly with sons (Langlois & Downs, 1980), showed more concern with cognitive achievement for sons than for daughters in one set of studies (Block et al., 1974) and showed more concern with cognitive achievements for daughters than for sons in another (Mazur, 1980).

There is little evidence from either area of recent research to support the traditional view of parental roles, as revealed in the previously discussed studies of children's perceptions of parent behavior—that is, the fathers are more restrictive, punitive authority figures, and mothers are nurturant and accepting sources of warmth who control by indirect and psychological means rather than by coercive means. This may be because such rules do not emerge in relating to infants, with whom control is hardly an issue, and because a laboratory environment with a prescribed task or agenda for parents and young children very likely precludes or inhibits displays of authoritarian behavior. However, little research has been done on parent-child interaction in unstructured situations, and with older children, in which, presumably, a wider range of naturally occurring behaviors might be expected to occur. The research that has been published suggests only that mothers in five cultures are in more frequent and closer contact with children than fathers are (Mackey & Day, 1979) and that fathers attend more frequently and positively to sons than to daughters (Margolin & Patterson, 1975).

To understand the different influences fathers and mothers may have on children's social and emotional development, it is important to go beyond the study of parents with infants and preschoolers and to observe the everyday patterns of parent behavior that emerge in relation to older children who have entered the complex worlds of school and community. Such an approach was followed in the research presented here. The present article, which represents part of a larger study of parent–child relationships in a provincial city in central Mexico, focuses on mothers' and fathers' interactions with their school-aged children, in the home. It considers whether or not there are substantial differences between fathers' and mothers' behavior toward children, whether these behaviors correspond to those found in studies of parents in other cultures, with younger children, and whether parental roles that are traditionally ascribed to the Mexican culture in fact emerge. These roles are not very different from the descriptions children provided of parents in the U.S. studies mentioned earlier. The mother is thought of as the more nurturant and affectionate parent, self-sacrificing to her children, who in turn place her on a pedestal. The father, on the other hand, is thought to be more aloof, more likely to provide discipline, and overall, more likely to maintain an authoritarian relationship with his children and with his wife, all of whom respect and obey him (Diaz-Guerrero, 1955; Fromm & Maccoby, 1970; Staton, 1972).

Based on some of the more consistent findings discussed earlier and on available descriptions of traditional Mexican parental roles, it was hypothesized that the following patterns would emerge from the data analysis of the present study:

Hypothesis 1.   Mothers would show more nurturant, affectionate, and supportive behaviors than fathers.

Hypothesis 2.   Fathers would show more restrictive, punitive, and dominant behaviors than mothers.

Hypothesis 3.   Mothers would show more subtle, psychological means of controlling children than fathers would, especially with daughters.

Hypothesis 4.   Fathers would show more directive and informative behaviors than mothers.

Hypothesis 5.   Fathers would differ more than mothers in their behaviors toward girls and boys, in particular showing more attention toward sons—both restricting and punishing them more and showing greater cognitive/intellectual involvement with them.

Though previous research would lead one to conclude that fathers tend to spend a greater proportion of their interaction time with children in play-type activities than mothers do, this finding was not hypothesized for the present study, because it was so at odds with the traditional picture of the aloof, authoritarian Mexican father.

Method

Subjects

The sample consisted of 78 parent–child dyads—22 father–son, 15 father–daughter, 26 mother–son, and 15 mother–daughter—in 19 families of lower and middle socioeconomic levels. Families at the lower end of the economic spectrum had annual incomes of $2,000 to $3,000 and lived in two-room houses with no inside plumbing. Families at the upper end had annual incomes of $12,000 to $15,000, lived in six- to eight-room houses, and had cars, servants, and numerous electrical appliances. Lower income fathers were miners (mining was the city's main industry) or construction workers; middle-income fathers were professionals or middle-level managers.

All but one of the middle-income families lived as independent nuclear units. In lower income families, however, the nuclear unit tended to be embedded in an extended kinship cluster, with up to 24 people living in the same compound or in adjacent quarters. Each nuclear unit had both parents living there, (though two fathers proved to be unavailable for observation), with two to five children, with the exception of one family, which had nine. Target children included all those between 7 and 12 years of age, with an average age of 9 for both girls and boys.

Observation Method

Five native observers were trained in two concurrent systems for the act-by-act scoring of interaction. The first, developed at the research locale with the help of local advisors, consisted initially of 81 observable behaviors, both verbal and nonverbal (such as agreeing, instructing, scolding, and ignoring), which were judged likely to occur in interaction between Mexican parents and children. The second was a modified and abbreviated version of Bales's system for measuring interpersonal behavior (Bales, 1970; Bales, Cohen, & Williamson, 1979) in which acts were evaluated according to three dimensions of affective style, here labeled Dominant versus Submissive, Positive versus Negative (or friendly vs. unfriendly), and Expressive versus Controlled (or perceivably expressing vs. controlling emotion). All acts were categorized according to both systems. An "act" was defined as an observable verbal or nonverbal behavior that communicated essentially one message: it could be as brief as a nod of the head or several sentences long, but most generally, it consisted of a single sentence or nonverbal response.

Reliability of the two systems was established during trial runs, in which pairs of field workers observed parent–child interaction in nonsample families for half-hour segments. Agreement on an act-by-act basis between different pairs of observers for the 81 behavior categories ranged from 68% to 86% ($M = 74\%$). On the Bales dimension, agreement ranged from 53% to 88% ($M = 73\%$) for the Dominant/Submissive dimension, from 70% to 81% ($M = 77\%$) for the Positive/Negative dimension, and from 42% to 83% ($M = 60\%$) for the Expressive/Controlled dimension. More detailed description of the observation method, instruments, and reliability have been presented elsewhere (Bronstein-Burrows, 1981).

Procedure

Each observer, assigned from three to five families, observed and tape recorded six 15-min segments of interaction between parents and all target children in each family—twice with the mother present, twice with the father present, and twice with both parents present. If the parent who was not scheduled to be observed in a given session happened to be present, then his or her interactions with the children were scored as well and later included in the analysis. Other people were allowed to be present, though acts involving them were not scored. However, if a target child or a parent scheduled for a given session were not at home, the field worker did no observations and rescheduled the session. Attempts were made to schedule observation sessions at different times of the day; however, because of fathers' work schedules, these attempts were often unsuccessful, so that the sampling of observation times was not very well distributed. During the observation session, the field worker, after retiring to an unobtrusive corner, wrote down the initiator and recipient of every act between target children and parents, with a brief indication of the verbal or nonverbal content (e.g., "M–J sit down" represented a longer act in which mother told son Juan to sit down and finish his dinner). Afterwards, away from the family, the worker transcribed the tape recording of the family's interactions and then scored all acts at his or her own pace from the transcription, with the help of the notations made during the observation session. One hundred nine sessions of parent–child interaction were observed, with two sessions dropped from the final analysis because of inadequate data. In all, there were approximately 18,000 scored acts.

Data Analysis

During the data analysis, the number of behavior categories was reduced from 81 to 25 by eliminating or subsuming low-frequency categories. Total frequencies for each behavior and each polar direction of the Bales dimensions were tabulated for each parent–child dyad across all sessions in which that dyad was present, irrespective of whether one or both parents were there, with parent totals and child totals computed separately. To adjust for the differences between dyads in total time observed, percentage scores were calculated for the individual behavior categories, for the Bales measures of affective style, and for behavior clusters formed from an exploratory factor analysis of the categories. The scores indicated what percentage of a parent's acts to a given target child were in a particular category—for example, that 12% of a mother's acts to her oldest son were scored as Disagrees. These percentage scores were used in all subsequent data analyses.

In addition, two measures were adopted to compensate for the fact that including 78 dyads from 19 families violates the usual statistical assumption of independence of cases.[1] First, to assure that families with several same-sex children in the study were not unduly "weighting" the data, each parent's scores for interactions with same-sex children were averaged. This created a new set of dyad scores that represented interaction with a composite "son" or "daughter," so that each parent now had at most one set of scores representing interactions with sons, and one representing interactions with daughters. Specifically, this meant that in six families, parent–child interactions were averaged over two or three sons, in two families they were averaged over two daughters, and in one family they were averaged separately over two daughters and two sons. Second, in determining statistical significance, the number of *families* involved (19) was used to determine the degrees of freedom rather than the number of dyads.

To see whether there were significant differences between mothers' and fathers' patterns of behavior toward children, *t* tests were run on appropriate dyad subgroupings (mothers–children vs. fathers–children for Hypotheses 1–4, and mothers–daughters vs. mothers–sons for Hypothesis 3). For each dependent variable, the set of *t* tests is equivalent to a Parents × Children factorial analysis of variance (ANOVA), including simple effects; *t* tests were chosen as a more direct approach, given that the analysis was designed to address specific hypotheses. However, because Hypothesis 5 relates directly to the interaction term of a Parents × Children factorial design, an ANOVA was used to examine this effect.

Results

Hypothesis 1:   Mothers would show more nurturant, affectionate, and supportive behavior than fathers.

Mothers were, in fact, significantly higher than fathers on a measure of *physical nurturance*, which included offering food, grooming, and showing concern for safety, $t(17) = 1.85, p < .05$.[2] However, contrary to the traditional image of Mexican family

---

[1] Field work in another culture, when time and resources are limited, is likely to involve trade-offs between sample size and depth of investigation. In order to obtain both a wide sampling of parent–child behaviors and an in-depth understanding of individual family contexts, the present study included all parent–child dyads that had target-age children rather than just one dyad per family. The analysis was designed to explore the interaction patterns that emerged and to compare them cross-culturally, with no claims for generalizability to a larger population of Mexican families. It should also be mentioned that true independence of cases is often impossible to achieve in field locales with small, highly stable populations; even if only one dyad per family were included in the sample, the families would often be known to one another, with friends and relatives in common.

[2] Probability estimates, unless otherwise noted, are one-tailed. However, for unpredicted findings, two-tailed estimates are provided.

roles, fathers in this sample were significantly higher than mothers on the behavior cluster Warm Egalitarianism, which consisted of agreeing, complying, showing affection, encouraging, participating with, acting playful, explaining, giving opinion, and suggesting, $t(17) = 2.51$, $p < .05$, two-tailed. In addition, fathers were somewhat higher than mothers on showing a Positive affective style, though the trend did not quite reach statistical significance. All the above results, as well as the ones that follow, remained the same when an arcsine transformation was applied to the data.

Hypothesis 2:   Fathers would show more restrictive, punitive, and dominant behaviors than mothers.

There was no difference between fathers and mothers on the behavior cluster Punitive Authoritarianism, which consisted of scolding, criticising, ordering, threatening, interrogating, and acting hostile. Nor was there any difference on the behavior cluster Instrumental Direction, which consisted of ordering and prohibiting or on showing a Dominant or Negative affective style.

Hypothesis 3:   Mothers would show more subtle, psychological means of controlling children than fathers would, especially with daughters.

There was no difference between fathers and mothers on the behavior cluster Psychological Control, which consisted of moralizing, correcting, pressuring, manipulating, asking opinion, interrogating, and belittling. Nor were mothers higher toward girls than toward boys on this behavior.

Hypothesis 4:   Fathers would show more directive and informative behaviors than mothers.

Fathers were significantly higher than mothers in giving information to children, $t(17) = 1.75$, $p < .05$, but no different from mothers in instructing or ordering. On the behavior cluster Cooperative Instruction, which consisted of instructing, participating with, agreeing, and complying, the trend for fathers to be higher did not quite reach statistical significance. Findings relevant to Hypotheses 1–4 are summarized in Table 1.

Hypothesis 5:   Fathers would differ more than mothers in behaviors toward girls and boys, in particular showing more attention to sons—both restricting and punishing them more and showing greater cognitive/intellectual involvement with them.

Although the ANOVAs relevant to this hypothesis did not produce significant interactions, the means and t values, which are presented in Table 2, are suggestive for future research. Examination of the means and t values suggests that mothers tended to treat girls and boys similarly, whereas fathers treated girls in a distinctly different manner from the way they treated boys. Father–son dyads were significantly higher than father–daughter dyads on the behavior cluster Punitive Authoritarianism, which consisted of scolding, criticising, ordering, threatening, interrogating, and acting hostile, $t(17) = 2.01$, $p < .05$, the behavior cluster Instrumental Direction, which consisted of ordering and prohibiting, $t(17) = 2.39$, $p < .05$, and on show-

Table 1 ▓ **Mean Percentage Scores and *t* Test Results for Mothers'
and Fathers' Behavior Toward Children**

Behaviors	Mothers–children Mean	Fathers–children Mean	t
Behavior clusters			
Punitive authoritarianism	22.50	17.60	1.39
Instrumental direction	14.90	12.06	1.01
Psychological control	17.97	16.85	0.31
Cooperative instruction	6.93	10.81	1.54
Warm egalitarianism	17.27	26.20	2.51*
Individual behaviors			
Physical nurturance	3.42	1.95	1.85*
Gives information/explains	5.94	8.75	1.75*
Instructs	1.21	1.19	0.03
Orders	11.86	9.07	1.15
Affective style			
Positive	40.41	48.10	1.46
Negative	26.61	24.07	0.75
Dominant	46.62	44.40	0.46

Note. N = 54 (28 mother–child dyads and 26 father–child dyads).
*$p < .05$.

ing a Dominant affective style, $t(17) = 2.08$, $p < .05$. However, these findings were due to fathers' extremely gentle treatment of daughters, compared with all other dyad combinations, rather than to relative harsh treatment of sons; in fact, fathers were significantly lower than mothers on Punitive Authoritarianism, $t(17) = 2.34$, $p < .05$, two-tailed, and Instrumental Direction, $t(17) = 2.04$, $p < .05$, two-tailed, to daughters.

Fathers also differed toward girls and boys on measures of attention and cognitive/intellectual involvement. They instructed sons more frequently, $t(17) = 1.85$, $p < .05$, though there was no difference on the behavior cluster Cooperative Instruction, and the trend for fathers more frequently to ask sons to explain or give information did not reach statistical significance. Toward daughters, they were higher on the behavior cluster Inattentive Parentalism, which consisted of precautioning, proposing, giving opinion, disagreeing, interrupting, ignoring, and giving monosyllabic answers, $t(17) = 2.6$, $p < .05$. Mothers, on the other hand, differed much less on these measures, though with the exception of Instructs, the differences were in the same direction as fathers'. Neither parent explained or gave information to sons more than to daughters.

Table 2   ■   **Mean Percentage Scores and *t* Test Results for Mothers'
and Fathers' Behaviors Toward Children**

Behaviors	Mothers–daughters Mean	Mothers–sons Mean	t	Fathers–daughters Mean	Fathers–sons Mean	t
Behavior clusters						
Punitive authoritarianism	20.03	24.35	1.07	11.91	22.48	2.01*
Instrumental direction	14.46	15.23	0.18	7.57	15.91	2.39*
Cooperative instruction	8.25	5.94		10.62	10.98	0.08
Inattentive parentalism	24.56	19.69	1.40	28.86	15.53	2.60**
Individual behaviors						
Instructs	1.75	0.81	1.39	0.18	2.05	1.85*
Asks for information	14.27	15.38	0.42	12.54	17.62	1.23
Gives information/explains	5.71	6.12	0.29	8.27	9.16	0.30
Affective style						
Dominant	44.81	47.98	0.51	36.34	51.31	2.08*

Note. N = 54 (12 mother–daughter dyads, 16 mother–son dyads, 12 father–daughter dyads, and 14 father–son dyads).
*$p < .05$.   **$p < .01$.

Discussion

What emerges from this study of naturally occurring parent–child interaction in Mexican families are findings that are remarkably similar to those obtained in recent observational research on parents and their infants and preschoolers in this country. Mothers spent a greater proportion of their interactions in caretaking activities than fathers did, and fathers spent a greater proportion of their interactions in playful, participatory activities than mothers did. Further, fathers were no less warm or affectionate than mothers, and in fact (relevant perhaps to the kinds of activities they engaged in), they were somewhat higher than mothers on showing friendly affect. In addition, fathers' interactions, more than mothers', involved explaining or giving information to children. Finally, fathers did differ significantly in their interactions with girls and boys, whereas mothers did not. As was found by Kotelchuck (1976), Lamb (1977b, 1977c), Parke and O'Leary (1976), and others, fathers paid more interested attention to sons than to daughters, and as found by Block et al. (1974), they showed more cognitive/achievement orientation with them. In addition, their low relative frequency of dominant, restrictive, and punitive behaviors to daughters suggests that, as found by Tauber (1979) and Block et al. (1974), fathers may have interacted in a more sociable manner with daughters than with sons.

What these findings reveal within their own cultural context is that fathers in these Mexican families played a distinct and salient role of their own, different from mothers, and very different from the traditional view of the aloof Mexican patriarch.

Although there is no measure of the hours per day each father in the present sample spent at home, most did seem to spend most of their nonworking hours and their days off there or in recreational pursuits with their families. Furthermore, when they were with their children, many of the fathers seemed genuinely involved with them, in friendly, nonauthoritarian interaction. They joked and talked with them, showed them how to shoot a marble or polish their shoes, and in the homes where there were sufficient money and space for toys and hobbies, they played dominoes with them or looked at a coin or rock collection together.

Why they were significantly more playful and companionable with their children than mothers were is an interesting question. At least part of the answer lies in the separation of parents' work domains. Though several of the mothers had part-time work outside the home, all had primary responsibility for the household work and child care and thus were more likely than fathers to be involved in doing chores or overseeing chores done by children or servants (depending on the economic level of the family) when they were at home. For fathers, on the other hand, being at home meant being entirely removed from their own work domains, generally with no household chores that they were expected to attend to—which thus allowed them more time and attention for playful, companionable interaction with children.

In addition, a number of researchers are beginning to question the traditional image of the dominant, authoritarian Mexican father. Hawkes and Taylor (1975), in a study comparing the husband–wife power structure in Mexican and Mexican–American farm labor families in the United States, found the prevalent pattern to be egalitarian and concluded that the dominance–submission patterns are much less universal than had previously been assumed. Mirandé (1979) has made a strong case for the reexamination of the male role in the Mexican and the Mexican–American family, claiming that the traditional view is based on unsupported myths and stereotypes held by both social scientists and the public at large.

The other main finding, that fathers but not mothers differed in their behaviors toward girls and boys, suggests that Mexican fathers may play an important role in the socialization of their children for traditional sex roles. Boys were listened to and shown how to do things, which would seem to convey the message that what they have to say is important and that they are capable of mastering new skills. Girls, on the other hand, were treated especially gently, and at the same time, with a lack of full attention and an imposing of opinions and values. The gentle treatment would seem to convey the message that they are fragile and docile—a paternal viewpoint that emerged in this country in earlier self-report studies of fathers' perceptions of children (e.g., Rubin, Provenzano, & Luria, 1974; Tasch, 1952, 1955). The inattention and imposing of opinion would seem to communicate the view that what females have to say is less valuable than what males have to say, so that females need to be told more what to think and do, and can more readily be interrupted or ignored. Thus in this sample of Mexican families, very different messages were being transmitted to girls and boys—about their roles, their temperaments, their thinking, and their expected behavior—and fathers were the main transmitters of those messages. The findings are also similar to ones emerging from U.S. observational studies of parent–child interaction, in which "adults, particularly fathers, act in more instrumental, task-oriented, mastery-emphasizing ways with their sons and in more expressive, less intellectually rigorous ways with their daughters" (Block, 1979). In addition, it should be mentioned that fathers' greater tendency to give information, explanations, and directions to children presents a knowledgeable and mastery-oriented image as a male role model.

What is striking about the findings of the present study is the consistency of fathers' behavior patterns, across different methodologies, cultures, and ages of children. The findings do not match very well with *reports* of fathers' behaviors by children, mothers, and fathers themselves (e.g., Bronfenbrenner, 1961; Devereux et al., 1974; Kagan, Hosken, & Watson, 1961), in which fathers were generally described as being less warm and more strict and punitive than mothers. Instead, they support those findings of recent observational studies of parents and very young children, which show that whereas fathers did significantly less caretaking than mothers, they were nonetheless involved, participatory parents who had positive, companionable, and instructive relationships with their children. In addition, the findings support those self-report and observational measures that found fathers but not mothers to differ in their attitudes and behaviors toward girls and boys, particularly with regard to gender-related areas. How widespread these patterns may be across cultures and across different family structures and ages of children are questions worthy of further investigation.

References

Armentrout, J. A., & Burger, G. K. (1972). Children's reports of parental child-rearing behavior at five grade levels. *Developmental Psychology, 7,* 44–48.

Bales, R. F. (1970). *Personality and interpersonal behavior.* New York: Holt, Rinehart & Winston.

Bales, R. F., Cohen, S. P., & Williamson, S. A. (1979). *SYMLOG: A system for the multiple level observation of groups.* New York: Free Press.

Bellinger, D. (1980). *Sex differences in parental directives to young children.* Paper presented at the annual meeting of the American Psychological Association, Montreal.

Block, J. H. (1979). *Socialization influences on personality development in males and females.* Invited address presented at the annual meeting of the American Psychological Association, New York.

Block, J. H., Block, J., & Harrington, D. (1974). *The relationship of parental teaching strategies to ego-resiliency in pre-school children.* Paper presented at the annual meeting of the Western Psychological Association, San Francisco.

Bronfenbrenner, U. (1961). Some familial antecedents of responsibility and leadership in adolescents. In L. Petrullo & B. M. Bass (Eds.), *Leadership and interpersonal behavior* (pp. 239–271). New York: Holt, Rinehart & Winston.

Bronstein-Burrows, P. (1981). Patterns of parent behavior: A cross-cultural study. *Merrill-Palmer Quarterly, 27,* 129–143.

Clarke-Stewart, K. A. (1978). And daddy makes 3: The father's impact on mothers and young children. *Child Development, 49,* 466–478.

Clarke-Stewart, K. A. (1980). The father's contribution to children's cognitive and social development in early childhood. In F. A. Pedersen (Ed.), *The father–infant relationship: Observational studies in the family setting* (pp. 111–146). New York: Praeger.

Devereux, E. C., Shouval, R., Bronfenbrenner, U., Rogers, R. R., Kav-Venaki, S., & Kiely, E. (1974). Socialization practices of parents, teachers, and peers in Israel: The kibbutz vs. the city. *Child Development, 45,* 269–281.

Diaz-Guerrero, R. (1955). Neurosis and the Mexican family structure. *American Journal of Psychiatry, 112,* 411–417.

DiPietro, J., Jacklin, C. N., & Maccoby, E. E. (1981). *Sex-typing in parent and child interaction.* Paper presented at the biennial meeting of the Society for Research in Child Development, Boston, MA.

Droppelman, L. F., & Schaeffer, E. S. (1963). Boys' and girls' reports of maternal and paternal behavior. *Journal of Abnormal and Social Psychology, 67,* 648–654.

Fagot, B. (1978). The influence of sex of child on parental reactions to toddler children. *Child Development, 49,* 459–465.

Field, T. (1978). Interaction patterns of primary versus secondary caretaker fathers. *Developmental Psychology, 14,* 183–185.

Fromm, E., & Maccoby, M. (1970). *Social character in a Mexican village: A sociopsychoanalytic study.* Englewood Cliffs, NJ: Prentice-Hall.

Greif, E. G. (1979). *Sex differences in parent–child conversations: Who interrupts whom.* Paper presented at the biennial meeting of the Society for Research in Child Development, San Francisco.

Hawkes, G. R., & Taylor, M. (1975). Power structure in Mexican and Mexican–American farm labor families. *Journal of Marriage and the Family, 37,* 807–811.

Kagan, J., Hosken, B., & Watson, S. (1961). Child's symbolic conceptualization of parents. *Child Development, 32,* 625–636.

Kotelchuck, M. (1972). *The nature of the child's tie to his father.* Unpublished doctoral dissertation, Harvard University.

Kotelchuck, M. (1976). The infant's relationship to the father: Experimental evidence. In M. E. Lamb (Ed.), *The role of the father in child development* (pp. 329–344). New York: Wiley.

Lamb, M. E. (1977a). Father–infant and mother–infant interaction in the first year of life. *Child Development, 48,* 167–181.

Lamb, M. E. (1977b). The development of mother–infant and father–infant attachment in the second year of life. *Developmental Psychology, 13,* 637–648.

Lamb, M. E. (1977c). The development of parental preferences in the first two years of life. *Sex Roles, 3,* 495–497.

Lamb, M. E. (1980). The development of parent–infant attachments in the first two years of life. In F. A. Pedersen (Ed.), *The father–infant relationship: Observational studies in the family setting* (pp. 21–43). New York: Praeger.

Langlois, J. H., & Downs, A. C. (1980). Mothers, fathers, and peers as socialization agents of sex-typed play behaviors in young children. *Child Development, 51,* 1217–1247.

Mackey, W. C., & Day, R. D. (1979). Some indicators of fathering behaviors in the United States: A cross-cultural examination of adult male–child interaction. *Journal of Marriage and the Family, 41,* 287–298.

Margolin, G., & Patterson, G. R. (1975). Differential consequences provided by mothers and fathers for their sons and daughters. *Developmental Psychology, 11,* 537–538.

Mazur, E. (1980). Parent–child interaction and the acquisition of lexical information during play. *Developmental Psychology, 16,* 404–409.

Mirandé, A. (1979). A reinterpretation of male dominance in the Chicano family. *The Family Coordinator, 28,* 473–479.

Osofsky, J. D., & O'Connell, E. J. (1972). Parent–child interaction: Daughters' effects upon mothers' and fathers' behaviors. *Developmental Psychology, 7,* 157–168.

Parke, R. O., & O'Leary, S. E. (1976). Father–mother–infant interaction in the newborn period: Some findings, some observations, and some unresolved issues. In K. Riegel & J. Meacham (Eds.), *The developing individual in a changing world: Vol. 2. Social and environmental issues* (pp. 653–663). The Hague, The Netherlands: Mouton.

Parke, R. D., & Sawin, D. B. (1980). The family in early infancy: Social interactional and attitudinal analyses. In F. A. Pedersen (Ed.), *The father–infant relationship: Observational studies in the family setting* (pp. 44–67). New York: Praeger.

Pedersen, F. A., & Robson, K. S. (1969). Father participation in infancy. *American Journal of Orthopsychiatry, 39,* 466–472.

Power, T. G., & Parke, R. D. (1981). Play as a context for early learning: Lab and home analyses. In L. M. Laosa & I. E. Sigel (Eds.), *The family as a learning environment* (pp. 147–178). New York: Plenum Press.

Rebelsky, F., & Hanks, C. (1971). Fathers' verbal interaction with infants in the first three months of life. *Child Development, 42,* 63–68.

Rendina, I., & Dickerscheid, J. D. (1976). Father involvement with first-born infants. *Family Coordinator, 25,* 373–379.

Rubin, J. Z., Provenzano, F. J., & Luria, Z. (1974). The eye of the beholder: Parents' views on sex of newborns. *American Journal of Orthopsychiatry, 44,* 512–519.

Staton, R. D. (1972). A comparison of Mexican and Mexican–American families. *The Family Coordinator, 21,* 325–330.

Tasch, R. J. (1952). The role of the father in the family. *Journal of Experimental Education, 20,* 319–361.

Tasch, R. J. (1955). Interpersonal perceptions of fathers and mothers. *Journal of Genetic Psychology, 87,* 59–65.

Tauber, M. A. (1979). Sex differences in parent–child interaction styles during a free-play session. *Child Development, 50,* 981–988.

Questions for Thought

1. Bronstein found that fathers spent a greater proportion of their time with their children in playful activities than mothers did. What were her explanations for this finding?

2. In this study fathers (but not mothers) treated their daughters differently than their sons. Describe how fathers behaved toward each sex. What messages about gender might this pattern of paternal behavior communicate to children?

3. Select a family you know fairly well (your own or another). Describe how the father and the mother interact with their children. Were sons and daughters treated differently? What effect do you think this has had on the children?

4. Bronstein found striking similarities in the ways that Mexican and American parents treat their children. This suggests that Mexico and the United States may share certain values and beliefs about raising children. Discuss what these common values and beliefs might be.

5. Briefly describe the observational methodology used by Bronstein. It would have been easier to ask parents to describe how they treat their children rather than observing their actual behavior. What are the advantages of observation over self-report? What might be the disadvantages of an observational methodology?

6. If parents want to raise their children in a nontraditional, egalitarian way, what lessons can they learn from this research?

7 Raising Confident and Competent Girls
One Size Does Not Fit All

Sumru Erkut

Fern Marx

Jacqueline P. Fields

Rachel Sing

Liking and feeling good about ourself is an important component of psychological well-being. This study examines self-esteem among teenage girls from African American, Caucasian, Chinese American, and Latino backgrounds. The researchers used standardized tests to assess both overall feelings of self-esteem ("global self worth") and feelings about specific aspects of the self such as one's physical appearance, scholastic competence, and acceptance by peers. In addition, to provide richer descriptions of girls' experiences, the researchers organized group discussions about "a girl who likes sherself." The results illustrate how our cultural background can shape the standards we use to evaluate ourselves and our accomplishments.

In recent years there has been much academic and popular interest in girls' self-esteem. Girls' high self-esteem has been associated with motivation to achieve (academically and in a career) and confidence in their ability to achieve (AAUW, 1991; Baruch, 1975; Phillips & Zimmerman, 1990). While some research indicates that an adolescent's self-concept generally remains positive (Marsh & Gouvernet, 1989), other research notes a low point in many girls' self-regard beginning in early adolescence (AAUW, 1991). Longitudinal studies have found that a decline in positive

An earlier version of this paper appeared in 1996 as No. 282 in the Wellesley College Center for Research on Women Working Papers Series. Copyright 1997 by Sumru Erkut, Fern Marx, Jacqueline P. Fields, and Rachel Sing. Used by permission. The Raising Competent Girls research was funded by grants from the Remmer Family Foundation. Zaida Rivera, Heidie A. Vázquez García, Rosie Love, Wanda Guzman, and Barbara Phillips participated in the data collection. Comments of Laura Szalacha, Scott Van Manen, and Jacklyn Blake Clayton on an earlier draft are gratefully acknowledged.

self-regard among adolescent girls contrasts not only with males' experiences, but with younger girls' self-confidence and optimism about their lives (Brown & Gilligan, 1992; Phillips & Zimmerman, 1990).

Increasingly, being female is being defined as a factor that puts a young person "at risk" (Earle, Roach, & Fraser, 1987), and early adolescence is regarded as a critical time in girls' lives (AAUW, 1991; Brown & Gilligan, 1992). Studies have reported that dissatisfaction with one's body, eating disorders, depression, and suicide attempts all occur at much higher rates for adolescent girls than for adolescent boys (Gans & Blyth, 1990; Reinherz, Frost, & Pakiz, 1990).

Gilligan and her colleagues (1992) view early adolescence as a "crossroads" for girls. They describe it as a time of crisis when girls become uncertain of what they know and what they can say in public. At this age girls are becoming conscious of growing up in a patriarchal society that undervalues women. Consequently, girls lose confidence in themselves; their public voices become muted (Brown & Gilligan, 1992; Debold, Wilson & Malave, 1993; Gilligan, Rogers & Noel, 1992). Brown and Gilligan (1992) have argued that girls' self-silencing and "taking their knowledge underground" is a strategy of acquiescence that girls employ to remain acceptable to others.

Gilligan and her colleagues' views on girls' declining confidence in early adolescence were originally formulated on the basis of qualitative research primarily carried out with White girls from middle-class backgrounds. Later research, which included girls of color (Robinson & Ward, 1991; Sullivan, 1996; Taylor, 1996), has led them to expand the original formulation of self-silencing in order to hold on to relationships to include both overt and covert resistance to societal dictates. However, Gilligan and her colleagues' belief that early adolescence is a time of a "crisis in confidence" for girls has remained largely unchanged.

The work of Gilligan and her colleagues and the results of the AAUW survey (1991) that showed older girls having lower self-esteem than younger girls, heightened concern over adolescent girls' development. This concern has coincided with a virtual "cottage industry" that has been decrying the gender gap in self-esteem and offering a variety of strategies to ameliorate the situation (see Flansburg, 1991; Orenstein, 1994; Pipher, 1994; Steinem, 1992). Today, one can rarely find a program designed to uplift "at-risk" youth that does not have a self-esteem component.

On the other hand, research has not always shown adolescent girls to lag in self-esteem. A number of researchers have not found a decline in self-esteem among adolescent girls of color (see Powell, 1985; Rosenberg & Simmons, 1972; Tashakkori, 1993; Taylor, 1976), while others have reported inconsistent findings with respect to the effects of race and gender on self-esteem (Martinez & Dukes, 1987; Tashakkori & Thompson, 1991; Wade, 1991).

It is not clear from the existing literature whether the drop in self-esteem found by some researchers (but not others) in early- to middle-adolescent girls is an artifact of how self-esteem has been operationalized and measured. Also, it appears doubtful that one general notion or measure of satisfaction with self could adequately capture the diverse underpinnings of self-evaluations in different sociocultural milieus and across different domains of competence.

This chapter is based on exploratory research designed to examine different components of girls' positive self-evaluations—that is, their views on what it means for a girl to feel good about herself—among middle-school students from diverse racial and ethnic backgrounds. Our primary hypotheses are that (1) liking one's self, as a young adolescent, can have different meanings depending on the social context of one's life, and that (2) the dimensions of one's self-esteem can be different among girls from different racial and ethnic groups.

Following Harter (1990), we view self-esteem as the evaluation of the self, influenced by both one's self-perceived competence in important domains (see James, 1892) and feedback and support from significant others (see Cooley, 1902; Mead, 1934). We distinguish between evaluations of specific domains of competence on the one hand, and global self-evaluation on the other (see Harter, 1990; Rosenberg, Schooler, Schoenbach & Rosenberg, 1995). Rosenberg and his colleagues (1995) concur with Harter that global self-esteem and competence in specific domains cannot serve as surrogates for one another. On the other hand, we make this distinction bearing in mind that it is generally accepted that overall self-esteem and competence in specific domains are interrelated. As William James (1892) maintained over a century ago, a person's overall sense of self-esteem is derived from self-judged competence in domains the person views as important components of the self. For example, a girl who believes it is important to excel academically and perceives herself to be doing well in school will have a higher overall self-esteem than a classmate who also values academic excellence but judges herself to be an academic failure. However, another girl who is failing in school but does not believe getting good grades is important may still give herself high self-esteem ratings if she judges herself to be good in other domains such as physical attractiveness, athletic ability, and/or social acceptance.

Unless otherwise specified, we use the terms *self-esteem, self-confidence, self-worth, positive self-regard,* and *feeling good about one's self* interchangeably to referr to a *global* or overall sense of one's worth. Throughout the chapter we make a distinction between this global sense of self-confidence and the self-evaluations on specific dimensions of competence. Dimensions of competence that are relevant to self-esteem are bound by culture and historical time. In the research reported here, we have adopted domains proposed by Harter (1988) based on her interviews with adolescent girls and boys—these dimensions are described in the Data Collection Instruments section below. It is our belief that the distinction between overall self-esteem and competence in specific domains is important for an examination of differences in the underpinnings of self-esteem among girls from diverse backgrounds.

Methods

The research was designed to include both quantitative (questionnaire) and qualitative (focus-group interview) methods of data collection among four racial/ethnic groups of girls in the seventh and eighth grades. The racial and ethnic groups included in the study were Caucasian, African American, Puerto Rican, and Chinese American, because they are the largest racial and ethnic groups in the greater Boston area.

Sample

A total of 164 middle-school girls took part in the study. We have complete data available on 161 subjects (3 failed to complete the Harter Self-Perception scales satisfactorily). Approximately one-third of the respondents were in the eighth grade and two-thirds in the seventh grade. Respondents were recruited primarily through their schools with the assistance of the school administration, guidance counselors, and bilingual education teachers, and secondarily through community contacts. We were granted permission to collect data in six public school systems and one private school in the greater Boston area. The sample included 33 African Americans, 46 Caucasians, 40 Chinese Americans, 19 Puerto Ricans, and 25 girls from other race/ethnic groups. "Others" included Armenians, Cape Verdians, Jamaicans, non–Puerto Rican Latinas, and girls who reported mixed racial/ethnic heritage. Due to the heterogeneity in the "other" group, the comparative analyses were restricted to the four major racial/ethnic groups.

The study schools differed not only in terms of racial/ethnic composition but along other dimensions as well. Consequently, our subsamples were not comparable with respect to a number of important demographic variables such as socioeconomic status (SES). The majority of the African American and Puerto Rican girls were from lower-income inner-city neighborhoods. The majority of Caucasian girls were from middle-class suburbs and lower-middle-class satellite cities in the greater Boston area. Most of the Chinese American girls were either from lower-income inner-city neighborhoods or from a lower-middle-class satellite city. Also, the majority of Puerto Rican and Chinese American girls were from recent immigrant families where English was not the primary language spoken at home. Moreover, recruitment procedures, which involved acquiring parental permission via letters sent home with each student, yielded a volunteer sample of relatively "organized" students who remembered to take the letter home, show it to their parents, bring it back signed, and turn it in. Therefore, we obtained convenience samples which cannot be viewed as representative of the schools or the racial/ethnic group.

Data Collection

Quantitative Data

Quantitative data were collected by means of a questionnaire set that included Harter's Adolescent Self-Perception Profile (1988). The Self-Perception Profile is a 40-item scale that taps domain-specific judgment of competence in eight separate domains, briefly described below, each measured by a 5-item subscale plus a separate 5-item scale of Global Self-Worth. The items are rated on a 4-point scale. Harter (1988) reports adequate internal consistency coefficients for each of the subscales (Cronbach's alpha .79 or higher) based on data from middle-school students. The Scholastic Competence subscale measures an adolescent's perception of her competence in doing class work and how smart or intelligent she feels in school. Social Acceptance taps perceptions of how well she is accepted by peers and whether she feels popular. Athletic competence taps her perception of her competence in sports and athletic activity. The subscale of Physical Appearance measures an adoles-

Table 1   ▧   Internal Consistency (alpha) Estimates for Domains of Self-Perception

Domains of Self-Perception	Harter's Sample B (n = 99)[a]	Caucasian (n = 46)	African American (n = 33)	Chinese American (n = 40)	Puerto Rican (n = 19)
Scholastic Competence	.81	.80	.81	.68	.52
Social Acceptance	.81	.69	.74	.59	.48
Athletic Competence	.89	.90	.86	.84	.43
Physical Appearance	.85	.92	.78	.84	.67
Behavioral Conduct	.78[b]	.80	.35	.48	.63
Close Friendship	.79	.78	.75	.75	.57
Global Self-Worth	.80	.90	.79	.72	.68

[a] Harter's Sample B is made up of 48 female and 51 male eighth-graders, approximately 90% of whom are Caucasian (1988, p. 12).
[b] From Harter's Sample D, made up of 60 female and 63 male ninth-graders, approximately 90% of whom are Caucasian (1988, p. 12).

cent's happiness with her looks, body image, and perceptions of attractiveness. Behavioral Conduct is intended to measure perceptions of individual behavior, such as whether an adolescent likes the way she behaves, does the right thing, acts the way she is supposed to, and avoids getting into trouble. The Close Friendships subscale measures ability to make close friends with whom she can confide and share secrets. Finally, Global Self-Worth is a separate subscale that measures the overall global judgment of an adolescent's personal worth, instead of competence in specific domains. This subscale taps the extent to which an adolescent likes herself as a person, is happy with the way she is leading her life, and her general happiness. Given the grade level of our respondents—seventh- and eighth-graders—we omitted the Romantic Appeal and Job Competence subscales from the domains we measured. Romantic Appeal contains items about dating and Job Competence about paid employment; in pilot testing we found these two domains to be less relevant to middle-school girls' lives.

Table 1 presents the internal consistency (alpha) estimates of subscales from Harter's Self-Perception scale that were employed in this study. The first column consists of the estimates from one of Harter's samples, her Sample B. This sample was composed of 48 girls and 51 boys in the eighth grade, which is the sample closest in age to the seventh- and eighth-grade girls in this study. Harter reports that approximately 90 percent of her samples were Caucasians drawn from primarily lower-middle-class to upper-middle-class neighborhoods in Colorado (1988, p. 13). Our Caucasian sample is the one most similar to Harter's Sample B with respect to race/ethnicity and SES. Indeed, with the exception of the Social Acceptance domain, our Caucasian sample's internal consistency estimates are the most similar to those reported by Harter. In other words, items measuring the different domains appear to be tapping the same underlying dimension in samples of middle-class Caucasians.

Data from other racial/ethnic groups in our sample did not always yield adequate internal consistency estimates (see Table 1). Because the relatively small size of racial/ethnic subsamples can suppress these scores by limiting variability within, we decided that an alpha of .65 or above would be evidence of an adequate level of internal consistency for this exploratory study, instead of the more traditional cut-off of .70 (see DeVellis, 1991; Nunnally, 1978). Even with this low cut-off point of .65, the African American sample had one subscale with an unacceptably low internal consistency (Behavioral Conduct = 35); the Chinese American sample had two (Social Acceptance, = .59 and Behavioral Conduct, = .48) and the Puerto Rican sample, with the smallest sample size (N = 19), had five (Scholastic Competence = .52; Social Acceptance, = .48; Athletic Competence, = .43; Behavioral Conduct, = .63; and Close Friendship, = .57). Subscales with unacceptably low alpha estimates were eliminated from subsequent statistical analyses.

Qualitative Data

The qualitative data were gathered in focus-group interviews lasting approximately one hour. A subset of the sample, 93 girls, participated in 20 groups, which varied in size from two to nine. The groups were homogeneous with respect to the race/ethnicity of the girls and interviewer.

Field testing questions for the focus-group interview highlighted the difficulty of using terms such as *self-esteem, competence, self-worth,* and *positive self-evaluations* with seventh- and eighth-grade students. The blank stares from the girls made it clear that we needed to employ plain English. With input from both middle-school girls and our colleagues, we settled on the words *a girl who likes herself* to capture the essence of positive self-evaluations.

Testing the phrase *a girl who likes herself* in several groups revealed that girls did not readily talk about whether they liked themselves, but were quite vocal when it came to talking as "experts" on the topic. That is, each girl was reluctant (or unable) to talk about whether she liked herself, but had lots of opinions on the more general topic of a girl's liking herself. Therefore, the focus groups elicited these girls' self-esteem *ideology* rather than their subjective evaluations of themselves.

Focus-group discussions were prompted by the interviewer saying, "Think about a girl who likes herself; what is she like?" This was followed up by "How did she become that way?" and ended with asking advice on how to raise a girl so she'll grow up to like herself. The audio-taped and transcribed interviews were analyzed for emergent themes, which led to the construction of coding categories. Answers to the question about the characteristics of a girl who likes herself were analyzed with respect to the following categories: (1) positive personal qualities, (2) negative personal qualities, (3) physical characteristics, (4) sexuality-related characteristics, and (5) preferred activities. Responses to the follow-up question of how she got to be that way were coded into (1) family influences, (2) peer influences, and (3) personal attributes. Coding categories for analyzing responses to the third question regarding advice to parents were (1) parents' jurisdiction, (2) child's jurisdiction, (3) reward and punishment—do's and don'ts, (4) value systems, (5) what girls need, (6) authoritative style of child rearing, (7) communication about sexuality, and (8) safety concerns. Independent coding of 10 percent of the transcript material yielded inter-coder agreement of 90 percent.

Results

In this exploratory study, we have analyzed the results by race and ethnicity as one of the ways of operationalizing social background. The results of the racial/ethnic analyses are intended to be suggestive and illustrative, not definitive, and not solely, or even primarily, attributable to race/ethnicity. This is because the four groups of girls in the study were not randomly selected and differed on relevant dimensions (such as SES and urbanization) other than simply race and ethnicity. For this reason, in our data analyses we have refrained from using inferential statistics, to avoid a suggestion that the sample means are indicators of the population means. On the other hand, we present quantitative and qualitative descriptions of the samples to provide a context for interpreting observed relationships among variables within each sample.

Quantitative Analyses

Table 2 presents the mean scores for self-perception domains as measured by Harter's Self-Perception Profile for each racial/ethnic group. The African American subsample had the most positive self-evaluations, Chinese American girls had the least positive views. Puerto Rican and Caucasian girls fell in between the two extremes. The Global Self-Worth scores followed the same pattern, with African American girls having the highest scores.

The racial/ethnic groups also differed in the areas in which girls gave themselves the highest ratings. African American girls had high scores on the following domains of Self-Perception: Social Acceptance ($m = 3.41$), Scholastic Competence ($m = 3.20$), and Physical Appearance ($m = 3.12$). Caucasian girls' ratings were the

Table 2 ▩ **Mean Self-Perception Ratings by Racial/Ethnic Group**

	African American M (n = 33)	Caucasian M (n = 46)	Chinese American M (n = 40)	Puerto Rican M (n = 19)
Domains of Self-Perception				
Scholastic Competence	3.20	2.97	2.67	a
Social Acceptance	3.41	3.06	a	a
Athletic Competence	2.72	2.77	2.11	a
Physical Appearance	3.12	2.28	2.16	2.65
Behavioral Conduct	a	3.03	a	a
Close Friendship	3.13	3.36	2.91	a
Global Self-Worth	3.36	2.90	2.63	2.96

[a] means are omitted because alphas were less than .65.

Table 3 ■ **Correlations of Domains of Self-Perception with Global Self-Worth**

	African American M (n = 33)	Caucasian M (n = 46)	Chinese American M (n = 40)	Puerto Rican M (n = 19)
Scholastic Competence	.75**	.37*	.28	a
Social Acceptance	.32	.28	a	a
Athletic Competence	.47*	.22	.18	a
Physical Appearance	.47*	.82**	.30	.73**
Behavioral Conduct	a	.58**	a	a
Close Friendship	−.08	.17	.42*	a

*p < .01
**p < .001
a Correlation not reported because alpha estimates were less than .65.

highest in the domains of Social Acceptance (*m* = 3.06), Behavioral Conduct (*m* = 3.03), and Close Friendship (*m* = 3.36). For Puerto Rican girls, the highest self-rating was in the domain of Physical Appearance (*m* = 2.65). For Chinese American girls, the domain on which they rated themselves the highest was Close Friendship (*m* = 2.91).

An examination of the correlations in Table 3 reveals that, overall, Physical Appearance is the domain most closely associated with Global Self-Worth. There were also some noteworthy differences among correlations with Global Self-Worth. For African American girls, the strongest correlation was with Scholastic Competence (*r* = 75), while for both Caucasian and Puerto Rican girls it was with Physical Appearance (*r* = .82 and *r* = .73, respectively). Among Chinese American girls, Close Friendship was moderately related to Global Self-Worth (*r* = .42).

Qualitative Analyses

African American Girls   Among African American girls, "a girl who likes herself" was described primarily in terms of interpersonal qualities, which included being a good friend, having friends, giving and getting respect, being a good student, and her physical appearance/attractiveness.

> She sings well, she's smart, and gets good grades, so she gets compliments. She gives respect to others, so others give her respect. She has manners . . .

> She's polite, dresses good, smart, pretty . . . she has good friends—she is a good friend, she's friendly.

How she got to be that way was credited to her family upbringing, role models, her personal accomplishments, and receiving compliments, as well as being physically attractive.

> Her friends and family that talk a lot to her and really care about her; good parents help—a good father and mother roles.

> Maybe her boyfriend makes her feel good about herself—tells her how nice she looks that day. Maybe her mother too.

Advice to parents centered on the major themes of teaching respect, having open communication between parents and the daughter, and showing interest in her education. Having ground rules but not smothering the girl with too many rules was seen as important. Additionally, African American girls talked about having "freedom" from parental protectiveness. While their comments suggested an acceptance of the limits imposed by parents, they just wanted their parents to ease up on the controls a little.

> Take the time to look at her work and go to her open houses and talk to her teachers.

> Make sure that she takes the time to study.

> Be reasonably strict. Don't smother her: Let her breathe.

> Do not watch her 24/7 (24 hours a day, seven days a week).

> Trust her, you know. Don't make . . . don't always try to keep her in the house . . . because all this violence in here and violence in there.

Responses additionally touched on providing guidance in relation to violence, drugs, sex education, and racism.

> They also have to be raised with values, otherwise she's nobody but a statistic. Being Black is a tough thing, but you need to teach her not to be discriminative and prejudiced.

> Tell her, like, about everything . . . everyday life. Like, what happens when you use drugs and what happens when you're gonna have sex, and . . . and plus her education.

> Should raise her with self-defense, and if you don't fight in a situation where you don't have to, it's fine but sometime you will have to fight for yourself.

Scholastic Achievement scores, which emerged as the most powerful correlate of African American girls' Global Self-Worth ratings ($r = 75$), were echoed in the focus-group discussions on girls' advice to parents to be supportive of their daughter's education. Moreover, African American girls' comments in the focus-group discussion on the role of being attractive and getting compliments corroborate the moderate correlation between Physical Appearance and Global Self-Worth ($r = .47$).

Caucasian Girls   Among Caucasian respondents, "a girl who likes herself" was described primarily in terms of a strong sense of individuality and independence, both of which suggest that Caucasian respondents connected feeling good about one's self to being one's own person.

> She has confidence and doesn't care about what others think, sure of herself, not afraid to speak out, does not care about what others think about her (her opinions, her clothes, etc.).

Takes pride in herself, not afraid to wear different clothes; not afraid to be different.

Positive interpersonal qualities, which included how she treats others and is treated by them, were secondary themes in the discussion.

They care about what you say, respect you, and would readily defend you despite what others think or say. They would want to hear what you have to say in class.

How she got to be that way was credited to parents who raised the girl in a supportive and respectful environment.

Their upbringing—she was raised that way. A supportive family equals a family that cares and respects you. Parents can show they respect you by trusting you.

She [mother] makes her [daughter] feel important.

Supportive friends who care about you, listen to you, and are loyal. They don't try to ignore you (would not listen to others if others started bad mouthing you). They would defend you.

Having good friends, a role model, and someone who will listen to and understand them were also mentioned as positive influences.

They [friends] are interested in your opinions. They would give you constructive criticism and won't tell you you're stupid.

Advice to parents included loving the girl, encouraging and supporting her, and trying to understand her. Caucasian respondents wanted parents to foster independence and individuality while maintaining some limits.

When she does something good let her know and show her you are proud.

Discipline them by encouragement, not by punishment. Make sure they understand what they did wrong, as well as what they did right so they will know for the next time.

Have her tell them [parents] who and where and when if they do let her go [out at night].

Don't repeat things 10 million times.

For Caucasian girls, the results of the quantitative analyses and themes that emerged in the focus-group discussions generally agree, except on the issue of physical appearance. While in their discussion, Caucasian girls said that a girl who likes herself is too independent to care about what others think about her looks, quantitative data showed that scores on the Physical Appearance domain were very highly correlated with Global Self-Worth.

Chinese American Girls   The main themes that emerged from focus-group interviews with Chinese American respondents described a girl who likes herself as "her own person," meaning immune to criticism, defiant, does what she believes is right, and is able to take care of herself. Paradoxically, this quest for independence was closely related to having the freedom to form close connections with friends and to have one's own thoughts and "space" for one's own feelings. Thus the Chinese respondents view a girl who likes herself as one who is independent enough to be able to take care of herself as well as others. Additional characteristics mentioned included a girl who was born in the United States and speaks English well.

> She does what she wants to. Like if you tell her to, like you peer pressure her, she won't do it. And she understands people's feelings and how they react to her, reacts to a certain comment. But she is still confident in what she thinks and she does her own thing.

> I know a person who believes in what she thinks and she does a lot of things different from other people. She doesn't try to change herself to become like them. She says that she is an anarchist because she believes in herself instead of others and she works hard at a lot of things and tries to, um, make people happy and helps out a lot.

How she got to be that way was described as requiring both "space" (i.e., freedom from close family supervision) and support. The space allows a girl to become her own person in relationship to others beyond her family. Support refers to adults understanding her (i.e., being there for her but also letting her make certain choices for herself), providing access to a good education, and allowing her to explore options and activities which can be fun.

> She is unsure of what she wants to be, but she knows that she wants to be something. She wants to be successful and she wants to make a difference in the world and in life. And, um, she has a positive attitude and it's because she gets, like, support most of the time. And she takes [parents'] ideas into mind but then she makes up the decision at the end.

> Your parents start you off. . . ; Like, you do nothing, what's so fun about that? You have to be a fun person to feel good about yourself. So, like, do fun things; like, enroll in special classes, like sports or something. Things everyone else is doing 'cause if you do that, you'll feel good, you'll feel proud. And then you'll feel good about yourself.

> (What if you can't do these things? Then what do you do?)

> Then it's your parents' fault.

> (Okay, but how would you feel about yourself?)

> I'd feel really bad.

A number of participants spoke of the need for freedom to be with friends and to interact with peers, including male peers, on an informal basis.

> . . . Give her freedom.

> (What do you mean by "freedom"?)

Like, she, like, I mean, like, not lots of freedom but sort of, like, letting her stay . . . let her hang out with friends, but not too late. Just give her a little time. Let her get used to freedom.

Not too much freedom! [Laughter]

I know!

Thus, the Chinese respondents saw a girl who likes herself as one who knows how to conduct herself and is independent enough to be able to take care of herself as well as her friends. This importance attached to friends in focus-group discussions was borne out by the quantitative data wherein Global Self-Worth was most closely related to scores on the Close Friendship domain.

Puerto Rican Girls   Among Puerto Ricans, a girl who likes herself was described primarily in terms of social/interpersonal qualities; that is, she is popular, has lots of friends, and gets along well with people. A strong, second theme was being well behaved, including the ability to stay out of trouble.

Okay! I know this girl that she's always happy and she makes people feel happy the same way that she is and she don't put people down—like some people do, and she's nice.

And she doesn't get into trouble, you know [pause, other girls offering answers, someone says "fights"], yeah, into fights.

How she got to be that way was credited to how she is treated by family and friends—people treat her well.

Yeah, like the way people treat her, that's the way she feels. And if people treat her nice and she, then that comes along with, um, . . . if you feel good about yourself then that comes along with making friends and everything.

'Cause they say what goes around comes around and, like, if you give love then you get love. You treat people like you want to be treated.

Advice to parents centered on teaching the girl right from wrong, being there for her, and teaching her to respect herself and others. Another theme was teaching daughters to be streetwise. This included teaching girls about the dangers of drugs and premature sexual activity, as well as being able to defend oneself physically.

Teach her right from wrong and you know, don't do something you'll regret later.

[Tell your daughter:] Don't do drugs, sex, alcohol.

Like, don't go to bed with the first guy you see. And if you have sex, use a condom and make sure you love that person. And don't get into trouble.

I would teach my kid to defend him or herself in a bad situation. I don't consider that to be a bad thing, if she or he uses it for good.

. . . the girl's gotta be streetwise.

For Puerto Rican girls and the others as well, the analyses of qualitative data from the focus-group interviews generally supported the results of the quantitative analyses. The only divergent information was found for Caucasian girls' views on physical appearance (for a more detailed discussion of the focus-group outcomes, see Erkut & Marx, 1995).

Discussion

Taken together, the quantitative and qualitative results point to four conclusions. First girls from different racial/ethnic groups use different standards to judge self-worth. The qualitative data from focus-group discussions, where girls were asked to take the "expert" position, were informative about the self-esteem ideology of girls from different racial/ethnic groups. Because the focus groups were homogeneous with respect to race/ethnicity and led by a same-race/ethnicity facilitator, values particular to their racial/ethnic subculture were likely salient in the discussions. Therefore, the focus-group data yielded information about a particular racial/ethnic group of girls' perceptions of what a girl who likes herself *ought* to be like. In other words, we obtained information on the *standards* the girls use for evaluating themselves.

The results show that there are some similarities in these standards; for example, all girls talked about the importance of having friends and being well behaved. However, even these general themes took on different meaning in the discussions. Moreover, there were also notable differences in the standards of self-evaluation. We interpret these differences in terms of the social and physical context of the girls' lives.

For example, the Caucasian girls, who in our sample lived in the relative safety of middle-class suburbs or lower-middle-class satellite cities, placed a high emphasis on independence, individualism, being one's own person, and not bowing to peer pressure. In contrast, the African American and Puerto Rican girls, who in our sample lived in lower-income urban environments, did not stress independence in the same way that Caucasian girls did. Instead, their comments suggested a keen awareness of the physical dangers that surround their urban existence as well as the threats posed by racism. A girl who likes herself was described by African American and Puerto Rican girls as a nice girl who stays out of trouble but is also able to fight to defend herself if necessary. The "freedom" African American girls wanted was not only about being one's own person, it was as much about freedom from being constantly watched and monitored by parents concerned for their safety.

Chinese American girls also talked about wanting "freedom." Yet the context and the meaning were, again, different. Whereas for African American girls it was a quest for their parents to trust them and to let up on controls so that they could have more freedom and be more on their own, for Chinese American girls, wanting space appeared to be a quest for freedom to *connect* with peers and friends outside of their family circles. That is, Chinese American girls did not want to be left alone by their parents to be independent. Rather, they wanted the freedom to form connections outside the family.

We have interpreted Chinese American girls' quest for freedom in the context of their acculturation struggles. Many in our sample were recent immigrants, and

English was not the first language spoken in most of these girls' homes. It appears that the Chinese American girls experienced a discontinuity between home and the outside world and felt that, as much as they respected their parents and accepted and appreciated parental values, they needed to find role models and sources of support outside the family to be able to learn to make their way in mainstream American culture. The "space" they sought was permission to make connections with friends and peers who could teach them about how things are done in U.S. mainstream culture and the opportunities and options that are there for them.

The second noteworthy finding, derived from the quantitative data, was that each racial/ethnic group of girls presented a different profile of self-perceived strengths on Harter's domains of competence. Our sample of African American girls rated themselves as highly competent—average ratings of 3.12 and above on a 4-point scale—in the domains of Social Acceptance, Scholastic Competence, and Physical Appearance. They also had the highest Global Self-Worth ratings of all racial/ethnic groups (3.36 on a 4-point scale). While high global self-esteem was found among African American girls in the 1991 AAUW sponsored survey, the same study had shown African American girls to lag in confidence in their scholastic abilities, which our research contradicts.

Caucasian girls in our sample gave themselves high ratings on the Social Acceptance, Behavioral Conduct, and Close Friendship domains. This pattern of findings suggests that they perceived themselves to be well liked by their peers and close friends and that they saw themselves as well behaved. In spite of this, their Global Self-Worth ratings were only moderately high, 2.90 on a 4-point scale. It may be that their perceived strengths in being well-liked, good girls were diminished by the relatively low ratings they gave themselves in Physical Appearance (2.28).

Our sample of Chinese American girls gave themselves lower ratings on most of the domains compared with other groups and, also, had the lowest Global Self-Worth scores of all. Close Friendship was the domain on which they rated themselves the highest, but even this was only 2.91 out of 4. Relative to the other groups, it appears that Chinese American girls did not see themselves as measuring up to the standards to which they aspire.

Puerto Rican girls in our sample ratings were fairly even across domains and did not show any particular area of strength or weakness. Even though they did not see themselves as particularly strong on any one domain, their average Global Self-Esteem of 2.96 was comparable with that of Caucasian girls' (2.90) who, by contrast, had rated themselves quite highly on several domains. On the other hand, these results need to be viewed with caution because five out of the seven subscale scores on the self-perception profile had low reliability.

The third noteworthy finding was that physical attractiveness appears to be a source of conflict for Caucasian girls. In their focus-group discussion, Caucasian girls were vehement in their insistence that a girl who likes herself would not bow to peer pressure in terms of how she looks and dresses. Yet their ratings on the Physical Appearance domain were very highly correlated with Global Self-Esteem scores ($r = .82$), which suggest that for Caucasian girls, Global Self-Worth is almost the same thing as perceiving one's self as physically appealing. This contradiction points to a strong ambivalence about the role of being physically attractive among Caucasian girls. In contrast, Puerto Rican girls, among whom Physical Appearance and Global Self-Worth scores also were highly correlated ($r = .73$), showed no ambivalence in their attitude toward being attractive: They stressed the importance of being attractive in focus-group discussions and generally gave themselves high ratings on Physical Appearance.

Chinese American girls were also consistent in their attitudes toward physical attractiveness. They did not bring it up as part of the discussion of a girl who likes herself, they did not rate themselves highly on this domain, nor did their scores on Physical Appearance correlate strongly with Global Self-Worth.

Our findings on Caucasian girls' ambivalence about physical attractiveness suggests that the majority culture's narrow and unrealistic standards of physical beauty— e.g., the image captured in caricature in the original Barbie doll—may be most undermining of Caucasian girls' evaluations of their worth. As Wade (1991) points out, media images of feminine beauty ideals have mostly reflected White standards in the United States, hence most relevant to Caucasian girls' self-evaluations. In contrast to the narrow Caucasian standard of beauty, until recently, non-White images were scarce in mainstream media, which gave many girls of color the option to choose standards of beauty from the wide range of people in their lives. In the past few years, there has been an increase in the number of non-White models depicted by mainstream media and the fashion industry, some portraying a wide range of skin color, hair style and texture, and facial features. Moreover, in the past few decades, non-White girls have enjoyed the added bonus of seeing themselves depicted in not only a range of skin colors, facial features, and hair styles, but also body image (the full-figured woman) in magazines such as *Ebony* and *Essence* and on television programs such as "Living Single" with Queen Latifah. The depictions of a wider array of what is attractive—when compared with the narrow Caucasian standard—may allow non-White adolescents a greater range of self-acceptance in how they view their physical appearance.

The fourth finding was the widespread endorsement of girls' need for support but also for parental limit-setting. Seventh- and eighth-grade girls' advice to parents for raising a girl who will grow up to like herself stressed giving her freedom but not too much; trusting her to go out but adhering to a curfew; watching her closely but not all the time. It appears that, at least during the middle-school years, girls believe that both love and limits are necessary ingredients for successful childrearing.

Conclusions

The findings of this research are that (1) girls from different racial and ethnic groups use different standards to judge self-worth; (2) girls from different racial and ethnic groups view themselves as having different strengths; (3) Caucasian girls have the most conflicted attitudes toward the role played by physical attractiveness in determining self-worth; and (4) middle-school girls widely endorse "love and limits" as the best child-rearing approach for raising daughters who will grow up to like themselves. Differences we have highlighted in the ways girls from diverse social backgrounds perceive what it means to like one's self underscore the important role played by contextual variables. The results have led us to postulate that not only race/ethnicity, but also the level of danger in the neighborhood, the nature of family boundaries, recency of immigration, and media images of feminine beauty can play a role in the composition of self-evaluations. The general conclusion to be drawn from this exploratory research is that an understanding of the social forces a girl faces is essential for an understanding of what that particular girl needs in order to like herself.

Because our subsamples were relatively small and not comparable with respect to many relevant variables such as family composition, social class, and urbanization of residence, the pattern of findings discussed cannot be solely or primarily attributed to racial/ethnic differences. We recommend that future research employ larger representative samples to more accurately assess the meaning and determinants of middle-school-aged girls' positive self-evaluations.

We believe that documenting the diversity in girls' conceptions of positive self-regard has significant consequences for understanding girls from diverse backgrounds, because what may appear on the surface to be similar phenomena may, on closer inspection, reveal subtle but important differences (see Erkut, Fields, Sing & Marx, 1996). Therefore, it is important to arrive at a more differentiated understanding of the diversity in girls' lives and subsequent conceptions of positive self-regard, because one size does not fit all.

One of the practical outcomes of a clearer understanding of the underpinnings of self-evaluations among adolescent girls will be a rethinking of current prevention and intervention programs for bolstering girls' self-esteem. It may well be that, when measured using context-sensitive definitions and instruments, many girls from backgrounds other than White middle-class already have an adequate level of self-esteem and may not benefit from intervention programs designed for White middle-class girls. Also, given that there are multiple configurations of self-esteem in diverse groups, programs that work from a single, essentialist notion of what it means to like one's self may in fact be ineffective for girls from different backgrounds. Any program designed to bolster self-esteem should explicitly define the important dimensions of competence for its target population. Finally, to the extent that self-esteem is both global and also has specific domains, interventions can be designed to be specific to the domains of interest. For example, in our sample of African American girls, Global Self-Worth was most highly correlated with the domain of Scholastic Achievement. This finding suggests that for a sample with a similar profile, an academic enrichment program is likely to yield the most return in terms of boosting global self-esteem. For the Caucasian sample, the highest correlation was between Global Self-Worth and Physical Appearance. In a sample with this particular profile, most gains in overall self-esteem are likely to be attained by addressing controversies surrounding physical attractiveness, rather that by providing academic enhancement.

Results of the current study have several implications for future research on girl's self-esteem. First, there is a need for psychometrically sound measurement tools that are valid and reliable for use with diverse populations. Second, it is necessary to tease out the separate effects of such demographic variables as race/ethnicity, SES, immigration, and urbanization of residence, which we touched on in the research reported here. Future research should additionally explore the role played by sexual orientation, gender roles, and being physically and/or mentally disabled. Third, longitudinal studies are needed to document the relative stability or instability of global self-worth throughout adolescence, as well as to examine which domains are the sources of strength for which groups of girls during early, middle, and late adolescence. Finally, the very same research questions can be asked about boys' self-esteem, because adolescent boys are no more monolithic a group than are girls. Future research needs to examine the developmental trajectory of global self-esteem as well as its specific underpinnings among boys from diverse backgrounds.

Middle-school girls seem to agree that parents should provide support and freedom for a daughter if they want her to grow up liking herself. Almost in the same breath, they add that the freedom should be within limits. Thus, middle-school girls' advice to parents for raising confident and competent girls is the "love and limits" approach to child rearing. The basic finding of this study is that what constitutes loving support and limited freedom for a given girl depends on the social realities of her life. The particular pattern of differences we found in this research may be unique to the samples studied and not generalizable to the population. Nevertheless, in view of the multiple and varying underpinnings of self-esteem in girls from different backgrounds, the findings underscore the weaknesses of an essentialist approach to girls' self-esteem. The question concerning a decline in girls' self-esteem in early adolescence is then turned into a need to examine the relative stability of global self-evaluation throughout adolescence among different groups of girls, as well as which domains of competence are sources of strength during early, middle, and late adolescence.

References

American Association of University Women (1991). *Shortchanging girls, shortchanging America.* Washington, DC: AAUW, The Analysis Group, Greenberg-Lake.

Baruch, G. K. (1975). Girls who perceive themselves as competent: Some antecedents and correlates. Unpublished paper. Shrewsbury, MA: Worcester Foundation for Experimental Biology.

Brown, L. M., & Gilligan, C. (1992). *Meeting at the crossroads: Women's psychology and girls' development.* New York: Random House.

Cooley, C. H. (1902). *Human nature and the social order.* New York: Charles Scribner's Sons.

Debold, E., Wilson, M., & Malave, I. (1993). *Mother daughter revolution: From betrayal to power.* Reading, MA: Addison Wesley.

DeVellis, R. F. (1991). *Scale development: Theory and applications.* Beverly Hills, CA: Sage Publications.

Earle, J., Roach, V., & Fraser, K. (1987). *Female dropouts: A new perspective.* Alexandria, VA: National Association of State Boards of Education.

Erkut, S., Fields, J. P., Sing, R., & Marx, F. (1996). Diversity in girls' experiences: Feeling good about who you are. In B. Leadbetter & N. Way (Eds.), *Urban adolescent girls: Resisting stereotypes.* New York: New York University Press.

Erkut, S., & Marx, F. (1995). *Raising competent girls: An exploratory study of diversity in girls' views of liking one's self.* Wellesley, MA: Center for Research on Women Special Report #10.

Flansburg, S. (1991). Building a self: Teenaged girls and issues of self-esteem. *Women's Educational Equity Act Publishing Center Digest.* Newton, MA: Education Development Center, Inc.

Gans, J., & Blyth, D. (1990). *America's adolescents: How healthy are they?* Chicago, IL: American Medical Association.

Gilligan, C., Rogers, A. G., & Noel, N. (1992, February). *Cartography of a lost time: Women, girls, and relationships.* A paper presented at the Lilly Endowment Conference on Youth and Caring, Miami, Florida.

Harter, S. (1985). Processes underlying the construct, maintenance and enhancement of the self-concept in children. In J. Suls & A. Greenwald (Eds.), *Psychological perspectives on the self: Vol. 3.* Hillsdale, NJ: Lawrence Erlbaum.

Harter, S. (1988). Developmental process in the construction of self. In T. D. Yawkey & J. E. Johnson (Eds.), *Integrative process and socialization: Early to middle childhood* (pp. 45–78). Hillsdale, CA: Laurence Erlbaum Associates.

Harter, S. (1990). Causes, correlates, and the functional role of global self-worth: A life-span perspective. In J. Kolligian Jr. & R. J. Sternberg (Eds.), *Perceptions of competence and incompetence across the life-span.* New Haven, CT: Yale University Press.

James, W. (1892). *Psychology: The briefer course.* New York: Henry Holt.

Marsh, H., & Gouvernet, P. (1989). Multidimensional self-concepts and perceptions of control: Construct validation of responses by children. *Journal of Educational Psychology, 81*(1), 57–69.

Martinez, R., & Dukes, R. L. (1987). Race, gender and self-esteem among youth. *Hispanic Journal of Behavioral Sciences, 9,* 427–443.

Mead, G. H. (1934). *Mind, self, and society.* Chicago: University of Chicago Press.

Nunnally, J. (1978). *Psychometric theory,* 2nd ed. New York: McGraw-Hill.

Orenstein, P. (1994). *School girls: Young women, self-esteem, and the confidence gap.* New York: Doubleday.

Phillips, D. A., & Zimmerman, M. (1990). The developmental course of perceived competence and incompetence among competent children. In R. J. Sternberg & J. Kolligian Jr. (Eds.), *Competence considered* (pp. 41–66). New Haven, CT: Yale University Press.

Pipher, M. (1994). *Reviving Ophelia: Saving the selves of adolescent girls.* New York: Ballantine.

Powell, G. J. (1985). Self-concepts among Afro-American students in racially isolated minority schools: Some regional differences. *Journal of the American Academy of Child Psychiatry, 24,* 142–149.

Reinherz, R., Frost, A., & Pakiz, B. (1990). *Changing faces: Correlates of depressive symptoms in late adolescence.* Boston: Simmons College School of Social Work.

Robinson, T., & Ward, J. V. (1991). "A belief in a self far greater than anyone's disbelief": Cultivating healthy resistance among African American female adolescents. In C. Gilligan, A. G. Rogers, & D. Tolman (Eds.), *Women, girls, and psychotherapy: Reframing resistance* (pp. 87–103). Binghamton, NY: Harrington Park Press.

Rosenberg, M., Schooler, C., Schoenbach, C., & Rosenberg, F. (1995). Global self-esteem and specific self-esteem: Different concepts, different outcomes. *American Sociological Review, 60,* 141–156

Rosenberg, M., & Simmons, R. (1972). *Black and white self-esteem: The urban school child.* Rose Monograph Series. Washington, DC: American Sociological Association.

Steinem, G. (1992). *Revolution from within: A book of self-esteem.* Boston: Little, Brown.

Sullivan, Amy M. (1996). From mentor to muse: Recasting the role of women in relationship with urban adolescent girls. In B. J. R. Leadbetter & N. Way (Eds.), *Urban girls: Resisting stereotypes, creating identities* (pp. 226–249). New York: New York University Press.

Tashakkori, A. (1993). Gender, ethnicity, and the structure of self-esteem: An attitude theory approach. *The Journal of Social Psychology, 133*(4), 479–488.

Tashakkori, A., & Thompson, V. D. (1991). Race differences in self-perception, and self-devaluation in depression: A factor analytic study among Iranian college students. *Personality and Individual Differences, 14,* 341–354.

Taylor, R. L. (1976). Psychosocial development among black children and youth: A reexamination. *American Journal of Orthopsychiatry, 46,* 4–19.

Wade, T. J. (1991). Race and sex differences in adolescent self-perceptions of physical attractiveness and level of self-esteem during early and late adolescence. *Personality and Individual Differences, 12,* 1319–1324.

Questions for Thought

1. Explain the concept of self-esteem and how it was measured.

2. How did recent immigration and the level of danger in her neighborhood affect a girl's sense of self-esteem?

3. Select one of the four ethnic groups of girls. Based on this article, discuss the cultural traditions and life experiences that are relevant to self-esteem among girls in this group.

4. The researchers report that being physically attractive is especially likely to be a source of conflict for Caucasian girls. What evidence do they present to support this conclusion? Explain why Caucasian girls might experience more conflict about their looks than other girls.

5. The researchers collected both quantitative data (standardized test scores) and qualitative data (comments during focus-group discussions). Discuss the strengths and weaknesses of each kind of data.

6. These researchers studied girls, but self-esteem is also important to the psychological development of boys. Discuss how the six specific domains of self-esteem (e.g., physical attractiveness, behavioral conduct) might affect the global self-worth of boys. Be specific about the ethnicity of the boys you discuss.

The Path to Math

Gender and Racial-Ethnic Differences in Mathematics Participation from Middle School to High School

Sophia Catsambis

By high school graduation, boys are more likely than girls to have taken advanced math courses and to pursue careers in math and science. How does this gender gap in math develop? Catsambis uses national survey data to trace the "path to math" for boys and girls from eighth grade to tenth grade. Her detailed analyses focus on three factors: students' opportunities to learn math, their achievement in math courses and on standardized tests, and their interest in math. Catsambis identifies different barriers to success in math for White, Latino, and African American girls and boys. Her findings underline the intertwined effects of gender and ethnicity in determining math success.

This study traced the development of gender differences in learning opportunities, achievement, and choice in mathematics among White, African American, and Latino students using data from a nationally representative sample of eighth-grade students who were resurveyed in the 10th grade. It found that in this age group, female students do not lag behind male students in test scores and grades and that White female students are exposed to more learning opportunities in mathematics than are male students. However, all female students tend to have less interest in mathematics and less confidence in their mathematics abilities. Gender differences are the largest among Latinos and the smallest among African Americans. Furthermore, the major barriers to mathematics achievement for White female students are attitudes and career choices and for minority students of both sexes, they are limited learning opportunities and low levels of achievement.

Adapted from *Sociology of Education*, 1994, 67, 199–215. Copyright 1994 by the American Sociological Association. Used by permission.

Women still trail men in their participation in mathematics and related fields (Friedman 1989; Marsh 1989; National Science Foundation, NSF, 1988; Sadker, Sadker, and Klein 1991). Oakes (1990) provided a useful conceptualization for explaining this gender gap: "opportunities, achievement, and choice." In mathematics, women's limited involvement in learning opportunities, relatively low levels of achievement, and lack of interest eventually affect their underrepresentation in the field. Logically, if the opportunity structure benefits men, one should be able to identify some mechanisms of disadvantage by documenting differences between males and females in these three conceptual areas.

Gender differences in the domains of opportunity, achievement, and choice emerge during the middle grades, but little is known of the exact and developmental nature of their interrelationship (Oakes 1990). This lack of knowledge is due mainly to limitations in research that has not been longitudinal in scope, generalizable in extent, and ethnic-race specific (Clewell and Anderson 1991; Oakes 1990).

Berryman (1983), for example, discussed these limitations when she suggested that girls' interests and career choices before ninth grade may develop independently of their achievements. The relationship between interests and achievement may differ for older students, since in high school, career choices and attitudes toward academic subjects may influence participation in the more advanced elective courses. Berryman cautioned, though, that these conclusions were tentative because they were based on data that may not be generalizable.

To be certain of the causal direction between and the relative importance of opportunity, achievement, and choice, one needs nationally representative longitudinal data that measure students from the middle grades on, when the pool of mathematics and science talent is formed (Berryman 1983; Oakes 1990). With the addition of an oversampling of minority students, one could examine the relative contributions of each of these conceptual domains for all students who remain underrepresented in mathematics and other quantitative fields (Berryman 1983; Clewell and Anderson 1991; Oakes 1990). Most research has focused on gender differences in general, and for that reason the portrayal of any one group is inaccurate (Oakes 1990). In thinking about equity, one needs research that investigates the "path to math" for different types of women and men. It is only since 1988 that nationally representative data bases satisfying these conditions have been available.

This article reports on a study that used data from a large, national survey to examine race- and ethnic-specific gender differences in a cohort of eighth-grade students. The aim of the study was to explore the process by which women's participation in mathematics begins to drop during adolescence, by tracing students' mathematics-related learning opportunities, attitudes, and achievements from middle school to the early years of high school.

Emergence of Gender Differences

Although gender differences in mathematics achievement are most evident during secondary and postsecondary education, they may develop much earlier (Kahle and Lakes 1983; Steinkamp and Maehr 1984). For middle school students, gender differences in performance and course work are minimal, but strong differences exist in attitudes and perceptions of the usefulness of mathematics (Lockheed, Thorpe, Brooks-Gunn, Casserly, and McAloon 1985; Oakes 1990). For example, beginning in middle school, girls show less interest in mathematics and science and have more negative attitudes toward these fields. They have relatively high levels of performance anxiety and little confidence in their personal abilities, and they attribute their success to luck, rather than to their own efforts and abilities (Cross 1988; Fennema 1980, 1984; Fox 1980; Lockheed et al. 1985; Norman 1988; Schronberger 1980). Girls' negative attitudes toward mathematics and limited academic confidence may influence their later career choices and steer them away from mathematics-related fields.

Some researchers (see, for example, Steinkamp and Maehr 1984) who investigated students' attitudes toward mathematics in the middle school years suggested that gender differences emerge partly as a result of the new learning environment that students face when they enter middle school. At this level, students are exposed to a greater number of male teachers and to a more competitive and unstructured learning environment that may undermine girls' self-esteem and confidence in their academic abilities. Therefore, this new learning environment could contribute to subsequent inequalities in male and female students' performance and participation in mathematics during high school, when students can choose advanced mathematics courses as electives. Also at the middle school level, little is known about gender differences in learning opportunities (such as course work, ability-group placement, and extracurricular activities) and how such learning opportunities are related to students' further achievements and attitudes.

At the high school level, young women often limit their opportunities to learn mathematics by completing only the minimal mathematics courses required for graduation (Fox 1980; Fennema 1984; Norman 1988; Reyes 1980). Women's inadequate participation in mathematics courses during high school explains a substantial part of the gender differences in mathematical achievement (Berryman 1983; Fennema 1980; Jones 1987; Oakes 1990; Pallas and Alexander 1983; Smith and Walker 1988).

Unlike research on middle school students, studies of high school students have made some attempt to link opportunities to learn through participation in courses to gender differences in mathematics achievement. The causal direction in the relationship between learning opportunities, achievement, and attitudes remains unclear, however (Oakes 1990). One might assume that female students participate less in learning opportunities and do less well in mathematics because they are not interested in this subject. It is also possible that female students develop negative attitudes toward mathematics because of their relatively low levels of achievement and limited participation in learning opportunities.

Race and Ethnic Variations

Studies of developmental differences in opportunities, achievement, and choice by gender may be further qualified for race and ethnicity; women of color are the most underrepresented group in mathematics and science, but few researchers have specifically studied their educational experiences. The literature generally treats race and ethnicity by excluding gender as a variable or does not focus on what stage in a student's education gender and racial or ethnic interactions occur (Clewell and Anderson 1991; Lockheed et al. 1985).[1]

Some research has found that African American and Latino students tend to have positive attitudes toward mathematics, despite their low levels of achievement in the subject (Clewell and Anderson 1991; Mickelson 1990; Oakes 1990). Thus, the relationship between achievement in mathematics and attitudes toward this subject may not exist for all groups of students.

The few studies that have been done have indicated that female minority students perform poorly on mathematics achievement tests. Minority students, in general, participate in few learning opportunities, such as extracurricular activities and advanced course work, in mathematics (Clewell and Anderson 1991). Therefore, these students decrease their opportunities for further course work in high school and for careers in scientific and quantitative fields (Clewell and Anderson 1991).

Among African Americans, gender differences in mathematics achievement and course participation either do not exist or favor female students (Clewell and Anderson 1991; Mathews 1984). If indeed such findings are confirmed through nationally representative data, the generalization that young women underachieve in mathematics in relation to young men may misrepresent the educational experiences of the variety of students who attend our nation's schools. The interrelationships among the conceptual domains of opportunity, achievement, and choice, as well as gender differences in each domain, may vary considerably according to students' racial or ethnic backgrounds.

The study presented here sought to advance understanding of the processes leading to inequities in participation in mathematics by examining the development of differences in opportunity, achievement, and choice for male and female students of specific racial and ethnic groups. I expected that the opportunity structure leading to participation in mathematics and related fields varies for these groups.

Source of Data

I used data from the base year and first follow-up surveys of the National Educational Longitudinal Study of 1988 (NELS:88), sponsored by the National Center for Education Statistics. NELS:88 makes available survey and testing data for a national probability sample of eighth-grade students. Its design includes plans to resurvey these same students at two-year intervals (for detailed information on this data set, see Ingels, Scott, Lindmark, Frankel, and Myers 1992).

The NELS:88 sample is a two-stage stratified, nationally representative sample

---

[1] It may be assumed that differences in mathematics participation by race and ethnicity are grounded in the broader determinants of economic development, as cross-national studies (Baker and Perkins Jones 1993) found for gender differences. In the United States, educational and labor market opportunities may vary considerably according to race and ethnicity (Braddock 1990; Ogbu 1978). Ogbu found that castelike minority groups, such as those in African American and some Latino communities, face a job ceiling that does not permit them to obtain jobs that are commensurate with their educational credentials. The limited occupational and educational opportunity structures of these groups affect both their educational performance and their attitudes toward education.

of approximately 1,052 schools and 24,500 students who were interviewed in 1988 and 1990. I used data from the base-year student, parent, and teacher surveys and the first follow-up student survey. The student surveys included information about the students' socioeconomic backgrounds, perceptions of self, school life and educational experiences, and career aspirations. The students also completed a battery of cognitive tests developed by the Educational Testing Service. The base-year parent survey yielded information about the nature and extent of parental support for students' educational activities. The base-year teacher survey probed teachers' perceptions of the sampled students' classroom performances, information about the curricular content of the teachers' classes, instructional methods and materials used, and teachers' backgrounds. Information from their mathematics teachers is available for about half the students in the sample.

Data analyses for this study were restricted to students attending public schools because a number of studies have indicated that differences in the academic and social organization of private schools, especially Catholic schools, influence students' academic behavior (Coleman and Hoffer 1987; Coleman, Hoffer, and Kilgore 1982; Lee and Bryk 1988). The base-year sample included approximately 19,000 students in public schools; of these students, approximately 14,000 were still enrolled in public schools in the 10th grade.[2]

Variables

Measures of Opportunity, Achievement, and Choice

A number of variables were used to indicate these three domains.

Mathematics achievement refers to students' scores on mathematics tests in the eighth and 10th grades and students' mathematics grades from the sixth to the 10th grade.

Learning opportunities in mathematics refers to (1) eighth-grade class ability levels, (2) the type of curriculum in which students are enrolled in the 10th grade, and (3) students' enrollment in Algebra I, Algebra II, and Geometry by the 10th grade. Regarding eighth-grade class ability levels, the mathematics teachers were asked to respond to the following question: "Which of the following best describes the achievement level of the eighth graders in this class in comparison with the average eighth-grade student in this school?—higher achievement levels, average, lower, or widely differing achievement levels."

Although the teachers' responses may be prone to some error regarding the existence of ability grouping, they generally tend to be more reliable than are the students' responses. Comparative analyses of teachers' and students' responses in the NELS:88 data revealed that minority and low-achieving students tended to underrepresent their placement in low-ability groups (Braddock and Mac Iver 1991).

---

[2]All the data were weighted by the appropriate sampling weights provided by the National Opinion Research Center (BYQWT, F1PANLWT). The weights were standardized (for example, BYQWT/mean BYQWT) to obtain appropriate sample sizes for tests of significance.

These discrepancies make the use of teachers' responses a more desirable alternative to students' self-reports.

Choice and attitudes toward mathematics refer to eighth graders' aspirations to a mathematics- and science-related career, attitudes toward mathematics (whether students look forward to mathematics class, whether they are afraid to ask questions in mathematics courses, and whether they think that mathematics will be useful for their future), and a composite of students' participation in relevant extracurricular activities (mathematics and computer clubs). The 10th-grade survey did not repeat these items, but introduced new items regarding students' interests and judgments of their own performance in mathematics: student-reported reasons for enrolling in their mathematics course, a series of statements indicating students' perceptions of their performance in mathematics, and students' reports of how hard they try in mathematics classes.

Independent Variables

Social background characteristics refer to the student's socioeconomic status (a composite variable consisting of parents' education, occupation, and family income); parents' responses to whether they expect their eighth grader to attend postsecondary school; student's expectations for taking an academic high school curriculum; and the student's year of birth, gender, and racial and ethnic characteristics.

Eighth-grade teacher evaluation is a composite variable indicating teachers' ratings of each student's problematic classroom behavior.

Results and Discussion

The analyses revealed several significant race- and ethnic-specific gender differences in opportunity, achievement, and choice for the eighth- and 10th-grade students.

Patterns for Eighth-grade Students

Achievement   Concerning achievement, male and female eighth graders tend to have similar scores on mathematics tests. This gender equity exists even when the girls receive better grades in mathematics, as is the case of White students (see Table 1).

At this stage of schooling, differences in mathematics achievement occur mostly among racial-ethnic groups, rather than between male and female students; girls perform equally well, or even better, in mathematics than do boys. The strongest gender differences, though, occur in learning opportunities, which are represented here by ability-group placement; placement in classes of different ability levels favors female, rather than male, students.

Learning Opportunities   The indicator of learning opportunities shows that students of both genders are equally likely to enroll in average-ability mathematics

Table 1 ■ **Eighth-grade Mathematics Achievement and Learning Opportunities (Ability Grouping), by Gender and Race-Ethnicity**

	White Students		African American Students		Latino Students	
	Male	*Female*	*Male*	*Female*	*Male*	*Female*
Mathematics Test Scores						
Mean	51.54	51.36	43.42	43.67	45.90	44.69
Mathematics Grades (Grades 6–8)						
Mean	3.87	3.96[a]	3.73	3.77	3.74	3.73
Average N	5,802	5,708	1,136	1,033	1,208	1,210
Ability-group Placement (percentage)[b]						
High	27.0	30.2	14.2	17.5	16.7	17.8
Average	39.9	39.6	32.3	32.7	40.0	40.9
Low	19.0	16.5	35.6	29.6	28.9	23.8
Mixed	14.1	13.7	18.0	15.7	14.5	17.4
N	2,862	2,797	552	570	582	563

[a] Gender differences statistically significant at $p < .05$.
[b] Chi-squares statistically significant at $p < .05$.

classes. However, a higher proportion of boys are enrolled in low-ability classes, and a higher proportion of girls are enrolled in high-ability classes. Even when the educational, social background, or social-psychological characteristics of students are held constant, female students are still more likely to enroll in high-ability mathematics classes than are male students. These gender differences are fairly consistent among all three racial-ethnic groups, even though African American and Latino students are, in general, overrepresented in low-ability classes. White female students have the highest enrollment in high-ability classes, and African American male students have the highest enrollment in low-ability classes. These differences are important because they show that both female and White students have greater opportunities to learn mathematics, since they are more often exposed to the rigorous and demanding curricula of high-ability classes.

Unfortunately, the NELS:88 data set does not provide information on the criteria that schools use to assign students to ability groups. Students' performance on relevant achievement tests would be an important placement criterion, but given the lack of gender differences in this variable, it may not explain the female advantage in ability-group enrollment. It is possible that additional assignment criteria are used that tend to distinguish female students from their male classmates. Students' prior grades, their age (which indicates the probability of their having been retained in previous grades), and their classroom behavior may influence the decisions of school personnel. Girls, who are more diligent students and exhibit less-disruptive classroom behavior, may be placed in higher-ability groups than may boys. Students' socioeconomic background may also be an important factor that may influence the differential placement of male and female students, especially through parental involvement in school. Parents of high socioeconomic status tend to intervene effectively on behalf of their children's placement in high-ability tracks (Useem 1992a). . . .

Assigning students to mathematics classes that are grouped by ability is a practice that has important consequences for students and is extensively used in the middle grades. Over 80 percent of school administrators report that they use ability grouping for eighth-grade mathematics classes (Braddock 1990). Given the cumulative nature of learning mathematics, enrollment in a high-ability class may influence students' academic preparation and future participation in mathematics (Gamoran 1987; Kulik and Kulik 1984; Useem 1992b). In high-ability classes, students receive more intensive academic training and are exposed more often to topics such as algebra. These learning opportunities allow them to pursue a more rigorous mathematics sequence in high school and to gain access to quantitative and science-related college majors (Sells 1980; Useem 1992b). Thus, the advantage that White and African American females gain over comparable males by being placed in high-ability classes may be crucial for their participation in mathematics in high school and college.

Previous studies reported either no gender differences in ability-group placement and curriculum tracking or placement that favored male over comparable female students (Alexander and Cook 1982; Alexander, Cook, and McDill 1978; Alexander and McDill 1976; Hallinan and Sørenson 1987). It is possible that this trend was reversed in the late 1980s, since Gamoran and Mare (1989) found a similar advantage for females in enrollment in the academic curriculum in high school.

Choice   Measures of choice of and attitudes toward mathematics show that young women's persistence in advanced mathematics course work during high school may actually depend on their earlier decisions about careers and attitudes toward this subject. By the eighth grade, fewer female students than male students have decided to pursue mathematics and science careers (see Table 2). Students' career choices show strong gender differences among all three racial-ethnic groups. Although few students are interested in mathematics- and science-related careers, twice as many male students as female students are interested. Female African American and Latina students are the least likely to aspire to such careers, and White male students are the most likely to do so.

Male students also have more positive attitudes toward the subject of mathematics and are more likely to enroll in relevant extracurricular activities than are female students. More male than female students report that they look forward to mathematics classes, whereas more female than male students report that they are afraid to ask questions in class. These gender differences are the strongest among Latino students. Among African Americans, there are no gender differences with regard to whether students are afraid to ask questions, and thus African American young women may have less anxiety about mathematics than do their White or Latina coun-

Table 2   ■   Measures of Eighth-grade Choice, by Gender and Race-Ethnicity

	White Students		African American Students		Latino Students	
	Male	Female	Male	Female	Male	Female
Career Aspirations for a Mathematics/Science-related Field						
% aspiring	8.5	3.4[a]	5.3	2.4[a]	6.3	2.5[a]
Attitudes toward Mathematics (percentage of students who agree)						
I look forward to math class	54.8	51.3[a]	72.2	68.5[b]	67.8	59.6[a]
Afraid to ask questions in math class	17.0	22.6[a]	22.3	21.5	24.9	32.6[a]
Math will be useful in my future	88.6	86.5[a]	90.0	88.0	89.6	89.4
Extracurricular Activities						
% participating in math or computer clubs	9.2	6.2[a]	16.4	14.8[a]	15.7	9.5[a]
Average sample size	5,976	5,997	1,121	1,218	1,286	1,274

[a] Gender differences statistically significant at $p < .001$.
[b] Gender differences statistically significant at $p < .05$.

terparts.[3] The majority of eighth graders seem to recognize the importance of mathematics for their future, with small gender differences existing for Whites and African Americans.

Participation in extracurricular activities represents students' exposure to further learning opportunities, but also reveals students' interest in mathematics. Although few students participate in such activities, male students are more likely than are female students to do so. Again, these differences are the strongest among Latinos. It is also important to note that both Latinos and especially African Americans have high levels of extracurricular participation and very positive mathematics attitudes, despite their low levels of achievement in this subject. Since I found that minority students with particularly high levels of extracurricular participation are

---

[3] This pattern of gender differences in students' attitudes seems to be specific to mathematics and does not represent students' general attitudes toward school. For example, there are few gender differences among students who are afraid to ask questions in English and social studies; with regard to English, the percentages of male and female students, respectively, who are afraid to ask questions are 14 percent and 15 percent for Whites, 20 percent and 15 percent for African Americans, and 20 percent and 21 percent for Latinos.

concentrated in urban areas, it is possible that minority students' high participation in these activities may be explained by their concentration in large, urban schools that may offer a variety of clubs. It is doubtful, though, that in the absence of other instructional programs, extracurricular activities would substantially improve students' achievement.

The positive attitudes of minority students toward mathematics and science have also been noted in earlier studies (Clewell and Anderson 1991; Mickelson 1990). Although most researchers have suggested that there is a direct relationship between students' achievement in mathematics and their attitudes or participation in relevant activities, these relationships may not exist for African American or other minority students. Elements of these students' family environments, communities, and schools may be more crucial for the students' underachievement in mathematics than may the students' attitudes toward this subject.

A number of factors may influence students' "choice" (interest in mathematics), which may actually mask differences among male and female students. Socioeconomic status is an important predictor of both mathematics achievement and career decisions, especially for female students (Oakes 1990). Moreover, students' level of achievement and placement in low-ability groups have also been found to have a negative effect on students' social-psychological makeup and attitudes toward academic subjects (Braddock 1990; Gamoran 1987; Oakes 1985). Learning opportunities that give students greater exposure to mathematics may positively affect students' attitudes toward these subjects. Thus, female students' advantages in ability-group placement may positively influence their career choices and attitudes toward mathematics.

The gender differences in the choice of mathematics and science careers are fairly strong among students with similar achievement levels, attitudes toward mathematics, and social background characteristics. Among all three racial-ethnic groups, young women have much lower probabilities of choosing a mathematics- or science-related career than have comparable young men.

Students' gender also affects their attitudes toward mathematics, even when achievement, ability-group placement, and social background are taken into account. Female students are less likely to enjoy their mathematics classes, and White female students are less likely to believe that these classes will be useful for their future than are comparable male students. White female and Latina students also show higher levels of anxiety than do their male counterparts. The effect of gender is somewhat stronger on participation in extracurricular activities. Among all three racial-ethnic groups, young women have much lower probabilities of participating in relevant extracurricular activities than do comparable young men. Except for beliefs about the usefulness of mathematics, gender differences in these variables remain the strongest among Latinos. . . .

If one considers the developmental pathway to mathematics participation, one sees that during the middle grades, gender differences in achievement and learning opportunities are either nonexistent or favor female students. However, gender differences in various indicators of choice provide some clues to the eventual decline in women's participation in mathematics. These findings begin to clarify the nature of the relationships among opportunity, achievement, and choice. As Berryman (1983) tentatively suggested, attitudes toward mathematics and career decisions develop independently of the other two dimensions. Gender differences in attitudes and orientations could affect further learning opportunities during high school, where students are relatively free to choose their own courses.

Patterns for 10th-grade Students

Achievement and Learning Opportunities The further development of gender differences during high school is shown by data from the first follow-up of the NELS:88 study. Indicators of mathematics achievement (average test scores and grades) show few gender differences among students in the 10th grade (see Table 3). The small gender differences in the average test scores of African American and Latino students disappear in multivariate analyses controlling for students' background characteristics. Again, in the 10th grade, racial and ethnic differences in achievement and learning opportunities are much stronger than are gender differences.

Male and female students are generally exposed to similar learning opportunities in enrollment in courses, but female students are somewhat advantaged in enrollments in the academic curriculum. In logistic regression analyses that controlled for students' achievement levels, social background, and aspirations, the advantage of female students remained statistically significant only among White students (odds of $1/1.16, p < .01$).

Although historically a similar proportion of males and females enrolled in the academic curriculum (NSF 1988), Gamoran and Mare (1989) found that among the 1980 high school sophomores, females had a 4 percent higher chance of enrolling

Table 3 ▓ **10th-grade Mathematics Achievement and Learning Opportunities, by Gender and Race-Ethnicity**

	White Students		African American Students		Latino Students	
	Male	Female	Male	Female	Male	Female
Mathematics Test Scores						
Mean	51.75	51.61	43.22	44.71[a]	46.28	44.64[a]
Mathematics Grades Since the Ninth Grade						
Mean	4.89	4.74[a]	4.65	4.77	4.44	4.60
Curriculum and Course Work Enrollment (percentage enrolled)						
Academic curriculum	32.1	35.5[a]	20.8	31.0[a]	22.5	25.5
Algebra I	68.7	69.6[a]	60.9	62.6	65.9	68.9
Geometry	48.8	51.0[b]	36.1	44.4[a]	37.7	35.9
Algebra II	27.5	27.0	20.1	21.0	25.5	23.3
Average sample size	4,504	4,546	807	851	635	651

[a] Gender differences statistically significant at $p < .01$.
[b] Gender differences statistically significant at $p < .05$.

Table 4 ■ **10th-Graders' Measures of Choice (Percentages), by Gender and Race-Ethnicity**

Measure of Choice	White Students		African American Students		Latino Students	
	Male	Female	Male	Female	Male	Female
Reason for Taking Mathematics[a]						
Not taking math	3.1	2.5	2.0	1.0	3.2	2.4
Required	55.9	60.6	61.3	63.1	56.4	69.5
My choice	33.1	28.9	26.1	26.7	23.3	18.6
Recommended or assigned	8.0	8.0	10.5	9.2	17.1	9.6
Judgments of Mathematics Performance and Effort (percentage who agree)						
Math is one of my best subjects.	64.5	54.2[b]	69.3	62.1[b]	63.7	44.8[b]
I've always done well in math.	68.4	71.2[b]	72.0	69.4	65.5	50.7[b]
I get good grades in math.	70.4	66.7[b]	73.9	71.9	70.3	56.8[b]
I do badly in math tests.	27.2	31.3[b]	26.0	32.9[b]	32.7	33.7
I try hard in math almost daily.	45.6	60.6[b]	52.1	74.6[b]	50.1	64.6[b]
Average sample size	4,610	4,503	782	829	606	648

[a] Chi-squares are statistically significant for Whites and Latinos at $p < .01$.
[b] Gender differences significant at $p < .01$.

in the academic curriculum than had males. These authors suggested that changes in cultural expectations about gender roles may have eliminated gender biases in track placements. The advantage of White females in enrollment in the academic curriculum has important implications because enrollment in such programs ensures a greater exposure to both basic and advanced mathematics courses (NSF 1988; Oakes 1990).

Choice   Tenth-grade measures of mathematics choice and attitudes, however, indicate that greater gender differences in mathematics participation may indeed appear, once students complete their mathematics course requirements (see Table 4).

High school students are likely to continue to take required courses in mathematics up to the 10th grade. Although more than half the respondents reported taking such courses because they were required to do so, a higher percentage of females than of males did so. Again, the differences were the weakest among African Americans and the strongest among Latinos. Almost 70 percent of the Latina students said that they took mathematics because they were required to do so. The White male students seemed to have the greatest interest in this subject, since one-third of them reported choosing to enroll in mathematics.

Female students tended to have less confidence in their mathematics performance than did their male classmates. These differences were especially strong among Latinos; young Latinas responded more negatively than did any other group of students, especially to the statements indicating whether mathematics was one of their best subjects and whether they had always done well in mathematics. Fewer gender differences were found among African Americans, with the exception of students' estimation of their own mathematics effort. Almost 25 percent more African American female students than male students reported that they tried hard almost daily in mathematics. Overall, most female students reported that they tried hard almost daily in mathematics, but they did not judge their mathematics performance to be as high as did the male students.

Racial and ethnic differences are also striking with regard to the students' judgments of their mathematics performance. Despite their low mathematics test scores (shown in Table 3), the minority students, especially the African Americans, had a positive image of their academic performance in this subject. About 70 percent or more of the African American male students reported that mathematics was one of their best subjects and that they had always done well and received good grades in mathematics. These minority students also had positive attitudes toward this subject and participated in relevant extracurricular activities at higher rates than did other students in the eighth grade.

Some gender differences exist among African Americans' self-concept of performance, in a direction similar to that found for Whites and Latinos. The reasons for these gender differences are not entirely clear. A number of factors could influence the formation of these social-psychological characteristics. As the relevant literature suggests, socioeconomic status and associated parental encouragement and aspirations may be important factors, especially for the mathematics self-concept of female students. Other studies have shown that mother's education and socioeconomic background are important predictors of young women's success and persistence in mathematics (Oakes 1990). On the other hand, students' achievement levels, grades, and academic effort would also be important influences on students' judgments of their school performance.

Multivariate analyses can explore whether gender differences in students' judgments of academic performance and effort are influenced by these factors. I combined the original variables into an additive index indicating students' self-concept of mathematics performance. I treated students' reports of how hard they try in this subject as a separate dependent variable because of the strong gender differences in it.

The White female students and Latina students had a lower self-concept of their mathematics performance than did their male counterparts, irrespective of socioeconomic status, achievement, and levels of homework. Once these variables were controlled for, gender differences in mathematics self-concept disappeared among the African American students, although the African American female students remained much more likely than did their male counterparts to report that they tried hard in mathematics. This gender effect was present for the other two groups and remained strong even when the amount of time spent on homework was controlled for. That is, despite the similar levels of achievement and effort (as indicated by the amount of time spent on mathematics homework), all the female students believed more strongly than did the male students that they tried hard in mathematics courses. The White female and Latina students also judged their mathematics performance to be lower than did the male students. Thus, it is probable that fewer female students than male students would choose advanced mathematics courses as electives.

In earlier cohorts of high school seniors, fewer female than male students enrolled in advanced courses, such as Trigonometry, Precalculus, and Calculus (Armstrong 1985; Miller 1991). At the time of this study, NELS:88 data were not available for 1992, when this cohort of students reached their senior year. However, data from the National Assessment of Educational Progress indicated that there were significant gender differences, especially for the White high school seniors of 1992, in average levels of achievement. Similar differences also existed in the proportion of students who reached advanced levels of mathematics achievement (Mullis, Dossey, Owen, and Phillips 1993).

Overall, gender and racial-ethnic interactions regarding students' mathematics-related attitudes and educational experiences are important. The factors leading to the underrepresentation of students in advanced mathematics courses and related careers may actually differ according to students' gender and race-ethnicity. Latinas tend to be the most disadvantaged group, since they face barriers in all three domains: opportunity, achievement, and choice. For African American students, both female and male, the barrier to mathematics participation may prove to be their limited exposure to learning opportunities and their low levels of mathematics achievement. Attitudes and early career choices may be the major barrier for the mathematics participation of White female students, who have equal levels of achievement with White male students and are exposed to greater learning opportunities from the middle grades to the early years of high school.

Conclusion

I return to my initial premise that an intensive understanding of equity in mathematics requires caution in applying general findings for gender to any one race or ethnic group. The analyses reported in this article, though, indicate that some similar patterns of gender differences in opportunity, achievement, and choice exist for all three groups. Up to the early years of high school, female students of White, African American, and Latino backgrounds do not lag behind their male classmates in mathematics achievement and are actually advantaged in learning opportunities in mathematics. However, this gender equity, or even female advantage, may be due *not* to young women's interest in mathematics but, rather, to school placements and course requirements. Young women of all three groups may be reluctant participants in mathematics learning. Gender differences in the decision to pursue a mathematics-related career and in attitudes toward mathematics are already apparent in the eighth grade. Strong gender differences in students' judgments of their mathematics performance also exist in the early years of high school. These gender differences may lead to a decline in women's mathematics participation later in school, when enrollment in such courses is optional.

Of key importance is the finding that students' attitudes toward and self-confidence in mathematics vary greatly by gender, as well as by race and ethnicity. Although Latinos and African Americans have relatively low levels of achievement and limited exposure to learning opportunities, their attitudes toward mathematics are positive. This attitude-achievement paradox has also been noted by other researchers (Clewell and Anderson 1991; Mickelson 1990), but the reasons for its existence are not clear. Mickelson provided a theoretical explanation by introducing the distinction between abstract and concrete attitudes toward education: Whereas African Americans' abstract attitudes reflect the dominant achievement ideology, their concrete attitudes are more pessimistic and reflect the limited returns of education for minority groups. In her study, she measured the concrete attitudes of African American students, which reflected their estimation of the probable returns of education for themselves, as opposed to abstract beliefs about the value of education. The concrete attitudes of these students were close to their levels of achievement. This distinction does not explain the attitude-achievement paradox found in my study, however. African American students and, to a lesser extent, Latino students responded positively to statements about the importance of mathematics for their own future and their own mathematics performance, despite their low test scores in this subject. At this point, I can only speculate that minority students may judge their performance on the basis of their reported grades, which seem to be relatively high, as well as on other positive messages that they may receive within their school environments.

Gender differences in mathematics attitudes not only vary by race and ethnicity, but are strongest among Latino students. Along with limited learning opportunities and low levels of achievement, Latinas seem to be the students with the most negative attitudes toward mathematics and toward their own academic ability in this subject. Gender differences in the Latino population seem to follow traditional patterns that may no longer exist among White or African American populations. Although little is known about the educational experiences of Latinas, researchers have noted that within many Latino cultures, traditional gender roles and orientations tend to persist (Acosta-Belén 1986; Bose 1986). Latinas in the United States also tend to have relatively low levels of education and to work in blue-collar and service occupations that are segregated by gender (Bose 1986; Pessar 1987). Thus, both the culture and the job-opportunity structure that many Latinas face may not provide opportunities that encourage young Latinas to aspire to nontraditional gender roles and occupations.

There is some research evidence that the school experiences of Latinas may also place them at a disadvantage. Studies of Mexican American children indicate that girls may have greater difficulty than boys adjusting to the achievement-oriented and competitive environment of schools. However, it is encouraging to note that these girls are also quite responsive to positive interventions, such as bilingual and bicultural programs, that tend to enhance their self-concept significantly (Nieto Senour 1977).

The opportunity structures available to women and men from different social backgrounds, as well as ethnic-specific gender roles, seem to interact in their influence on students' interest in and performance of mathematics. Racial and ethnic differences in cultural, economic, and educational factors may actually translate into differences in opportunity, achievement, and choice.

In sum, the findings presented here have elucidated the interrelationships and relative importance of the three conceptual domains of opportunity, achievement, and choice for equity in mathematics participation. It is possible that different gender and racial-ethnic groups are at different stages of development in terms of equity in mathematics achievement and participation. For male and female minority students, learning opportunities and levels of achievement are the most important barriers to mathematics participation. Their relatively high interest in mathematics could provide educators with an important opportunity to engage these students in more intensive academic efforts. Latinas seem to be the most disadvantaged group, since they are faced with additional limitations in attitudes toward mathematics and toward their own academic abilities.

White women are the most advantaged of the three groups of women considered in this article, and many have overcome the formal barriers that opportunity and achievement represent. In terms of opportunity, they may often be even more advantaged than their White male classmates (as in the case of eighth-grade ability-group placement and 10th-grade academic curriculum enrollment). For them, it is attitudes toward mathematics and career choices that may undermine their future participation in mathematics-related fields.

The findings regarding White women show that increased opportunities to learn, such as placement in high-ability tracks, may indeed eliminate the gender gap in mathematics achievement, especially when enhanced opportunities are coupled with a common core curriculum, such as the one usually found in the middle grades. However, although educational opportunities and high achievement may provide the necessary conditions for mathematics participation, early career choices and attitudes toward these fields may become equally important during the last years of high school and beyond. These career decisions and attitudes seem to develop independently of students' learning opportunities and achievement levels and may cast the deciding vote on whether White women pursue further study in mathematics. All three parts of the equation—opportunities, achievement, and choice—are important for gaining gender equity in mathematics, although the influence of each one may be manifested at different stages of schooling and may vary by race-ethnicity. The "path to math," as Oakes suggested, is a conditional relationship between mathematics choices and participation, one that becomes important only when students have high levels of achievement and ample opportunities to learn.

References

Acosta-Belén, Edna. 1986. "Puerto Rican Women in Culture, History, and Society." Pp. 1–25 in *The Puerto Rican Woman: Perspectives on Culture, History, and Society,* edited by Edna Acosta-Beléen. New York: Praeger.

Alexander, Karl L. and Martha A. Cook. 1982. "Curricula and Coursework: A Surprise Ending to a Familiar Story." *American Sociological Review* 47:626–40.

Alexander, Karl L., Martha A. Cook, and Edward L. McDill. 1978. "Curriculum Tracking and Educational Stratification." *American Sociological Review* 43:47–66.

Alexander, Karl L. and Edward L. McDill. 1976. "Selection and Allocation within Schools: Some Causes and Consequences of Curriculum Placement." *American Sociological Review* 41:963–80.

Armstrong, J. M. 1985. "A National Assessment of Participation and Achievement of Women in Mathematics." Pp. 59–94 in *Women and Mathematics: Balancing the Equation,* edited by S. F. Chipman, L. R. Brush, and D. M. Wilson. Hillsdale, NJ: Lawrence Erlbaum Associates.

Baker, David and Deborah Perkins Jones. 1993. "Creating Gender Equality: Cross-National Gender Stratification and Mathematical Performance." *Sociology of Education* 66:91–103.

Berryman, Sue E. 1983. *Who Will Do Science? Minority and Female Attainment of Science and Mathematics Degrees: Trends and Causes.* New York: Rockefeller Foundation.

Bose, Christine E. 1986. "Puerto Rican Women in the United States: An Overview." Pp. 147–169 in *The Puerto Rican Woman: Perspectives on Culture, History, and Society,* edited by Edna Acosta-Belén. New York: Praeger.

Braddock, Jomills H., II. 1990, February. "Tracking in the Middle Grades: National Patterns of Grouping for Instruction." *Phi Delta Kappan,* pp. 445–49.

Braddock, Jomills H., II, and D. Mac Iver. 1991, April. "Student Grouping in the Middle Grades: Analysis from the NELS88 and Principals' Supplement." Paper presented at the Annual Meeting of the American Educational Research Association, Chicago.

Clewell, Beatriz C. and Bernice Anderson. 1991. *Women of Color in Mathematics, Science and Engineering: A Review of the Literature.* Washington, DC: Center for Women Policy Studies.

Coleman, James C. and Thomas Hoffer. 1987. *Public and Private High Schools.* New York: Basic Books.

Coleman, James C., Thomas Hoffer, and Sally Kilgore. 1982. *High School Achievement: Public, Catholic, and Private Schools Compared.* New York: Basic Books.

Cross, R. T. 1988. "Task Value Intervention: Increasing Girls' Awareness of the Importance of Mathematics and Physical Science for Career Choice." *School Science and Mathematics* 88:397–412.

Fennema, Elizabeth. 1980. "Sex-related Differences in Mathematics Achievement: Where and Why." Pp. 76–93 in *Women and the Mathematical Mystique,* edited by Lynn Fox, Linda Brody, and Dianne Tobin. Baltimore: Johns Hopkins University Press.

———. 1984. "Girls, Women, and Mathematics." Pp. 137–164 in *Women and Education: Equity or Equality?* edited by Elizabeth Fennema. Berkeley, CA: McCutchan.

Fox, Lynn, H. 1980. *The Problem of Women and Mathematics.* New York: Ford Foundation.

Friedman, Lynn. 1989. "Mathematics and the Gender Gap: A Meta-Analysis of Recent Studies on Sex Differences in Mathematical Tasks." *Review of Educational Research* 59:185–213.

Gamoran, Adam. 1987. "The Stratification of High School Learning Opportunities." *Sociology of Education* 60:135–55.

Gamoran, Adam and Robert D. Mare. 1989. "Secondary School Tracking and Educational Inequality: Compensation, Reinforcement, or Neutrality?" *American Journal of Sociology* 94:1146–83.

Hallinan, Maureen T. and Aage B. Sørenson. 1987. "Ability Grouping and Sex Differences in Mathematics Achievement." *Sociology of Education* 60:63–72.

Ingels, Steven J., Leslie A. Scott, Judith T. Lindmark, Martin R. Frankel, and Sharon L. Myers. 1992. *National Educational Longitudinal Study of 1988: First Follow-Up Data File User's Manual.* Washington, DC: U.S. Department of Education.

Jones, Lyle. 1987. "The Influence of Mathematics Test Scores, by Ethnicity and Sex, on Prior Achievement and High School Mathematics Courses." *Journal for Research in Mathematics Education* 18:180–86.

Kahle, Jane B. and Marsha K. Lakes. 1983. "The Myth of Equality in Science Classrooms." *Journal of Research in Science Teaching* 20:131–40.

Kulik, J. A. and C. C. Kulik. 1984. "Effects of Accelerated Instruction on Students." *Review of Educational Research* 54:409–25.

Lee, Valerie E. and Anthony S. Bryk, 1986. "Effects of Single-Sex Secondary Schools on Student Achievement and Attitudes." *Journal of Educational Psychology* 78:381–95.

———. 1988. "Curriculum Tracking as Mediating the Social Distribution of High School Achievement." *Sociology of Education* 61:78–94.

Lockheed, Marlaine E., Margaret Thorpe, J. Brooks-Gunn, Patricia Casserly, and An McAloon. 1985. *Sex and Ethnic Differences in Middle School Mathematics, Science and Computer Science: What Do We Know?* Princeton, NJ: Educational Testing Service.

Marsh, Herbert. 1989. "Sex Differences in the Development of Verbal and Mathematics Constructs: The High School and Beyond Study." *American Educational Research Journal* 26:191–225.

Mathews, Westina. 1984. "Influences on the Learning and Participation of Minorities in Mathematics." *Journal for Research in Mathematics Education* 15:84–95.

Mickelson, Roslyn, A. 1990. "The Attitude-Achievement Paradox Among Black Adolescents." *Sociology of Education* 63:44–61.

Miller, John D. 1991, April. "Persistence in High School Mathematics." Paper presented at the annual meeting of the American Educational Research Association, Chicago.

Mullis, Ina V. S., John A. Dossey, Eugene H. Owen, and Gary W. Phillips. 1993. *NAEP 1992: Mathematics Report Card for the Nation and States.* Washington, DC: National Center for Education Statistics.

National Science Foundation. 1988. *Women and Minorities in Science and Engineering* (NSF 86-301). Washington, DC: Author.

Nieto Senour, Maria. 1977. "Psychology of the Chicana." Pp. 329–43 in *Chicano Psychology,* edited by J. L. Martinez. New York: Academic Press.

Norman, Colin. 1988, July 22. "Math Education: A Mixed Picture." *Science* 241: 408–09.

Oakes, Jeannie. 1985. *Keeping Track: How Schools Structure Inequality.* New Haven, CT: Yale University Press.

———. 1990. "Opportunities, Achievement, and Choice: Women and Minority Students in Science and Mathematics." *Review of Research in Education* 16: 153–222.

Ogbu, John, U. 1978. *Minority Education and Caste.* New York: Academic Press.

Pallas, Aaron M. and Karl L. Alexander. 1983. "Sex Differences in Quantitative SAT Performance: New Evidence on the Differential Coursework Hypothesis." *American Educational Research Journal* 20: 165–82.

Pessar, Patricia, R. 1987. "The Dominicans: Women in the Household and the Garment Industry." Pp. 103–29 in *New Immigration in New York,* edited by N. Foner. New York: Columbia University Press.

Reyes, Laurie H. 1980. "Attitudes and Mathematics." In *Selected Issues in Mathematics Education,* edited by Mary Montgomery Linguist. Berkeley, CA: McCutchan.

Sadker, Myra, David Sadker, and Susan Klein. 1991. "The Issue of Gender in Elementary and Secondary Education." *Review of Research in Education* 17: 269–334.

Schronberger, Ann K. 1980. "Sex-Related Issues in Mathematics Education." Pp. 185–98 in *Selected Issues in Mathematics Education,* edited by Mary Montgomery Linguist. Berkeley, CA: McCutchan.

Sells, Lucy. 1980. "The Mathematics Filter and the Education of Women and Minorities." Pp. 66–75 in *Women and the Mathematical Mystique,* edited by L. N. Fox, L. Brody, and D. Tobin. Baltimore: Johns Hopkins University Press.

Smith, Stuart E. and William J. Walker. 1988. "Sex Differences on New York State Regents Examinations: Support for the Differential Course-taking Hypothesis." *Journal for Research in Mathematics Education* 19: 81–85.

Steinkamp, Marjorie W. and Martin L. Maehr. 1984. "Gender Difference in Motivational Orientations Toward Achievement in School Science: A Quantitative Synthesis." *American Educational Research Journal* 21: 39–59.

Useem, Elizabeth. 1992a. "Middle Schools and Math Groups: Parents' Involvement in Children's Placement." *Sociology of Education* 65: 263–78.

———. 1992b. "Getting on the Fast Track in Mathematics: School Organizational Influence on Math Track Assignment." *American Journal of Education* 100: 325–53.

Questions for Thought

1. Three factors influence the gender gap in math: opportunities, achievement, and choice. Explain what each term means and how Catsambis measured it in this study.

2. In eighth grade, more girls than boys are in high-ability math classes and fewer girls than boys are in low-ability classes (see Table 1). What may be an explanation for this pattern?

3. Describe how gender and ethnicity affect students' choice or interest in math in eighth grade (Table 2) and tenth grade (Table 4).

4. In the conclusion to this article, the author discusses the "attitude-achievement paradox" among Latino and African American students. Explain this concept.

5. Catsambis did not collect the data for her study. Rather, she made use of an existing data set collected by others. What were the advantages of using this data archive? What might be the disadvantages of using data collected by other researchers?

6. Design an intervention program to encourage White girls and Latina girls in math. What factors would you take into account for girls in each group? What strategies would you propose to foster math success for girls in each group?

Ethnic-Minority and Sexual-Minority Youths

Ritch C. Savin-Williams

In this review paper, Savin-Williams describes the dilemmas faced by lesbian, gay, and bisexual teenagers who come from ethnic minority backgrounds. A Latina lesbian and a Chinese gay teenager are "double minorities"—neither heterosexual nor White. These youths may experience ethnic prejudice and discrimination within the predominantly White lesbian, gay, or bisexual community. They may also encounter homophobia within their own ethnic communities. This dilemma may be complicated by a fear of "coming out" to one's family and jeopardizing family relationships, an important support system for many ethnic minority youths.

Regardless of ethnic or sexual identification, individuals experience major life changes during the period of adolescence. One task that is central to both ethnic- and sexual-minority youth is the consolidation of a reference group orientation (Cross, 1991). According to Cross, reference group orientation (RGO) includes aspects of self-concept "that are culture, class, and gender specific. . . . It seeks to discover differences in values, perspectives, group identities, lifestyles, and world views" (p. 45). Reference group identity refers not to how one feels in general, "but how one orients oneself or how one feels regarding specific values, preferences, or symbols" (p. 46). In combination, personal and group identity compose the essential features of one's self-concept (Cross, 1991).

Espin (1987) noted that for ethnic group members, healthy development includes the "acceptance of an external reality that can rarely be changed (e.g., being

Black, Puerto Rican, Jewish, or Vietnamese), but also an intrapsychic 'embracing' of that reality as a positive component of one's self" (p. 35). This aspect of self-concept may be more or less salient to individuals depending on the centrality of a particular reference group in their lives. Living as a minority group member in Anglo North American society often creates a sense of group distinctiveness and community.

Ethnic-minority adolescents with same-sex attractions must negotiate an additional formidable task in the development of a mature self-concept. They must integrate personal identity and reference group orientation within the context of two, at times competing and antagonistic, group identities: being lesbian, gay, or bisexual and an ethnic minority (Icard, 1986; Johnson, 1981; Tremble, Schneider, & Appathurai, 1989). Espin (1987) noted further complexities faced by female ethnic-/sexual-minorities:

> By definition in the context of a heterosexist, racist, and sexist society, the process of identity development for Latina lesbian women entails the embracing of "stigmatized" or "negative" identities. Coming out to self and others in the context of a sexist and heterosexist American society is compounded by coming out in the context of a heterosexist and sexist Latin culture immersed in racist society. (p. 35)

Hence, three tasks that ethnic-minority lesbian, bisexual, and gay youth face are: developing and defining a sexual and an ethnic identity; resolving potential conflict in allegiance within both reference groups or communities; and negotiating homophobia and racism.

Issues Confronting Ethnic Lesbian, Gay, and Bisexual Youth

Being an ethnic minority and a sexual minority within a White, heterosexual social world can tax even the strongest of youths. Espin (1987) noted that Latina lesbians fear stigmatization and loss of support from both Hispanic and gay and lesbian communities. They often feel that they must choose which of two groups will be their primary identification. Coupled with conflicting pressures from peers and the mass media to assimilate by acting White and heterosexual, youths from ethnic communities who are gay, bisexual, or lesbian struggle between who they are and that which they feel they must be in order to avoid a stigmatizing identity. The progress toward a healthy and positive gay identity is not an easy transition for these youths.

A sexual- and ethnic-minority youth may want to identify closely with both communities but feel that the two place demands that are inherently oppositional. Each community may present an adolescent with conflicting information about "appropriate" sexual or ethnic behavior and the importance of choosing one identity over the other. A youth may thus feel that it is impossible to be both a sexual and an ethnic minority.

Johnson (1981) documented this conflict among Black gay men. In his research, 60% of the men primarily identified themselves according to their race/ethnic community ("Black identified"). The rest affirmed their gay reference group identity ("gay identified"). Both groups had comparable levels of mental health—self-acceptance, happiness, loneliness, and depression—but differed on social behavioral measures. The Black-identified gay men were more likely to have Black lovers and friends, live in and celebrate the Black community, and prefer traditional, subtle modes of expressing affection among gay men. The gay-identified Black men were more likely to have White lovers, live in the gay community, and favor public displays of affection among gay men. Each felt estranged from a central aspect of who he is—from the gay or Black community (Johnson, 1981).

At an Asian Lesbian Conference in Bangkok, Thailand (Historic Meet, 1991), many participants noted the problems of dual identities. "The feeling of isolation, invisibility, ostracism by society, the pain of having to lead double lives, problems of coming out to the family were common to all despite some cultural differences" (p. 5). Many felt that their invisibility handicapped their ability to network with each other. The absence of community support and the opportunity to explore and assert their sexuality within the historic Asian context of forced marriages and strong family ties prevented them from creating their own identity.

Unfortunately, because inadequate research has been conducted with ethnic-minority lesbian, bisexual, and gay youth, little is known about the ways in which the formation of a self-concept is compounded by status within an ethnic group and the racism often inherent in lesbian and gay communities. Thus, much must be extrapolated from information derived from research conducted with lesbian, bisexual, and gay ethnic adults. Several of these issues are also discussed in recent reviews by Manalansan (1996) and Greene (1994).

Both authors warned their readers of the dangers of inferring that all nationalities within an ethnic group are identical. Greene (1994) noted that "African Americans are a diverse group of people with cultural origins in the tribes of Western Africa, with some Indian and European racial admixture" (p. 245). Thus, "gross descriptions of cultural practices may never be applied with uniformity to all members of an ethnic group" (p. 244). Mindful of this warning, which Manalansan (1996) discusses at length, the present review emphasizes the common dilemmas shared by lesbian, bisexual, and gay youths from various ethnic communities. These include racism in gay and lesbian communities, homophobia in ethnic communities, unique problems of coming out to family, limitations imposed by sex role expectations, and cultural shifts in levels of support for ethnic/sexual minority youths. Only within the last several years has the ultimate reference group network formed: ethnic communities for sexual-minority individuals.

Racism in Gay and Lesbian Communities

Many of the difficulties experienced by lesbian, gay, and bisexual youth of color emanate from the social prejudice and institutional discrimination that are inherent in White society. Racist attitudes and beliefs permeate even liberal lesbian and gay communities. Consequently, ethnic-minority individuals with same-sex attractions may be rejected when among other lesbians and gays because of their minority status or may be expected to place their sexual identity and allegiance foremost in their lives.

In a survey of Third World gays and lesbians in San Francisco, Morales and Eversley (cited in Morales, 1983) reported that 85% perceived themselves as having been discriminated against by both heterosexual and lesbian and gay communities. As a group, ethnic gays and lesbians ranked discrimination as one of the most persistent problems in gay and lesbian communities. More recently, one African American lesbian noted:

> In the gay community, I feel that the majority of the White women are prejudiced just as much as they are in the straight world. So I don't care to deal with them, really, you know, unless I feel that they are really, really sincere in what they are saying and that it doesn't make a difference the color that I'm Black and she's White. Otherwise, I just deal with my own people. (Mays, Cochran, & Rhue, 1993, pp. 9–10)

The racism experienced by this woman was often subtle, such as the failure of White lesbians to recognize cultural differences between themselves and Black lesbians.

Two other examples of racism are attitudes sometimes held about Jews and Asians. Rofes (1989) observed that anti-Semitic insensitivities are common among many gay men and lesbians who are ignorant or callous about Jewish issues, such as the Holocaust. Rofes noted that a speaker at a gay political event commented that gay men should not go to their deaths from AIDS without protest, "like six million Jews did in the Holocaust" (p. 201). Although Rofes reported feeling "stunned, unable to move," and deeply hurt, he sat in silence unwilling to protest. Many Jews feel that they are supposed to assimilate into lesbian and gay communities, hiding their unique Jewish characteristics and sensitivities. As a result, the World Congress of Gay and Lesbian Jewish Organizations was founded 15 years ago (Cooper, 1989/1990).

The Japanese American gay men in Wooden, Kawasaki, and Mayeda's (1983) sample described stereotypes of Asians in gay male communities. One said, "They see us as fitting the 'Madame Butterfly' role and that of the 'good oriental'" (p. 240). Another reported, "They believe we are passive, docile, faithful, and responsible for more 'housewifey' jobs" (p. 240). Other stereotypes listed included: feminine, small genitals, youthful, easy pickups, polite, and secretive. One man concluded, "Their view is that Japanese only like Caucasian men sexually, and they associate femininity with being oriental" (p. 240).

Too frequently lesbian and gay communities do not acknowledge the presence of non-Anglo members. When acknowledgment is offered, all too often the majority culture members assume that their unique ways of conceptualizing, understanding, and enacting lesbian and gay issues are applicable for *all* ethnic group members simply because they share homoerotic attractions and identities. Thus, for ethnic-minority adolescents, a very important aspect of their identity is not recognized (Chan, 1989; Pamela H., 1989).

For example, the pressure applied by Anglo gay men and lesbians on Latino/a gays and lesbians to be activists negates an essential feature of their ethnic heritage. Hidalgo and Hidalgo-Christensen (1976/1977) argued that Puerto Rican lesbians are not visible in activist networks because they do not want to disgrace their families through public disclosure of their homosexuality. Within many Latino/a cultures, the significance of the family extends beyond the immediate biological family to include distant kin. To be publicly out affects many generations and carries a heavy cultural burden.

A gay Chinese adolescent best summarized the feelings of many ethnic-/sexual-minority youths: "I am a double minority. Caucasian gays don't like gay Chinese, and the Chinese don't like the gays. It would be easier to be white. It would be easier to be straight. It's hard to be both" (Tremble et al., 1989, p. 263).

Homophobia in Ethnic Communities

An ethnic community seldom provides a youth refuge from homophobic prejudice because negative views toward homosexuality may, in fact, be more pervasive in such communities than in mainstream White culture (Clarke, 1983; Espin, 1987; Icard, 1986; Morales, 1983; Poussaint, 1990). In the African American community, Gates (1993) labeled this "blacklash." One African American lesbian (Mays et al., 1993) noted her dilemma:

> Instead of accepting me for the person I am, they look at me as being a lesbian and look at me as being with another woman, and they see that as being very sinful and very bad. I told them to not judge me because I am gay, to look at me for who I am inside and not just judge me on . . . what they've heard on the news or what they've heard from other people or what they've read in books. (p. 6)

Homophobia may be derivative of attitudes that exist in an ethnic-minority member's native culture. For example, gay life in Cuba must exist primarily in prostitution and the underworld (Arguelles & Rich, 1989) because there is considerable repression and animosity against gays and lesbians (for personal, vivid accounts see Arenas, 1993, and Ramos, 1994). Within Judaism, homosexuality is often considered unnatural and undesirable; there are no traditional celebrations of same-sex committed relationships or instruction for lesbians and gays to become rabbis or cantors. These points were dramatically illustrated by Raphael (1990) in his collection of short stories, *Dancing on Tisha B'av,* and by Marder, a rabbi who led a gay shul. Marder noted:

> The message conveyed to my congregants by the community to which they belong is clear: you are welcome as long as you are invisible. We will tolerate your homosexuality, but we will certainly not hold you up as role models to be admired and emulated. (1989, p. 216)

Homosexuality may be more tolerated in other groups than in one's own ethnic group. Although liberal attitudes may be expressed toward lesbians and gays in general, the "live and let live" attitude seldom extends to homosexuality within one's own community (Wooden et al., 1983). The reasons for this ethnic-group homophobia are complex and beyond the scope of this chapter, but they likely reside in the unique religious values and cultural beliefs carried over from the "homeland" as well as the tribulations that ethnic minorities have experienced surviving in the dominant Anglo culture of North America (for elaboration see Gates, 1993; Greene, 1994;

Manalansan, 1996). For example, Gates (1993) noted that an antihomosexual ideology has been characteristic of the Black nationalist movement in the U.S. He quoted Professor Asante of Temple University as saying:

> Homosexuality is a deviation from Afrocentric thought, because it makes the person evaluate his own physical needs above the teachings of national consciousness. . . . [W]e can no longer allow our social lives to be controlled by European decadence. (p. 44)

Not uncommonly, parents view homosexuality as a sign that the younger generation has become too assimilated and has lost touch with their heritage (Pamela H., 1989). After a Korean daughter came out to her parents, they admonished her: "Being gay is a white disease. We're Korean; Korean people aren't gay" (Pamela H., 1989, p. 284). Tremble et al. (1989) noted that many find it "inconceivable" that anyone in their ethnic community could be "homosexual":

> Being black, Muslim, Greek, and so forth, and being homosexual, are perceived to be mutually exclusive. . . . To resolve the dissonance created by a gay or lesbian child, ethnic parents may blame the dominant culture. A 20-year-old Pakistani-Canadian male explains, "My parents are hurt. They see homosexuality as being against the Muslim faith. They think of it as a white people's thing. Being gay is something I picked up from my white friends." (p. 260)

Parents often blame a decadent, urban society; homosexuality is the price some pay for the privilege of living in North America. In their state of vulnerability, the children have been seduced by Anglo-American culture (Carrier, Nguyen, & Su, 1992). Homosexuality may also be considered by parents to be a manifestation of adolescent rebellion against traditional culture.

When their family holds such views, ethnic-minority youths experience increased fear and anxiety about their same-sex attractions and coming out to others. They may anticipate that parents will not believe them if they disclose their sexual orientation. Consequently, according to Morales (1983), youths experience inordinate pain: "To live as a minority within a minority leads to heightened feelings of isolation, depression and anger centered around the fear of being separated from all support systems including the family" (p. 2).

Many ethnic-minority youths must contend with maintaining the family honor, fulfilling expectations of marriage, and satisfying cultural definitions of masculinity and femininity. Yet, increasingly, these cultural expectations are shifting, easing pressure on ethnic-minority youth and thus allowing them to celebrate their unique sexual status.

The Family

Morales (1983) argued that the primary difference between traditional American and ethnic family constellations

> . . . centers around the integration of the extended family within its support system. The ethnic family support system resembles more of a tribe with mul-

tiple family groups rather than a nuclear family structure consisting solely of parents and children. For the ethnic person the family constitutes a symbol of their basic roots and the focal point of their ethnic identity. (p. 9)

Thus, coming out to the family may be a very onerous experience for ethnic youths who normally rely on the family as the primary support system during "the arduous times of experiencing discrimination, slander and inferior treatment" (Morales, 1983, p. 9). To alienate the family jeopardizes a youth's intrafamily relationships, associations with other ethnic-group members, and progress toward a healthy sense of self.

The Significance of the Family

For ethnic-minority youths to successfully negotiate the development of a positive lesbian, gay, or bisexual identity, it is often paramount to come out to the family. However, this is seldom an easy task. One of Wooden et al.'s (1983) subjects noted, "Japanese are taught humility and being gay is often associated with shame. You tend to keep it quiet so you don't bring shame to your family" (p. 241).

In ethnic communities, family is defined more broadly than nuclear family members. Extended family members, including grandparents, aunts, uncles, and cousins, provide child care, advice, role models, support, and other specialized roles. The significance of the extended family in the lives of youths has been persistently documented in Asian families. If an Asian youth disgraces herself or himself, shame is brought not only to the immediate family but to all past generations, living and dead (Carrier et al., 1992; Chan, 1989; Pamela H., 1989; Morales, 1983; Tsui, 1985). The family's honor is tarnished; it is not the children who have failed but the parents.

This view has been noted as well in other ethnic communities (Espin, 1987; Medina, 1987; Yeskel, 1989). Yeskel (1989), a Jewish lesbian, recalled that when she came out she felt "as if I was throwing a huge wrench into the parental plan. I thought about killing myself just about every day. How could I destroy my parents' happiness?" (p. 43). African American, Asian American, Jewish, and Latino/a families strongly emphasize loyalty, honoring parents, and extended family ties.

Given the importance and centrality of the extended family, some youths feel that they are forced to choose between their ethnic affiliation and a gay or lesbian identity. Tremble et al. (1989) noted that minority youths often "excluded themselves from cultural activities in order to avoid shaming the family in front of friends" (p. 261). This may be particularly acute among Asian women, some of whom feel they must leave their ethnic community to be a lesbian, thus forfeiting the support of family and extended kin (Pamela H., 1989). Many decide to participate in lesbian rather than Asian activities because they fear rejection more from ethnic than lesbian communities.

Coming Out to the Family

A youth may thus feel that he or she can never come out publicly for fear of humiliating that which is most important in his or her life: the close-knit family that extends beyond immediate members to include multiple generations. Chicana poet Torres (1980) expressed this sentiment in response to pressure from lesbians to come out to her parents:

Somehow it would be disrespectful to say to them, "Look, I'm a lesbian, and you're going to have to deal with it." I don't have the right to do that. They've been through so much in their lives about being Chicanos and living in this society. They've just taken so much shit that I won't do that to them until I feel like it can be said. (p. 244)

In a state of near desperation, one Latina lesbian, Rodriguez (1980), came out to her mother in the twelfth grade:

I told my mother, "Look, I'm freaking out. Do you know why I'm freaking out? It's not because I'm on dope; it's not because I listen to acid rock; it's because I'm a lesbian. And if I get your understanding, then I'll be able to clean my life up. I can take this cover off."

She told me, "I always knew you were. If you're going to be a lesbian, be a good lesbian." And then she started crying. At first she was so glad that I wasn't freaking out because of her or dope, it was like, "Phew." Then it hit her, "Oh! A lesbian! That's just as bad. Aaaaaaaah!" She cried and cried. (p. 110)

As Rodriguez illustrated, parents who suspect that their child is lesbian or gay may be hesitant to publicly raise the issue for fear of embarrassing relatives and their community. Thus, a wall of silence is likely to form around a family with a lesbian daughter, gay son, or bisexual child. Even if a youth advances to the point of self-recognition of her or his sexual status, the inhibitions against stating this publicly may block further self-development.

Part of this can be accounted for by the fact that sex is often a taboo topic in Asian and Latino communities. Sexual issues in general are considered to be a highly sensitive and delicate subject, open at best to awkward discussion (Pamela H., 1989; Ratti, 1993; Tsui, 1985; Wooden et al., 1983). Without a tradition of talking about sexuality, it is very difficult for an ethnic-/sexual-minority youth to discuss sexual identity, beliefs, and practices with family members.

Japanese don't seem to discuss sex or personal things with their children, although the family unit tends to be closely knit. Coming out was difficult, because I felt I was odd. I also felt that it was wrong and I would be a disgrace to the family. (Wooden et al., 1983, p. 240)

In fact, many ethnic-minority youths delay self-disclosure or never come out to their parents. Several investigations have reported that siblings, usually sisters, are told before, and perhaps in lieu of, parents. For example, Chan's (1989) sample of Chinese, Japanese, and Korean young adults found that almost 80% had come out to a family member, usually a sister; only one quarter had come out to parents. Similar results were found with samples of Puerto Ricans (Hidalgo & Hidalgo-Christensen, 1976/1977) and Japanese Americans (Wooden et al., 1983). A primary reason for coming out to nonparent family members was noted in the former study: They can become confidants and invaluable sources of support. A reason for not coming out was offered by an individual in the latter study: "They would never understand and I would be disowned and denied seeing my younger sister" (p. 239).

There is a strong expectation in many ethnic communities that children will marry and have children. Girls are expected to play the roles of wife and mother and to be dutiful, loyal, and obedient; boys, father and procreator of heirs (Chan, 1989; Pamela H., 1989; Icard, 1986; Medina, 1987; Ratti, 1993; Tsui, 1985). Homosexuality is considered detrimental to the fulfillment of these expectations. To neglect these obligations indicates that a youth is selfish, having only his or her own pleasure in mind rather than the community good.

Cultural Expectations of Appropriate Sex-Role Behavior

Ethnic communities frequently have traditional expectations regarding appropriate masculine and feminine roles. For lesbian, gay, and bisexual youths who cannot meet these expectations, this may well be another way in which their ethnic and sexual identities are incongruent. For example, a traditional virtue common in Latino communities is that Latino males should appear defiantly heterosexual—embracing and enacting the social construct of "machismo" (Carrier, 1989; Parker, 1989). Males are expected to personify traditional masculine sex roles, such as aggressiveness, dominance, power, courage, and invulnerability (Carrier, 1989).

In Hispanic culture, *same-sex behavior* per se is not sufficient to be labeled gay (Magana & Carrier, 1991). Rather, male homosexuality is equated with effeminacy and assuming the passive (receiver) role in sexual relations. If, for example, a Mexican (Magana & Carrier, 1991) or Cuban (Young, 1981) male assumes the inserter role in anal intercourse, he will not likely be considered deviant or gay. Because he embraces traditional masculine macho behavior, it is also unlikely that he will consider himself to be gay.

Carrier (1989) suggested that Mexican males who are feminine in behavior and who never think of themselves as heterosexual may experience an easier time self-identifying as gay in adulthood. Males who behave in a masculine manner may find it easier to rationalize that they are heterosexuals who occasionally enjoy insertive anal intercourse with other males. If and when they eventually self-identify as gay, they may experience a much more difficult time accepting and embracing their new identity. Bisexuality, particularly the assumption of the dominant (inserter) position, is more acceptable (Carrier, 1989).

Etiqueta, the proper sex role for Latina females, prescribes patience, nurturance, passivity, and subservience. Women are showpieces to be adorned. They are virgins until married, docile, inferior, and faithful. Not surprisingly, traditional Hispanic views of lesbians are negative. Latina lesbians are likely to be considered man-haters—acting macho and trying to overthrow men and masculine cultural heritage. They are perceived to engage in foreign ways and to be headstrong and independent. Sexually, lesbians are thought to be promiscuous, unchaste, and selfish (Hidalgo & Hidalgo-Christensen, 1976/1977; Ramos, 1994; Romo-Carmona, 1994). One Latina lesbian (Romo-Carmona, 1994) noted several cultural expectations:

> As Latinas, we are supposed to grow up submissive, virtuous, respectful of elders and helpful to our mothers, long suffering, deferring to men, industrious and devoted. We also know that any deviation from these expectations constitutes an act of rebellion, and there is great pressure to conform. Independence is discouraged, and we learn early that women who think for themselves are branded "putas" or "marimachas" [sluts or butches].

Being a lesbian is by definition an act of treason against our cultural values. (p. xxvi)

In some Asian communities, a discrepancy between behavior sanctioned in the homeland and its subsequent interpretation following immigration to the U.S. is not uncommon. For example, in Vietnam, homosexuality is equated with femininity and being half male, half female. Nonetheless, some adolescent males engage in same-sex behavior such as mutual masturbation and fellatio. Close physical contact, holding hands, and sleeping together in the same bed are considered normal and socially sanctioned, suggesting that little is implied about future sexual identification (Carrier et al., 1992). In North America, however, a "masculine" Vietnamese adolescent male who engaged in these otherwise "normal" same-sex activities would raise considerable concern among peers and family.

In Mexico, male youths who display gender atypical or nontraditional behavior at a young age "are eventually, if not from the beginning, pushed toward exclusive homosexual behavior" (Carrier, 1989, p. 227). The ethnic-minority youths interviewed by Tremble et al. (1989) were preoccupied with reconciling homoerotic desires with their sex role behavior:

Often these youngsters are victimized by the stereotypes within their own culture. They believe that being gay or lesbian implies a gender-role reversal. They go through a phase of extreme cross-gender behavior, which distresses or alienates their parents, or may leave them open to harassment or victimization. (p. 263)

These pressures can undermine psychological integrity and identity formation and sabotage the maturation of a healthy self-concept. However, there are indications of cultural shifts regarding expectations and acceptance within some ethnic-minority communities.

Cultural Shifts

Attitudes toward homosexuality can alter. The increasing visibility and diversity of lesbian and gay life may well be changing the rigid stereotypes of gays and lesbians preserved in some ethnic communities. Tremble et al. (1989) suggested that

. . . cultural sanctions are not fixed values. They are perceived and interpreted by individuals, families, communities, and are modified in application by the perceived characteristics of the individual involved. . . . Herein, lies the flexibility to come to terms with homosexuality. (p. 257)

Changes in cultural perspectives are not a recent phenomenon but the consequence of gradual shifts over many years. Arora (1980) noted this increasing liberalization 15 years ago:

Today the potential for a gay person to declare his sexuality is much wider— there seems to be a more "liberal" atmosphere. No child or teenager grows up without knowing—reading—hearing the word "gay." But for a person who is homosexual, the trauma of facing social derision and alienation is by no means less. (p. 23)

Newman and Muzzonigro (1993) suggested that more important than ethnicity in the coming-out process are traditional values such as an emphasis on religion, marriage, and bearing children. Even those "traditional values," however, are mutating. Although the Catholic church has traditionally been one of the bulwarks of traditional values, change is slowly occurring. One Latina lesbian noted:

> When I was thirteen, I confessed to a priest that I was a lesbian. I thought it was a sin so I should confess it, but he said that it was alright and that he was gay. He said, "God isn't going to condemn you. God is all good. How can he condemn something that he's made?" (Gonzalez, 1980, p. 184)

One Japanese American linked changes in attitudes to generational differences:

> I feel this can be categorized into two classifications—attitudes of the first and second generations, and those of the third and fourth generations. I think those of the first and second generations are more rigid and non-accepting. They feel we are perverts and child-molesters. Those of the third and fourth are more accepting. Attitudes are changing. (Wooden et al., 1983, p. 240)

Ethnic roots, religion, social class, and date immigrated are factors that appear to matter most in predicting a liberal attitude toward homosexuality among Vietnamese (Carrier et al., 1992).

Tremble et al. (1989) found that parents from Asian, Portuguese, Greek, Italian, and Indo-Pakistani cultural backgrounds who adjusted best to their offspring's homosexuality prioritized and reinterpreted their values, maintaining, "You are my child and I love you no matter what" (p. 259). Preserving family unity was given first priority. Other parents who accepted their gay or lesbian children found precedents for homosexuality among lesbian and gay friends and family members. A third mechanism for acceptance was less satisfactory:

> Attributing homosexuality to an external source does not make parents any happier, nor could these rationales be called a real understanding, but they do seem to remove responsibility from themselves and their child. The child can be accepted as part of the family, albeit uneasily at times. (p. 261)

Cultural shifts in ethnic communities toward a more liberal attitude can be life affirming for youths striving to accept homoerotic attractions without rejecting their family and ethnic community.

Conclusion

It is important to understand the dual identities, multiple roles, emotional conflicts, and psychological adjustments that result from the complex situations in which lesbian, bisexual, and gay ethnic-minority youths find themselves. Such youths endure two stigmas, being an ethnic minority and being bisexual, gay, or lesbian. Consequently, they encounter racism in gay and lesbian communities and homophobia in their cultural communities. It is a risky venture with profound repercussions for a healthy integration of personal and group identities.

Ideally these adolescents should have the opportunity to acquire information and social support from two distinct and rich sources. They should receive support from lesbian and gay communities that their cultural community would otherwise be unable to provide, including affirmation of sexuality and sexual identity; a place in which to relax and talk openly about same-sex relationships; and information about social organizations and networks that cater to other sexual-minority individuals. Similarly, familial, racial, ethnic, and cultural ties should reinforce a cultural identification, offer a deep sense of heritage and values, and provide a sense of self (Morales, 1983).

A version of this ideal reality is occurring as an increasing number of ethnic-minority youths are finding support and encouragement from non-Anglo gay and lesbian communities. Almost every major ethnic-/sexual-minority group in North America sponsors, at least in large urban areas, various support and political organizations for its community. Also available are newsletters and magazines.

Forming an integrated multiple self-identification that includes ethnic and sexual identities is a protracted developmental process. Learning the skills to integrate and manage one aspect of a dissonant group identity, such as an ethnic-minority status, may facilitate the subsequent integration and management of a second dissonant group identity, such as sexual-minority status. Rofes (1989) noted that growing up Jewish, an "outsider" in a Gentile world, proved "indispensable to me as a gay man living in a world that often prefers that I not exist" (p. 198). Being targeted as a Jew was "useful preparation for later experiences of being much more overtly targeted as gay" (p. 199). Having experienced the difficulties of being ethnically "different," ethnic-/sexual-minority youths may develop coping skills that assist them to manage being sexually "different."

References

Arenas, R. (1993). *Before night falls*. New York: Penguin.

Arguelles, L., & Rich, B. R. (1989). Homosexuality, homophobia, and revolution: Notes toward an understanding of the Cuban lesbian and gay male experience. In M. B. Duberman, M. Vicinus, & G. Chauncey, Jr. (Eds.), *Hidden from history: Reclaiming the gay and lesbian past* (pp. 441–455). New York: Penguin.

Arora, D. (1980, August). When "gay" is not happy! *Society*, pp. 20–23.

Carrier, J. M. (1989). Gay liberation and coming out in Mexico. *Journal of Homosexuality, 17,* 225–252.

Carrier, J., Nguyen, B., & Su, S. (1992). Vietnamese American sexual behaviors and HIV infection. *The Journal of Sex Research, 29,* 547–560.

Chan, C. S. (1989). Issues of identity development among Asian-American lesbians and gay men. *Journal of Counseling and Development, 68,* 16–20.

Clarke, C. (1983). The failure to transform: Homophobia in the Black community. In B. Smith (Ed.), *Home girls: A Black feminist anthology* (pp. 197–208). New York: Kitchen Table Press.

Cooper, A. (1989/1990). No longer invisible: Gay and lesbian Jews build a movement. *Journal of Homosexuality, 18,* 83–94.

Cross, W. E. (1991). *Shades of Black: Diversity in African-American identity*. Philadelphia: Temple University Press.

Espin, O. M. (1987). Issues of identity in the psychology of Latina lesbians. In Boston Lesbian Psychologies Collective (Eds.), *Lesbian psychologies: Explorations and challenges* (pp. 35–55). Urbana, IL: University of Illinois Press.

Gates, H. L., Jr. (1993, May 17). Blacklash? *The New Yorker*, pp. 42–44.

Gonzalez, M. (1980). Maria Gonzalez. In R. Baetz (Ed.), *Lesbian crossroads* (p. 184). New York: William Morrow.

Greene, B. (1994). Ethnic-minority lesbians and gay men: Mental health and treatment issues. *Journal of Consulting and Clinical Psychology, 62,* 243–251.

H., Pamela. (1989). Asian American lesbians: An emerging voice in the Asian American community. In Asian Women United of California (Eds.), *Making waves: An anthology of writing by and about Asian American women* (pp. 282–290). Boston: Beacon Press.

Hidalgo, H. A., & Hidalgo-Christensen, E. (1976/1977). The Puerto Rican lesbian and the Puerto Rican community. *Journal of Homosexuality, 2,* 109–121.

Historic Meet. (1991). *Bombay Dost, 1,* 5–6.

Icard, L. (1986). Black gay men and conflicting social identities: Sexual orientation versus racial identity. *Journal of Social Work and Human Sexuality, 4,* 83–93.

Johnson, J. M. (1981). Influences of assimilation on the psychosocial adjustment of Black homosexual men (Doctoral dissertation, California School of Professional Psychology, Berkeley, 1981). *Dissertation Abstract International, 42* (11B), 4620.

Magana, J. R., & Carrier, J. M. (1991). Mexican and Mexican American male sexual behavior and spread of AIDS in California. *The Journal of Sex Research, 28,* 425–441.

Manalansan, M. F. (1996). Double minorities: Latino, Black, and Asian men who have sex with men. In R. C. Savin-Williams & K. M. Cohen (Eds.), *The lives of lesbians, gays, and bisexuals: Children to adults.* Ft. Worth, TX: Harcourt Brace College Publishers.

Marder, J. R. (1989). Getting to know the gay and lesbian shul: A rabbi moves from tolerance to acceptance. In C. Balka & A. Rose (Eds.), *Twice blessed: On being lesbian, gay, and Jewish* (pp. 209–217). Boston: Beacon Press.

Mays, V. M., Cochran, S. D., & Rhue, S. (1993). The impact of perceived discrimination on the intimate relationships of Black lesbians. *Journal of Homosexuality, 25,* 1–14.

Medina, C. (1987, January/February). Latino culture and sex education. *SIECUS, 15,* 3.

Morales, E. S. (1983, August). Third World gays and lesbians: A process of multiple identities. Paper presented at the 91st Annual Convention of the American Psychological Association, Anaheim, CA.

Newman, B. S., & Muzzonigro, P. G. (1993). The effects of traditional family values on the coming out process of gay male adolescents. *Adolescence, 28,* 213–226.

Parker, R. (1989). Youth, identity, and homosexuality: The changing shape of sexual life in contemporary Brazil. *Journal of Homosexuality, 17,* 269–289.

Poussaint, A. (1990, September). An honest look at Black gays and lesbians. *Ebony*, pp. 124, 126, 130–131.

Ramos, J. (1994). *Compañeras: Latina lesbians.* New York: Routledge.

Raphael, L. (1990). *Dancing on Tisha B'av.* New York: St. Martin's Press.

Ratti, R. (Ed.). (1993). *A lotus of another color: An unfolding of the South Asian gay and lesbian experience.* Boston: Alyson.

Rodriguez, D. (1980). Dolores Rodriguez. In R. Baetz (Ed.), *Lesbian crossroads* (pp. 110–112). New York: William Morrow.

Rofes, E. E. (1989). Living as all of who I am: Being Jewish in the lesbian/gay community. In C. Balka & A. Rose (Eds.), *Twice blessed: On being lesbian, gay, and Jewish* (pp. 198–204). Boston: Beacon Press.

Romo-Carmona, M. (1994). Introduction. In J. Ramos (Ed.), *Compañeras: Latina lesbians* (pp. xx–xxix). New York: Routledge.

Torres, A. (1980). Ana Torres. In R. Baetz (Ed.), *Lesbian crossroads* (pp. 240–244). New York: William Morrow.

Tremble, B., Schneider, M., & Appathurai, C. (1989). Growing up gay or lesbian in a multicultural context. *Journal of Homosexuality, 17,* 253–267.

Tsui, A. M. (1985). Psychotherapeutic considerations in sexual counseling for Asian immigrants. *Psychotherapy, 22,* 357–362.

Wooden, W. S., Kawasaki, H., & Mayeda, R. (1983). Lifestyles and identity maintenance among gay Japanese-American males. *Alternative Lifestyles, 5,* 236–243.

Yeskel, F. (1989). You didn't talk about these things: Growing up Jewish, lesbian, and working class. In C. Balka & A. Rose (Eds.), *Twice blessed: On being lesbian, gay, and Jewish* (pp. 40–47). Boston: Beacon Press.

Young, A. (1981). *Gays under the Cuban revolution.* San Francisco: Grey Fox Press.

Questions for Thought

1. Describe the problems that an ethnic minority lesbian or gay man might experience in predominantly White lesbian or gay communities.

2. Describe the problems that an ethnic minority gay man or lesbian might experience in his or her ethnic community.

3. Explain how the concepts of "machismo" and "etiqueta" affect attitudes toward homosexuality in Latino communities.

4. Discuss possible similarities and differences in the experiences of an African American lesbian with a same-race romantic partner and an African American lesbian with a romantic partner of another race.

5. What personal strengths might an ethnic minority gay man or lesbian develop as a result of being a "double minority."

6. The great importance given to the family in many ethnic communities can create dilemmas for gay, lesbian, and bisexual adolescents. But strong family ties can also create problems for heterosexuals who violate family expectations, for instance, by marrying outside their ethnic or religious group, or by espousing strong feminist beliefs. Discuss how Savin-Williams's analysis of the family might apply to ethnic minority heterosexuals.

10

"Outsider Within" the Firehouse

Subordination and Difference in the Social Interactions of African American Women Firefighters

Janice D. Yoder

Patricia Aniakudo

What is it like to be an African American woman firefighter? These women are invariably "tokens"—differing in both race and gender from the White male majority in the firehouse. Using quotations taken from personal interviews, Yoder and Aniakudo describe the distinctive encounters that Black women firefighters have with White women, White men, and Black men co-workers. Three main themes emerge in this qualitative analysis of the experiences of Black women firefighters: exclusion, token difference, and the inseparability of race and gender.

From the perspective of African American women firefighters, the authors examine the social interactions that make them excluded "outsiders within" their firehouses and different from not only dominant White men but also other subordinated groups of Black men and White women firefighters. Drawing on extensive survey data from 24 Black women career firefighters nationwide and detailed interviews with 22 of these, the authors found persistent and pervasive patterns of subordination through the exclusion of Black women, reflected in insufficient instruction, coworker hostility, silence, close supervision, lack of support, and stereotyping. Perceived differences of Black women from White and Black men as well as White women created strained relations, especially when Black men and White women gained some acceptance by virtue of their gender and race, respectively, and thus reportedly distanced themselves from Black women. The experiences of African American women firefighters highlight the omnirelevance and intertwining of race and gender.

Reprinted from *Gender and Society*, 1997, *11*(3), 324–341. Copyright 1997 by Sociologists for Women in Society. Published by Sage Publications. Used by permission of Sage Publications.

Early feminist theory described woman as "other" in contrast to a normative man (de Beauvoir 1952). Two critical assumptions are implicit in this conceptualization: first, that women and men are homogeneous groups, and second, that differences between the two mutually exclusive groups are accounted for by gender alone. Subsequent feminist theorists and researchers have challenged both assumptions by arguing for a more complex approach to recognizing and understanding differences among women based on race/ethnicity, class, sexual orientation, and so on (e.g., see Anderson and Collins 1995; Moraga and Anzaldua 1981). Spelman (1988) argued that there is no raceless, classless, generic woman. This was illustrated empirically by Landrine (1985), who documented that stereotypes of a presumably generic woman actually reflect assumptions about the target's race (White) and class (middle).

Given the diversity of women (and men), the study of difference has moved beyond simple comparisons of women and men to a more complex, nuanced view. Focusing on race and gender, a few theorists have regarded these as distinct and additive statuses such that, within American society, White women are subordinated on one count (gender) in contrast to African American women, who are doubly jeopardized (Pak, Dion, and Dion 1991) or paradoxically advantaged (Epstein 1973). This perspective implies that race and gender can be separated and that the gender portion is shared similarly by all women. Empirically, this approach leads us to expect that White and African American women will experience similar patterns of gender discrimination and that the latter simply will experience heightened levels, given their double oppression.

In contrast, West and Fenstermaker (1995) describe an ethnomethodological perspective to "doing difference" that conceptualizes gender, race, and class as omnirelevant and as working simultaneously to organize women's lives. Although gender, race, and class take on varying degrees of salience within different social contexts, West and Fenstermaker (1995) argue that each is potentially omnirelevant such that all social exchanges are affected to some degree by the confluence of all three. For example, gender may be especially salient when a lone woman works in a group of men of the same race and class, yet her race and class help shape her gender enactments and the expectations of others. Continuing with this example, if the lone woman is White and middle class (as well as heterosexual), a possible expectation may be that she is fragile and in need of paternalistic protection (Martin 1994). On the other hand, if this lone woman is African American (and even if her colleagues share her race), a possible expectation may be that she is strong and self-reliant (Hurtado 1989). Thus, gender cannot be enacted separately from race and class, even though it may be the obvious differentiating factor in a specific social context.

The purpose of this study is to explore the omnirelevance, inseparability, and confluence of gender and race in the social workplace interactions of African American women firefighters. These interactions will be probed for evidence of subordination, difference, and the intertwining of race and gender, drawing on theory and research from two interrelated strands of work.

The first strand explores subordination by conceptualizing race and gender as status variables (Berger et al. 1977) constructed through social exchanges (West and Fenstermaker 1995) such that African American women are subordinated in an occupation that is dominated and defined by White men. Collins (1986) captures the marginalization of African American women in White male-dominated groups by describing them as "outsiders within" who ultimately offer an alternative vision by sharing their personal and cultural biographies. Marginalized others offer a unique perspective on the events occurring within a setting because they perceive activities from the vantages of both nearness (being within) and detachment (being outsiders). Insiders tend to confide in outsiders in ways unthinkable with other insiders, and outsiders may see patterns that those too close to the center cannot discern. The stories of outsiders within can tell us both about their own experiences and about aspects of group functioning that pass unnoticed by those immersed in the setting. Thus, the experiences of African American women firefighters in this study will inform us both about their marginalized position and about the intimate day-to-day workings of a nontraditional work setting.

Examining the perspective of the outsider within, Hurtado (1989) theorizes that African American women's subordination will be experienced as exclusion in contrast to White women, who she speculates are subordinated through seduction, that is, through co-optation by their privileged racial status relative to dominant White men. Documentation of the exclusion of African American women as a means of subordination was provided by Martin (1994), who examined the social-work relations of African American policewomen. Martin (1994, 390) enumerated the forms their exclusion took: "They faced insufficient instruction, co-worker hostility, and the 'silent treatment'; . . . close and punitive supervision; exposure to danger and lack of backup; and paternalistic overprotection [stereotyping]." Each of these will be explored with our sample of African American women firefighters.

A second strand of relevant theory and research, focused on work group composition and differences among coworkers, provides a basis from which we can explore ongoing group processes—in this study, from the vantage of the outsider within. Early tokenism theory (Kanter 1977) conceptualized marginalization as one consequence of token difference, defined as proportional underrepresentation (less than 15 percent) in a skewed work group. Token difference originally was defined by Kanter (1977) as using any categorizing factor, but most empirical work used gender as the defining difference between tokens and dominants. Although Kanter (1977) speculated that tokenism processes would occur for any underrepresented group, including White men, recent reviews concluded that tokenism processes are not gender neutral (Yoder 1991; Zimmer 1988). With tokenism outcomes limited to proportionally scarce women, theorists began to consider the interaction of token numbers with gender as a subordinated status (Laws 1975; Reskin 1988). This refined view renewed interest in other ascribed statuses, such as race (Cox and Nkomo 1990; Greenhaus, Parasuraman, and Wormley 1990; Nkomo 1992). Given West and Fenstermaker's (1995) argument that gender and race cannot be studied in isolation, we propose that tokenism theorists and researchers consider the intertwining of differences in work group composition, such as tokens who differ from their coworkers along both racial and gender lines (cf. Dugger 1988; Gooley 1989; King 1988; Palmer 1983; Reid 1988; Segura 1992; Spelman 1988; Dill 1983).

What results is a more expansive exploration of tokenism processes. While prior research was confined to exploring differences between token women and dominant men in male-dominated work settings, we propose that theorists and researchers consider multiple intertwining differences (and similarities) between tokens and dominants. This becomes most obvious in the case of African American women in White male-dominated occupations. Analyses can no longer be confined to differences between presumably generic (White?) women and generic (White?) men. Rather, explorations of work group interactions encompass the relations of African American women with White men, African American men, and White women co-workers. In this article, token difference will be examined from the vantage point of African American women themselves across these three relations.

Professional firefighting is an especially fertile area in which to study social interaction. Firefighters rely heavily on team cohesiveness and support, often in life and death situations. Social exchanges are intensified by the demands of shift work—units spend 24 hours or longer together in shared quarters. In fact, the prevalence rate for diagnosable posttraumatic stress disorder (PTSD) in firefighters (16.5 percent) is 1 percent higher than PTSD rates among Vietnam veterans (DeAngelis 1995).

Furthermore, professional firefighting has a long history of discriminatory access, assignment, and assessment. Although women have long served as volunteer firefighters, the first woman career firefighter was hired in 1974 (Women in the Fire Service 1991) at a time when the occupation itself was moving toward greater professionalization and integrating men of color (McCarl 1985). In a 1990 survey of 356 career women firefighters, fully 16 percent reported that they gained entry to the fire service as the result of a successful equal employment opportunity complaint (Armstrong et al. 1993). Recently, the Los Angeles Fire Department was spotlighted by the media for commissioning and using a training video that repeatedly showed women failing miserably ("L.A. Fire Training Tape" 1994). It is not surprising that, as an occupation, professional firefighting remains highly skewed: More than 95 percent of all workers in fire protection nationwide are men; 83 percent are White (*American Statistical Index* 1992). It is estimated that there are more than 3,000 women in the fire service nationwide, and 11 percent of these are African American (Armstrong et al. 1993).

Research Participants and Design

Because we know of no comprehensive (or even rudimentary) list of career women firefighters nationwide, we began our search for African American women firefighters at the 1992 meetings of the International Association of Black Professional Firefighters (IABPFF), a loosely organized group of mostly Black male firefighters. With the help of the head of the women's caucus within the IABPFF and a handful of attendees at these meetings, we started with a list of 15 names of African American women firefighters. From these beginnings and by using snowball sampling, we generated a list of 48 Black women across all regions of the United States who work in a range of small to large metropolitan firehouses. Of these 48 women (50 percent), 24 returned an hour-long survey (a respectable return rate for African American women) (Cannon, Higginbotham, and Leung 1988); 22 of the 24 engaged in an hour-long phone interview.

The median age of these African American women firefighters was 32 years (range = 26–42), and their median length of service was more than 5 years (range = 1–16). Regarding their family arrangements, 12 percent were married, 42 percent were divorced or separated, 38 percent were never married, and 52 percent had children. Finally, the majority (74 percent) were gender-defined tokens (less than 15 percent women), and 46 percent were the first woman in their firehouse.[1]

Black women averaged 14.87 weeks of firefighting training. Three were high school graduates, 14 (58 percent) had some college, and 7 (29 percent) held B.A.s or more. One-third of the Black women worked in White-dominated houses of more than 65 percent Whites, half worked with balanced numbers of Whites (36–65 percent), and the remaining 4 (17 percent) worked in Black-dominated houses of less than 35 percent Whites (28–35 percent). Although 71 percent of the Black women were not the first African American in their firehouse, only three worked with another Black woman.[2]

In collaboration with two African American women firefighters, we developed a 20-page mail survey that included demographic information and items exploring differential treatment, sexual harassment, work group race and gender composition,[3] tokenism outcomes, mentoring relations, beliefs about affirmative action, and ratings of chilly climate focused on both race and gender. Participants were paid $35 for completing both the survey and interview. Upon return of the survey, 22 hour-long phone interviews were conducted by the second author, who is African American, has a sister who is a firefighter, and did preliminary field observation of the daily routines of firefighters before interviewing.

The interview schedule consisted of three questions that were given to the Black women interviewees prior to the prearranged phone call. (1) "What influenced you to become a firefighter?" was included as an icebreaker. (2) "Have you ever been treated differently because you are Black or a woman?" was included to parallel its use by prior researchers (Brooks and Perot 1991; Essed 1991; Rosenberg, Perlstadt, and Phillips 1993) to sensitively elicit reports of racial discrimination. (3) "Do you know of any rumors that have circulated about you as a firefighter?" was asked because prior research with firefighters (Gruber 1992; McCarl 1985) identified rumors as a way to embellish or diminish a firefighter's reputation on a team. Respondents voluntarily spent the most time responding to the second question.

Firehouse Interaction

Three global themes emerged from our analysis of African American women firefighters' responses: (1) subordination through exclusion, (2) a more encompassing definition of difference, and (3) the omnirelevance, inseparability, and confluence of race and gender.

Subordination through Exclusion

Paralleling the findings of Martin (1994) with policewomen, the subordination of African American women firefighters was expressed throughout these women's stories in examples of insufficient instruction, coworker hostility, silence, close supervision, lack of support stereotyping and differential treatment.

Insufficient Instruction   An undercurrent of colleagues' animus was exposed in several accounts of training by Black women firefighters. Several recounted examples of training exercises that they alone endured. The Black woman with the least amount of formal training in our sample (only six weeks) described how she was duped into chopping down a live tree under the pretext of testing her ability to swing an ax. A Californian reported that she filed a grievance when the shelf, onto which she had been trained to hoist a hose, grew 5 inches before her formal testing. A third Black woman described how, when she naively asked a senior White male colleague for help with a leaking air pack, she received no constructive instruction, was subsequently written up for presumed negligence, and was referred for additional training. She recalls thinking:

> I can't go ask for help unless it gets written up that something was wrong. You know, so I really don't know how I can trust you guys.

Coworker Hostility   The message that underlied the above training experiences was one of hostility. All too often, no attempt was made to cloak coworkers' disdain. A 16-year veteran vividly recalled her first encounter with her White male captain:

> The first day I came on, the first day I was in the field, the guy told me he didn't like me. And then he said: "I'm gonna tell you why I don't like you. Number one, I don't like you cuz you're Black. And number two, cuz you're a woman." And that was all he said. He walked away.

Such blatant confrontations were not isolated incidents but rather appeared across many interviews with Black women:

> I've been told a number of times that I'll never make it [in a firehouse of four Black men and two White men].

> They [nine White men and seven Black men] let me know: "You don't belong here, but since you're here, just stay out of the way. We get a fire, I don't want you touching nothing. I don't want you doing nothing. Just stay out of the way."

> [After a few minutes in the bathroom of a firehouse with five White men and seven Black men, a woman reported hearing]: "We don't need no woman over here. I told y'all we don't need no woman in here. We don't have no space for a woman. She's in the restroom 20 minutes!"

> They [six White men] kept telling me that I shouldn't be here, that I was taking up a man's job.

> The majority of the guys, like I said, make it highly known that they do not want women on the job. . . . It's been, you know, stated to me directly to my face that I shouldn't be here. You know, just for the simple fact that I am a woman, and God forbid that I'm a Black female.

Three Black women reported that peers sought transfers to avoid being paired with them. Another described a White male captain who "fought tooth and nail to make sure I was not gonna get on his shift." A fifth Black woman described notes she would find on her bed in a firehouse with three White men and four Black men: "You're not going to sleep because this spot is reserved for someone else." A sixth Black woman claimed that she was denied materials for a promotion exam that she directly requested and had seen being shared among her colleagues. A seventh Black woman in a firehouse of nine White men, one Black man, one other Black woman, and one other man was literally left sleeping at the station "because they want to see me fail, you know."

Silence   The "silent treatment" is another expression of enmity keenly felt by firefighters. A 40-year-old woman in an Eastern metropolitan area, who was the first woman and the first African American in her firehouse, which now included four Black men and three White men, described the persistence of silence:

> No one really talked to me. It was difficult the first, I'd say, six months, because I was basically alone. I'd walk in and everything would get quiet. I'd go to eat; everybody leaves the room. Once they saw I was not going anywhere and I was there to stay, slowly guys started coming around, you know, talking. As I said, I've been on the job now seven years, and there're still guys that don't talk to me. They speak and that's it. Haven't really accepted the fact that yes, we do have women on the department.

There is some evidence that what started as imposed exclusion became self-sustaining. Many of these women's stories of silence began on their first day of work. Years later, these women seem to have excluded themselves so that one could easily look at these women now and blame them for failing to interact with their colleagues. For one firefighter, the initial message from nine White men and seven Black men was clear: "You don't belong here, but since you're here, just stay out of the way." Ten years later she says, "Now, like I said, I stay to myself as much as I possibly can."

Close Supervision   The close and often punitive supervision of Black women firefighters was captured well by a 12-year veteran serving in a firehouse of five White men and two Black men. She describes the alleged practice of "pencil whipping":

> It was a process of what they call being "pencil whipped." Where if they keep writing enough damaging information about you, then it will give them justifiable reason to say . . . "We've tried and train her. We've tried to do this, and she's just not going to be able to handle this job."

Repeatedly, these women complained that they were closely observed, held to the letter rather than the spirit of rules and regulations, and quickly and needlessly chastised for their failings. A driver (in a small firehouse of three White men and one Black man) was forced by her White male captain to recertify after skidding into a pole during an ice storm, while a male colleague was absolved of blame for accidentally killing an elderly pedestrian crossing a street. Others recounted the following:

> I was always written up for whatever I did.

> He's [a White male lieutenant] writing up forms when he feels that you're doing badly, but when he feels you're doing well, he's not writing up reports.

A man can make a mistake and it will be covered up or will not be discussed . . . [for me,] they try to make things out of nothing. It's always something out of nothing.

He [a White male captain] just decided to take it out on me by using the rules and regulations.

Although no firefighter told a story of being physically endangered by colleagues, few felt supported. Most felt that they were given assignments designed to discourage them, that coworkers subtly questioned their competence, and that accommodations were seemingly made for White women but not for Black women. Two Black women interpreted their assignments to blatantly racist areas of large metropolitan cities as a signal to quit. Others viewed assignments to firehouses dominated by White men as attempts to isolate and discourage them:

It just seems to me too coincidental that I would be sent to a house [of nine White men and four Black men] where problems were, you know, hatred. I mean hatred.

Lack of Support   Lack of backup from colleagues appeared in gestures that subtly raised questions about the competence of these Black women firefighters. Although most (75 percent) felt that affirmative action facilitated their hiring, none reported that this undermined their own feelings of competence. In contrast, fully 79 percent of Black women felt that others believed that affirmation action influenced their hiring, and the majority (58 percent) believed that this fueled uncertainties in other firefighters about the women's competence. As a firefighter of nine years who was the first African American in her house described,

They felt that I had been given special preference to get onto the job. And those were the types of rumors that I heard as time went on: that I was hired because I was a Black woman, that I could not perform.

The repeated challenge for many Black women was to "prove myself." They felt pressured to prove their physical prowess, knowledge of firefighting, and commitment to the cohesiveness of the team. No one "proof" ever seemed sufficient, nor was it generally recognized:

Every time I have to go out someplace I have to prove myself just because I'm a woman . . . no matter, you know, how many times you go out and you do a great job and you do everything right . . . but that one time, that one time that you have a slight little problem or you need just a little bit of help or something might go wrong on your end, that's what they're gonna remember you for, not all the good things that you did, just that one bad thing. You know, and they're going to build on that.

Many Black women noted dissatisfaction with sleeping and bathroom facilities (54 percent) and the sizing of gear (54 percent). Yet, African American women felt that progress in each of these areas came more readily when White women appeared on the scene:

The first [restroom] facility that was built wasn't done until 1987, and it was done in a firehouse that had only White females.

When White females started coming on the department in great numbers, all of a sudden sexual harassment classes were given; women's clothes were purchased.

Stereotyping and Differential Treatment   Almost all women (92 percent) felt that they were treated differently than other firefighters because they were women; none reported that this difference was positive. Not surprisingly, similarly high proportions of Black women (96 percent) noted differential treatment based on race; again, none regarded this difference positively.

The influence of race and gender on the stereotyping of Black women was evident in how stereotyping was expressed. In contrast to prior research with White women who coped with stereotypic paternalistic overprotection (Martin 1994; Yoder, Adams, and Prince 1983) and sexualization (MacCorquodale and Jensen 1993; Tallichet 1995), Black women firefighters dealt with denigrating stereotypes of themselves as welfare recipients and "beasts of burden" (Dill 1979).

> I am a woman, and God forbid, I'm a Black female. . . . [Others in her firehouse of eight White men and one other man said]: "You're taking a spot away from, you know, some White male who has a family. A White male who needs this job" . . . So just because I'm a Black female, I don't need this job? So in other words you're telling me that I should be on welfare and I should fit into that stereotype. . . . I should be at home, you know, having babies, and let some man have this position.

> I would end up with more chores than another female would. And she would happen to be White there. And . . . the [White male] lieutenant would assign me to carry heavier things.

Token Difference

When subordinated difference is defined along interlocking lines, contrasts multiply such that African American women experience strained relationships with at least three distinct groups of differing statuses: White men, Black men, and White women. Each is explored within our data from the perspective of Black women as outsiders within.

Relations with White Men   Although Black women tended to work in racially integrated firehouses, the majority of Black women (71 percent) worked with at least 50 percent White men (median = 57 percent, range = 28–86 percent). Examining a composite measure of work group atmosphere developed within the tokenism literature (Yoder 1994), Black women reported that overall work relations were less favorable as the proportion of White men in their firehouse increased ($r = -.49$, $p < .05$). Specifically, as the percentage of White men increased, Black women reported less encouragement from team members to seek promotion ($r = -.61$,

$p < .01$), less favorable expected reactions from team members to their own promotion ($r = -.63, p < .01$), less discussion of general topics with teammates ($r = -.46$, $p < .05$), less acceptance as a colleague ($r = -.57, p < .01$), less acceptance by coworkers' families ($r = -.42, p < .05$), and less leisure time spent with peers ($r = -.47, p < .05$). Similarly, Black women felt that their own competent work was more likely to be ignored in the presence of greater numbers of White men ($r = .59$, $p < .01$). Although there was no relationship between the proportion of White men in the firehouse and both chilly climate toward women ($r = .33$, n.s.) and incidents of sexual harassment ($r = .04$, n.s.), Black women did note a negative association between more White men and heightened chilly climate toward Blacks ($r = .61$, $p < .01$).[4] In sum, then, these correlations paint a picture of increasingly strained relations between Black women and White men as the representation of the latter increases.

Relations with Black Men   African American women firefighters' relationships with Black men typically were mixed. Most of our Black women interviewees reported having at least some supportive relationships with their Black male colleagues. Of the 19 (79 percent) noting in the survey that they had a mentor, 15 were mentored by Black men,[5] and all described these mentors as very helpful to them both personally ($M = 6.42, SD = 1.22$) and professionally ($M = 6.74, SD = .56$) on 7-point Likert scales. Black women noted that Black men broke the racial ground for them. As one woman in a Southern department with a solid Black representation of four Black men (and two White women) noted,

> I think that the Black men that were there, they had to struggle because they made it possible for us to come on.

Black women firefighters described two scenarios involving their interactions and Black men's interactions with White men. In the first, Black men served as intermediaries between Black women and White men. Black women reported that some Black men seemingly traded on their commonality with both Black women and White men and thus mediated between them. For example, a sole Black woman (on a team with four Black men and nine White men) recounted that a Black male colleague warned his White coworker:

> "You know what? You guys are gonna keep pushing her, and one day, you're gonna find yourself out of a job because she's gonna file harassment charges." And he said, "You see that book she's keeping? Don't think your name is not in there."

In the second scenario, Black women perceived that male bonding was achieved at the expense of Black women. Black women felt that their inclusion may have helped to reduce the gap between Black and White men who became united, to some degree, by virtue of their shared gender and opposition to women firefighters. The same woman who spoke of a Black male defender immediately above and who was in a large Midwestern department summed this up:

> Before women came on this job . . . the big picture was White and Black, and you have some Hispanic. And, that was it. . . . That's the big picture. Before

we came on the job, the Blacks were having a lot of trouble. Now the women are on the job, the White guys say, "Come on, guys. We're all one now. Look at those women. They aren't, you know, they can't do this. Look at that." And you got some of the Black guys believing this. You got some of them believing that women don't belong on the job. Of course, you will find some who don't, but then you will find a lot of men who do.

Overall, from the perspective of African American women, relations of Black women with Black men reflected their relative positions within a race-gender power hierarchy:

> Black men [seven Black men with five White men] on the fire department . . .
> have been the underdogs . . . for so long. Now there's a group of people under
> them who they consider the underdogs . . . the Black woman. . . . And you
> know how it is; I explained it to the children: how the big brother gets picked
> on, how he picks on the little brother, and the little brother to the baby . . . it's
> that kind of effect.

Relations with White Women   Given that firefighting is a highly skewed, male-dominated occupation, it is rare for women to work together in the same firehouse, and only 1 of the 24 women in our sample worked directly with a White woman firefighter. However, African American women firefighters did encounter White women in positions related to firefighting (e.g., dispatchers and paramedics), in training programs, and across companies. Reports about these relationships describe divisions among women, separated by race, that have been documented elsewhere (Giddings 1984; hooks 1984; Martin 1994; Poster 1995). Such disunity was echoed by a 34-year-old firefighter of 10 years with no direct female peers:

> It's just a shame that we can't be just women on the fire department as op-
> posed to Black women and White women.

This lack of unity has been attributed by African American women to racism and to the tendency for White women, paralleling that of Black men, to trade on their racial solidarity with higher-status White men (Martin 1994).

The impact of others' racism on the formation of relationships between Black and White women was illustrated in the following anecdote from a lone woman firefighter of three years:

> I can tell you about the first day I walked into my firehouse. Here I am a
> Black woman, the first woman in the firehouse. . . . Just being there, being
> the first woman, I was treated a lot differently than anybody else. We have
> a White woman who's on the ambulance, and she's been there, and they never
> spoke to her before. She would bring things into the firehouse, like pies or
> cookies or things she'd make at home. They would never eat them. They
> wouldn't even talk to her. As soon as they knew I was coming, and I walked
> in the door, all of a sudden they're talking to her and they really don't have a
> lot of conversation with me. And I worked with them on the same apparatus,
> and she's on something totally different. I mean, I felt that was a blow right
> there. I really did. And I never really found out, I didn't know if it was just me

thinking that or what, but the guys, some of the Black guys on the job, told me. . . . "That's the way it is."

Although the Black woman who told this story recognized that her problems with this White woman began with the sexism of her male colleagues, it was race that drove a wedge between these women and that co-opted the White woman in the eyes of our Black respondent.

A second reason women can be divided along racial lines is because White women are perceived by African American women to be co-opted by White men who share their race. Two stories from our interviews with Black women illustrate this point clearly. First, a 29-year-old firefighter described her 14 weeks of training:

> In the academy, I had a friend. Her name was [Jane]. And, we used to be really tight. White girl. We were really tight. Because I don't have anything against being White or anything else. And we were good friends until all of a sudden a White guy tells her to be snooping around, because there was four Black women in our class, and one White woman. And we all participated; we all went out to drink together, to eat together, whatever. We baked for each other. But in the academy, they told her to find out if we had any information on a test. For her to be snooping through our stuff. And one of the girls caught her doing that. So then all of a sudden, she was accepted by a White peer group, and she no longer needed us. And everything changed. But before that, we were like really good friends. It was so weird.

Second, a 10-year veteran talked about promotion exams:

> On the first test we took, only Black women were taken because we were the ones who had the most seniority. The second test, there was a couple of White women that did take the test. . . . We kept hearing things about this one particular girl. They were calling her, believe it or not, they were calling her their "great White hope." They grilled her . . . now of course this is just rumor, but she got a lot of study material that wasn't available to everyone else.

Both anecdotes illustrate how Black women believe that White women's race can serve simultaneously to unify them with White men, however tenuously, and to separate them from Black women.

The Intertwining of Race and Gender

The omnirelevance and inseparability of racism and sexism in constructing the forms of Black women firefighters' exclusion and token difference appear throughout the descriptions of social interactions presented here. Although a few quotations from African American women realistically could be attributed to White women, most cannot. Race is either clearly noted as a contributor to the point being made by the interviewee, or it hovers in the background as a subtle but omnirelevant influence (West and Fenstermaker 1995).

The inseparability and confluence of race and gender for Black women became blatantly clear in our interviews when we asked women to indicate whether the incidents of differential treatment they had just described were attributable to their race *or* gender. Almost universally, these women rejected our assignment, claiming instead that such a distinction was artificial:

> It's hard to say whether it was just specifically because I was Black. With it being a double edge: being Black and being female [in a firehouse with all (six) White men].

> But I don't know if I had been White, would the situation [have] been any different? I don't know. Only because I got the same treatment from both sides. I wasn't just one of the group [of four Black men and two White men].

> Being a Black female . . . it was like two things that needed to be proven [to two Black men and five White men].

> We just seem to be the lowest on the totem pole when it comes to any type of support on this job [from four Black men and nine White men].

The same sentiments, expressed almost verbatim, appeared in Martin's (1994, 393) interviews with Black women police officers:

> Sometimes I couldn't tell if what I faced was racial or sexual or both. The Black female is the last one on the totem pole in the department, so if things are okay you thank God for that.

Our sense is that more was happening here than the confounding of race and gender as underlying causes of the events reported. The question itself seemed foreign to our respondents, as if we were trying to impose a distinction they simply did not share. Only one woman describing the incident in which she was required to recertify as a driver after a minor accident attributed her experience exclusively to her gender. All other responses described events in terms of being Black and being a woman. The assignment to distinguish between the two was ignored.

Conclusion and Implications

Research with African American women firefighters highlights patterns of social interaction that involve subordination, token difference, and the intertwining of race and gender. A series of processes—including insufficient, unnecessary, and hypercritical training; open and subtle coworker hostility; silence; exacting supervision; lack of support; and demeaning stereotyping with negative treatment—combine to send a clear message of exclusion to Black women firefighters.

Noting these women's vantage as outsiders within (Collins 1986), their stories suggest that the persistence of exclusion makes their withdrawal from their coworkers ultimately self-sustaining. Only from the perspective of African American women themselves can we see that what now appears to be the rejection of the group by the Black women is instead a coping strategy to deal with repeated past experiences of subordination through exclusion. This interpretation, as well as others throughout these women's narratives, reflect Black women's self-definition and self-valuation and produces an understanding of African American women firefighters that can counter potential misinterpretations of their actions by nonmarginalized insiders (Collins 1986). As Zinn et al. (1986) sagely note, misinterpretations, such as the alleged positive status afforded Black women professionals as affirmative action double-counts (Epstein 1973), "double jeopardy," and firefighters' self-exclusion, are formulated and promulgated only by those uninformed and unresponsive to the perspective of outsiders within. One valuable use of the present data is to provide this outsiders' perspective.

Unlike many studies of token difference, we defined difference along both racial and gender lines by considering Black women's relations with White men, Black men, and White women. Although African American women's relations with White men predictably are strained, and although this strain is reduced somewhat with the inclusion of coworkers other than White men, the presence of Black men is in no way a panacea for African American women. Black men may provide mentoring to Black women, but they also may contribute to their exclusion, at least from the perspective of Black women. Furthermore, although most of the direct agents of discriminatory treatment identified by Black women were White men, the mere presence of Black men, even as a proportional majority, did not seem to discourage hostile behavior from White men, especially when the White male transgressors were in positions of higher rank. Similarly, African American women report that contact with White women does not automatically lead to gendered solidarity. These data, along with other studies (e.g., South et al. 1982), argue that more than number balancing must be done to reduce the negative impact of token proportions.

Throughout the present explorations of both subordination and token difference, it becomes clear that race and gender are omnirelevant, inseparable, and intertwined (West and Fenstermaker 1995). One does not "control for" gender by comparing Black and White women (Spelman 1988; Yoder and Kahn 1993), nor do discussions of Black women's relations with White men support additive or interactive views of "double jeopardy." Black women firefighters work as Black women, not as Black *women* or as *Black* women.

The stories of these African American women challenge the extensive literatures on subordination and token difference that have relied on comparisons of presumably generic women with presumably generic men. Subordination does not take the form of protection, co-optation, and sexualization, as has been documented with White women vis-à-vis White men. Nor are token processes limited to relations between White women and White men (or even between African American women and White men). These findings not only call into question the generalizability of prior findings that have been blind to race or that have presumably controlled for race by holding it constant but also raise questions about the ways in which being White reflects racial influences in and of itself (Frankenberg 1993; Roman 1993).

Such analyses pave the way for future research to openly and systematically explore the impact of the privileges afforded by whiteness in a Eurocentric society (McIntosh 1992). Studies of subordination and token difference must be revisited with these considerations in mind. For example, African American women believe that White women and Black men can parlay their race and gender, respectively, to gain some acceptance, however tenuous, with dominant White men. Empirical data are needed to confirm if these perceptions accurately reflect the privileges afforded whiteness and maleness in American society and to detail how each affects our understanding of gendered relations.

Considering the present findings as they relate to strategies for social change, these African American women's stories support the idea that there are no "automatic concepts of connection" (Jordon 1985, 46) linking Black women with Black men and Black women with White women. It is paradoxical that solidarity must be forged with an unwavering recognition of difference (Lorber 1994; Lorde 1992). Furthermore, our analyses suggest that social change aimed at countering discrimination based on subordinated gender or subordinated race alone will continue to exclude Black women or, worse yet, use them as pawns in a competition for redress (Martin 1994). In addition, it will continue to perpetuate the false sense that only people of color experience race and only women of all colors experience gender, when in fact we all experience gender and race (as well as class, physical ability, sexual orientation, etc.) throughout our working and personal lives (Spelman 1988; West and Fenstermaker 1995). When Black women hastily are grouped with White women as women or with Black men as Blacks, and when Black women are not heeded as outsiders within, we believe that the subordination and token difference illustrated here will remain unchallenged.

Notes

1. These patterns for African American women parallel those for both a sample of 356 women responding to a survey sent to 1,300 women firefighters from Women in the Fire Service (WFS) (Armstrong et al. 1993), 91 percent of whom were White, and a sample of 39 White women who completed our survey in response to a call for volunteers we ran in the newsletter of WFS in 1995. Our smaller White sample parallels the 1990 sample along all demographic dimensions studied. WFS, incorporated in 1983, is a nonprofit network of and for women firefighters, mostly in the United States and Canada.

2. Our sample of African American women differed from our White sample along these three dimensions. White women averaged less training (11.39 weeks), $t(59) = 2.06$, $p = .04$. All White women had at least some college, and 51 percent held at least a B.A., χ^2 (2) = 7.10, $p = .03$. White women tended to work in settings with more Whites: 54 percent worked only with Whites; all but one worked with at least 65 percent Whites, χ^2 (2) = 32.41, $p < .001$, and 41 percent worked with at least one other White woman.

Although the above identifies some likely differences between Black and White women involving training, education, and racial composition of their firehouses, all firefighters used in these comparisons have voluntarily joined organizations emphasizing gender (e.g., WFS) or race (e.g., IABPFF). This differentiates them from the majority of women firefighters. Our sense is that many Black women feel that they are not well represented by either organization; for example, the head of the Black women's caucus of the IABPFF earned her title by being the only woman in the room when the idea of a women's caucus was discussed. In addition, not one African American woman responded to our call for volunteers sent to the 1,050 members (about 750 of whom are women in the fire service) of WFS through their monthly newsletter. Thus, we speculate that the African American women in our sample, generated mainly through IABPFF contacts and all but one of whom are members of the IABPFF, have strong racial identities that motivate them to join a racially focused organization. Thus, race may be an especially salient component in their reports of their experiences.

3. To measure this accurately, we asked respondents to complete a matrix by writing the initials of the members of "your current house and the other firefighters on your team" down the leftmost column, then noting the race (Black, White, other), sex, and approximate age (in decades) of each

individual in three other columns. Thus, each row described a specific individual. The first four rows were labeled for their department chief, battalion chief, captain, and lieutenant, and up to 13 remaining rows could be used to describe other firefighters.

4. Twenty-four items of the Working Environment Scale (Stokes, Riger, and Sullivan 1995) focused on both gender and racial climate. The composite of racial items summed agreement on five items: increasing number of minorities will lead to reverse discrimination, people treat minorities equally (reverse coded), racially demeaning joking would be criticized (reverse coded), racial discrimination is a big problem here, and those who complain about racial discrimination are not supported. Seven behavioral indicators of sexual harassment, defined by the U.S. Merit Systems Protection Board (1987), were used to measure incidence.

5. Two were mentored by White men and the remaining two by other Black women.

References

American statistical index. 1992. Bethesda, MD: Congressional Information Services.

Andersen, Margaret L., and Patricia Hill Collins. 1992. Preface. In *Race, class and gender: An anthology,* edited by Margaret L. Andersen and Patricia Hill Collins. Belmont, CA: Wadsworth.

Armstrong, Dee S., Brenda Berkman, Terese M. Floren, and Linda F. Willing. 1993. *The changing face of the fire service: A handbook on women in firefighting.* Washington, D.C.: U.S. Fire Administration.

Berger, Joseph, M. Hamit Fisek, Robert Z. Norman, and Morris Zelditch, Jr. 1977. *Status characteristics in social interaction: An expectation status approach.* New York: Elsevier.

Brooks, Linda, and Annette R. Perot. 1991. Reporting sexual harassment: Exploring a predictive model. *Psychology of Women Quarterly* 15:31–47.

Cannon, Lynn Weber, Elizabeth Higginbotham, and Marianne L. A. Leung. 1988. Race and class: Bias in qualitative research on women. *Gender & Society* 2:449–62.

Collins, Patricia Hill. 1986. Learning from the outsider within: The sociological significance of Black feminist thought. *Social Problems* 33:S14–S32.

Cox, Taylor, and Stella M. Nkomo. 1990. Invisible men and women: A status report on race as a variable in organization behavior research. *Journal of Organizational Behavior* 11:419–31.

DeAngelis, Tori. 1995. Firefighters' PTSD at dangerous levels. *APA Monitor,* February, 36.

de Beauvoir, Simone. 1952. *The second sex.* Translated by H. M. Parshley. New York: Knopf.

Dill, Bonnie Thornton. 1979. The dialectics of Black womanhood. *Signs: Journal of Women in Culture and Society* 4:543–55.

———. 1983. Race, class and gender. Prospects for an all-inclusive sisterhood. *Feminist Studies* 9:131–50.

Dugger, Karen. 1988. Social location and gender-role attitudes: A comparison of Black and White women. *Gender & Society* 2:425–48.

Epstein, Cynthia Fuchs. 1973. Positive effects of the double negative: Explaining the success of Black professional women. In *Changing women in a changing society,* edited by Joan Huber. Chicago: University of Chicago Press.

Essed, Philomena. 1991. *Understanding everyday racism: An interdisciplinary theory.* Newbury Park, CA: Sage.

Frankenberg, Ruth. 1993. *White women, race matters: The social construction of whiteness.* Minneapolis: University of Minnesota Press.

Giddings, Paula. 1984. *When and where I enter: The impact of Black women on race and sex in America.* New York: Morrow.

Gooley, Ruby Lee. 1989. The role of Black women in social change. *Western Journal of Black Studies* 13:165–72.

Greenhaus, Jeffrey H., Saroj Parasuraman, and Wayne M. Wormley. 1990. Effects of race on organizational experiences, job performance evaluations, and career outcomes. *Academy of Management Journal* 33:64–86.

Gruber, James E. 1992. A typology of personal and environmental sexual harassment: Research and policy implications for the 1990s. *Sex Roles* 26:447–64.

hooks, bell. 1984. *Feminist theory: From margin to center.* Boston: South End.

Hurtado, Aida. 1989. Relating to privilege: Seduction and rejection in the subordination of White women and women of color. *Signs: Journal of Women in Culture and Society* 14:833–55.

Jordon, June. 1985. Report from the Bahamas. In *On call: Political essays.* Boston: South End.

Kanter, Rosabeth Moss. 1977. *Men and women of the corporation.* New York: Basic Books.

King, Deborah K. 1988. Multiple jeopardy, multiple consciousness: The context of a Black feminist ideology. *Signs: Journal of Women in Culture and Society* 14:42–72.

L.A. fire training tape demeaning, women say. 1994. *The Milwaukee Journal,* 8 December, A2.

Landrine, Hope. 1985. Race × class stereotypes of women. *Sex Roles* 13:65–76.

Laws, Judith Long. 1975. The psychology of tokenism: An analysis. *Sex Roles* 1:51–67.

Lorber, Judith. 1994. *Paradoxes of gender.* New Haven, CT: Yale University Press.

Lorde, Audre. 1992. Age, race, class, and sex: Women redefining difference. In *Race, class, and gender: An anthology,* edited by Margaret L. Andersen and Patricia Hill Collins. Belmont, CA: Wadsworth.

MacCorquodale, Patricia, and Gary Jensen. 1993. Women in the law: Partners or tokens? *Gender & Society* 7:582–93.

Martin, Susan E. 1994. "Outsider within" the station house: The impact of race and gender on Black women police. *Social Problems* 41:383–400.

McCarl, Robert. 1985. *The District of Columbia Fire Fighters Project: A case study of occupational folklife.* Washington, D.C.: Smithsonian Institution Press.

McIntosh, Peggy. 1992. White privilege and male privilege: A personal account of coming to see correspondences through work in women's studies. In *Race, class, and gender: An anthology,* edited by Margaret L. Andersen and Patricia Hill Collins. Belmont, CA: Wadsworth.

Moraga, Cherrie, and Gloria Anzaldua, eds. 1981. *This bridge called my back: Writings by radical women of color.* Watertown, MA: Persephone.

Nkomo, Stella M. 1992. The emperor has no clothes: Rewriting race in organizations. *Academy of Management Review* 17:487–513.

Pak, Anita Wan-Ping, Kenneth L. Dion, and Karen K. Dion. 1991. Social psychological correlates of experienced discrimination: Test of the double jeopardy hypothesis. *International Journal of Intercultural Relations* 15:243–54.

Palmer, Phyllis Marynick. 1983. White women/Black women: The dualism of female identity and experience in the United States. *Feminist Studies* 9:151–70.

Poster, Winifred R. 1995. The challenges and promises of class and racial diversity in the women's movement: A study of two women's organizations. *Gender & Society* 9:659–79.

Reid, Pamela T. 1988. Racism and sexism: Comparison and conflicts. In *Eliminating racism: Profiles in controversy,* edited by Phyllis A. Katz and Dalmus A. Taylor. New York: Plenum.

Reskin, Barbara F. 1988. Bringing the men back in: Sex differentiation and the devaluation of women's work. *Gender & Society* 2:58–81.

Roman, Leslie G. 1993. White is a color! White defensiveness, postmodernism, and anti-racist pedagogy. In *Race identity and representation in education,* edited by Cameron McCarthy and Warren Crichlow. New York: Routledge & Kegan Paul.

Rosenberg, Janet, Harry Perlstadt, and William R. Phillips. 1993. Now that we are here: Discrimination, disparagement, and harassment at work and the experience of women lawyers. *Gender & Society* 7:415–33.

Segura, Denise A. 1992. Chicanas in white-collar jobs: You have to prove yourself more. *Sociological Perspectives* 35:163–82.

South, Scott J., Charles W. Bonjean, William T. Markham, and Judy Corder. 1982. Social structure and intergroup interaction: Men and women of the federal bureaucracy. *American Sociological Review* 47:587–99.

Spelman, Elizabeth V. 1988. *Inessential woman: Problems of exclusion in feminist thought.* Boston: Beacon.

Stokes, Joseph, Stephanie Riger, and Megan Sullivan. 1993. Measuring perceptions of the working environment for women in corporate settings. *Psychology of Women Quarterly* 19:533–50.

Tallichet, Suzanne E. 1995. Gendered relations in the mines and the division of labor underground. *Gender & Society* 9:697–711.

U.S. Merit Systems Protection Board. 1987. *Sexual harassment of federal workers: An update.* Washington, D.C.: Government Printing Office.

West, Candace, and Sarah Fenstermaker. 1995. Doing difference. *Gender & Society* 9:8–37.

Women in the Fire Service. 1991. Brochure. [Available from WFS, P.O. Box 5446, Madison, WI 53705]

Yoder, Janice D. 1991. Rethinking tokenism: Looking beyond numbers. *Gender & Society* 5:178–92.

———. 1994. Looking beyond numbers: The effects of gender status, job prestige, and occupational gender-typing on tokenism outcomes. *Social Psychology Quarterly* 57:150–59.

Yoder, Janice D., Jerome Adams, and Howard T. Prince. 1983. The price of a token. *Journal of Political and Military Sociology* 11:325–37.

Yoder, Janice D., and Arnold S. Kahn. 1993. Working toward an inclusive psychology of women. *American Psychologist* 48:846–50.

Zimmer, Lynn. 1988. Tokenism and women in the workplace: The limits of gender-neutral theory. *Social Problems* 35:64–77.

Zinn, Maxine Baca, Lynn Weber Cannon, Elizabeth Higginbotham, and Bonnie Thornton Dill. 1986. The costs of exclusionary practices in women's studies. *Signs: Journal of Women in Culture and Society* 11:290–303.

Questions for Thought

1. The researchers report that Black women firefighters experienced "subordination through exclusion." What does this concept mean? What behaviors in the firehouse conveyed this theme of exclusion?

2. African American women firefighters were different from three groups of co-workers: White men, Black men, and White women. Describe their relations with co-workers from each of these groups.

3. The authors emphasize that the effects of race and gender are not additive, but rather "omnirelevant and inseparable." Explain and illustrate what this means.

4. How might the experiences of these African American women firefighters be similar to or different from the experiences of the first White women to be hired in all-male law firms or the first Black man to become an astronaut in the predominantly White U.S. space program?

5. How did Yoder and Aniakudo recruit the participants in their study? What are possible advantages and limitations of their sample?

6. This study focused on the experiences and perceptions of Black women firefighters. The researchers offer hints that the women's co-workers may have interpreted interactions in the firehouse differently than the Black women did, for instance, by perceiving the Black women as withdrawing from other co-workers. Discuss possible ways in which White women, White men, and Black men may have had different perspectives on their interactions with Black women in the firehouse.

7. Suggest three ways to reduce the exclusion felt on the job by African American women firefighters.

Meanings of Political Participation Among Black and White Women
Political Identity and Social Responsibility

Elizabeth R. Cole

Abigail J. Stewart

Will the campus activists of today be more politically involved than their peers at age 40? In this study Cole and Stewart examine the impact that the women's movement and the civil rights movement of the 1960s had on the political lives of Black and White women 20 years later. The researchers describe Black and White college women's involvement with feminist and civil rights activities, and assess women's beliefs about social responsibility, their political identity, and other attitudes relevant to political involvement. The authors find that the specific factors that encouraged political involvement at midlife differed for Black and White women.

This study examined the correlates of midlife political participation among 64 Black and 107 White women of the college classes of 1967–1973. Compared with White women, Black women scored higher on political participation, generativity, power discontent, and politicization. Factor analysis of personality and political attitude variables yielded three factors labeled *Political Identity, Power Discontent,* and *Social Responsibility.* Adult political participation was regressed on level of student activism and index scores of political identity, power discontent, and social responsibility. For both racial groups, social responsibility was associated with midlife political participation. For White women, political identity was also related; for Black women, student activism bore a significant relationship. The findings suggest that Black and White women's historical and political contexts imbued their political activities with different meanings.

Adapted from *Journal of Personality and Social Psychology,* 1996, *71,* 130–140. Copyright 1996 by the American Psychological Association, Inc. Used by permission.

During the late 1960s and the early 1970s, three social movements simultaneously developed and gained momentum in the United States: resistance against the war in Vietnam; the women's liberation movement; and the Black power movement, which grew out of the civil rights movement of the 1950s and 1960s. The goals and tactics of these latter two movements shared much in common: Each aimed to redefine the roles and broaden the privileges of historically disadvantaged groups and worked to accomplish these ends through the redefinition of the constituent groups' identities and political consciousness (Carroll, 1989; Cohen, 1985; Morris, Hatchett, & Brown, 1989). The emphasis on the transformation of the identity and consciousness of individual group members is well captured by each of the movements' best known slogans: The Black power exhortation that "Black is beautiful" rejects a conferred stigmatized racial identity, whereas the feminist assertion that "the personal is political" recasts women's private experiences within the traditional family in terms of public relations of power.

Given the focus of both the women's movement and the civil rights movement on issues of group identity, it might be expected that these movements would have had different meanings and hence different long-term impact for individuals of different social groups. Much of the research on these two movements has been framed theoretically by Mannheim's (1928/1952) essay on generations (e.g., Braungart & Braungart, 1990; Jennings, 1987), which argued that periods of youth movement result from the combined effects of the circumstances of the historical moment in which a cohort comes of age, the shared cultural experiences of the cohort, and the particular demographic characteristics of the cohort. Although the members of a generation may be influenced by the same historical events, Mannheim (1928/1952) suggested that within any birth cohort there are subgroups, or "generation units [who] work up the material of their common experiences in different specific ways" (p. 304). Thus, for example, Stewart and Healy (1989) pointed to the difference in the meaning of the Vietnam War for those who fought it and those who opposed it (despite the fact that it was laden with meaning for both groups). Although several researchers have explored the long-term impact of the social movements of this era on those who participated as compared with those who did not (e.g., Abramowitz & Nassi, 1981; Fendrich, 1974, 1976, 1977; Franz & McClelland, 1994; Hoge & Ankney, 1982; Jennings, 1987; Nassi, 1981; Nassi & Abramowitz, 1979), little of this research has addressed the unique experiences of women or explored the differential effect of participation in these movements on the later lives of Black and White protesters. The present study addressed these gaps in the literature, exploring the ways in which social movements, coinciding with personal development, may be related to differences in political belief and involvement for members of divergent subcultures with distinct political statuses.

Student Activism Among Women and African Americans

Sherkat and Blocker (1994) found that women were relatively underrepresented among movement activists of this era; however, this difference was largely accounted for by differences in gender socialization (including political efficacy and religiosity) and lower rates of college attendance. In contrast, studies based on interviews with women who were active (Cable, 1992; Thorne, 1975) suggest that many women were dissuaded from participation by being relegated to the most trivial and menial tasks by the mostly male leadership. Longitudinal research that followed the activists into adulthood suggests that despite the fact that women faced gender discrimination even within liberatory social movements, participation in the movements of this era had a long-term impact on both the later political participation and personal development of the women who were activists.

Franz and McClelland (1994) found that at 41 years of age, women who were activists as students seemed better adapted than did their male activist peers, both in terms of occupational status and levels of strain reported; they speculated that the women's movement empowered women and increased their opportunities for satisfying work lives. McAdam (1992) followed up applicants to the "Freedom Summer" campaign of 1964, a program in which college students from Northern states traveled to Mississippi to register Black voters and bring national attention to the denial of civil rights in the South. McAdam found that women were less likely than men to participate in the program, in part because of gender discrimination in the application process. However, among those who did participate, the experience was deeply meaningful. Indeed, despite the fact that participation in the program was predictive of later activism for men but not for women, women described the experience as more personally significant than did men. McAdam attributed the source of this discrepancy to the different historical meaning of Freedom Summer for men and women. Because the development of the women's movement subsequent to the Freedom Summer program heightened the women's identities as activists, they accorded their Freedom Summer experience greater personal significance in their retrospective biographical accounts than did their male peers. Braungart and Braungart's (1991) findings based on interviews with women who had been active in both left- and right-wing organizations during the 1960s similarly suggest that the movements had a long-term impact on women's commitment to women's political concerns; they observed that, in addition to pursuing the ideological commitments of their youth, many of the former activists from both groups had also become active in women's issues.

Little research has explored racial differences in the impact of the social movements of this era. Fendrich (1976, 1977) compared a sample of White male students from the early civil rights era with a contemporaneous sample of male African American alumni from the same school 10 years after graduation. He found that variance in the degree of student activism predicted later leftist attitudes and political behavior among both the Black and White alumni. However, Fendrich (1976) also found that student activism was a stronger predictor of adult participation in leftist politics for White men than for Black men.

Taken together, these few studies suggest that civil rights activism in the 1960s bears a weaker relationship to adult political participation for women and for African Americans than it does for White men in this cohort; however, this is not because women were relatively unaffected by their experience. On the contrary, we argue that because women and African Americans bore a different, and more direct, relationship to the civil rights and women's movements, variables other than student activism might be equally important in predicting their continued participation later in life.

Predicting Midlife Political Participation

We expected that White women who graduated from college in the late 1960s would view the women's movement as having had a strong effect on their lives and that the civil rights movement would have been significant as well (see evidence from another similar sample presented in Stewart & Healy, 1989). In contrast, because the leadership of the women's movement was dominated by White women and much of the movement's energy focused on issues of much greater interest to middle-class White women than to any other group (e.g., the critique of the middle-class domestic role of housewife), we expected that Black women graduating from college during this same era would view the women's movement as having been a less important influence. Instead, because of the importance of the civil rights movement to African Americans in general (see Schuman & Scott, 1989), we expected that Black women would perceive this series of events as having been an important influence on their later lives. We anticipated that for both groups, though, involvement in political activity in late adolescence would be related to their identities and later lives.

Two separate lines of theory and research suggest that student movements of the 1960s that focused on gaining rights for women and African Americans would strongly affect, or politicize, the identities of members of those groups who were on college campuses at that time. First, theory and research in social psychology indicate that a central mechanism through which social movements mobilize is the creation of a collective identity that not only enlarges individual identity but also connects the participant to the social group, cementing his or her commitment (Gamson, 1992). When individuals share a common identity, and hence a sense of common fate with a group, they act to protect group interests (Gurin & Townsend, 1986). Theory and research that specifically address the women's movement and the civil rights–Black power movement similarly emphasize the centrality of collective identity. Cross (1991) observed that the Black power phase of the Black social movement attempted to transform the stigmatized Black identity into a new one based on pride in African American culture and experience; he argued that this pattern of transformation characterizes the development of individual Black identity as well (this premise has been extensively tested empirically; see Helms, 1993; Ponterotto & Wise, 1987). More generally, Cohen (1985) argued that recent political struggles, notably feminism, differ from earlier forms of leftist movement in that they invoke an activist identity that shapes and is shaped by participants' own experiences of group identity, rather than being strictly based on class membership (see also Mueller, 1987).

Second, research based on a model of life span development suggests that the period of late adolescence and young adulthood is a critical time for the development of identity, including the commitment to values, ideologies, and groups. Stewart and Healy (1986, 1989) suggested that events of historical significance experienced during this period are likely to affect cohort members' developing identities. Speaking specifically of this cohort, Erikson (1968b) argued that the student movements represented an attempt by that generation to develop its own ideology and rituals of passage, making the connection between identity development, social change, and political participation explicit. This premise found empirical support in Duncan and Agronick's (1995) longitudinal analyses based on women of this cohort. They found that women who actively explored different identities available at age 21 (i.e., who were classified in the stages of identity achievement and identity moratorium) rated the women's movement as being more personally meaningful at midlife. Similarly, Jennings's (1987) study of the "protest generation" found evidence both for the persistence of the hypothesized "cohort" definition through the life course and for a particularly strong shaping effect of cohort or generation for those who participated in student activism. This influence is thought to be quite general and diffuse, including and integrating particular attitudes and stances toward social life (e.g., social dominance orientation; see Prato, Sidanius, Stallworth, & Malle, 1994; Sidanius, Prato, & Bobo, 1994).

We use the term *political identity* to describe a pattern of beliefs related to the social and structural relationships that connect the individual to social groups: specifically, that human existence is interconnected, that disadvantaged groups are limited by systemic obstacles rather than individual shortcomings, that the political realm is personally relevant and meaningful, and that collective actions are the best responses to social problems. Because college-educated Black women of this cohort were expected to be powerfully influenced by both the civil rights and women's movements, whereas White women were expected to be more strongly influenced by the women's movement, we hypothesized that Black women would show a higher level of political identity but that political identity would be associated with midlife political activism for both groups.

Power discontent, or dissatisfaction with the power one's group holds relative to other groups, provides an affective component to political participation. This construct taps the individual's view of her own personal stake in political action and was hypothesized to be related to level of midlife political involvement. We anticipated that Black women would have higher levels of power discontent than White women because they suffer both race- and gender-based disadvantages (consistent with the racial differences found by Gurin, Miller, & Gurin, 1980) but that power discontent would play a similar role for both groups of women in motivating political participation. Both Gurin and Townsend's (1986) group consciousness model and Crosby's (1976, 1982) and others' (e.g., Gurr, 1968, 1970; Runciman, 1966) relative deprivation models assume that a sense of grievance is an important precondition for political mobilization.

The construct of power discontent, like much of the traditional research on social movement participation, is based on a conceptualization of participants as being motivated primarily by their own personal material interests. However, more recently, scholars have argued that individuals profit from movement participation not only through the tangible achievements won but also in terms of the development of a shared collective identity, and this felt connection to others may motivate individuals to act on behalf of group interests (Gamson, 1992). This observation suggests that a final aspect of political participation concerns the desire to act individually for the benefit of the larger group and the belief in one's own ability to do so effectively; we label this construct *social responsibility.*

The notion of social responsibility was addressed empirically in a few articles during the 1950s and 1960s; however, recent research on this topic has been scant except in discussions of the related notions of generativity (for exceptions, see

Chebat, 1986; Witt, 1990). Early research by Gogh, McClosky, and Meehl (1952) and by Berkowitz and Lutterman (1968) painted a distinctive portrait of the socially responsible personality. Such people are concerned with social and moral issues, are committed to working for the good of groups rather than just for personal gain, and have a sense of trust in society in general. In this way, they may be considered generative, which is in part defined by a "belief in the species, concern for the next generation, [and the] cultural demand" that individuals contribute their resources to the long-term societal good (McAdams & de St. Aubin, 1992, p. 1004). Socially responsible people demonstrate a form of personal efficacy in the public realm that Gogh et al. (1952) characterized as "greater poise, assurance and personal security" (p. 77). Perhaps most importantly, they may be described as having a strong sense of community; they are active participants in their communities, representing the antithesis of the alienated citizen. In addition, these researchers speculated that socially responsible individuals are likely to be highly conventional, by virtue of their respect for and attention to communally held social values and norms. However, they recognized that other forms of social responsibility might exist, in particular one characterized by the willingness to participate in principled dissent, seen in the examples of Abraham Lincoln and Mahatma Gandhi (Berkowitz & Lutterman, 1968).

Social responsibility is related to the Eriksonian (Erikson, 1963) concept of generativity, particularly as it may be expressed in political activity. Generativity is the desire to make a lasting contribution to ensure the well-being of future generations, which at midlife would provide a developmental press to act politically, particularly for those who had made political and ideological commitments in youth. Research in the field of political science suggests that political activity does increase throughout the adult life span, peaking at midlife (Conway, 1985; Milbrath & Goel, 1982). This pattern is largely attributed to the decreased demands of family life that may be experienced during this period. Similarly, Flacks (1988) argued that people participate politically to the extent that such activities may be negotiated with the responsibilities of daily life. However, these mundane concerns are not incongruent with the argument that generative concern may press individuals to act politically: Such relaxation of the everyday demands of family life may allow individuals to consider what their contributions to future generations will be (McAdams, 1988) and what they can create that will "outlive the self" (Kotre, 1984). Indeed, research has demonstrated that midlife adults express higher levels of generative concern than do either older or younger respondents (McAdams, de St. Aubin, & Logan, 1992).

In the present study, we operationalized social responsibility to include the elements of political efficacy, sense of community, and generativity; we hypothesized that this measure would be related to higher levels of political activism for both White and African American women. Because there is considerable theoretical and empirical literature linking these constructs to midlife personality in general (see, e.g., Erikson, 1968a; Haan, 1989; Mitchell & Helson, 1990; Neugarten, 1968)—although there is virtually no empirical evidence from Black samples—we did not anticipate racial differences.

This study tested the following hypotheses:

Hypothesis 1:   At midlife, Black women who were young adults during the social movements of the late 1960s and the early 1970s will report that the civil rights movement had a larger impact on their lives than did the women's movement. Conversely, we expect that White women of this cohort will endorse the women's movement as having had a greater impact on their subsequent lives than did the civil rights movement.

Hypothesis 2: Level of political participation at midlife will be predicted by student activism for both Black and White women.

Hypothesis 3: High scores on measures tapping the construct of political identity will be associated with midlife political participation in women of both racial groups.

Hypothesis 4: Black women will endorse higher levels of power discontent than will White women; however, power discontent will be associated with midlife political participation for both groups.

Hypothesis 5: Social responsibility will be related to midlife political participation for both Black and White women.

Method

Participants

The study was based on responses to mailed questionnaires administered to two samples of women who were alumnae of the University of Michigan. The measures discussed here were embedded in a larger questionnaire that included items pertaining to respondents' occupational and family history, health, and life satisfaction; thus, the questionnaire was not obviously focused on political attitudes and behavior.

First, the measures discussed here were administered to the White women in the sample as part of the fourth wave of the Women's Life Paths Study, a longitudinal study initiated in 1967 by Tangri (1969). Current addresses for the alumnae were obtained with assistance from the University of Michigan's alumni association. Of the original 200 women in the sample, 107 participated in this wave. Three of the original sample members had died, and 48 were no longer locatable; thus, the response rate from those receiving the questionnaire was 72%. Follow-up respondents in this wave did not differ from nonrespondents from the initial sample on six demographic variables available from the 1967 waves: levels of mothers' and fathers' education, number of siblings, parents' income, mothers' employment, and family religion.

Because the original longitudinal sample did not include any African Americans, 64 African American participants from the same era were recruited through the assistance of the alumni association, including a solicitation in the university's Black alumni newsletter. Because of the method of recruitment, there was no way to compute a response rate analogous to that for the longitudinal sample. Women who graduated between 1967 and 1973 were included in the sample, because substantial numbers of Black women were recruited to the university only beginning in 1970. The data were collected through questionnaires mailed to the respondents in the fall of 1992.

Preliminary analyses indicated that the Black and White samples were comparable on most demographic variables. There were no significant differences between the groups' mean levels of education, personal income, and number of children. However, the White women in the sample were more likely to be married or living with a partner (84% for the White women vs. 56% for the Black women), $\chi^2(1, N = 166) = 15.90, p < .01$. White women were significantly older ($M = 47.91$ years, $SD = 0.43$ years), than Black women ($M = 44.52$ years, $SD = 2.49$ years) $F(1, 166) = 185.51, p < .001$, but the difference was not large. Because of the discrepancies between the two samples on the mean and the variance of age, we performed analyses to determine whether there were significant age differences within the African American sample on the variables of interest; t tests comparing older and younger African American women (based on a median split) revealed no significant differences in their mean scores on student activism, adult political participation, political identity, power discontent, and social responsibility. Thus, the African American sample was treated as a single cohort.

Measures

Impact of the Movements   To assess racial differences in experiences of the civil rights and women's movements, we asked respondents whether they had participated in each movement and to rate the impact of these movements on their lives on a scale ranging from 1 (*very little*) to 5 (*very much*).

Student Activism and Adult Political Participation   Student activism and adult political participation were measured as continuous variables on the basis of self-reports of the frequency with which respondents engaged in specific political behaviors. The scale was developed by Fendrich and Lovoy (1988), who found that former civil rights activists and student government leaders reported higher levels of political involvement on this measure than did their less active classmates 10 years after graduation.

For the measure of student activism, we asked respondents how often as college students they had engaged in each of nine different political behaviors that Fendrich and Lovoy (1988) characterized as protest and community activism. They responded on a 4-point scale ranging from 0 (*never*) to 3 (*regularly*). Responses were summed and divided by the number of items; therefore, scores ranged from 0 to 3. The behaviors were as follows: joined in a protest march, attended protest meetings, participated in any form of political activity that could lead to arrest, was a candidate for office, worked with others on local problems, formed a group to work on local problems, contacted local officials on social issues, contacted a local state or federal official about a particular personal problem, and went with a group to protest to a public official. Because this measure was administered retrospectively, we calculated its correlation with an item administered to the White sample in 1970 measuring exposure to the women's movement. The item asked how they had "heard about the new women's rights movement." Responses ranged in proximity to the movement: from a low score of 1 (*through the media*) to high scores of 4 (*attended activities*) and 5 (*had helped organize for the movement*). This item was treated as a continuous variable assessing relative proximity of exposure to and involvement in the women's movement; its correlation with student activism was .37 ($N = 85$, $p \leq .001$). This single item served only as a proxy for a measure of involvement; however, it lent some support to the validity of the retrospective measure of student activism.

Adult political participation was defined as encompassing a wider array of behaviors, including participation in the electoral process, and was measured similarly using an expanded list of 17 political behaviors. All of the behaviors listed above were included in this measure as well as items tapping party and campaign work (e.g., "took an active part in a political campaign" and "participated in a political party between elections") and political communication (e.g., "kept informed about politics" and "sent messages to a political leader when they were doing well or poorly"). Respondents were asked to indicate how often they had engaged in each type of behavior during the past 2 years. As before, responses were summed and divided by the number of items. Internal consistency reliability (α) for the student activism measure was .85; for the adult political participation index, it was .87.

Political Identity   Political identity was conceptualized as the belief that the political realm is personally relevant and meaningful, human existence is interconnected, collective actions are the best responses to social problems, and disadvantaged groups are limited by systemic obstacles rather than individual shortcomings. Five measures were used to operationalize this construct.

Political Salience   Political salience was assessed using a measure adapted from Stewart and Healy's (1989) study, in which respondents were asked to judge how personally meaningful (1 = *not at all*, 2 = *somewhat*, 3 = *very*) they found each of nine historical events of the 20th century, such as the Vietnam War and the freeing of Nelson Mandela. The reliability of this nine-item scale was .76.

Collective Orientation   Collective orientation was measured using a scale adapted from studies by Lykes (1984) and by Gurin et al. (1980) to measure the extent to which the respondents believed that human existence is essentially relational, rather than individualistic (Lykes, 1984). Seven items, stated either as proverbs (e.g., "'paddle your own canoe' is a good principle to live by") or as generalized ideas about human nature and existence (e.g., "if you think about life, you realize that each person is a separate individual leading his or her own individual life"), were rated on 7-point scales (1 = *strongly disagree*, 7 = *strongly agree*). Two items were taken from the 1972 National Election Study (Gurin et al., 1980); these assessed agreement with collective action as a strategy to improve the social and political situation of Blacks and women. The reliability of the resulting nine-item measure was .70.

System Blame   Two measures of system blame, one pertaining to race and the other to sex, developed by Gurin et al. (1980), gauged the extent to which respondents located the cause of social inequalities within social and political systems, rather than within individuals (on 7-point Likert-type scales). Seven items measured system blame with respect to inequities experienced by women ($\alpha = .72$); eight items assessed system blame with respect to inequities faced by Blacks ($\alpha = .76$).

Left–Right Ideology   Finally, left–right ideology, the position on the left–right political continuum, was rated by respondents on a 6-point scale ranging from *very conservative* to *radical*. Because the movements under study were generally associated with "left" political attitudes (see Jennings, 1987), women's endorsement of these political attitudes is an important component of their politicization by these events. High scores corresponded to a liberal or leftist political orientation; low scores indicated more conservative views.

Power Discontent   An affective sense of relative deprivation, or grievance, was expected to be related to political involvement. This component was operationalized as power discontent and was assessed using items developed by Gurin et al. (1980). Respondents were asked to judge the relative amount of influence in American life and politics held by various groups. Specifically, they were asked to judge the relative power held by women in general (gender-based) and by women of their own racial group (race- and gender-based) on a scale ranging from 1 (*low discontent*) to 5 (*high discontent*).

Social Responsibility   Social responsibility was conceptualized as including the generative desire to improve the world for future generations as well as a sense of political efficacy (or empowerment) and a feeling of connection to a community. A six-item version of the Loyola Generativity scale (McAdams & de St. Aubin, 1992; Nakagawa, 1992) was administered to measure generativity. Respondents were asked to rate their agreement with the six items on 7-point scales. Items tapped generative concern with making a contribution that extended beyond the self through teaching ("I have important skills that I try to teach others"), caring for future generations ("if I were unable to have children of my own, I would like to adopt children"), or through the products of one's creative endeavors ("I have made and created things that have had an impact on other people"). Internal consistency reliability of this scale was .70.

Internal Political Efficacy   Internal political efficacy, the sense that the individual can successfully affect the political system relative to the ability of other individuals to do so, was measured using a scale developed by Craig and Maggiotto (1982). The five-item measure asked participants to rate their agreement with statements like "I feel like I could do as good a job in public office as most of the politicians we elect." They responded on scales ranging from 1 (*strongly disagree*) to 7 (*strongly agree*). The internal consistency of the measure was .76.

Sense of Community   Sense of community, encompassing feelings of community attachment and belongingness, was chosen to capture the communal aspects of social responsibility and was measured using a scale developed by Bachrach and Zautra (1985). Respondents were asked to select the community that was most important to them and to rate eight attitudes toward this community on a 7-point scale ranging from 1 (*not at all*) to 7 (*very much*). Items concerned the sense of community belongingness, connection, and contentment as well as the feeling that one shares commonalities with others in the community. Reliability for the eight items was .84.

Table 1 ▦ **Mean Levels of Participation in Political Movements of the 1960s and 1970s, by Race**

Variable	White women		Black women		Significance of differences
	Mean	%	Mean	%	
Participated in women's movement		61		42	$\chi^2(1, N = 167) = 5.67^{**}$
Effect of women's movement	3.4		3.3		$F(1, 164) = 0.40, ns$
Participated in civil rights movement		48		92	$\chi^2(1, N = 168) = 33.88^{***}$
Effect of civil rights movement	2.9		4.7		$F(1, 165) = 108.54^{***}$
Level of student activism	0.3		1.2		$F(1, 157) = 93.17^{***}$
Level of midlife activism	0.9		1.1		$F(1, 160) = 4.11^{*}$

$^{*}p < .05$ $^{**}p < .01$ $^{***}p < .001$

Results

First, we consider evidence that the proposed predictor variables did assess the underlying constructs: political identity, social responsibility, and power discontent. Next, we examine evidence for racial differences in political activism and in the measures of personality, attitudes, and political identity. Finally, we present the pattern of relationships between the hypothesized predictors and midlife political participation. . . .

Racial Differences in Political Activism and Predictors

The results of analyses pertaining to student activism and participation in the civil rights and women's movements are presented in Table 1. Beginning with participation in the movements, a chi-square analysis showed that significantly more White women than Black women participated in the women's movement; however, a *t* test indicated that the groups rated the effect of the movement on their lives as equally important. Not surprisingly, significantly more Black women reported having participated in the civil rights movement than did their White counterparts; similarly, Black women rated the movement as having had a greater effect on their lives.

T tests showed that compared with their White classmates, Black women participated in more student activism and reported higher rates of midlife political participation; however, at midlife, the difference in their rates of participation had narrowed.

Multivariate analyses of variance assessed racial differences in political identity, power discontent, and social responsibility. As is shown in Table 2, the hypothesized racial differences in political identity and power discontent were revealed; also as hypothesized, there was no racial difference in social responsibility. All of the indicators of political identity were significantly different in the two groups, except for collective orientation.

Table 2   Multivariate Analyses of Variance on Political Identity, Power Discontent, and Social Responsibility

| | Mean score | | | |
	White women	Black women	F	p
Variable				
Political identity				
Political salience	1.95	2.14	8.41	.004
Collective orientation	−0.77	−0.21	0.40	ns
System blame: Sex	19.81	21.66	5.57	.02
System blame: Race	20.57	22.64	6.09	.02
Left–right ideology	3.25	3.58	4.72	.03
Total			2.73	.02
Power discontent				
Women in general	4.28	4.21	0.35	ns
Women of own race	4.07	4.46	8.70	.004
Total			6.65	.002
Social responsibility				
Generativity	−0.59	0.48	2.77	.10
Sense of community	45.93	46.43	0.17	ns
Political efficacy	21.80	23.13	2.36	ns
Total			1.28	ns

Note. Scores for collective orientation and generativity are aggregates of standard-scored items, with means of 0 and standard deviations of 1.

On power discontent, the measure of within-race power discontent showed a racial difference (with Black women endorsing higher discontent with the power of their own group than did White women); there was no racial difference for the measure of discontent with the power of women in general. It should be noted that both groups reported high levels of both types of discontent. . . .

Correlates of Midlife Political Participation

Table 3 presents the simple correlations of student activism and the index scores of political identity, power discontent, and social responsibility with midlife political participation for the two samples separately by race. For both groups, student activism and midlife social responsibility were significantly and positively correlated with midlife political participation; for the White women, political identity was also a significant positive correlate.

Midlife political participation was regressed on level of student activism and the index scores of political identity, power discontent, and social responsibility, separately by race. These results are presented in Table 3 as well.

Table 3 ▨ **Multiple Regression Analysis of Active Political Participation at Midlife, by Race**

Variable[a]	White women[a] (n = 101)		Black women[b] (n = 61)	
	r	β	r	β
Level of student activism	.23*	.00	.50***	.47***
Political identity	.43***	.38**	.04	−.03
Power discontent	−.05	−.13	−.16	−.04
Social responsibility	.41***	.31**	.37**	.33**

Note. All variables were entered simultaneously. Ns are based on pairwise deletion of missing data.
[a]$R^2 = .29$; $F(4, 78) = 8.10$, $p \leq .001$.   [b]$R^2 = .36$; $F(4, 45) = 6.46$, $p \leq .001$.
*$p \leq .05$ **$p \leq .01$ ***$p \leq .001$

For White women, the multivariate model explained 29% of the variance in midlife political participation. Political identity and social responsibility were significantly related to midlife activism. Note that although level of student activism was significantly and positively correlated with midlife activism, when all variables were included in the model, student activism was not a significant predictor of political participation at midlife.

For Black women, this model predicted 36% of the variance in midlife political participation. For this group, level of student activism and social responsibility were significantly related to midlife political involvement. Note that for Black women, political identity was not significantly associated with midlife activism in the bivariate correlation nor in the multivariate model.

Discussion

These findings support the notion that Black and White women of this generation were similarly affected by some historical events of this era but there were important differences between them as well. Although White women were more likely to have participated in the women's movement (as expected), both groups rated the women's movement as having had a similar, moderate impact on their lives. As predicted, Black women were more likely to have participated in the civil rights movement and rated the movement as having had a much stronger impact on their lives than did White women. The finding that Black women were similar to their White counterparts on measures of the impact of the women's movement and power discontent with respect to sex is particularly noteworthy. It contradicts the popular perception that Black women are relatively unconcerned about gender issues because of their overriding concern with racial injustice. It supports, instead, the contention that African American women have a "multiple (political) consciousness" corresponding to the "multiple jeopardy" they experience as members of two relatively disempowered groups (King, 1988).

For both racial groups, the construct of social responsibility, including midlife generativity, contributed to political involvement, independent of its relationship to political identity. The multivariate analysis suggests that within both racial groups, those who are politically active at midlife are those who are empowered by a sense of personal efficacy to create change, who feel a strong connection to the communities to which they belong, and who are concerned with making a lasting contribution to future generations. This finding casts both midlife political involvement and its student antecedent in a positive light, in contrast to the stereotype of activists as malcontents (see, e.g., Rothman & Lichter, 1982).

As expected, political identity showed a significant relationship to White women's midlife political involvement. However, for Black women, the index score based on the political identity variables was not related to midlife political activism. This finding should not be interpreted as suggesting that Black women in the sample were not politically conscious; indeed, they scored significantly higher than their White counterparts on all but one of the political identity variables. Rather, political identity did not distinguish the activists from the less active among Black women. Black women's higher endorsement of historical events as personally meaningful and their more homogeneous scores on the political identity variables of political salience and system blame with respect to race suggest that, in general, Black women in the sample shared a relatively politicized identity or worldview.

Unexpectedly, level of involvement in student activism was not a significant predictor of White women's midlife political participation, although it was predictive of Black women's political involvement later in life. Considered together with the findings concerning political identity, this suggests that among White women, the politically active were discernible from their less active peers by their level of politicization; among Black women, those who were active politically were characterized by their continuity of participation over time, rather than by a distinctive ideology.

For both groups, power discontent (the sense of personal grievance on behalf of one's group) was unrelated to midlife political participation, perhaps partly because power discontent was generally so high within the sample; the average rating for both racial groups on both types of discontent was more than 4 on a 5-point scale. It is important, though, that power discontent was not related to midlife political participation, because it supports Crosby's argument that a sense of collective grievance is often not readily or directly translated into political action (see especially Crosby, Pufall, Snyder, O'Connell, & Whalen, 1989).

We cannot assume that the findings of this study can be readily generalized to Black and White women at other places and in other times. Nevertheless, the findings presented here have important implications for thinking about the meaning of Black and White women's political involvement and thought and may serve as an important source of hypotheses for future study. The findings suggest not only that Black and White women may have different ideological perspectives on race and gender politics but also that ideology itself may have a different relationship to political participation for Black and White women. This may be due, in part, to the ways in which Black and White women experienced the significant movements of this era, particularly the civil rights movement and the women's movement.

The women's movement emphasized the importance of transformation of ideology, making consciousness raising a principal part of its practice (Popkin, 1990). Hence, it is not surprising that among White women in the sample, political identity was significantly related to midlife political participation, independent of its correlation with earlier political activism during the college years. In contrast, although the Black power movement of the late 1960s emphasized the importance of consciousness raising, the movement was actually an outgrowth or later phase of the civil rights movement (Morris et al., 1989), which historians view as the expression of a longstanding shared culture of ideological and, at times, behavioral resistance among African Americans (Harding, 1991). In this cultural context, ideology may not be the most important determinant of political involvement; instead, cultural norms may support continued commitment to political participation. Many Black feminist theorists have called for work to deepen our understanding of the distinctive ideology of African American women (King, 1988; Robinson, 1987); this study underscores the importance of this line of research.

These findings also suggest that greater study of the relationship between political activism and social responsibility in women is warranted. Some feminist scholars have argued that women are predisposed to work to maintain peace and to use the tactics of nonviolent action as a natural extension of the work that they do within families; this could be understood as a form of social responsibility, particularly in its generative aspects (Elshtain, 1982; Ruddick, 1985). However, others have argued that this view is limiting in its essentialism (Lott, 1990); moreover, the diversity of political positions taken by women belies this argument (Tilley & Gurin, 1990). Instead, the relationship between women's social responsibility and political activism might be better understood within particular social and historical contexts. For example, Kerber (1980) argued that the concept of "republican motherhood" arose in the earliest years of the American republic, specifying that women's political role in the new polis was to educate their sons to perform as virtuous and public-spirited citizens.

Research in disciplines outside of psychology supports the contention that political participation among African Americans may be related to a sense of social responsibility. First, several African American feminist theorists have posited that social responsibility is a key component of Black women's activism (e.g., Collins, 1990; hooks, 1984). They have conceptualized African American women's activism as an extension of the daily resistance that was historically necessary to ensure the wellbeing of their families under oppressive conditions. Thus, Black women's activism is grounded in their desire to ensure the survival of their immediate and extended families. Second, the idea that all striving represents a struggle toward the larger goal of racial uplift (Giddings, 1984), long cultivated in Black communities, is inherently generative. In this context, political activism can easily be understood and experienced as generative behavior. Finally, within African American culture generally and within Black activist cultures particularly, the community has popularly been viewed as a kind of extended family (see Harding, 1991); thus, Black women may be especially likely to view political activity as an appropriate domain of generative endeavor.

Although there is less theoretical work explicitly addressing the ways in which race might shape the political values of White women, a number of scholars have written about women in general in terms that apply to contemporary White women in particular. For example, in discussing gender differences in political participation, Jennings (1979) commented that "the rearing of the young is still predominantly the prescriptive and descriptive province of mothers. Becoming involved in the politics of education serves as an extension of this primary role" (p. 769). The traditional role for women as homemakers and culture bearers may, then, have permitted women to gradually become politicized through work taken on at first as part of their roles as mothers, on behalf of their own children. Consistent with this notion, Franz and McClelland (1994) found that at age 31, White women who had been active in social movements of the 1960s rated "the importance of teaching children the value of being free to develop one's full potential" (p. 203) more highly than did their less active peers. Viewing the question of the role of gender socialization in shaping political participation more broadly, Constantini and Craik (1972) commented that political activism in women (implicitly or predominantly White) is experienced as service to others and a "labor of love" whereas it is experienced by men as a "vehicle for personal enhancement and career advancement" (pp. 234–235).

In short, social responsibility played an important role in both Black and White women's midlife political participation, but cultural and other factors may have operated differently to link these two domains for these two groups. Moreover, it is important to clarify whether gender is indeed an important moderator of this relationship. Even if social responsibility is an equally important factor in Black and White men's political participation, perhaps the specific racial and gender-based socializations they experience shape their understanding of social responsibility in ways that are consequential for their political activities.

In response to crises pertaining to poverty, violent crime, and corruption among political elites, there have recently been bipartisan calls for a reexamination of the values of obligation, citizenship, and social responsibility. These range from George Bush's entreaty to the "thousand points of light" to a recent conference sponsored by the Clinton Administration on "Character Building for a Democratic, Civil Society." This study suggests that further research on this topic as it relates to personality development is desirable. On the basis of 25 years of follow-ups of Black and White male activists who were veterans of the earliest phase of student movements in the 1960s, Fendrich (1993) observed that in adulthood the former activists were "ideal citizens," more socially and politically active than others of their generation, including former student government leaders. He argued that this continuity of participation resulted because "political identities and commitments originate in collective political experience, not the other way around. The problem is not the political apathy of individuals, but the poverty of collective opportunities to act democratically" (Fendrich, 1993, p. 144). Our findings, based on women of a later cohort, support this argument and the notion that identity (in this case, political identity) may be an important source of continuity in political behavior. Moreover, they indicate that the concept of social responsibility, encompassing a commitment to one's community and to future generations, taken together with a sense of political efficacy or empowerment may be an important mediator between active political participation in young adulthood and in midlife. In other words, participation in student activism may, in part, produce a sense of commitment and capacity to act, which in turn promotes active political participation later in life. In this light, student protestors may be seen not as society's malcontents but as tomorrow's exemplars of social responsibility.

References

Abramowitz, S. I., & Nassi, A. J. (1981). Keeping the faith: Psychosocial correlates of activism persistence into middle adulthood. *Journal of Youth and Adolescence, 10,* 507–523.

Bachrach, K. M., & Zautra, A. J. (1985). Coping with a community stressor: The threat of a hazardous waste facility. *Journal of Health and Social Behavior, 26,* 127–141.

Berkowitz, L., & Lutterman, K. G. (1968). The traditional socially responsible personality. *Public Opinion Quarterly, 32,* 169–185.

Braungart, M. M., & Braungart, R. G. (1990). The life-course development of left- and right-wing youth activist leaders from the 1960s. *Political Psychology, 11,* 242–282.

Braungart, M. M., & Braungart, R. G. (1991). The effects of the 1960s political generation on former left- and right-wing youth activist leaders. *Social Problems, 38,* 297–315.

Cable, S. (1992). Women's social movement involvement: The role of structural availability in recruitment and participation processes. *The Sociological Quarterly, 33,* 35–50.

Carroll, S. J. (1989). Gender politics and the socializing impact of the women's movement. In R. S. Sigel (Ed.), *Political learning in adulthood: A sourcebook of theory and research* (pp. 306–339). Chicago: University of Chicago Press.

Chebat, J. (1986). Social responsibility, locus of control and social class. *Journal of Social Psychology, 126,* 559–561.

Cohen, J. L. (1985). Strategy or identity: New theoretical paradigms and contemporary social movements. *Social Research, 52,* 663–716.

Collins, P. H. (1990). *Black feminist thought.* Cambridge, MA: Unwin Hyman.

Constantini, E., & Craik, K. H. (1972). Women as politicians: The social background, personality and political careers of female party leaders. *Journal of Social Issues, 28,* 217–236.

Conway, M. M. (1985). *Political participation in the United States.* Washington, DC: Congressional Quarterly.

Craig, S. C., & Maggiotto, M. A. (1982). Measuring political efficacy. *Political Methodology, 8,* 85–109.

Crosby, F. J. (1976). A model of egoistical relative deprivation. *Psychological Review, 83,* 85–113.

Crosby, F. J. (1982). *Relative deprivation and working women.* New York: Oxford University Press.

Crosby, F. J., Pufall, A., Snyder, R. C., O'Connell, M., & Whalen, P. (1989). The denial of personal disadvantage among you, me, and all the other ostriches. In M. Crawford & M. Gentry (Eds.), *Gender and thought* (pp. 79–99). New York: Springer-Verlag.

Cross, W. E. (1991). *Shades of Black: Diversity in African-American identity.* Philadelphia: Temple University Press.

Duncan, L. E., & Agronick, G. S. (1995). The intersection of life stage and social events: Personality and life outcomes. *Journal of Personality and Social Psychology, 69,* 558–568.

Elshtain, J. B. (1982). Feminist discourse and its discontents: Language, power and meaning. *Signs, 3,* 342–367.

Erikson, E. H. (1963). *Childhood and Society* (2nd ed.). New York: Norton.

Erikson, E. H. (1968a). Generativity and ego integrity. In B. L. Neugarten (Ed.), *Middle age and aging* (pp. 85–87). Chicago: University of Chicago Press.

Erikson, E. H. (1968b). *Identity: Youth and crisis.* New York: Norton.

Fendrich, J. M. (1974). Activists ten years later: A test of generational unit continuity. *Journal of Social Issues, 30,* 95–118.

Fendrich, J. M. (1976). Black and White activists ten years later. Political socialization and adult left-wing politics. *Youth and Society, 8,* 81–104.

Fendrich, J. M. (1977). Keeping the faith or pursuing the good life: A study of the consequences of participation in the civil rights movement. *American Sociological Review, 42,* 144–157.

Fendrich, J. M. (1993). *Ideal citizens: The legacy of the civil rights movement.* Albany: State University of New York Press.

Fendrich, J. M., & Lovoy, K. L. (1988). Back to the future: Adult political behavior of former student activists. *American Sociological Review, 53,* 780–784.

Flacks, R. (1988). *Making history: The radical tradition in American life.* New York: Columbia University Press.

Franz, C. E., & McClelland, D. C. (1994). Lives of women and men active in the social protests of the 1960s: A longitudinal study. *Journal of Personality and Social Psychology, 66,* 196–205.

Gamson, W. A. (1992). The social psychology of collective action. In A. D. Morris & C. M. Mueller (Eds.), *Frontiers in social movement theory* (pp. 53–76). New Haven, CT: Yale University Press.

Giddings, P. (1984). *When and where I enter*. New York: Morrow.

Gogh, H. G., McClosky, H., & Meehl, P. E. (1952). A personality scale for social responsibility. *Journal of Abnormal and Social Psychology, 47*, 73–80.

Gurin, P., Miller, A., & Gurin, G. (1980). Stratum identification and consciousness. *Social Psychology Quarterly, 43*, 30–47.

Gurin, P., & Townsend, A. (1986). Properties of gender identity and their implications for gender consciousness. *British Journal of Social Psychology, 25*, 139–148.

Gurr, T. R. (1968). A causal model of civil strife: A comparative analysis using new indices. *American Political Science Review, 62*, 1104–1124.

Gurr, T. R. (1970). *Why men rebel*. Princeton, NJ: Princeton University Press.

Haan, N. (1989). Personality at midlife. In S. Hunter & M. Sundel (Eds.), *Midlife myths* (pp. 145–156). Newbury Park, CA: Sage.

Harding, V. (1991). Community as a liberating theme in Civil Rights history. In A. L. Robinson & P. Sullivan (Eds.), *New directions in Civil Rights studies* (pp. 17–29). Charlottesville: University Press of Virginia.

Helms, J. E. (1993). The measurement of Black racial identity attitudes. In J. E. Helms (Ed.), *Black and White racial identity: Theory, research and practice* (pp. 33–48). Westport, CT: Praeger.

Hoge, D. R., & Ankney, T. L. (1982). Occupation and attitudes of former student activists ten years later. *Journal of Youth and Adolescence, 11*, 355–371.

hooks, b. (1984). *Feminist theory: From margin to center*. Boston: South End Press.

Jennings, M. K. (1979). Another look at the life cycle and political participation. *American Journal of Political Science, 23*, 755–771.

Jennings, M. K. (1987). Residues of a movement: The aging of the American protest generation. *American Political Science Review, 81*, 365–382.

Kerber, L. K. (1980). *Women of the republic*. Chapel Hill: University of North Carolina Press.

King, D. (1988). Multiple jeopardy, multiple consciousness: The context of Black feminist ideology. *Signs, 14*, 42–72.

Kotre, J. (1984). *Outliving the self: Generativity and the interpretation of lives*. Baltimore: Johns Hopkins University Press.

Lott, B. (1990). Dual natures or learned behavior: The challenge to feminist psychology. In R. T. Hare-Mustin & J. Marecek (Eds.), *Making a difference: Psychology and the construction of gender* (pp. 65–101). New Haven, CT: Yale University Press.

Lykes, M. B. (1984). *Autonomous individualism versus social individuality: Towards an alternative understanding of the self*. Unpublished doctoral dissertation, Boston College.

Mannheim, K. (1952). The problem of generations. In *Essays on the sociology of knowledge* (pp. 276–322). London: Routledge & Kegan Paul. (Original work published 1928.)

McAdam, D. (1992). Gender as a mediator of the activist experience: The case of Freedom Summer. *American Journal of Sociology, 97*, 1211–1240.

McAdams, D. P. (1988). *Power, intimacy and the life story: Personological inquiries into identity*. New York: Guilford Press.

McAdams, D. P., & de St. Aubin, E. (1992). A theory of generativity and its assessment through self-report, behavioral acts, and narrative themes in autobiography. *Journal of Personality and Social Psychology, 62*, 1003–1015.

McAdams, D. P., de St. Aubin, E., & Logan, R. L. (1992). Generativity among young, midlife, and older adults. *Psychology and Aging, 8*, 221–230.

Milbrath, L. W., & Goel, M. L. (1982). *Political participation: How and why do people get involved in politics* (2nd ed.). Washington, DC: University Press of America.

Mitchell, V., & Helson, R. (1990). Women's prime of life: Is it the fifties? *Psychology of Women Quarterly, 14*, 451–470.

Morris, A. D., Hatchett, S. J., & Brown, R. E. (1989). The civil rights movement and Black political socialization. In R. S. Sigel (Ed.), *Political learning in adulthood: A sourcebook of theory and research* (pp. 272–305). Chicago: University of Chicago Press.

Mueller, C. M. (1987). Collective consciousness, identity transformation and the rise of women in public office in the United States. In M. F. Katzenstein & C. M. Mueller (Eds.), *The women's movements of the United States and Western Europe* (pp. 89–108). Philadelphia: Temple University Press.

Nassi, A. J. (1981). Survivors of the sixties: Comparative psychosocial and political development of former Berkeley student activists. *American Psychologist, 36,* 753–761.

Nassi, A. J., & Abramowitz, S. I. (1979). Transition or transformation? Personal and political development of former Berkeley free speech movement activists. *Journal of Youth and Adolescence, 8,* 21–35.

Neugarten, B. L. (Ed.). (1968). *Middle age and aging.* Chicago: University of Chicago Press.

Ponterotto, J. G., & Wise, S. L. (1987). Construct validity study of the Racial Identity Attitude Scale. *Journal of Counseling Psychology, 34,* 218–223.

Popkin, A. (1990). The social experience of bread and roses: Building a community and creating a culture. In K. V. Harness & I. J. Philipson (Eds.), *Women, class and the feminist imagination* (pp. 182–212). Philadelphia: Temple University Press.

Prato, F., Sidanius, J., Stallworth, L. M., & Malle, B. F. (1994). Social dominance orientation: A personality variable predicting social and political attitudes. *Journal of Personality and Social Psychology, 67,* 741–763.

Robinson, D. M. (1987). *The effect of multiple group identity among Black women on group consciousness.* Unpublished doctoral dissertation, University of Michigan.

Rothman, S., & Lichter, S. R. (1982). *Roots of radicalism: Jews, Christians and the New Left.* New York: Oxford University Press.

Ruddick, S. (1985). Maternal work and the practice of peace. *Journal of Education, 167,* 97–111.

Runciman, W. G. (1966). *Relative deprivation and social justice.* Berkeley: University of California Press.

Schuman, H., & Scott, J. (1989). Generations and collective memories. *American Sociological Review, 54,* 359–381.

Sherkat, D. E., & Blocker, T. J. (1994). The political development of sixties' activists: Identifying the influence of class, gender, and socialization on protest participation. *Social Forces, 72,* 821–842.

Sidanius, J., Prato, F., & Bobo, L. (1994). Social dominance orientation and the political psychology of gender: A case of invariance. *Journal of Personality and Social Psychology, 67,* 998–1011.

Stewart, A. J., & Healy, J. M. (1986). The role of personality development and experience in shaping political commitment: An illustrative case. *Journal of Social Issues, 42,* 11–31.

Stewart, A. J., & Healy, J. M. (1989). Linking individual development and social changes. *American Psychologist, 44,* 30–42.

Tangri, S. S. (1969). *Role innovation in occupational choice among college women.* Unpublished doctoral dissertation, University of Michigan.

Thorne, B. (1975). Women in the draft resistance movement: A case study of sex roles and social movements. *Sex Roles, 1,* 179–195.

Tilley, L. A., & Gurin, P. (1990). Women, politics and change. In L. A. Tilley & P. Gurin (Eds.), *Women, politics and change* (pp. 3–32). New York: Sage.

Witt, L. A. (1990). Person–situation effects and gender differences in the prediction of social responsibility. *Journal of Social Psychology, 130,* 543–553.

Questions for Thought

1. Three key concepts in this research are political identity, power discontent, and social responsibility. Explain each concept and how it was measured.

2. Compare and contrast the involvement of Black and White women in the women's movement.

3. Based on this research, describe the characteristics of Black women and of White women who are politically active in midlife.

4. What role did social responsibility play in the midlife political participation of Black and White women?

5. Describe how the researchers recruited Black and White women for their study. How comparable were their Black and White samples? What factors might limit the generalizability of these findings to other college students?

6. What social movements today are affecting the lives of college students? Select one contemporary social movement. Drawing on the work of Cole and Stewart, discuss how participation in this movement may affect the attitudes and future political involvement of today's young adults.

Aging Minority Women

12

Deborah Padgett

On average, aging ethnic minority women experience more poverty and a shorter life span than their White agemates. But Padgett's review also uncovers many areas of strength and resilience among these women, who are often actively involved with their families and ethnic communities.

This paper presents an overview of current knowledge about the economic, psychosocial and cultural dimensions of the aging process among minority women in the U.S. Attention is directed to the shorter life span of minority women and its implication for understanding aging, the reality of the "quadruple jeopardy" hypothesis, and the adaptative advantages minority women may have in dealing with growing older. The need to consider cohort effects and ethnic diversity in future research on minority women is stressed.

Clinicians, researchers, and policymakers know so little about the lives of aging Black, Hispanic, and Native American women that they are often left with little more than stereotypical pictures. While the literatures on aging, on women, and on minorities are abundant, the spotlight rarely falls on this seemingly invisible group.

This paper will attempt to synthesize what is known about the economic, psychosocial and cultural dimensions of the aging process among minority women in the United States. Due to the scarcity of empirical research, it will focus on broad thematic areas, highlighting important issues and suggesting topics for future research.

Adapted from *Women and Health*, 1989, *14*(3/4), 213–225. Copyright 1989 by The Haworth Press. Used by permission.

Three perspectives are presented, the first emphasizing the hardships shared by aging minority women ("quadruple jeopardy"), the second focusing on the adaptive psychosocial and cultural strengths which appear to characterize the surviving "old-old," and the third arguing for recognition of heterogeneity within groups and through successive cohorts. While discussion of these perspectives allows comparisons between aging minority women and their middle-class White counterparts, it also provides suggestions for future research.

Defining Terms: What Is Meant by "Minority" and "Aging"?

While no one will dispute the definition of "female," there is a need to discuss other terms used in this paper. The term "aging," which is usually defined as over 65 years of age, must here take into account the fact that members of minority groups have shorter life spans, may be functionally old well before age 65, and even consider themselves "old" at age 55 (Bengtson et al. 1977). Thus, the term aging rather than "old" or "elderly" is generally preferable when referring to this group. Furthermore, it is useful to distinguish two groups of minority women over age 55: (1) the "younger-aging" who constitute the majority, and (2) the "old-old," a much smaller group of survivors who live beyond age 75.

The term "minority" is used to identify members of ethnic and racial groups who share in common a relative lack of power and suffer the effects of discrimination based upon real or perceived racial or cultural differences (Wagley and Harris 1958). In the main, it refers to Blacks, Hispanics, and Native Americans, though Pacific Islanders and some Asian ethnic groups may be included in Federal government designations.

The fact that members of some White ethnic groups may also suffer from discrimination or that some Hispanic and Asian groups appear to be exempt from minority status, makes the concept difficult to operationalize. Nevertheless, it is a useful if less-than-perfect device for analysis. Whenever possible, the discussion will identify specific groups, e.g., Blacks or Hispanics.

The Quadruple Jeopardy Perspective on Aging Minority Women

One of the most salient descriptions of being an aging minority female in our society is embodied in the words "quadruple jeopardy," that is, to be old, poor, female, and of minority status. Jacqueline Jackson coined the term in 1971 specifically to refer to the experience of Black women, its origins linked to the earlier use of "double jeopardy" to draw attention to the plight of the Black aged in America (Talley and Kaplan 1956). However, Jackson's own critique of the concept leaves little doubt that it is problematic (1985).

Empirical tests of the double jeopardy and quadruple jeopardy hypotheses are hampered by a lack of relevant data on age, income, education, health and psychological well-being. Census data, for example, are considered suspect due to undercounting and inaccuracy in retrieving information from members of minority groups

(Bengtson 1979). However, we do know that the burden of poverty is greater for aging minority women. Eighty percent of Black women (Women's Equity Action League 1985) and fifty percent of Hispanic women (Berger 1983) live in poverty, compared with twenty percent of all aged women.

It is difficult to assess the relative effects of poverty and racial or ethnic status on the lives of aging minority women. Well-known comparisons of gender and race differences in mortality rates, for example, are not controlled by socioeconomic status. At first glance, these comparisons provide support for the concept of quadruple jeopardy, with Black women having an average life expectancy of 73.6 years compared with 78.9 years for White women (National Center for Health Statistics, August 24, 1987). However, the fact that shorter life expectancies for Black women are reversed by a "crossover" in mortality rates after age 85 weakens the notion of quadruple jeopardy as a correlate of life expectancy.

Jackson's inspection of suicide rates as crude indicators of life satisfaction also tends to undermine the quadruple jeopardy hypothesis. Age-adjusted suicide rates over age 65 broken down by age and sex reveal that Black women consistently have the lowest rates for all age categories. In 1979, for example, Black women over age 65 had an age-adjusted suicide rate (per 100,000) of 2.5, compared with 7.5 for White women, 12.8 for Black men, and 37.7 for White men (Jackson 1985).

Most primary research on double jeopardy has been cross-sectional rather than longitudinal, as exemplified by a survey conducted in southern California by Dowd and Bengtson in 1978. Their test of double jeopardy involved comparing Black, Mexican-American, and White elderly on four dimensions: income, health, social interaction, and life satisfaction. Evidence of double jeopardy was found in income and self-rated health, with minority respondents suffering greater relative declines than their White counterparts.

On the other hand, levels of social interaction and of life satisfaction were similar among all three groups, implying that aging does not necessarily entail greater losses in quality of life for minority group members (Dowd and Bengtson 1978). Farakhan et al. (1984) also found relatively high levels of life satisfaction among retired Black elderly in Kansas City. Similar results came from another large-scale multiethnic survey of the elderly in New York City, where Cantor and associates (1985) found higher levels of family assistance and family solidarity differentiated Hispanics from Blacks and Whites. Only in their tendency to give more financial assistance to children were Blacks and Hispanics distinct from their White counterparts.

In summary, the evidence from survey research and available national statistics offers mixed messages of support for the quadruple jeopardy perspective. Relative deprivation in income and self-reported health status is not necessarily linked with lower levels of social support, family interaction, self-reported life satisfaction, or higher mortality rates after age 85.

However, marked disparities in income have clear implications for the health and mental health status of aging minority women which deserve further discussion. Objective measures of health status reveal higher morbidity rates for specific conditions associated with lower income status such as diabetes, hypertension, and kidney disease which take their toll in increased disability and overall reductions in life expectancy.

There are no known studies comparing rates of mental disorders between aging minority and White women, but research in related areas suggests a higher degree of risk for those at lower income levels regardless of racial or ethnic status. The federally sponsored Epidemiological Catchment Area (ECA) studies conducted in three sites found that differences between Blacks and Whites in lifetime prevalence rates of psychiatric disorders were generally modest and rarely statistically significant (Robins et al. 1984). Indeed, Kessler and Neighbors argue that most racial and ethnic differences disappear when socioeconomic status is controlled (1983). The ECA findings of higher rates of mental disorders in inner-city areas as compared with suburbs and small town/rural areas (Robins et al. 1984) also support this emerging picture of income rather than race-related risk factors.

At the same time, the ECA studies yielded rates of mental disorders which declined with age, dropping sharply after age 45. Contrary to popular impression, the evidence is growing that prevalence of all psychiatric disorders except organic brain syndromes actually decreases with age (Myers et al. 1984).

Whether these lower rates of psychopathology apply to aging minority women remains an unanswered question, but a few words of caution are in order before any extrapolations are made. First, most epidemiological studies measure psychiatric disorders which meet strict DSM-III (Diagnostic and Statistical Manual of Mental Disorders, Third Edition) criteria. Dysphoric symptoms associated with medical problems and transient demoralized states which fall short of syndromes are not usually measured or reported. Second, the instruments or scales used in these population surveys have not been validated for use in different minority groups and are thus subject to inaccuracy due to cultural bias. Finally, the tendency of the aged and members of some ethnic groups to somatize symptoms of distress (attributing problems to physical rather than mental origins) may reduce estimates of prevalence based solely upon the disclosure of psychiatric symptoms (Katon et al. 1984). If we cannot state with certainty that the prevalence of mental disorders is greater for aging minority women, it does seem safe to say that the risks are higher for this group due to income-related factors.

The dilemma presented by juxtaposing low income and poor health with relatively high scores on social interaction and quality of life measures raises interesting questions for future research on quadruple jeopardy. More in-depth studies are needed which help us to understand how some minority women adopt psychosocial coping strategies which enhance their ability to age successfully despite the odds against them.

It appears that the premature mortality rates that adversely affect this group produce a select group of survivors who are, in all likelihood, more hardy than their White age counterparts. For these "hardy" older women the day to day problems of poverty and discrimination do not necessarily recede, but they do apparently become less threatening, thus explaining higher life satisfaction and lower rates of suicide.

Surveys of aging minority women which recognize an age stratum distinction between young-old and old-old offer possible tests of the hypothesis that some aspects of quadruple jeopardy lose salience in the latter group. Of course, longitudinal research is needed to fully study the complex process of survivorship. In the meantime, descriptive studies provide clues to the strengths possessed by these older women which enable them to adapt successfully.

Strengths for Survival: An Adaptive Perspective on Aging Minority Women

Statistics documenting the disparities in income and health status experienced by aging minority women obscure a more complex picture of survival and even successful aging for a select few. While the struggles and hardships do not let up, it appears that many aging minority women are able to draw on strengths—psychological, social, and cultural—which ease the transition to old age. They have spent their lives as strategists, marshalling scarce resources to cope with everyday demands and these coping strategies "pay off" later on in self-reliance.

Of course, those who died prematurely in their 50s and 60s faced the same pressures, and it remains unclear which set of biogenetic and socio-environmental factors shortened their lives. We can, however, learn a great deal by applying an adaptive perspective to those who did survive to identify factors which may enhance survival.

Support for an adaptive perspective on successful aging among minority women comes from a variety of sources, including the survey research mentioned earlier. Cantor et al. (1975), for example, suggest that sharing of limited economic and social resources by Hispanic and Black elderly is a positive adaptation to the pressures of poverty. More contextual evidence comes from ethnographic accounts of the lives of older Black and minority women provided by cultural anthropologists (Aschenbrenner, 1975; Clark and Mendelson, 1969; Stack, 1974). These studies emphasize strengths arising from family and social networks and shared ethnic identity.

In general, older minority women play integral roles in their family networks as "kintenders," providing instrumental and expressive support to their adult children and grandchildren. Stack (1974) notes that poor Black households are largely organized around women, with intergenerational ties maintained continuously over time. Family and household boundaries are flexible to meet shifting economic demands, but a core of female relatives retains domestic authority with older women at the center.

This theme of matrifocality is less applicable to Hispanics and Native Americans where males are more directly involved in family and household affairs. Nevertheless, women in these groups enjoy greater prestige and domestic authority as they grow older (Cuellar 1978). Providing and receiving social support in kin networks are important survival strategies for these women.

Ethnicity can be another important resource in successful aging. Cuellar's description of older Mexican-Americans in East Los Angeles (1978) illustrates how traditional cultural values reduce feelings of alienation in an Anglo-dominated society. Likewise, Cota-Robles Newton (1980) writes of the Hispanic values of "personalismo" and "dignidad" which characterize positive interaction between young and old and reinforce group identity.

How do minority women compare with their older White counterparts in adaptive strategies for aging? Earlier research in social gerontology, largely confined to the white middle-class, emphasized disengagement and images of decline and loss; but the more recent research cited earlier has challenged this negative picture with findings of extensive social interaction by White and non-White respondents alike (Cantor 1985; Dowd and Bengtson 1978). What *does* appear to distinguish the minority aged are higher familial contacts. While Whites have more interaction with friends and neighbors, Dowd and Bengtson (1978) found familial contacts to be highest among Mexican-Americans, followed by Blacks. In contrast, social interaction patterns of White elderly included both family and non-kin relationships.

Theories of adaptive aging based upon presumed higher overall levels of social interaction and social support among minorities have little support from empirical research. However, their immersion in kin networks and reliance on ethnic identity point to features which may coalesce to form adaptive strategies which are distinct from those of older Whites. From an adaptive perspective, this reliance on kinship and ethnicity is not a static carry-over of traditional ways, but is a dynamic response to a changing, often threatening environment.

Understanding the role of lifelong experiences and adaptive (or maladaptive) responses is critical. For minority women, just being alive and surviving to old age testifies to earlier successes in coping with deprivation and hardship. Older White women have not generally had to meet the same challenges; the need to develop strategies for survival has been far less over the course of a lifetime and tends to be greatest at retirement age when abrupt losses in income occur. However, the adaptive strategies of those who have endured lives of poverty and deprivation are likely to be similar to those of minority women.

Differences between minority and White women are more aptly described as occurring along a continuum rather than as discrete. What appears most important for understanding survival are the challenges posed by the surrounding environment and the strengths possessed by individuals—economic, social, and cultural—which enable them to adapt and survive to old age. While useful in some respects, minority-White comparisons entail the risk of obscuring important variation within these broadly-defined groups. Recognizing differences within as well as between groups and subgroups of aging women allows a more complete—and more complex—picture to emerge.

Heterogeneity and Cohort Perspectives on Aging: The Missing Links in Research on Minority Women

The key concepts embodied in these perspectives are diversity and change. Both constitute "missing links" in research due to an almost total reliance upon cross-sectional approaches which treat aging populations as homogeneous entities.

Aging women are in fact a highly diverse group, distinguished by inter- and intra-ethnic differences as well as by age stratum differences between the younger aging and the old-old. Black Americans, for example, may be native-born or come from West Indian, Jamaican, or Bahamian backgrounds. Hispanic groups include Mexican, Puerto Rican and Cuban Americans and many others from a variety of Central and South American countries. White ethnic groups may be Polish, Italian, Greek, or Hungarian, to name only a few.

The experiences of older women in America can also be usefully examined from a cohort perspective. As described by Riley (1985), this perspective takes into account changing social and historical circumstances which characterize the unique developmental experiences of each age cohort. Thus, just as modal patterns of aging differ cross-culturally, so do they differ in successive generations (Ryder 1964).

Aging minority women born in this country share certain experiences in common with their White native-born counterparts—two World Wars, the Great Depression—which have influenced them in unique ways. Both cohort groups also matured at a time when sex roles were sharply differentiated and women's work devalued.

Minority women are distinct, though, in having experienced the profound effects of inequality and racial/ethnic discrimination. The castelike stratification system described so eloquently by Myrdal (1956) lasted well into the 1960s and undoubtedly affected their life chances. The fact that so many older minority women have limited education and hold low-status service jobs attests to the effects of lifelong inequality. Indeed, their tendency to play family-tending roles as they age may be in part attributable to their exclusion from White society as both women and as minorities. Although those born abroad could not have experienced the full range of social and historical conditions of this native-born cohort of minority women, they have had to make similar adjustments to inequality further complicated by barriers of language and culture.

A number of changes have transformed American society in recent decades which are likely to affect future cohorts of aging minority women. These include increased equality for women and higher levels of labor force participation across all occupational strata. Whether these advances have "trickled down" to improve the lot of minority women is open to question, particularly since the acceleration of the feminization of poverty beginning in the early 1980s. The hazards of quadruple jeopardy are not likely to disappear overnight.

However, it is likely that future cohorts of minority women will be more educated and hold higher status jobs outside of the home. The overall emancipation of women and changing societal attitudes toward sex roles may well lead to increased mobility and reductions in the number of older women willing to occupy exclusively familial roles. Finally, future cohorts of minority women will almost certainly contain fewer foreign-born, opening the possibility of increased acculturation and more inter-ethnic interaction.

All of this is, of course, speculation. Only longitudinal research can provide answers to questions of how future generations of minority women will make the transition to old age. In the meantime, the cohort perspective offers useful lessons for challenging the fallacious view of aging as a static, universal process. . . .

References

Aschenbrenner, J. (1975). *Lifelines: Black Families in Chicago.* Prospect Heights: Waveland Press.

Bengtson, V. L. (1979). Ethnicity and aging: Problems and issues in current social science inquiry. In *Ethnicity and Aging: Theory, Research and Policy.* D. E. Gelfand and A. J. Kutzik (Eds.) New York: Springer, 9–31.

Bengtson, V. L., Dowd, J. J., Smith, D. H. and Inkeles, A. (1977). Modernization, modernity, and perceptions of aging: A cross-cultural study. *Journal of Gerontology,* 30; 688–695.

Berger, P. (1983). The economic well-being of elderly Hispanics. *Journal of Minority Aging,* 8; 36–46.

Cantor, M. H. (1985). The informal support system of New York's inner city elderly: Is ethnicity a factor? In *Ethnicity and Aging: Theory, Research and Policy*. D. E. Gelfand and A. J. Kutzik (Eds.) New York: Springer, 153–174.

Cantor, M. H., Rosenthal, K. and Wilker, L. (1975). Social and family relationships of Black aged women in New York City. Paper presented at the 28th annual meeting of the Gerontological Society, Louisville, Kentucky.

Cota-Robles Newton, F. (1980). Issues in research and service delivery among Mexican-American elderly: A concise statement with recommendations. *The Gerontologist,* 20; 208–212.

Clark, M. and Mendelson, M. (1969). The Mexican-American aged in San Francisco: A case description. *The Gerontologist,* 9, 90–95.

Cuellar, J. (1978). El Senior Citizens' Club: The elderly Mexican-Americans in the voluntary association. In *Life's Career: Aging*. B. G. Myerhoff and A. Simic (Eds.) Beverly Hills: Sage, 207–230.

Dowd, J. J. and Bengtson, V. L. (1978). Aging in minority populations: An examination of the double jeopardy hypothesis. *Journal of Gerontology,* 33, 427–436.

Farakhan, A., Lubin, B. and O'Connor, W. A. (1984). Life satisfaction and depression among retired Black persons. *Psychological Reports,* 55, 452–454.

Jackson, J. J. (1985). Poverty and minority status. In *The Physical and Mental Health of Aged Women*. M. Haug, A. B. Ford, M. Sheafor (Eds.) New York: Springer, 166–182.

Katon, W., Ries, R. K. and Kleinman, A. (1984). The prevalence of somatization in primary care. *Comprehensive Psychiatry,* 25, 208–214.

Kessler, R. and Neighbors, H. W. (1983). Special Issues Related to Racial and Ethnic Minorities in the United States. Position Paper submitted to the National Institute of Mental Health, Institute for Social Research, University of Michigan.

Myers, J. K., Weissman, M. M., Tischler, G. L., Holzer, C. E., Leas, P. J., Orvaschel, H., Anthony, J. C., Boyd, J. H., Burke, J. D., Kramer, M., and Stoltzman, R. (1984). Six month prevalence of psychiatric disorders in three communities. *Archives of General Psychiatry,* 41, 969–970.

Myrdal, G. (1956). *An American Dilemma*. Boston: Beacon Press.

National Center for Health Statistics: Annual Summary of Births, Marriages, Divorces and Deaths, U.S. 1986. Monthly Vital Statistics Reports. Vol. 35, No. 13, DHHS Pub. No. (PHS) 87-1100. Public Health Service, Government Printing Office, August 24, 1987.

Riley, M. W. (1985). The changing older woman: A cohort perspective. In *The Physical and Mental Health of Aged Women*. M. Haug, A. B. Ford, and M. Sheafor (Eds.) New York: Springer, 3–15.

Robins, L., Helzer, J. E., Weissman, M. M., Orvaschel, H., Greenberg, E., Burke, J. D., and Regier, D. A. (1984). Lifetime prevalence of specific psychiatric disorders in three sites. *Archives of General Psychiatry,* 41, 949–958.

Ryder, N. B. (1964). Notes on the concept of a population. *American Journal of Sociology,* 69, 447–463.

Stack, C. B. (1974). Sex roles and survival strategies in an urban black community. In *Woman, Culture, and Society*. M. Z. Rosaldo and L. Lamphere (Eds.) Stanford: Stanford University Press, 113–128.

Talley, T. and Kaplan, J. (1956). The Negro Aged. Newsletter, Gerontological Society, 3.

Wagley, C. and Harris, M. (1958). *Minorities in the New World*. New York: Columbia University Press.

Women's Equity Action League (WEAL). (1985). Facts on Social Security. Washington, D.C.: WEAL.

Questions for Thought

1. Explain the concept of "quadruple jeopardy." What are two ways in which aging ethnic minority women are disadvantaged relative to Whites? What are two ways in which aging women are similar regardless of ethnicity?

2. Padgett presents an "adaptive perspective" on aging minority women. Explain and provide illustrations of this concept.

3. How might the life experiences of a 75-year-old woman born in the 1920s differ from those of a woman of your own generation (born the same year as you) when she is 75?

4. Padgett emphasizes that there are many differences among older women. Identify at least seven important ways in which aging women may differ from one another. How might these affect the physical health and social life of older women?

5. Identify at least three TV shows, commercials, movies, or books that depict older women. Describe the images of aging women in each one, for instance, their ethnicity, income, education, and social life. Evaluate these media depictions of aging.

Gender Differences in Standards for Romantic Relationships
Different Cultures or Different Experiences?

Anita L. Vangelisti

John A. Daly

Do men and women have such different values and goals that each sex can be thought of as having its own distinct "culture"? Popular books such as Men Are From Mars, Women Are From Venus *seem to promote the idea that women and men are utterly different from each other, especially when it comes to love relationships. In this article Vangelisti and Daly investigate this issue among adults in long-term heterosexual relationships. The authors test two alternative models of male-female relationships. The "different cultures" model suggests that women and men have very different standards or ideals for relationships. For instance, women might value emotional openness and self-disclosure much more than men do. In contrast, the "different experiences" model suggests that men and women have similar standards but different experiences in their relationships. For instance, both sexes may value self-disclosure equally, but women may actually reveal more to their partners than men do. As a result, men may be more likely than women to feel that their relationship standards are fulfilled by their partner. This study offers an empirical test of these two perspectives.*

Why is it that women often report more problems in their romantic relationships than do men? One explanation apparent in the literature is that women may view different standards as important for relationships than do their male counterparts and, as a consequence, women may be less likely to have their standards met. A second explanation is that while women and men may not differ in terms of the importance they associate with various standards, the experiences they have in their romantic relationships may lead women to believe their standards are not

Reprinted from *Personal Relationships*, 1997, *4*, 203–219. Copyright 1997 by The International Society for the Study of Personal Relationships. Used by permission of Cambridge University Press.

fulfilled as often as do men. The current study offers a preliminary test of these two rival explanations and found greater support for the latter. Analyses of two composite measures and more detailed factor-based measures generally indicated that the standards held by women and men involved in heterosexual romantic relationships were rated similar in importance. Women, however, tended to note that their standards were met less fully than did men. Further, compared to men, women reported a greater discrepancy between the importance they associated with various standards and the extent to which the standards were fulfilled in the context of their relationship. The ability of two different theoretical models to predict and explain these findings is discussed, as are the implications of the results for future research.

Research suggests that women report more problems in their romantic relationships than do men (Levinger, 1979; Macklin, 1978; Rubin, Peplau, & Hill, 1981), are more lonely in the context of marriage (Peplau, Bikson, Rook, & Goodchilds, 1982; Rubenstein & Shaver, 1982; Tornstam, 1992), and initiate relational separations more frequently than do men (Fletcher, 1983; Harvey, Wells, & Alvarez, 1978; cf. Rusbult, Zembrodt, & Iwaniszek, 1986). Why is it that women seemingly experience more difficulty in their long-term romantic relationships than do their male counterparts? Many, if not most theories of interpersonal relations suggest the response to this question involves the standards women and men hold for their close relationships. It may be, for instance, that women see many relational standards as more important than do men. Alternatively, it may be that women find the criteria they have for "good" relationships often are not met. In the study described in this article we examine the association between standards and relational satisfaction, the importance women and men associate with various standards for long-term romantic relationships, and the degree to which men and women believe their standards are fulfilled.

Relational standards—the beliefs or criteria people hold about the qualities relationships *should* have (Baucom, Epstein, Sayers, & Sher, 1989; Ellis, 1962)—figure prominently in social exchange (Homans, 1961; Huston & Burgess, 1979; Nye, 1979), equity (Adams, 1965; Hatfield, Traupman, Sprecher, Utne, & Hay, 1985; Walster, Walster, & Berscheid, 1978), interdependence (Kelley & Thibaut, 1978; Thibaut & Kelley, 1959), and investment (Rusbult, 1980, 1983) theories. As defined in the current study, standards reflect individuals' goals and aspirations for their romantic relationships and involve what Higgins and his colleagues term "criteria of excellence" (Higgins, Strauman, & Klein, 1986, p. 30). As such, standards provide people with a means for evaluating their affiliations with others. They serve as a basis for the feelings people have about their partner (Beck, 1988; Duck, 1990; Epstein & Eidelson, 1981; Fletcher, 1996; Lederer & Jackson, 1968). Theorists argue that when people's relational standards are met or exceeded, partners will be relatively satisfied with their relationships. In contrast, when their standards are not fulfilled, they are likely to become dissatisfied or disillusioned.

The literature yields two different models that might predict and explain gender differences associated with the standards individuals hold for their personal relationships. The first model, labelled the *different cultures* view by Burleson and others (see Aries, 1996; Burleson, Kunkel, Samter, & Werking, 1996; and Kunkel, 1995, for critiques of this model), suggests that men and women approach personal relationships from two different cultural perspectives—that they have been social-ized to construct and perceive relationships in very different ways (Maltz & Borker, 1982; Tannen, 1990; Wood, 1994). Proponents of the different cultures model argue that women center their identity more closely around relationships than do men (Chodorow, 1978; Gilligan, 1982). Further, compared to men, women tend to be more aware of relational issues (Acitelli, 1992; Burnett, 1987), and they exhibit more complex thinking about relationships (Martin, 1991). Because women are socialized to place a relatively high premium on interdependence, communication and affect typically lie at the core of the way they define and evaluate intimacy. Compared to men, women rate positive affective behavior as more important to their relationships (Wills, Weiss, & Patterson, 1974), and they view talk as a more central and necessary component of their associations with others (Haas & Sherman, 1982; Johnson & Aries, 1983).

Alternatively, men, who have been socialized to value independence and com-petition, tend to organize their intimate relationships around shared activities (Cald-well & Peplau, 1982). Men rate positive instrumental behaviors as more important to their romantic relationships than do women (Wills et al., 1974). Indeed, some longitudinal research shows that men's satisfaction with instrumental concerns, such as the division of household labor, predicts changes in their love for their wives, whereas satisfaction with communication predicts changes in women's love for their husbands (Vangelisti & Huston, 1994). For those who adhere to the different cultures model, these and other findings imply that men and women have distinct ideas about what is important in their intimate relationships (Cutrona, 1996; Wood & Inman, 1993). The different cultures model, in short, suggests that women and men will differ in terms of the importance they assign to various relational standards.

By contrast, the second model apparent in the literature suggests that women and men enter romantic relationships with similar standards, but their relational experiences are often disparate. This model places *different experiences,* rather than different cultural perspectives, at the core of gender-based distinctions in romantic relationships. Those who advocate this view explain that women often enact a "care-taker" role in their relationships; they tend to take more responsibility for meeting the emotional needs of their partners than do men (Thompson & Walker, 1989). Indeed, Cutrona (1996) notes that "on average, women are better sources of social support than men" (p. 30). Based, in part, on women's more nurturant behavior, this model suggests that men are more likely than women to have their relational stan-dards fulfilled. Reis and his colleagues have found that women's interactions with one another tend to be more intimate than those of men and that people who spend more time with women tend to be less lonely (Reis, Senchack, & Solomon, 1985; Wheeler, Reis, & Nezlek, 1983). Helgeson, Shaver, and Dyer (1987) similarly found that in opposite-sex relationships, both women and men report feeling appreciation for their partner, but women are more likely than men to express that appreciation to their partner. These results suggest the possibility that interactions with women may be more amenable to meeting romantic partners' standards than those with men. Women appear to be better equipped to fulfill commonly held relational standards because their communication skills are more refined than are men's. Studies have dem-onstrated, for example, that women generally have greater skills in comforting others (Burleson, 1982), decoding and encoding nonverbal communication (Hall, 1978;

Rosenthal & DePaulo, 1979), listening (Miller, Berg, & Archer, 1983), and responding (Andersen & Bem, 1981) than do men. Although research suggests the magnitude of these gender differences is small (Canary & Hause, 1993; Hyde & Linn, 1988), they may give women an advantage over men in meeting their partner's relational standards. The different experiences model, in sum, suggests that dissimilarities in the attitudes and behaviors of women and men create a context in which relational standards are more often fulfilled for men than they are for women.

The purpose of this study was twofold. First, we sought to confirm the often demonstrated association (e.g., Kelley & Thibaut, 1978; Michalos, 1986; Nye, 1979; Rusbult & Buunk, 1993) between relational quality and the degree to which people believe their standards are fulfilled. Second, and more central to our concerns, we sought to explore, through a preliminary investigation, the extent to which one or both of the two models described in this paper help further understanding of women's and men's relational standards. If the different cultures model is predominant, we expect women and men will differ in the importance they associate with various relational standards. In contrast, if the different experiences model holds, we anticipate women and men will view various standards as of similar importance. Women, however, will report that their standards are less often fulfilled in their current relationship than will men, and the discrepancy between the importance women associate with standards and the degree to which those standards are met will be significantly greater for women than it will be for men.

Methods

Development of the Measure of Relational Standards

Several steps were taken to develop a measure of standards for long-term romantic relationships. First, research on measures of relational quality or satisfaction (e.g., Hendrick, 1988; Lewis & Spanier, 1979; Norton, 1983; Sabatelli, 1984) and studies focusing on the qualities people anticipate from romantic associations (Harvey, Agostinelli, & Weber, 1989; Jones & Gallois, 1989; Quick & Jacob, 1973; Tharp, 1963) were reviewed to obtain information about standards typically used to evaluate relationships. Second, 23 undergraduate students each interviewed four people (two college-aged students and two people older than the average college student) concerning the standards those people had for romantic relationships. Approximately one-half of the individuals interviewed were male and about one-half were female. The interviewers took notes, in the form of a list of standards, during the interviews and filled in the details or definitions they believed necessary. Third, the standards generated from the review of literature and the interviews were compiled into a single list so that similar standards were placed together. Thirty standards were identified and described. They are listed in Table 1, along with their definitions.

Debriefing discussions with the samples of undergraduate students and adults revealed six standards that were salient to a number of individuals, but were missing from the preliminary list. Because our effort was to generate as representative a listing as possible, these additional standards (Emotional Attachment, Adaptability, Physical Intimacy, Freedom, Relational Centrality, and Network Integration) were added to the revised list (see Table 1 for descriptions), for a total of 30.

Table 1 ▨ Typology of Standards for Long-Term Relationships

Category	*Description*
Adaptability*	Both people will be willing and able to adapt to the changing needs, demands, and desires of the other.
Privacy	Neither person will reveal personal data about the other to people not involved in the relationship.
Acquisition	The two people will acquire possessions together and will presume to jointly share and own them.
Freedom*	Each person will respect the other's rights; neither will presume upon the other. Each will allow the other his or her "own space" when desired.
Relational centrality*	For both people, the relationship will be more important than jobs, friends, others, etc. The relationship will be a very central part of their lives.
Fidelity	The two people will be emotionally and physically faithful to each other.
Impact	Each person in the relationship will significantly affect the other.
Contracts	Both people will abide by the various explicit and implicit contracts, rules, agreements, and arrangements the two have made with each other.
Presence	The two people will spend much time together.
Relaxation	Both people will feel comfortable and at ease with the other. There will be no need for pretensions or image consciousness. Both will be comfortable "letting their hair down" in the other's presence.
Acceptance	Both people will know and accept the other's faults and strengths; neither will take advantage of the other's weaknesses.
Respect	Both people will respect each other, provide credit where due, not be condescending or demeaning toward each other, not "put each other down."
Affection demonstration	Both people will show one another that they like and love each other.
Goal sharing	The two people will share similar plans, goals, and aspirations for the relationship.
Uniqueness	The people will believe their relationship to be different from other relationships. It is a unique and special relationship—not like others.
Reliability	Both people will be able to rely on the other; each will offer security and dependability for the other.
Differentiation	Both people in the relationship will fill certain roles. He will do X; she'll do Y. The roles will complement each other.
Physical intimacy*	The two people will be physically intimate with each other.
Openness	Both people will be willing to talk and comfortable talking with the other about wants and needs and things that are bothering them; each will be willing to self-disclose feelings and emotions.
Twosome	The two people will go and be together; neither will leave the other alone or behind.

Table 1 ■ (*Continued*)

Category	*Description*
Recognition	Others will recognize and know the two people as a couple.
Coping	Both people will be able to cope with problems, arguments, fights, discord, and disasters associated with the other and the relationship without sacrificing the relationship.
Predictability	Both people will know the other well enough to comfortably predict the other's likes, dislikes, and actions.
Frankness	Both people will be honest with the other. Neither person will lie to the other on important matters; each will be trustworthy.
Commitment	Both people will be committed to each other and their shared relationship.
Other-directedness	Each person will attempt to please and satisfy the other, make the other feel good, be helpful and unselfish.
Emotional attachment*	The two people will be emotionally tied to each other. Each will feel love for the other.
Network integration*	Each person will help the other become accepted in his or her circle of friends and relatives and each will accept the other's friends and relatives.
Enjoyment	The relationship will be fun and enjoyable.
Synchrony	The two people will mesh; they won't strongly disagree on major values and issues and they'll complement each other's tastes and needs.

*Standards with an asterisk were added after the initial pilot study.

Subjects

One hundred twenty-two adults enrolled in continuing education courses participated in this project. Of the total, 70 were women and 52 were men. Respondents reported they had been involved in an average of 2.33 ($SD = 1.15$) long-term romantic relationships (*range* = 1–6) and had been in their current relationships for an average of 11.94 years ($SD = 8.28$, *range* = 1–40). The age of participants ranged from 23 to 59 years (*mean* = 34.52, $SD = 7.44$).

Procedures

Respondents received a packet of materials containing a form of the Locke-Wallace measure of marital quality (Locke & Wallace, 1959) as well as a questionnaire about their standards for long-term romantic relationships. The Locke-Wallace scale has strong convergent validity with other measures of relational satisfaction (see, e.g., Norton, 1983). For this sample, the *alpha* reliability for the measure was .80. The questionnaire focusing on people's standards and the relational quality measure were randomly sequenced to prevent order effects.

To complete the questionnaire on standards, respondents were asked to read a description of each of 30 standards for long-term romantic relationships. Each description was followed by two 9-step Likert-type scales bounded by the phrases "very much" and "very little" (in all analyses, responses were calculated so that a high score indicated "very much" and a low score indicated "very little"). One of these two scales required participants to report how important they believed the standard was for successful long-term romantic relationships and the other asked that they rate the extent to which their current relationship reflected the standard. Table 1 contains descriptions of each of the standards, as they were presented to respondents.

Following previous work that has examined disparities between what partners anticipate and what they experience in their relationships (e.g., Ruble, Fleming, Hackel, & Stangor, 1988), two different approaches were taken to measure the extent to which people generally believed their relational standards were fulfilled. The first strategy, labelled by Kramer and Baron (1995) as the "direct" approach, involved calculating two composite measures: one for the importance individuals associated with the 30 relational standards and the other for the extent to which people believed their own relationships fulfilled the 30 standards. The *alpha* reliabilities for these two composite scales were .91 and .95, respectively.

The second measurement strategy, identified as the "discrepancy" approach (Kramer & Baron, 1995), involved calculating the difference between the degree to which participants held each standard and the extent to which they believed each was fulfilled in their relationship. The *alpha* reliability for the summed discrepancy measure was .97. As noted by Kramer and Baron, using the discrepancy approach along with the direct approach helps to alleviate some of the impact that social stereotypes and social desirability may have on respondents' ratings. By itself, direct questioning about whether standards are met may encourage participants to focus their attention on standards they believe others would find particularly important or problematic. The discrepancy approach reduces this bias by considering both the importance that respondents associate with relational standards and the extent to which they think their relationship reflects those standards.

Because composite measures such as these offer only a very general test of the two models raised in the introduction to this study, more in-depth analyses exploring possible variations among people's standards were also conducted. Similar to the tests done using the composite measures, these more detailed analyses used both direct and indirect approaches in examining the data. The more detailed analyses, however, did not presume a single underlying factor for standards. The responses to the importance ratings of each of the 30 items assessing individuals' relational standards instead were submitted to a factor analysis. The factors that emerged then were examined in terms of their relevance to both the different cultures and the different experiences models. This procedure contributed to the current investigation by highlighting patterns that may have been masked by using the composite measures. The analyses also yielded preliminary insights into the dimensional structure of people's relational standards.

The results of the factor analysis (varimax rotation) suggested that the 30 individual standards could be grouped into 7 general categories. This 7-factor solution accounted for 62.2% of the variance. These factors were labeled as *relational identity, integration, affective accessibility, trust, future orientation, role fulfillment,* and *flexibility*. The specific standards associated with each factor are shown in Table 2, along with

Table 2   ▨   Categories of Relational Standards

Name of Category and Standards Included	Alpha Coefficient for Importance	Alpha Coefficient for Fulfillment
Relational identity	.82	.88
Network integration Presence Acquisition Other-directedness Emotional attachment Recognition Relational centrality Uniqueness		
Integration	.78	.88
Acceptance Coping Respect Relaxation Synchrony		
Affective accessibility	.68	.68
Openness Affection demonstration Impact		
Trust	.73	.82
Fidelity Commitment Privacy Frankness		
Future orientation	.68	.62
Contracts Predictability Goal sharing		
Role fulfillment	.63	.70
Physical intimacy Twosome Differentiation Reliability		
Flexibility	.63	.65
Adaptability Freedom Enjoyment		

Categories are based on a factor analysis (varimax rotation). Each individual standard such as "Network integration" loaded .41 or higher on that factor; items listed first had the highest loading on that factor.

the alpha reliability coefficients for each factor. (Alphas were calculated both for respondents' ratings of the importance of their standards and for their ratings of the degree to which the standards were fulfilled in their relationships.)

Results

Standards and Marital Quality

Using the composite measure of standards (i.e., summing across standards), an analysis yielded a weak but marginally significant positive correlation between marital quality and the importance people associated with their standards for long-term romantic relationships ($r(91) = .14$, $p < .09$). There was a much stronger, positive, and significant association between relational quality and individuals' perceptions that their standards were fulfilled in the context of their relationships ($r(91) = .77$, $p < .001$). Further, as expected, the composite measure of the discrepancies between the importance people associated with various standards and the extent to which various standards and the extent to which people believed those standards were fulfilled was negatively and significantly associated with marital quality ($r(90) = -.72$, $p < .001$).

A similar pattern of results emerged using the seven more specific subscales drawn from the factor analysis of the standards measure. As can be seen in Table 3, the importance people associated with the various relational standards, for the most part, was not linked to marital quality. Only one of the factor-based subscales, *affective accessibility,* yielded a marginally significant positive correlation with the way participants reported feeling about the quality of their relationship. By contrast, people's assessments of whether or not the various factors were fulfilled were strongly and positively linked to relational quality. In addition, the discrepancies that individuals reported between the importance they associated with the standards reflected by each of the seven factor-based subscales and the degree to which each was fulfilled in their relationship were strongly and negatively associated with marital quality.

Table 3 ▓ **Correlations Between Factor-Based Subscales of Relational Standards and Marital Quality**

Subscales	*Importance*	*Fulfillment*	*Discrepancy*
Relational identity	.14	.67**	−.66**
Integration	.07	.68**	−.69**
Affective accessibility	.16[t]	.63**	−.61**
Trust	.12	.66**	−.61**
Future orientation	.07	.55**	−.65**
Role fulfillment	.12	.60**	−.64**
Flexibility	.07	.68**	−.63**

[t]$p < .10$; **$p < .001$

Table 4 ■ **Summary of Men's and Women's Mean Scores on Each Relational Standard Category and a Composite Measure**

	Importance		Fulfillment	
	Men	**Women**	**Men**	**Women**
Relational identity	63.10	61.14	63.12	56.78*
Integration	39.86	40.30	38.61	36.09*
Affective accessibility	24.37	24.05	23.76	22.12*
Trust	33.00	34.14*	32.72	31.51
Future orientation	23.37	23.08	23.24	21.44*
Role fulfillment	30.26	28.87ᶦ	29.82	26.99*
Flexibility	24.28	23.94	23.30	21.91*
Composite measure	239.30	234.90	235.26	215.57*

ᶦ$p < .12$; *$p < .05$

Gender Differences

Prior to testing potential gender differences in people's standards and their perceptions that those standards were fulfilled, an analysis was conducted to ensure that the women and men in the sample did not differ in terms of marital quality. Results indicated that there was no significant difference in marital quality for men and women who participated in the study ($F(1,97) = .002$; NS).

To begin to probe the relative merits of the two competing models presented at the outset of this paper, a 2×2 analysis of variance was calculated. The first factor was the sex of the respondents. The two levels of the second factor (a repeated or within subjects factor) were the respondents' ratings of (a) the importance of the standards and (b) the degree to which each standard was fulfilled in their current relationship. The different cultures model predicts that there will be a significant difference between men and women in the rated importance of their standards. In contrast, the different experiences model predicts an interaction such that there will be no significant difference between men's and women's importance ratings, but a significant dissimilarity in rated experience.

The 2×2 analysis of variance on the composite measures of standards yielded significant main effects for both sex ($F(1,102) = 7.32$; $p < .008$) and for the standards' rated importance versus fulfillment ($F(1,102) = 14.71$; $p < .001$). These main effects must be interpreted within the context of a significant interaction ($F(1,102) = 6.26$; $p < .01$) between the two variables. As expected from the different experiences model, individual comparisons used to probe the interaction found no significant distinctions between women and men in their importance ratings, but a significant difference ($F(1,103) = 9.74$; $p < .002$) between women and men in their ratings of the extent to which their standards were fulfilled. Men reported that their standards, overall, were met more fully in the context of their current relationship than did women. (Table 4 offers a summary of the relevant means.)

Seven additional 2 × 2 analyses of variance were calculated using the individual factor-based subscales. . . . The key interactions were all significant with one exception. The factor labelled *flexibility* had an interaction that approached significance ($p < .12$). In six of the seven cases, plots of the means offered greater support for the different experiences model: There were no significant differences between women's and men's ratings of the standards' importance, but there were significant distinctions between women and men on their fulfillment ratings. In each of the six cases, men believed their standards were fulfilled more than did women. Table 4 summarizes the mean comparisons across factors. As can be seen in the Table, *trust* was the only factor-based subscale that did not yield a significant difference in the degree to which men and women believed the standard was fulfilled in their relationship. Instead, there was a significant difference in the importance ratings associated with this subscale: Women believed *trust* was a more important standard than did men.

An alternative approach to testing possible gender differences in the gap between people's relational standards and the fulfillment of those standards is to examine the discrepancies between the importance women and men associate with various standards and the extent to which they believe the standards are met in their relationship. Consequently, an analysis of variance was conducted using the composite measure of the discrepancy between participants' importance ratings and their ratings of the degree to which their standards were fulfilled. As expected, there was a significant difference in the gap women and men perceived between the importance they associated with various standards and the fulfillment of those standards ($F(1,103) = 6.26$; $p < .01$). Women generally reported more of a discrepancy than did men. To test the extent to which this gender difference held up for different relational standards, the same analysis was conducted for each of the seven factor-based subscales. Not surprisingly, six of the seven subscales yielded the same pattern of results. Compared to men, women reported more of a discrepancy between the importance they associated with standards and the extent to which the standards were met in their relationship (*relational identity:* $F(1,110) = 6.31$, $p < .01$; *integration:* $F(1,111) = 6.56$, $p < .01$; *affective accessibility:* $F(1,115) = 4.43$, $p < .04$; *trust:* $F(1,115) = 7.06$, $p < .009$; *future orientation:* $F(1,112) = 6.79$, $p < .01$; *role fulfillment:* $F(1,116) = 4.00$, $p < .05$; and marginally, *flexibility:* $F(1,117) = 2.51$; $p < .12$). Table 5 summarizes the relevant means.

Taken together, the findings associated with the composite measures and the more specific factor-based subscales support the notion that women, more so than men, believe there is a gap between the importance they associate with relational standards and the extent to which those standards are met in their relationships. The men and women who participated in this study viewed relational standards as similarly important, but the women believed their standards were less often fulfilled.

Discussion

This study was conducted to (a) confirm previous findings concerning the association between the fulfillment of people's relational standards and relational quality, and (b) to investigate potential gender differences in relational standards and/or in the degree to which those standards are met. Analyses using both a composite mea-

Table 5 ▦ Summary of Men's and Women's Mean Discrepancy Scores on Each Relational Standard Category and a Composite Measure

	Discrepancy	
	Men	*Women*
Relational identity	−.02	4.27*
Integration	1.25	4.25*
Affective accessibility	.61	1.86*
Trust	.28	2.61*
Future orientation	.12	1.64*
Role fulfillment	.44	1.88*
Flexibility	.98	2.03ᵗ
Composite measure	4.04	19.19*

ᵗ$p < .12$; *$p < .05$

sure of standards and seven factor-based subscales revealed little association between the importance individuals associated with various standards and relational quality. Only the composite measure and one of seven subcomponents of people's standards (*affective accessibility*) were marginally and positively linked to the way individuals felt about their relationship. The lack of a substantial positive association between the standards people held and the quality of their relationships is not surprising in light of interdependence theory. Indeed, among others, Rusbult and Buunk (1993) argue that lower standards should be associated with higher relational satisfaction and commitment in part because lower standards are met with relative ease.

Predictably, the current findings did reveal strong, significant correlations between relational quality and both the degree to which individuals believed their standards were fulfilled, and the discrepancy between the importance people associated with standards and the extent to which those standards were met in their relationship. This pattern of findings was apparent when individuals' standards were examined as a composite, as well as when they were examined in terms of their more specific subcomponents. . . . When their relational standards are met or exceeded, people tend to evaluate their relationships in more positive ways.

The primary purpose of the study involved examining gender differences both in respondents' standards and in their perceptions of the degree to which those standards were met. The findings were more in line with a perspective labelled as the *different experiences* model than with one termed as the *different cultures* model. In brief, the different experiences model suggests that women's caretaker role (Thompson & Walker, 1989), their relatively intimate style of interaction (Caldwell & Peplau, 1982; Reis et al., 1985), and their communication skills (Andersen & Bem, 1981; Burleson, 1982; Hall, 1978; Miller et al., 1983; Rosenthal & DePaulo, 1979) create a relational context in which men's standards are more likely to be met than women's. In contrast, the different cultures perspective suggests that the importance of standards held by men and women differs in part because women and men enter romantic relationships with distinct views about what is central to those relationships.

Analyses of both composite measures and more detailed factor-based measures revealed that women and men did not differ in terms of the importance they associated with various standards (as hypothesized by the different cultures model), but rather that women believed their standards were fulfilled less often than did men (as predicted by the different experiences model). These findings are consistent with research conducted by Reis and his colleagues (Reis et al., 1985), which revealed that the criteria women and men used to judge intimacy did not differ, but that women's interactions were perceived (both by men and women) as more intimate than were those of men.

Obviously, there are limitations to the current study. For instance, causal statements cannot be made from these data. The processes by which people come to be dissatisfied in their relationships continue to be interesting and important ones for study. There is good evidence in a variety of literatures that discrepancies between people's standards and their perceptions of what they obtain influence their happiness or satisfaction (e.g., Michalos, 1986). However, at this point, either or both of two causal patterns may yield such findings. It is possible that when people's initial standards are not met, they become disillusioned. In contrast, it is just as probable that people who are dissatisfied with their relationships frequently note that their standards have gone unfulfilled. Very likely, both happen.

Another important limitation involves the type of data collected. Because the data are self-reports, they consist of people's perceptions of their standards and of the degree to which those standards were fulfilled. As a consequence, they do not provide information about whether, for example, women's relational partners actually failed to engage in behavior that met certain standards—the discrepancies between the importance people associated with standards and the fulfillment of those standards are perceptual. Although this clearly limits the scope of our claims, it does not negate the importance of our findings [see Sillars & Scott (1983) for a discussion of the centrality of perception to intimate relations]. As Cuber and Haroff (1965) argue, relational partners' perceptions are consequential because "they constitute reality for these people and are the bases for present and future courses of action" (p. 77).

In a similar vein, it is also possible that the women and men who participated in the study may have interpreted the descriptions of some of the standards in different ways. A strong version of the different cultures approach would proffer that women and men have very distinct meanings for standards. Men, for instance, might have a different interpretation than do women of a statement such as "Both people will be able to rely on the other; each will offer security and dependability for the other." To the extent that this is true, the results observed in the present investigation may not offer a definitive test of the different cultures model. Dealing with respondents' subjective interpretations is a potential problem anytime researchers examine self-reported group differences (e.g., due to gender, age, cultural background). Although this limitation definitely should be acknowledged, the findings of the current study are so consistent that broad interpretative differences seem unlikely. Certainly, a very thorough qualitative study will reveal if, and the extent to which, such differences actually exist.

In short, while the results of the present investigation are interesting, they represent only a small portion of a potentially expansive area of study. It is apparent that standards play a role in relational evaluations. But a number of scholars acknowledge that we know very little about how people use standards to formulate their assessments (Baucom et al., 1989; Ponzetti & Long, 1989). In discussing self-evaluation, for example, Higgins and his colleagues note that people likely use multiple standards at any given point in time and that evaluative processes are comprised of multiple stages (Higgins et al., 1986). Applying this theoretical framework to relational assessments raises a variety of issues for study. The process of selecting one or more standards over others, the influence of individual differences in the selection process, and the impact of selection on relationships all are issues that researchers have yet to explore thoroughly.

Similarly of interest are the ways both women and men assess whether or not their standards are being met and how they respond to those assessments. Evidence concerning attributional processing (e.g., Pyszczynski & Greenberg, 1981) suggests that, in at least some cases, unfulfilled standards are likely to result in individuals assessing the reason for the standard not being met and, based on that assessment, in re-evaluating their relational satisfaction. Given that women are more aware of relational issues (Acitelli, 1992; Burnett, 1987) and that they exhibit more complex thinking about relationships than do men (Martin, 1991), it is very possible that they also are more attentive to the extent to which their standards are met. The findings of the current study—that women more often than men believed their standards were not fulfilled—may have been due to women more closely monitoring the fulfillment of those standards. Women may have been more observant than men of where their relationship fell short.

Importantly, though, the women in this study were not more dissatisfied than their male counterparts. Clearly, dissatisfaction is not the only possible consequence of unfulfilled standards (see, e.g., Rusbult, Zembrodt, & Gunn, 1982). In some cases, unmet standards may lead one or the other person to leave (exit) the relationship. In others, where partners perceive their relational alternatives are limited, interdependence theory (Kelley & Thibaut, 1978; Thibaut & Kelley, 1959) suggests that dissatisfaction may set in and become the norm. Yet, in other cases, couples may cope with unmet standards in ways that allow them to maintain a certain level of relational satisfaction. Rusbult and her colleagues (Rusbult, Verette, Whitney, Slovik, & Lipkus, 1991) argue that accommodation—people's willingness to engage in constructive reactions and inhibit destructive reactions in the face of a partner's negative behavior—is key to maintaining relational satisfaction.

Although the data collected for the current study do not provide information about partners' coping strategies, they point to the notion that such strategies represent a potentially important outcome measure for how partners deal with (or preclude) relational disappointment. Some people may maintain relatively high levels of satisfaction in the face of significant problems through the judicious application of coping strategies. Further, the stability of romantic relationships, in the long run, may be evidenced by the sort of coping strategies devised by relational partners. Certain patterns of coping may be indicators of something akin to "relational hardiness." For example, Buehlman, Gottman, and Katz (1992) found that couples who "glorify" the struggles they experienced were more likely to stay together than couples who did not. In such cases, it is possible that the critical variable in determining stability is not the fulfillment of standards per se, but rather the way both partners cope with unmet standards.

The focus of most research on relational standards has been on what happens when partners perceive that their standards are not fulfilled. People's hopes for their relationships are shattered or reduced and this, in turn, is associated with lower relationship quality. It is also possible, however, that in some instances partners' standards are exceeded. Assuming individuals sometimes perceive their relationship exceeds their standards (and for a small subset of the current sample they did), a better understanding of the evaluative processes associated with such perceptions would be useful for those interested in relational maintenance.

Although the current study leaves a great deal to be done, it does make two important contributions to the literature. First, it confirms the oft cited association between the degree to which people's standards are met and their relational quality (e.g., Kelley & Thibaut, 1978; Michalos, 1986; Nye, 1979; Rusbult & Buunk, 1993). Second, and more relevant to our initial goals, the present study helps illuminate gender differences that may influence the link between partners' standards and their relational satisfaction. The findings indicate that women and men report that they have similar standards for their relationships, but that women are more likely than men to believe their standards are not fulfilled. These results support the notion that women and men have different experiences of romantic relationships and provide a testable explanation for why women suggest they have more problems in their relationships than do men.

References

Acitelli, L. K. (1992). Gender differences in relationship awareness and marital satisfaction among young married couples. *Personality and Social Psychology Bulletin, 18,* 102–110.

Adams, J. S. (1965). Inequity in social exchange. In L. Berkowitz (Ed.), *Advances in experimental social psychology* (Vol. 2, pp. 267–299). New York: Academic Press.

Andersen, S. M., & Bem, S. L. (1981). Sex typing and androgyny in dyadic interaction: Individual differences in responsiveness to physical attractiveness. *Journal of Personality and Social Psychology, 41,* 74–86.

Aries, E. (1996). *Men and women in interaction: Reconsidering the difference.* New York: Oxford University Press.

Baucom, D. H., Epstein, N., Sayers, S., & Sher, T. G. (1989). The role of cognitions in marital relationships: Definitional, methodological, and conceptual issues. *Journal of Consulting and Clinical Psychology, 57,* 31–38.

Beck, A. T. (1988). *Love is never enough: How couples can overcome misunderstandings, resolve conflicts, and solve relationship problems through cognitive therapy.* New York: Harper & Row.

Buehlman, K. T., Gottman, J. M., & Katz, L. F. (1992). How a couple views their past predicts their future: Predicting divorce from an oral history interview. *Journal of Family Psychology, 5,* 295–318.

Burleson, B. R. (1982). The development of comforting communication skills in childhood and adolescence. *Child Development, 53,* 1578–1588.

Burleson, B. R., Kunkel, A. W., Samter, W., & Werking, K. J. (1996). Men's and women's evaluations of communication skills in personal relationships: When sex differences make a difference—and when they don't. *Journal of Social and Personal Relationships, 13,* 201–224.

Burnett, R. (1987). Reflections in personal relationships. In R. Burnett, P. McGhee, & D. D. Clarke (Eds.), *Accounting for relationships: Explanation, representation, and knowledge* (pp. 74–93). London: Methuen.

Caldwell, M. A., & Peplau, L. A. (1982). Sex differences in same-sex friendship. *Sex Roles, 8,* 721–732.

Canary, D. J., & Hause, K. S. (1993). Is there any reason to research sex differences in communication? *Communication Quarterly, 41,* 129–144.

Chodorow, N. J. (1978). *The reproduction of mothering: Psychoanalysis and the sociology of gender.* Berkeley: University of California Press.

Cuber, J., & Haroff, P. (1965). *The significant Americans.* New York: Van Rees.

Cutrona, C. (1996). *Social support in couples.* Thousand Oaks, CA: Sage.

Duck, S. W. (1990). Relationships as unfinished business: Out of the frying pan and into the 1990's. *Journal of Social and Personal Relationships, 7*, 5–28.

Ellis, A. (1962). *Reason and emotion in psychotherapy.* New York: Lyle Stuart.

Epstein, N., & Eidelson, R. J. (1981). Unrealistic beliefs of clinical couples: Their relationship to expectations, goals and satisfaction. *The American Journal of Family Therapy, 9*, 13–22.

Fletcher, G. J. O. (1983). Sex differences in causal attributions for marital separation. *New Zealand Journal of Psychology, 12*, 82–89.

Fletcher, G. J. O. (1996). *Lay relationship ideals: Their structure and function.* Invited address presented at the International Conference on Personal Relationships, Banff, Canada.

Gilligan, C. (1982). *In a different voice: Psychological theory and women's development.* Cambridge, MA: Harvard University Press.

Haas, A., & Sherman, M. A. (1982). Reported topics of conversation among same-sex adults. *Communication Quarterly, 30*, 332–342.

Hall, J. A. (1978). Gender effects in decoding nonverbal cues. *Psychological Bulletin, 85*, 845–857.

Harvey, J. H., Agostinelli, G., & Weber, A. L. (1989). Account making and the formation of expectations about close relationships. In C. Hendrick (Ed.), *Close relationships* (pp. 39–62). Newbury Park, CA: Sage.

Harvey, J. H., Wells, G. L., & Alvarez, M. D. (1978). Attribution in the context of conflict and separation in close relationships. In J. H. Harvey, W. J. Ickes, & R. F. Kidd (Eds.), *New directions in attributional research* (Vol. 2, pp. 235–260). Hillsdale, NJ: Erlbaum.

Hatfield, E., Traupman, J., Sprecher, S., Utne, M., & Hay, J. (1985). Equity and intimate relations: Recent research. In W. Ickes (Ed.), *Compatible and incompatible relationships* (pp. 91–117). New York: Springer-Verlag.

Helgeson, V. S., Shaver, P., & Dyer, M. (1987). Prototypes of intimacy and distance in same-sex and opposite-sex relationships. *Journal of Social and Personal Relationships, 4*, 195–233.

Hendrick, S. S. (1988). A generic measure of relationship satisfaction. *Journal of Marriage and the Family, 50*, 93–98.

Higgins, E. T., Strauman, T., & Klein, R. (1986). Standards and the process of self-evaluation: Multiple affects from multiple stages. In R. M. Sorrentino & E. T. Higgins (Eds.), *Handbook of motivation and cognition* (pp. 23–63). New York: Guilford Press.

Homans, G. (1961). *Social behavior: Its elementary forms.* New York: Harcourt Brace Jovanovich.

Huston, T. L., & Burgess, R. L. (1979). Social exchange in developing relationships: An overview. In R. L. Burgess & T. L. Huston (Eds.), *Social exchange in developing relationships* (pp. 3–28). New York: Academic Press.

Hyde, J. S., & Linn, M. C. (1988). Gender differences in verbal ability: A meta-analysis. *Psychological Bulletin, 104*, 53–69.

Johnson, F., & Aries, E. (1983). The talk of women friends. *Women's Studies International Forum, 6*, 353–361.

Jones, E., & Gallois, C. (1989). Spouses' impressions of rules for communication in public and private marital conflicts. *Journal of Marriage and the Family, 51*, 957–967.

Kelley, H. H., & Thibaut, J. W. (1978). *Interpersonal relations: A theory of interdependence.* New York: Wiley.

Kramer, L., & Baron, L. A. (1995). Parental perceptions of children's sibling relationships. *Family Relations, 44*, 95–103.

Kunkel, A. W. (1995, November). *Assessing the adequacy of explanations for gender differences in emotional support: An experimental test of the different cultures and skill deficit accounts.* Paper presented at the annual meeting of the Speech Communication Association, San Antonio, TX.

Lederer, W., & Jackson, D. O. (1968). *The mirages of marriage.* New York: Norton.

Lewis, R. A., & Spanier, G. B. (1979). Theorizing about the quality and stability of marriage. In W. Burr, R. Hill, F. I. Nye, & I. Reiss (Eds.), *Contemporary theories about the family* (Vol. 2, pp. 268–294). New York: The Free Press.

Locke, H. J., & Wallace, K. M. (1959). Short marital-adjustment and prediction tests: Their reliability and validity. *Marriage and Family Living, 21,* 252–255.

Macklin, E. D. (1978). Review of research on nonmarital cohabitation in the United States. In B. I. Murstein (Ed.), *Exploring intimate lifestyles* (pp. 197–243). New York: Springer.

Maltz, D. N., & Borker, R. A. (1982). A cultural approach to male-female miscommunication. In J. J. Gumperz (Ed.), *Language and social identity* (pp. 196–216). Cambridge: Cambridge University Press.

Martin, R. W. (1991). Examining personal relationship thinking: The relational cognition complexity instrument. *Journal of Social and Personal Relationships, 8,* 467–480.

Michalos, A. C. (1986). An application of multiple discrepancies theory (MDT) to seniors. *Social Indicators Research, 18,* 349–373.

Miller, L., Berg, J. H., & Archer, R. L. (1983). Openers: Individuals who elicit intimate self-disclosure. *Journal of Personality and Social Psychology, 44,* 1234–1244.

Norton, R. (1983). Measuring marital quality: A critical look at the dependent variable. *Journal of Marriage and the Family, 45,* 141–151.

Nye, F. I. (1979). Choice, exchange, and the family. In W. Burr, R. Hill, F. I. Nye, & I. Reiss (Eds.), *Contemporary theories about the family* (Vol. 2, pp. 1–41). New York: The Free Press.

Peplau, L. A., Bikson, T. K., Rook, K., & Goodchilds, J. D. (1982). Being old and living alone. In L. A. Peplau & D. Perlman (Eds.), *Loneliness: A sourcebook of current theory, research, and therapy* (pp. 327–347). New York: Wiley.

Ponzetti, J. J., & Long, E. (1989). Healthy family functioning: A review and critique. *Family Therapy, 16,* 43–50.

Pyszczynski, T. A., & Greenberg, J. (1981). Role of disconfirmed expectancies in the instigation of attributional processing. *Journal of Personality and Social Psychology, 40,* 31–38.

Quick, E., & Jacob, T. (1973). Marital disturbance in relation to role theory and relationship theory. *Journal of Abnormal Psychology, 82,* 309–316.

Reis, H. T., Senchack, M., & Solomon, B. (1985). Sex differences in the intimacy of social interaction: Further examination of potential explanations. *Journal of Personality and Social Psychology, 48,* 1204–1217.

Rosenthal, R., & DePaulo, B. (1979). Sex differences in eavesdropping on nonverbal cues. *Journal of Personality and Social Psychology, 37,* 273–285.

Rubenstein, C. M., & Shaver, P. (1982). *In search of intimacy.* New York: Delacorte.

Rubin, Z., Peplau, L. A., & Hill, C. T. (1981). Loving and leaving: Sex differences in romantic attachments. *Sex Roles, 7,* 821–835.

Ruble, D. N., Fleming, A. S., Hackel, L. S., & Stangor, C. (1988). Changes in the marital relationship during the transition to first time motherhood: Effects of violated expectations concerning division of household labor. *Journal of Personality and Social Psychology, 55,* 78–87.

Rusbult, C. E. (1980). Commitment and satisfaction in romantic associations: A test of the investment model. *Journal of Experimental Social Psychology, 16,* 172–186.

Rusbult, C. E. (1983). A longitudinal test of the investment model: The development (and deterioration) of satisfaction and commitment in heterosexual involvement. *Journal of Personality and Social Psychology, 45,* 101–117.

Rusbult, C. E., & Buunk, B. P. (1993). Commitment processes in close relationships: An interdependence analysis. *Journal of Social and Personal Relationships, 10,* 175–204.

Rusbult, C. E., Verette, J. Whitney, G. A., Slovik, L. F., & Lipkus, I. (1991). Accommodation processes in close relationships: Theory and preliminary empirical evidence. *Journal of Personality and Social Psychology, 60,* 53–78.

Rusbult, C. E., Zembrodt, I. M., & Gunn, L. K. (1982). Exit, voice, loyalty, and neglect: Responses to dissatisfaction in romantic involvements. *Journal of Personality and Social Psychology, 43,* 1230–1242.

Rusbult, C. E., Zembrodt, I. M., & Iwaniszek, J. (1986). The impact of gender and sex-role orientation on responses to dissatisfaction in close relationships. *Sex Roles, 15,* 1–20.

Sabatelli, R. M. (1984). The marital comparison level index: A measure for assessing outcomes relative to expectations. *Journal of Marriage and the Family, 46,* 651–662.

Sillars, A. L., & Scott, M. D. (1983). Interpersonal perception between intimates: An integrative view. *Human Communication Research, 10,* 153–176.

Tannen, D. (1990). *You just don't understand: Women and men in conversation*. New York: William Morrow.

Tharp, R. G. (1963). Dimensions of marriage roles. *Marriage and Family Living, 25,* 389–404.

Thibaut, J. W., & Kelley, H. H. (1959). *The social psychology of groups*. New York: Wiley.

Thompson, L., & Walker, A. J. (1989). Gender in families: Women and men in marriage, work, and parenthood. *Journal of Marriage and the Family, 51,* 845–871.

Tornstam, L. (1992). Loneliness in marriage. *Journal of Social and Personal Relationships, 9,* 197–217.

Vangelisti, A. L., & Huston, T. L. (1994). Maintaining marital satisfaction and love. In D. J. Canary & L. Stafford (Eds.). *Communication and relational maintenance* (pp. 165–186). New York: Academic Press.

Walster, E., Walster, G. W., & Berscheid, E. (1978). *Equity: Theory and research*. Boston: Allyn & Bacon.

Wheeler, L., Reis, H., & Nezlek, J. (1983). Loneliness, social interaction, and sex roles. *Journal of Personality and Social Psychology, 45,* 943–953.

Wills, T. A., Weiss, R. L., & Patterson, G. R. (1974). A behavioral analysis of the determinants of marital satisfaction. *Journal of Consulting and Clinical Psychology, 42,* 802–811.

Wood, J. T. (1994). *Gendered lives: Communication, gender, and culture*. Belmont, CA: Wadsworth.

Wood, J. T., & Inman, C. C. (1993). In a different mode: Masculine styles of communicating closeness. *Journal of Applied Communication Research, 21,* 279–295.

Questions for Thought

1. The authors contrast two explanations of gender differences in close relationships—the "different cultures" model and the "different experiences" model. Explain and compare these two perspectives.

2. Describe how Vangelisti and Daly developed a measure of relationship standards. What clusters or subscales did they identify?

3. The authors believe that their results support the "different experiences" model rather than the "different cultures" model. Describe the main findings they present to support this claim.

4. Vangelisti and Daly investigated male-female romantic relationships. Consider how their approach might apply to same-sex platonic friendships. What would a "different cultures" model predict about male-male versus female-female friendships? What would a "different experiences" approach predict? What do you think research would actually find?

5. Many general-audience books about male-female relationships are available at your local library or bookstore (for example, *Men Are from Mars, Women Are from Venus* by John Gray and *You Just Don't Understand* by Deborah Tannen). Select one of these books. Read enough of the book to summarize the author's main thesis or point of view. Does this book present a "different cultures" or "different experiences" perspective on male-female relationships?

6. In America men are much more likely than women to commit violent crimes such as armed robbery, rape, and murder. Discuss how a "different cultures" perspective and a "different experiences" perspective would explain these male-female differences in terms of violent crime.

Power Structure in Mexican and Mexican American Farm Labor Families

Glenn R. Hawkes
Minna Taylor

*Mexican American marriages are often stereotyped as having a patriarchal power struc-
ture in which husbands are dominant, yet research has consistently challenged this view.
In this early study, researchers investigated the balance of power between husbands and
wives among Mexican and Mexican American farm workers in California. Most couples
had egalitarian relationships, with husbands and wives sharing in decisions about where
the family lives, how money is spent, and if the wife should work outside the home. More
recent research has replicated this finding, showing that an equal balance of power is common in Mexican American marriages.*

Familial power structure in Mexican and Mexican American farm labor families
was explored by standardized interview to determine if the commonly held view
of husband dominance could be substantiated. In 76 cases from California state-
operated migrant family labor camps egalitarianism was by far the most common mode in both decision-making and action-taking. Findings suggest that
dominance-submission patterns are much less universal than previously assumed
or never existed but were an ideal or are undergoing radical change.

During 1971–1973 we worked on a study of family patterns of California migrant
farm labor families as a part of a national study of disadvantaged families. In
answer to a series of questions about who made the decisions and who took the

Reprinted from *Journal of Marriage and the Family,* 1975, 37(4), 807–811. Copyright 1975 by the
National Council on Family Relations, 3989 Central Avenue NE, Suite 550, Minneapolis, MN 55421.
Used by permission.

action in the family the most common response was that the husband and wife decided or acted jointly. This struck us as unusual inasmuch as all but one of the respondents were Mexican or of Mexican descent.

In light of the descriptions in the literature of the patriarchal power structure in the Mexican and Mexican American family this was an unexpected finding. What follows is an analysis of our findings and an attempt to explain why a more egalitarian power structure was found than was expected.

The Mexican American family structure is described as a traditional patriarchy. It is supposedly modified only slightly from the structure found in Mexico, in which women are put on a pedestal, while being despised for their weakness and passivity. Husbands dominate their wives and carry out their family obligations as they see fit (Penalosa, 1968).

In the United States this set of patriarchal relations continues to exist. While the man may be a second-class citizen outside the family circle, at home he is a king, demanding and receiving unquestioning obedience from his wife and children. The husband is the authority figure in the family making all the decisions and disciplining the children. It is he who decides on financial matters and represents the household in dealings with the outside world. The wife, on the other hand, is expected to be submissive, chaste, and unworldly. She is expected to acknowledge her husband's authority and superiority, to place his needs and desires before her own and to carry out his decisions. This notion is so widely held that the Spanish term for male dominance, *machismo*,[1] is fast becoming a part of the vernacular American language (Jones, 1948; Clark, 1959; Madsen, 1964; Ruble, 1966; Staples, 1971).

In many of the studies on the Mexican American family it is clear that only a minority of families do not fit these norms. Usually these deviations are attributed to increasing Americanization and urbanization (Madsen, 1964; Tharp *et al.*, 1968; Staples, 1971), or to increasing financial independence of the women (Clark, 1959). But there is some evidence that while this patriarchal pattern was the ideal it was never the norm (Griffith, 1948; Woods, 1956; Grebler *et al.*, 1970). Thus three explanations have been put forth in the literature: (1) as the Mexican American family moves further away from its rural heritage, it becomes more like its egalitarian American counterpart; (2) as women become less dependent upon their husbands they exert more influence on family decisions; and (3) the described patriarchal family never truly existed, but was merely an ideal. These three possible explanations form the basis for the investigation of our unexpected findings.

Method

The data for this analysis came from a study of family living patterns of farm labor families residing in 12 state-owned and operated migrant family camps in California. To be eligible for the study a respondent had to be a female age 19 to 65 and responsible for at least one child under the age of 18. A woman of 18 or less would qualify

---

[1] Webster defines *machismo* (Spanish) as strong or assertive masculinity, characterized by virility, courage, aggressiveness, etc.

as a respondent if she were the mother of one of the children in the family. Interviews were conducted between September and November of 1971.

While ethnic origin was not an eligibility requirement, all but one of the interviewees was of Mexican or Mexican American origin. The one *Anglo* family studied is not included in the present analysis. This analysis was further restricted to include: (1) intact families—those in which both husband and wife were together; (2) respondents who answered all the questions about the family power structure; and (3) only those respondents who were interviewed without the husband being present. (In our attempt to get data for the power analysis which would be as pure as possible we decided to exclude those interviews where the husband was present.) The number of respondents remaining after these qualifications were met was 76.

The families were selected on a random basis from each of 12 migrant camps and interviews were conducted by bilingual (Spanish and English) women who were themselves residents of the migrant camp and who were specially trained to do the interviewing. The interviews covered many areas of family life in addition to conjugal power structure such as values and beliefs, family finances and demographic characteristics of the family. The power structure questions asked both about who in the family made the decision and who took the agreed-upon action.

The questions on decision-making asked who (husband, wife or husband and wife together) was mainly responsible for making the decisions in each of the following areas: (1) which friends the couple saw most often; (2) the best place for the family to live; (3) whether the wife should work outside the home; (4) the number of children wanted; (5) how the children should be handled; and (6) how the money should be used.

The questions in the area of action-taking asked who mainly (husband, wife, or husband and wife together): (1) tried to limit the number of children; (2) handled the children when both parents were home; (3) handled money matters (paid the bills, bought family necessities, etc.).

On each question a respondent received one point if the wife decided or acted alone, two points for a shared decision or action, and three points if the husband decided or acted alone. A mean decision-making score and mean action-taking score was computed for each respondent. These scores were used to assign respondents to decision-making and action-taking categories. For both decision-making and action-taking there were three categories: wife mainly decides (acts), both mainly decide (act), and husband mainly decides (acts). The decision-making and action-taking categories were further combined to yield a family pattern score and category for each family. Because there are three decision-making and three action-taking categories there are nine possible family pattern combinations: husband decides-husband acts; husband decides-both act; husband decides-wife acts; both decide-husband acts; wife decides-wife acts; wife decides-both act; wife decides-husband acts; both decide-wife acts; both decide-both act. Because there were no respondents in the wife decides-husband acts combination there are eight possible categories in our analysis. For correlation purposes these were assigned scores from eight to one, respectively. These family pattern categories were further reduced to six categories: (1) husband dominant which consists of the category husband decides-husband acts; (2) husband semi-dominant which consists of the categories husband decides-both act and both decide-husband acts; (3) husband decides-wife acts; (4) egalitarian which consists of

Table 1   ▓   **Decision-Making and Action-Taking**

	Husband %	Joint %	Wife %
Who mainly decides:			
1. Which friends visit	24	67	9
2. Where family lives	50	45	5
3. Should wife work	25	49	26
4. Number children desired	14	78	8
5. Disciplining of children	17	78	5
6. How money used	21	74	4
Who mainly acts to:			
1. Limit family size	12	75	13
2. Discipline children	22	60	17
3. Handle money matters	22	71	7

the category both decide-both act; (5) wife semi-dominant which consists of the categories wife decides-both act and both decide-wife acts; and (6) wife dominant which consists of the category wife decides-wife acts. Frequency distributions and correlations were used to analyze the data.

Findings and Discussion

It seems appropriate to begin by validating our initial assertion that an egalitarian power structure did exist in many of the Mexican American families. In answer to all but one of the questions about who decides or acts, a majority of the families responded that the decision or action was shared by husband and wife (see Table 1). The one area in which joint decision-making was not the most common response was deciding where the family should live. This was decided in the majority of homes by the husband alone. However, in nearly the same number of homes this too was a joint decision.

While the above information is indicative of an egalitarian power structure, it is not conclusive. More credence is lent to our assertion of an egalitarian power structure through examination of the decision-making and action-taking categories and the overall family patterns.

In both decision-making and in action-taking the majority of families fall into the categories of shared power (83 percent shared decision and 67 percent shared action-taking).[2] In 5 percent of the families the women had the decision-making

[2] That these powers were shared does not necessarily indicate that the decision was made or the action taken together. For instance, if the wife made half the decision or took half the action and the husband the other half, the family would have been assigned to this category.

Table 2 ■ Percentage of Each Family Type

Family Pattern Type	Percent
1. Husband dominant	7
2. Husband semi-dominant	9
3. Husband decides-wife acts	3
4. Egalitarian	62
5. Wife semi-dominant	17
6. Wife dominant	3

power and in 20 percent she had the action-taking power. The man held these powers in 12 percent and 13 percent of the families.

The overall family pattern (see Table 2) for most families (62 percent) is again an egalitarian one—one in which both the decision-making and the action-taking powers are shared. The next most frequent categories were wife semi-dominant and husband semi-dominant. The majority of this semi-dominance for both husbands and wives comes from cases in which decision-making is shared but action is generally taken by one spouse. This is true for 11 of the 13 cases of wife semi-dominant, and 5 of 7 cases of husband semi-dominant. From these data it is clear that egalitarianism among Mexican American farm labor families, far from being the exception, is the rule.

Having established that an egalitarian pattern does indeed exist among these families, and that it is far more extensive than is generally believed, we turn to factors which could account for it. Probably the most common explanation is that of increasing acculturation and urbanization. We have two indicators of differential acculturation: (1) citizenship, and (2) language spoken in the home. We have assumed that, on the average, U.S. citizens would be more acculturated than Mexican citizens, and that those who spoke English and Spanish in the home would be more acculturated than those who spoke only Spanish. (None of the respondents in this study spoke only English.)

Turning first to citizenship, we find differences in the expected direction. For both U.S. and Mexican citizens the majority of families are egalitarian; however, U.S. citizens tend to be somewhat more egalitarian than their Mexican counterparts in decision-making, action-taking and overall family patterns. None of these differences are statistically significant. Citizenship explains six percent of the decision-making variance, one percent of the action-taking variance, and three percent of the family pattern variance.

The second indicator of acculturation—language spoken in the home—reveals a similar pattern. Here again the majority of both Spanish-speaking and bilingual homes are egalitarian in decision-making, action-taking, and overall family patterns. However, the bilingual homes are more likely to be wife-dominated and less likely to be egalitarian than are homes in which Spanish is the only spoken language. But again, as with citizenship, none of the differences are significant. Language accounts for one percent of the decision-making variance, two percent of the action-taking variance, and one percent of the family pattern variance.

Increasing urbanization of Mexican Americans has also been put forth as an explanation for the egalitarian power structure found in some families. Since the original study was concerned with rural poor and since farm labor is by definition a rural occupation we have only one inadequate indicator of urban living. This is the number of years the respondent had lived in nonrural areas. If urban living were to account for the egalitarian power structure we would suppose that those who had lived part of their lives in nonrural areas would be more egalitarian than those who had lived in rural areas only. In fact, there is essentially no difference in our respondents. Number of years lived in nonrural areas accounts for none of the decision-making variance, 1 percent of the action-taking variance and 0.2 percent of the family pattern variance.

A third explanation found in the literature for an egalitarian pattern is the decreasing dependence of women upon their husbands in this country. Some of this independence is thought to come from the wife's opportunity to work outside the home. We used two measures of wifely independence: (1) whether or not the wife works outside the home; and (2) the difference in years of education between a wife and her husband. It was assumed that a working wife would be less dependent than a nonworking wife, and therefore, the families of working wives should be more egalitarian. It was also assumed that a wife would be more dependent upon a husband better educated than she was and less dependent if she were better educated than her husband.

The families of working wives are indeed more likely than those of nonworking wives to be egalitarian in decision-making, action-taking and overall family patterns. But, as with our previous differences, none of these are statistically significant. Whether or not a wife worked accounted for 2 percent of the decision-making variance, 0.06 percent of the action-taking variance, and 0.7 percent of the family pattern variance.

Families in which both spouses had received the same amount of education were the most egalitarian in decision-making, action-taking and family pattern. Wives who had more education than their husbands were more likely to have families in which decisions were shared than were wives whose husbands had more education than they did. Educational differences between spouses, however, made no difference in the amount of egalitarianism in their action-taking or family pattern.

Differential education accounted for 4 percent of the decision-making variance, 0.1 percent of the action-taking variance and 3 percent of the family pattern variance.

Summary and Conclusions

Scientific and popular literature have stressed the dominant role of the male in the Mexican and Mexican American culture. Studies of the husband role in the family have indicated the pervasiveness of this dominance in family functions and patterns. Complementing the male dominance has been the traditional submissive role of the wife. Her submission has been assumed to be as pervasive as his dominance.

The present study samples decision-making, action-taking, and family patterns of 76 Mexican and Mexican American farm labor families. Findings suggest that dominance-submission patterns are much less universal than previously assumed. Either they never existed but were an ideal or they are undergoing radical change. The traditional forces of change—acculturation and urbanization—were not found to be responsible for the results of this study.

We suggest that many of the traditional stereotypes of groups such as ethnic minorities noted in the literature and in public assumptions need more adequate verification. It is possible that more sophisticated methods of research may negate many of our previous assumptions. It is also possible that changing human conditions have modified roles without public and scientific awareness.

References

Clark, Margaret. 1959. *Health in the Mexican-American Culture.* Berkeley and Los Angeles: University of California Press.

Grebler, Les, Joan W. Moore, and Ralph Guzman. 1970. *The Mexican-American People: The Nation's Second Largest Minority.* New York: Free Press.

Griffith, Beatrice. 1948. *American Me.* Boston: Houghton Mifflin Co.

Jones, Robert C. 1948. "Ethnic family patterns: The Mexican family in the United States." *American Journal of Sociology* 53: 450–452.

Madsen, William. 1964. *The Mexican American of South Texas.* New York: Holt, Rinehart and Winston.

Ruble, Arthur J. 1966. *Across the Tracks.* Austin: University of Texas Press.

Staples, Robert. 1971. "The Mexican-American family: Its modification over time." *Phylon* 32: 179–192.

Tharp, R. G., Meadow, A., Lennhoff, S. G., and Satterfield, D. (1968). "Changes in marriage roles accompanying the acculturation of the Mexican-American wife." *Journal of Marriage and the Family,* 30(3), 404–412.

Woods, Sister Frances Jerome. 1956. *Cultural Values of American Ethnic Groups.* New York: Harper and Brothers.

Questions for Thought

1. The authors distinguish between the concepts of *patriarchy* and *machismo.* Explain and give an example of each term.

2. The researchers studied families living in 12 migrant worker camps in California. Interviews with wives were conducted by bilingual women who were also residents of the camp. Interviewers asked questions about decision-making and action-taking in several different areas. What are the advantages of this methodology? What are the potential limitations or biases of this methodology?

3. The researchers tested several explanations for the egalitarian pattern of decision-making that they found. Briefly summarize three of these explanations and the major findings reported by Hawkes and Taylor.

4. Many of these couples shared in decision-making. It is still possible, however, that they followed traditional patterns in other aspects of their family life. Who do you think did most of the housework and child care in these families? Explain your answer.

5. Today many Americans endorse the ideal of power-equality in dating and marriage. At the same time, some individuals prefer more traditional patterns of male dominance. Discuss the potential advantages and disadvantages of each pattern for women and for men.

6. Research has found that an egalitarian balance of power is common in families ranging from the relatively poor farm labor families studied by Hawkes and Taylor to middle-class couples. We know little, however, about the balance of power among very wealthy families. What do you think studies of the upper class would find? Explain your answer.

Korean Immigrant Women's Challenge to Gender Inequality at Home

The Interplay of Economic Resources, Gender, and Family

In-Sook Lim

What happens when Korean couples, accustomed to a pattern of male dominance and female economic dependence in marriage, move to the United States? Drawing on in-depth interviews with husbands and wives, Lim provides a rich portrait of the complex issues faced by immigrant families as wives gain greater economic independence and challenge traditional family roles. This fascinating report illustrates some of the benefits of qualitative research methods.

Based on in-depth interviews with 18 Korean immigrant working couples, this study explores Korean immigrant working wives' ongoing challenge to male dominance at home and to the unequal division of family work. A main factor in wives' being less obedient to their husbands is their psychological resources such as pride, competence, and honor, which they gain from awareness of their contribution to the family economy. Under immigrant family circumstances in which working for family survival is prioritized, wives feel that their neglect of family work, rejection of the superwoman ideal, and perceived right to demand their husbands' help with family work is legitimized. However, Confucian patriarchal beliefs lead these wives to place limits on the degree of challenge. The findings highlight the interplay of wives' psychological resources, gender norms, and the social standing of being immigrant families in affecting wives' challenge to gender inequality at home. Differences in effects among Korean immigrant families are explored.

Previous research has found that Korean immigrant husbands rarely participate in family work and are dominant over their wives; they demonstrate that Korean immigrant families are not gender egalitarian. However, one study reveals that Korean immigrants point to male dominance and men's nonparticipation in family work as Korean cultural traits that they need to modify (Hurh and Kim 1984); it suggests that Korean immigrant wives are aware of gender inequality at home and may attempt to challenge it.

This study aims to explore the stability and changes in gender inequality among Korean immigrant working couples by examining wives' challenges to their husbands' dominance and the unequal division of family work. Ideologies and structures of patriarchy are still powerful enough to hinder possible changes in the status quo of gender hierarchy, and women may not have yet succeeded in bringing about gender equality at home. Nevertheless, some changes may have occurred. Accordingly, this study analyzes the nature of Korean immigrant working wives' desire for change, their attempts to change marital relations, their tendency to resign themselves to their status quo, and husbands' responses to their wives' challenges.

A broader purpose of this study is to explore the interplay of Korean immigrant wives' economic resources, patriarchal cultural traditions, and immigrant family circumstances in facilitating or hindering wives' challenges. Resource theory suggests that working women attain the ability to challenge gender inequality at home through their participation in the paid labor force. However, gender theories suggest that the increase in women's economic resources does not necessarily guarantee more power for them because patriarchal gender norms and beliefs constrain women from maximizing their power and options. Furthermore, research on racial-ethnic minority or immigrant families suggests that despite the universal presence of patriarchy, men exercise varying degrees of power and women resist in diverse ways (Zinn et al. 1986; Collins 1990; Hondagneu-Sotelo 1992).

This study examines the changes as well as stability in gender inequality among Korean immigrant families by exploring the following issues: how Korean immigrant working wives experience the shift in their relative economic resources in the United States; how wives' employment affects their desire to challenge male dominance and the unequal division of family work; how Korean immigrants' strong attachment to patriarchal tradition constrains women from challenging gender inequality at home; and how being immigrant families affects wives' challenge and resignation to the status quo.

In-depth interviews with 18 Korean immigrant working couples in the United States were conducted for the analysis. The data collected from both spouses in this study reveal gender dynamics more vividly than the data in previous research that focused on one spouse only. Interviews of both Korean immigrant husbands and wives also show their differential perceptions of the same marriage. This study, which integrates Korean immigrants' unique cultural traditions such as Confucian ideologies with their social standing as immigrants, also highlights the importance of contextual understanding of gender.

Background of the Study

Korean Immigrant Families

Korean immigrants are characterized by strong ethnic attachment to the native culture, which is typically attributed to racial-ethnic segregation in the United States (Hurh and Kim 1984; Min 1995). High levels of affiliation with ethnic churches (around 67 percent in a 1986 survey in Los Angeles), which play the role of a "pseudo-extended family" for Korean immigrants, are one example of Korean immigrants' efforts to preserve their ethnicity (Kim 1981, 199). While Ferree (1979) claimed that assimilation to Western culture, which entails more egalitarian values, creates some variation in the patterns of division of labor among immigrant families, Korean immigrants' strong attachment to the high level of patriarchal tradition may constrain women from challenging gender inequality at home.

Gender inequality in Korea was intensified during the Chosun Dynasty (1392–1910), which adopted Confucianism as a ruling ideology of the era. Confucian patriarchy was characterized by the Rule of Three Obedience, which emphasized women's subordination to men: A woman should obey her father before her marriage, her husband after marriage, and her son(s) after her husband's death (Cho 1988). Therefore, women's assertiveness and disobedience were discouraged. A wife could be divorced if she was talkative or rebellious toward her parents-in-law, which included talking back to them. Since the principle of Distinction between Man and Woman was emphasized, even children over six years old were not expected to mix with the other gender. The principle of Distinction between Wife and Husband also demanded separate living and work spheres and accented the gendered power difference. Under these circumstances, a man ran the risk of losing face by participating in family work since the female work was regarded as degrading to men's prestige and dignity. These notions and principles were more strongly emphasized and more frequently practiced among the ruling class of the time.

Despite contemporary increases in women's employment and some men's participation in family work, the traditional notions are still pervasive in Korea. A comparative study reports that 71 percent of Korean married women agree with the statement "The husband should be the breadwinner, while the wife stays at home"; 34 percent of American women, 14 percent of Swedish women, and 71 percent of Japanese women agree (Korean Survey [Gallup] Polls Ltd. 1987). Therefore, Korean women still face strong resistance from men to participate in family work. While Korean working women spend four and a half hours per day on family work, men participate only 38 minutes. Consequently, Korean women work at both family work and paid work two months a year more than men, while American women work one month a year more than American men (Hochschild 1989).

In addition, unique social characteristics of Korean immigrant families may operate as factors hindering gender equality at home. The majority of Korean immigrants are engaged in small family businesses, which are run by a wife and husband without employees. Forty-five percent of Korean workers in Los Angeles, 61 percent of married males, and 49 percent of married females in New York City were in family businesses in the 1980s (Min 1991). Research on Chinese Americans in family business (Glenn 1983) found that collectivity is emphasized over the individual and a high premium is placed on cooperation rather than self-expression, which may precipitate conflicts. Further, Korean immigrant women in family businesses may not accumulate their own individual resources because they are unpaid workers regardless of their significant contribution to the family income. Considering that female control over income is a more important determinant of marital power than their employment or earnings (Blumberg 1991; Hertz 1986), Korean immigrant women in family businesses may be disadvantaged from the beginning in bargaining with their husbands.

Women's Economic Resources, Gender, and Family

Previous theory and research findings suggest the interplay of working wives' economic resources, gender norms, and family circumstances in wives' challenging gender inequality at home. According to resource theory, the relative resources of the spouses, such as education, income, or occupational status, are more viable determinants of marital power relations than the normative factor—that is, the husband's authority—in contemporary marriage (Blood and Wolfe 1960). The resources possessed by each spouse provide "leverage" in bargaining and negotiation between spouses, and affect marital power. A study by Blumstein and Schwartz (1983) revealed that the amount of money a spouse earns establishes relative power in any kind of relationship, except among lesbians.

As for the gender division of family work, resource theorists maintain that those members with greater resources can compel those with fewer resources to undertake the onerous work of the household (Berk 1985). Husbands' participation in family work is highest when spouses' incomes are similar (Haas 1987; Hood 1983; Scanzoni 1979). According to Ferree (1987), when women make a relatively substantial financial contribution to the family, this leads them to define their husbands' share of housework as too low and to articulate a desire for change. If this is the case, racial-ethnic minority or immigrant women may have a greater potential to challenge gender inequality at home. In these families, which experience racial discrimination and oppression in the job market, wives' earnings are more essential to their families, and the gap between a wife's earnings and husband's earnings is smaller than in dominant groups (Zinn 1990; Glenn 1987). Therefore, these women have an advantage in the relative economic resources of spouses, which may allow them a greater potential for bargaining to cope with male dominance in the family than other women.

However, the causal relationship between relative resources and bargaining power may be overly simplistic. Resource theory does not explain why some women are careful not to exploit their greater potential power to the fullest, despite their increased economic resources, consequently resulting in no significant change in gender relations (Hood 1983; Wallace and Wolf 1991).

Introducing the notion of patriarchy, gender theories explain how normative expectations in marriage operate as a form of subtle coercion that undermines the relationship between women's resources and their power in marriage (Komter 1989). In a society in which breadwinning is a social representation of manhood, wives whose husbands are not good providers often submit to their husbands' dominance because they feel guilty for contributing to their husbands' sense of failure. Hochschild (1989) found that wives whose husbands are underemployed, less ambitious, or earned less than their wives do not press their husbands to do more housework to establish a "balance." Rather, they attempt to soothe their husbands' threatened male ego, and they bolster their husbands' sense of self-worth. In these marriages, women's earnings are not considered a resource but a burden for the husband, and thus it does not influence marital power (Pyke 1994). Furthermore, as long as either the husband or the wife endorses the notion of "male-breadwinning and manhood," the husband is more powerful, regardless of his income (Blumstein and Schwartz 1983). Findings suggest that women still negotiate and adapt to the set of patriarchal rules that guide and constrain gender relations (Kandiyoti 1988).

Some women's challenge to gender inequality at home also may be constrained by their family circumstances. For example, among immigrant families who face a precarious economic environment, wives' employment is not a means for achieving independence from their husbands. Rather, it is an obligation for family survival and sacrifice necessary for the collective interests of the family (Ferree 1979; Glenn 1987; Kibria 1990). The members of immigrant families may perceive their families as a source of support in resisting oppression from outside institutions rather than a locus of gender conflict; any conflicts among family members may therefore be muted. For example, in a study of Vietnamese immigrants, Kibria (1990) found that the patriarchal family system is too valuable to give up because it adds income earners and extends resources. Furthermore, Vietnamese immigrant women find a fundamental appeal in the traditional patriarchal bargain—the authority to wield influence over the lives of the young.

These theories and research evidence led me to two research questions in this study. Firstly, I explore the changes as well as stability in gender inequality among Korean immigrant working couples by examining the challenge by wives to their husbands' dominance and unequal division of family work as well as their resignation to the status quo. Secondly, I explore how Korean immigrant working wives' economic resources, traditional gender norms, and the social standing of being immigrant families operate in these wives' challenges to gender inequality at home.

Methodology

Selecting the Sample and Characteristics of the Sample

In-depth interviews were conducted with 18 Korean immigrant working couples between December 1993 and August 1994 in Austin and Dallas, Texas. I contacted possible respondents using snowball sampling techniques and by random visits to Korean ethnic stores. Fifteen couples were obtained through the first method, while three couples were included through the second. In choosing couples to interview, several factors were considered that might be related to motivations, meanings, feelings, and justifications for wives' employment and husbands' family work: age, education, occupation, family income, years of marriage, years in the United States, the number and age of children, and helper(s) at home.

The four professional couples in this study have higher class characteristics in terms of family annual income, occupational prestige, and education levels than the three nonprofessional wage-earner couples and the family business couples. Among the latter were seven couples in which the wife and husband work full-time in the business and four couples in which the spouse works in his/her own business with part-time help of the other spouse who has a separate wage-earning job. Husbands of professional couples have a master's degree or higher and work in occupations such as engineer and publisher of a Korean ethnic newspaper. Wives of professional couples tend to graduate from a university and work as engineers, technicians, or nurses. Their family annual income ranges from $60,000 to $130,000. Family business couples work in a shoe-repair shop, restaurants, laundries, a flea market, a video rental shop, a wig shop, or a used appliance shop. Nonprofessional wage-earner couples work as building cleaners, technicians, or clerks. The family business couples and nonprofessional wage-earner couples tend to be high school graduates. Their family annual income ranges from $30,000 to $70,000. Wives and husbands range in age from 30 to 60 years.

There are recognizable distinctions in breadwinner role expectations between professional couples and the other couples. Professional couples still hold the traditional belief that breadwinning for their families is a husband's responsibility, while the nonprofessional couples emphasize that in the immigrant families, both a wife and a husband should share the breadwinning responsibility for their families. Wives of the former couples are secondary breadwinners, while wives of the latter couples play the role of equal breadwinners in their everyday lives. However, these distinctions are not salient in their attitudes toward and practices of homemaking among them. Both groups believe in the traditional notion that family work is generally a wife's responsibility and show no significant changes in men's participation in family work on a behavioral level. Even husbands whose wives equally contribute to the family economy do not necessarily share family work more than other husbands whose wives are secondary breadwinners.

Interviewing Procedures and Analysis

Interview schedules consisted of four parts. First, I asked interviewees a series of background questions about their family, jobs, marriage, and immigration. Second, I ascertained the practical experiences associated with breadwinning and homemaking in interviewees' families by asking who financially supported their families and who did what kinds of family work and to what extent. The third part focused on two themes: the meanings and feelings of wives working outside the home and husbands participating in family work, and the perceptions and feelings of changes in their marital relations. The interviews were conducted in a semistructured format, based on a series of open-ended questions. Finally, general attitudes toward the responsibility of the breadwinner/homemaker role were examined.

One may wonder whether my being a woman affected the levels of comfort of male interviewees, consequently affecting rapport building and the quality of this research. I do not believe that it did. Husbands were candid enough to reveal their fears of and complaints against wives' changes, their sense of relative deprivation of wives' services and caring, and their beliefs in traditional marital hierarchy. This exposure of these thoughts and feelings is a good indication of the successful rapport established between me and male interviewees. As for female interviewees, I believe the interviews were good for these wives in that they offered women new meanings and perspectives on taken-for-granted aspects of their marriage. During the interviews, many wives became aware and surprised at their husbands' nonparticipation and insensitivity when they responded to my questions of what kinds of family work their husbands perform. Many of them then expressed their feelings of anger, frustration, and resignation with marital relations.

Interviews were conducted at respondents' workplaces, houses, or the offices of several Korean ethnic churches. Husbands and wives were interviewed separately. All interviews were conducted in Korean because the majority of interviewees were first-generation immigrants and felt more comfortable speaking in Korean than in English. With permission from the interviewees, I taped each interview of approximately 90 minutes. Because of exposure of their private lives, I guaranteed my respondents anonymity and confidentiality, promising them to use pseudonyms in my study to protect their identity. I also assured interviewees that I would not discuss any of what they told me with their spouses. With an awareness of the inherent power imbalance between researchers and participants, I told my interviewees that they need not discuss topics that made them feel anxious or under stress (Gilgun, Daly, and Handel 1992). I reciprocated interviewees' time with a gift (an alarm clock to each couple valued at $15.00).

All interviews were transcribed from the audiotape in Korean. Then, I read and coded the interview transcripts carefully to catch major themes as well as unique aspects of interview content. To avoid misrepresentation of interviewees' responses, three follow-up calls were made when I needed clarification on what a respondent stated.

Findings

Wives' New Self-Expression and Marital Conflicts

Korean immigrant husbands in this study expressed consistent fears of wives' challenge to male dominance at home. Three factors contribute to the husbands' fears. One is the stereotypical image of America to Koreans. America has been portrayed as a Western society in which women enjoy equal rights and freedom. Therefore, Korean immigrant husbands have speculated that an exposure to Western culture will lead their wives to desire more power at home. Secondly, husbands whose wives change from a full-time homemaker to a working wife (nine wives in this study) have been afraid that their wives may bargain for new marital relations based on their newly derived earning power. Thirdly, newly immigrant husbands have often been warned by other Korean immigrant husbands, "Watch out for your wife. She may change a lot in the U.S. enough to think little of you." Therefore, they have been afraid that their wives will not be the same as they used to be in Korea.

Those husbands who have not yet found any change in their wives feel fortunate, and they do not hide their hostility against other wives who they feel use their moneymaking as an excuse to look down on their husbands. Those husbands who have already experienced their wives' changes express their displeasure. Choe, who is in his fifties and works with his wife in a shoe-repair and alteration shop, finds she is no longer the obedient wife she was in Korea. He is displeased with his wife's new "self-assertion":

> After she started working her voice got louder than in the past. Now, she says whatever she wants to say to me. She shows a lot of self-assertion. She didn't do that in Korea. Right after I came to the U.S., I heard that Korean wives change a lot in America. Now, I clearly understand what it means. However, it's wrong for women to think that they can control men in their own ways.

Choe's wife is in her forties and was a full-time housewife in Korea. She admits that since she has begun working in the United States, her "self-expression" has increased. Her comments imply that, with a growing sense of not being totally dependent on her husband for money, she no longer assumes a position of submission toward her husband. When she felt dependent on her husband as a full-time housewife, she obeyed her husband voluntarily. However, as she identifies herself as a working wife who contributes to her family as much as her husband, she has a different view of her marital relationship. She describes her changes:

> In Korea, wives tend to obey their husbands because husbands have financial power and provide for their families. However, in the U.S., wives also work to make money as their husbands do, so women are apt to speak out at least one time on what they previously refrained from saying.

The above statements by the Choe couple indicate that there is a gender difference in perception about the extent of wives' change. Choe feels that she does not speak out yet about all the things that she wants to say to her husband, while her husband perceives his wife's change as so evident that she says "whatever she wants to say." Yang, who is in his forties and runs an appliance repair shop, also claims that his wife is no longer naive in that she does not completely follow his orders as she did when she was a full-time housewife. He feels his decision-making power has become less secure since his wife began earning money. As she has worked hard to make a living, Yang's wife admits, she has become more aggressive and stronger than she was as a full-time housewife. She has a part-time job as an operator and helps in his repair shop. However, she claims that there is no great change in marital power since she still permits her husband to make final decisions in family matters. These findings suggest that even a little change in the marital power relation may not be perceived as trivial by husbands.

In addition to increasing self-expression, wives feel all right about spending money without their husbands' permission. This change is evident when Chung, who is in her thirties and runs a Japanese restaurant with her husband, says, "I feel differently spending money when I earn it. I have come to think I deserve to spend the money when I pick up something for my family. I feel honorable even when I send a gift to my own parents." Although wives feel that they can spend money in their own way, they tend to buy things for children or family members rather than for themselves. With tight family budgets and the pooled family accounting system, wives say, there is little discrete money that husbands as well as wives control for their own interests. In the case of family business couples, husbands often manage general spending related to the business. However, the control of money flow in their business is perceived not as a right of husbands but as a mental labor that demands a struggle with stringent budgets.

As Korean immigrant wives increasingly express their opinions, speak out against their husbands, or spend money without husbands' permission, marital conflicts increase. This is more evident among family business couples. Yu, a thirty-year-old who works with her husband in a laundry shop, says, "After we began working together in this business, we came to quarrel about even trivial things almost every day. I don't think it is desirable for both husband and wife to work together." Chung's husband understands the meaning of an old saying, "Don't be a business partner with a close person," through his experiences of working together with his wife.

Frequent conflicts among family business couples are related to both wives' newly acquired psychological resources and working conditions. Wives in family businesses are more likely to be defined as equal breadwinners by themselves and their husbands than their counterparts. As these wives are aware that they contribute to their family economy as much as their husbands, wives gain a sense of being honorable, fair, worthy, and proud, all of which allow them to express themselves actively. Since these immigrant families set a priority on income-generating work for family survival and value those who are involved in the work, wives feel competent as equal breadwinners. Bonacich, Hossain, and Park (1987) pointed out an ambiguity in the wife's position as co-operator of a family business—namely, she is both a co-owner and her husband's employee without even the benefit of a paycheck. They recognized that for many immigrant women, the latter role predominates and that their husbands could be exploiters of their wives' labor. However, wives of family business couples in this study think of themselves as co-owners of their business rather than unpaid employees of their husbands. Husbands also fully admit their wives' efforts to shoulder half of the burden of providing for their families by saying, "My wife also works as much as I do. Half and half, we contribute to the family economy."

The physically demanding work of family business couples also causes marital conflict to increase. As family business couples define their everyday lives as "nothing except eating, sleeping, and working," they feel so tired or stressed that they get easily angry at others. Also, the working condition, in which a wife and husband do similar work side by side in a small place, often leads them to meddle with each other. For example, a husband may question why his wife asks less money from her customers than he thinks she should or why she is not more efficient. However, these couples also mention merits of the working condition that allow the couples to share advice or consolation when they face difficulties with their business. In short, being coworkers offers the couples a sense of psychological interdependence as well as a source of conflict.

Wives' new self-expression and consequent marital conflicts suggest that Korean immigrant wives attempt to make a change in their husbands' dominance at home. However, it is important to recognize that Korean immigrant wives limit their attempts to change unequal marital relations. Although they try to check their husbands' monopoly at home, they do not intend to subvert the traditional sense of marital hierarchy itself. They believe that the authority of men as family heads should remain unchallenged for the family order. The distinction between attemptable change and avoided change is clear in the case of Yang. She reports her change from being a typical Korean wife who obeyed her husband "one hundred percent" into being a bold and competent woman after she had a job. However, she is still willing to defer to her husband's authority. When asked why, she replies:

> I don't think it is desirable for a woman to henpeck her husband even though she works outside the home. I want men to lead everything in their family. I think the authority of a family head needs to be secure at home.

The gap between a wife and husband in job prestige and earnings cannot explain her deference to her husband. Rather, her belief in the authority of the husband as a family head justifies the power difference in her marriage, consequently restraining her from challenging the overall system of male domination. Shin, who no longer perceives herself as a submissive wife, explicitly said, "I work just because I should. With my moneymaking, I do not covet a better position at home." In fact, among the majority of family business couples, wives' employment is regarded as a responsibility for the family, which they perceive as a "system of coexistence." For Korean immigrant families in this study, family survival often means not only securing food to eat, shelter, and clothes to wear, but also providing their children with the best education possible. Many immigrant wives cannot pass the buck to their husbands when they feel breadwinning is a joint responsibility of parents for their children. The notion of marital equality is never expressed directly by these wives.

Wives' Attempts to Change Husbands' Family Work

The majority of interviewees (30 out of 36) still believe that wives are responsible for family work in principle. However, the old belief that family work is unmanly and degrading to men's prestige is no longer dominant among them. Proudly reporting their attitudinal change toward family work in the United States, a husband states, "Nobody thinks that it is shameful for a husband to enter the kitchen because we live in the U.S. where wives as well as husbands have jobs." All but one wife depart from the traditional notion that family work should be done exclusively by themselves. While wives no longer take their husbands' insensitivity and nonparticipation in family work for granted, they perceive a right to demand that their husbands participate in family work.

The attitudinal change among Korean immigrant wives is linked to their awareness of their contribution to the family economy. As wives recognize that they share the traditional male activity, breadwinning, with their husbands, they think there should be a transformation in their husbands' family work. Emphasizing the differences in breadwinning experiences between working wives and full-time housewives, these wives tend to say, "In the case of wives as full-time housewives, family work is totally wives' work. But in the case of wives with jobs, husbands need to help their wives with family work."

The wives' reasoning does not necessarily imply that wives think their husbands should help them with family work to compensate for their inability to be sole breadwinners. Similarly, husbands do not think that wives can use their earning money as justification for demanding that husbands do more family work. Husbands' family work is mainly framed in terms of family cooperation or an adjustment to their employment. Family cooperation is understood to be the basis of survival and security for immigrant families, who begin rootless lives in a new land and face a precarious economic situation. Therefore, as wives work outside the home to reduce their husbands' burden of breadwinning, their husbands are expected to respond to wives' time shortage and fatigue.

Since husbands' outright resistance to sharing family work is no longer taken for granted as it used to be in Korea, resistant husbands are now perceived as selfish men who try to avoid another burden while wives bear two burdens: family work and a job. Under these circumstances, wives feel they work twice as hard as their husbands when they find their husbands' reluctance to share family work regardless of their employment. A sense of unfairness develops when they feel their lives relatively more burdened than their husbands.'

With a sense of injustice, wives attempt to change the unequal division of family work by demand or appeal to their husbands. Kim demanded that her husband help her with the family work. Kim, who is in her forties, financially supported her family by herself for five years when her family came to the United States for her husband's study for a Ph.D. degree. She had a hard time managing both family work and job because her husband rarely participated in family work. She passionately describes how she claimed her husband's help:

> I had always told him, "Isn't it ethical and humanistic for you to help me with family work when I feel tired? I can't manage it. Of course, I know that women are responsible for it. But I have to leave home to make money. I am doing the things men are responsible for. However, when I return from work to see family work left undone, as it was when I left home, I have to work twice as hard as you do."

Contrary to Kim, however, other wives do not actively defend the right to demand that their husbands participate in family work. When they try to introduce husbands to family work, they often use the "politics of appeal." They politely ask their husbands to help out by claiming their fatigue or time shortage due to their employment: "I am so tired. Will you please do the vacuuming?"; "Would you help me by taking out the garbage?" The politics of appeal, whereby women use stereotypical feminine traits, such as weakness and cautiousness, instead of assertiveness, is a strategy to change the unequal division of family work.

Wives' awareness that hurting men's self-respect or authority is ineffective to their interests factors into the politics of appeal. Wives are aware that when they demand that their husbands do something, their husbands may feel ordered about by a female, consequently damaging their pride. Husbands also admit that they tend to refuse their wives' requests for family work when they feel that their wives treat them without respect. Because doing family work traditionally means that women are "doing their gender" (Berk 1985), husbands try to show their wives the fundamental difference between men and women by rejecting family work. For example, Yu withdraws his participation in family work, saying, "No, how dare you think that men and women are the same!" He reclaims his authority as a man when he feels his wife hurt it. Through experiences, wives have learned that their husbands respond more to their appeals than to demands.

Furthermore, wives are aware that their demands may lead husbands to think that they lord their earning power over them. In Korea, the traditional notion that "only a stupid man makes his wife leave home to make money" is still pervasive, despite the increasing rate of women's employment. However, most men I interviewed did not reveal much feeling of shame at being dependent on their wives' earnings, since they regard the situation not as a consequence of personal failure but as an unavoidable reality that any immigrant family must face. Nonetheless, wives sense that their husbands' self-respect is not quite secure when the men are no longer sole breadwinners. Therefore, they try not to get on their husbands' nerves.

Wives also think it wiser for a wife to take care of most of the family work, at least in the presence of others, than to push her husband into the kitchen. As an old Korean saying goes, "If women or hens of a family run wild and speak with an air, the family will be ruined." There are ample warnings against female dominance and assertiveness among Korean immigrants, and because wives are aware of the social stigma attached to being dominant wives, they are careful not to give others the impression that they control their husbands. They also do not want their husbands to lose face; the women do not want to be ridiculed for emasculating their husbands publicly.

Women's Resignation to Unequal Division of Family Work

While all but one wife perceive that they have a right to demand their husbands' participation in family work, they do not necessarily try to defend this right in their everyday lives. Rather, these Korean immigrant wives expressed resignation to the unequal division of family work. Patriarchal gender ideas and immigrant family circumstances hinder women's attempts to challenge gender inequality at home.

The Belief in Women's Endurance and Sacrifice
Some wives' resignation to unequal division of family work is due to their deep-seated belief that women should endure any marital relations no matter how unfair they perceive them to be. Although they recognize the current unequal division of labor at home as unfair, they frame it as their "destiny" that they must embrace because they are women. Whenever they get irritated with their constant feelings of being rushed and fatigued with both a job and family work, they feel their lives more burdened than their husbands'. However, they say, "There is no other way. This is the life given to me." These wives tend to have been married for more than 20 years and are in their late forties or older.

When these wives recognize that younger husbands help their wives with family work, they express envy. However, the older women feel they cannot change the status quo. Rather, they regard their husbands' resistance against sharing family work as understandable. Their reasoning is that Korean men of their generation are not used to doing family work since they have been taught that family work is fundamentally a female obligation. Therefore, they think that it is not easy for husbands to change themselves all of a sudden.

The patriarchal belief in women's sacrifice for their families also contributes to wives' resignation. Those wives who experienced marital conflicts over the division of family work or other matters now want to avoid further conflict by resigning themselves to the status quo. For example, Lee's husband, who made less money than Lee for several years in the early stages of their immigration, constantly initiated quarrels and made Lee's life in the United States unbearable. Therefore, Lee gave up requesting her husband's help, because she felt it might create ill temper and result in more marital conflict, which would make her children unhappy.

This pattern parallels previous research on American women that reveals that women's low level of desire for men's participation in family work may reflect their resignation and wish to avoid marital conflict (Berheide 1984; Hochschild 1989; Komter 1989). However, there is a subtle difference between Korean immigrant women and American women in general. American women live in a society in which more than half of the marriages end in divorce, which is a primary factor in the increased poverty among women. Fears of divorce and a declining standard of living restrain them from demanding that their husbands help with family work (Hochschild 1989). However, fear of divorce is less salient among Korean immigrant women, who still have a low divorce rate.

Understanding Husbands' Time Shortage and Fatigue   As long as wives regard men's family work as a matter of help rather than a matter of responsibility, they cannot demand that their husbands help unless the men have extra time and energy. Therefore, husbands' absolute or relative time shortages and fatigue, which Korean immigrant wives recognize, affect the extent of their resignation.

Wives of family business couples, who work more than 13 hours per day at physically demanding jobs, admit that their husbands as well as they themselves have little time to do family work. These wives reveal sympathy for their husbands, saying, "I know how tired he is because I experience the same thing." The wives explicitly state that both their husbands and they themselves need to rest rather than spend their time doing family work. Their statements suggest that for Korean immigrant families, working for family survival is a priority that takes precedence over the matter of division of family work. Consequently, their husbands can limit their participation in family work to the extent that they put the dishes in the sink and put leftovers in the refrigerator after eating alone. The wives reveal that they also lower the quality and quantity of family work that they perform.

The findings suggest that working conditions of family business couples provide both an opportunity and a constraint for these wives' challenge to gender inequality at home. All but two wives of family business couples earn the title of equal breadwinners by working as much as their husbands in labor-intensive family businesses and are in a better position to bargain for new marital power than wives who are secondary breadwinners. However, the tough working conditions limit these wives' attempts to change the unequal division of family work.

The relative time shortage of husbands is more likely to be a reason for professional wives' giving up achieving husbands' help. Whang, who works part-time as an engineering consultant while her husband works full-time as an engineer, thinks it is fair for her to take care of most of the family work without her husband's help because she has relatively more time at home than her husband. Furthermore, she believes that her husband may be excused from family work because he needs to spend his time on his own work for career advancement. Instead of expecting help from her husband, she often gets household help from a maid.

Gatekeeping of Mothers/Mothers-in-Law   Some wives' resignation to the unequal division of family work is due to the presence of mothers or mothers-in-law at home. All of the mothers in this study (four mothers-in-law and two mothers) moved into the houses of respondents to help with child rearing and household tasks. In fact, four out of six families have children under seven years old. These grandmothers take care of most of the everyday child rearing. All but one do the everyday cooking and cleaning except on weekends when their daughters or daughters-in-law do not go to work. Therefore, these mothers are significant helpers. However, they are also gate-keepers who try to maintain the traditional way of doing family work. For these mothers, family work has been a culturally designated female job, obligating women to take care of it. They believe that when a wife is not able to do family work, she should manage it anyway with other women's help. Therefore, the mothers do not complain about their doing family work instead of their daughters or daughters-in-law. But they restrain their daughters or daughters-in-law from asking their husbands to help with family work, as the following comments of Park, who is in her forties, reveal: "My mother shouts at me and scolds me for making my husband do the family work, saying 'Why do you demand that your husband do family work even though there are two women in this house?'"

These mothers also do not want their sons to do family work at the demand of their daughters-in-law because they perceive that the daughters-in-law control their sons in their own way. According to Hong, who works at a building-cleaning job and flea market with his wife, their parents do not care about his voluntary participation in family work because they know that their son is a good cook and that he enjoys cooking. However, he cannot help being conscious of his parents when he tries to help his wife with family work at the request of his wife. He perceives that his mother does not like her daughter-in-law to be aggressive enough to demand that her son do something. At the same time, his wife recognizes that her mother-in-law expects her to be strong and aggressive enough to deal with employment in the United States. Hong's wife, a woman in her thirties who was a full-time housewife in Korea, recalls feeling pushed into working by her mother-in-law who had worked for more than 10 years in the United States. She feels that she was brainwashed by her mother-in-law, who repeatedly said, "From now on, never dream about living like a princess as you did in Korea. Here, in the U.S., women should be more aggressive and stronger than men."

These mothers also try to keep their sons or sons-in-law from doing family work, arguing that men lose face and self-respect when they are involved in traditionally female work. According to Chung, her mother-in-law interrupts her husband who tries to do dishes on Sunday, saying to him, "Leave it. Both of us [Chung and the mother-in-law] will take care of it. It's not good for men to do family work too much. You worked hard all week. You just take a rest, you look tired." However, the task is often done by Chung because she feels that it is proper for her as a daughter-in-law to take care of family work at least when she does not go to work.

As Chung's case reveals, some wives do recognize their mother-in-law's differential treatment of them and their husbands. Regardless of identical working hours and fatigue of their son and daughter-in-law, in the eyes of their daughters-in-law, mothers-in-law seem to care about only their own sons' fatigue. The mothers-in-law seem to believe that no matter how tired their daughters or daughters-in-law are, the exhaustion does not release them from family work responsibility. While wives feel differential treatment by their mothers-in-law, they do not argue against them. This is especially the case when the wives really appreciate the mothers for reducing their burden of family work and when they know it is disobedient for a daughter-in-law to talk back to parents-in-law.

Will women interviewed in this study be more generous to their future daughters-in-law than their mothers-in-law? When asked how she feels about her son helping her future daughter-in-law with family work, many wives say, "It's OK. No longer should women suffer lives as I did." Some wives emphasize that they ask their sons to do household chores so that the sons can naturally learn family work from an early stage in their lives. However, the ways in which family work is assigned to their children follows the traditional distinction between family work for men and family work for women. Sons older than 10 years perform such tasks as vacuuming, laundry, gardening, and taking out garbage by themselves or with their siblings, while doing the dishes or cooking are mainly performed by daughters. And a few wives admit a subtle difference between their feelings about their own sons' family work and that of their future sons-in-law. They may feel thankful to their future sons-in-law for helping their daughters with family work, while they may feel sorry for their sons' having a hard time with family work. These wives ambivalently desire change in men.

Husbands' Reluctance   Despite attitudinal change in men's family work, few husbands practice what they preach. Only one husband I interviewed voluntarily participates in family work, and if a husband participates in a household task, he is more likely to do it at his wife's request. Even when some men accept their wives' requests, they tend to control the time they are involved in family work. "Leave it undone. I will do it later" is a typical response of husbands to wives' requests. If wives push their husbands, the latter often argues, "Can't you do it, if you think it is really urgent?" The task is often done by wives who feel they cannot leave the task undone until the husbands do it. Husbands also control the task that they may accept at their wives' request. Korean immigrant husbands are most likely to vacuum, take out garbage, and do the gardening because they regard this as male work in that it occurs outside the house or it demands more or less physical strength. In contrast, they strongly resist doing laundry, cooking, and doing the dishes because they believe that these tasks are typically indoor work, related to women.

Facing their husbands' constant reluctance and resistance, some wives finally give up demanding help from their husbands. These wives recall the anger and frustration they felt begging for their husbands' help. Once they define their husbands as men who will never change, they feel further appeals to their husbands are just tiresome and meaningless. Kim, who says that the unequal division of family work has been the sole reason for marital conflict for 14 years of her marriage, declares her final resignation. Since her family can now afford it, she quit her full-time job, cutting back her work hours as a solution to her double burden of family work and job.

Husbands explain their reluctance to share family work in terms of the persistent influence of Korean traditions. They feel that since they are "Korean men" who used to take for granted strict gender division of work and patriarchal privileges of men, it is not easy to change themselves. Even after 16 years in the United States, Lee, who is in his sixties, still mentions his difficulty with being engaged in tasks that are traditionally defined as nonmasculine. His reluctance to change contrasts with his wife's fast change from a full-time housewife to a working wife two days after her arrival.

Being "immigrant men" also serves as an excuse for husbands' reluctance to change. Husbands mention their hardships as immigrants and consequent stresses; they have often felt depressed, angry, tired, and frustrated with the language barrier, underemployment, or racial discrimination. This is evident when Lee explains why he rejects his wife's requests:

> I will say "No" when I am not in the mood. How really tiring physically and psychologically the immigrant life in the U.S. is! I am always full of stress. It will burst into flames if anybody touches it.

The status of immigrant offers Lee elective affinity in viewing the changes in traditional marital roles. Since he perceived wives' employment as a required part of immigrant womanhood, he took his wife's change into a breadwinner for granted. However, the stress, anxiety, and tension that he feels as an immigrant man operate as excuses for his reluctant change into a sharing partner of family work.

No Longer Superwomen

As a coping strategy to combine their jobs and family work, most Korean immigrant wives in this study choose to neglect the quality and/or quantity of family work. This coping strategy is a self-resolution, with no significant changes occurring in their husbands' behaviors. Nonetheless, this is an indication of Korean immigrant women's attempt to change their share of family labor in that women's relinquishment of some family work is a step for them toward bargaining for equal sharing of household work with their husbands (Hood 1983).

Most wives (15 out of 18), do not change the types of family work they do but rather lower the standards they apply to their family work. These wives still take care of most household chores that are related to family sustenance, such as cooking, grocery shopping, and doing the dishes and the laundry. However, laundry is often delayed until clean socks are no longer available, the house is often messy, and just one side dish is prepared for dinner. Other wives neglect not only the standard of family work but also the kinds of family work. For example, Yu, who feels exhausted after 15 hours of hard work in a newly opened laundry, rarely does family work except grocery shopping. The only thing that Kong does is cooking dinner. Yu and Kong's abandoned tasks are taken over by her mother and her grown children (a 14-year-old daughter and an 18-year-old son).

These wives try to give up being a good housewife who always serves her family, regardless of her employment. Without hesitation, Kong, who runs a used appliance store with her husband, says, "I turn off the switch for family work. I now concern myself only with the business." As this quote suggests, Korean immigrant working wives reject the superwoman ideal, which their counterparts in Korea are still socially expected to follow.

A socially acknowledged priority of immigrant families, building a secure economic base as soon as possible, offers these wives a valid excuse for their neglect of family work. The notion that wives' employment is secondary and a matter of choice, which offers a basis for the superwoman ideal, is convincing to only affluent Korean immigrant families. Professional husbands in this study insist that their wives' first priority be their children and family work, but they do not oppose their wives having a job. However, husbands of family business couples or low-wage-earner couples admit that more commitment of wives to their jobs than to family work is unavoidable. Therefore, these wives are not afraid of the social stigmas attached to being absent mothers or having a poorly kept house.

With an awareness of their contribution to the family economy, these women also believe that their great effort and consequent hardships for family survival can compensate for their reduced effort in homemaking. Choe reveals that "In Korea, it might have been absurd for me to treat my husband to a humble dish when he came home from work. However, in the U.S., with the excuse that I am busy, it is natural for me to make my family a simple dinner. Under these circumstances I work as much as my husband does, there is no other way to this." Therefore, they do not feel sorry for their husbands, though they regret their limited time in caring for their children.

Their husbands also admit that they cannot complain about wives' reduced family work because they know it is unavoidable. However, there is a contradiction between what husbands think they "should feel" and what they "really feel" about their wives' reduced services and caring (Hochschild 1989). Husbands cannot help feeling deprived of their wives' full-time services in the United States, which they enjoyed in Korea and which their counterparts in Korea may still enjoy. This feeling of relative deprivation is, according to these husbands, the cost that they have to pay for by not being sole breadwinners. This is well illustrated by the following comments of Kang. He has spent most of the daytime for several years alone at home because he and his wife work on different shifts. He grieves about his misfortune:

> I just gave up on [my wife's services] rather than understand her. I can't help resigning. This is my life. I wish I lived in Korea because at least a husband is able to provide for his family with only his earnings, whatever job he has.

Discussion

Korean immigrant wives in this study no longer take for granted husbands' dominance at home and relief from family work. Many wives become less obedient to their husbands by expressing their opinions or speaking out against them, consequently resulting in marital conflicts. With an awareness of their contribution to the family economy, wives also believe that they deserve their husbands' help with family work. Most wives also believe that their great efforts toward family survival legitimize their own decreased effort in homemaking. Therefore, they do not practice the superwoman ideal and feel no guilt about this. These findings suggest an ongoing challenge by wives to gender inequality at home.

Resource theory, which explains the relationship between spouses' economic resources and bargaining power in a marriage, is confirmed in this study. However, it is important to recognize that the increase in wives' negotiating power is not a result of the increases in that amount of money that wives have or in their control over their earnings. In fact, few Korean immigrant wives in this study accumulate their own individual money to control because some are unpaid workers in family businesses and the majority of family accounting systems are pooled rather than discrete. Instead, psychological resources such as pride and honor, which Korean immigrant wives gain as they are aware of their contribution to the family, are more viable driving forces of wives' challenge.

These positive feelings are related to the immigrant family circumstances under which the hierarchy of paid work and unpaid family work is intensified. Among immigrant families who prioritize working for survival, wives recognize that their contribution to their families as working wives or mothers will never be trivialized by other family members. The socially acknowledged priority of immigrant families offers these wives a valid excuse for their neglect of family work. As immigrant women, who work as hard and as many hours as their husbands at labor-intensive jobs for family survival, many wives earn the title of equal breadwinners and thus gain a foothold to challenge gender inequality at home. While family cooperation is an emphasized ethos among these families that put a priority on family survival, it does not make wives keep silent. In the context of unequal marital relations, many Korean immigrant families experience conflict as well as cooperation.

It is important to recognize a difference between a wife's feeling about her job itself and her feeling about what she does for her family through the job. Those wives who work intensively at a laundry, flea market, or shoe-repair shop may not find satisfaction in their jobs. With physical hardships such as fainting spells, cramps in their legs, bloody noses, or emotional stress, they wish they could have a little recess or work at more comfortable jobs. Nonetheless, through their employment, they recognize themselves as fair contributors to their families and feel proud of themselves. Though these wives did not begin their jobs to secure a base of independence from their husbands, they find a new sense of not being totally dependent on their husbands through employment, consequently perceiving new rights to a voice at home and to demands for help from their husbands. This is a main reason all wives but one in this study desire to remain in the labor force even if their families no longer needed their earnings, thus confirming Ferree's (1984) assertion that having to work for the family does not preclude wanting to work.

In the process of challenging to gender inequality at home, Korean immigrant wives still draw boundaries that are not to be crossed, although they are stretching those lines. The goal of their ongoing challenge is not to subvert the marital hierarchy itself. The Confucian patriarchal ideology, that women should submit to their husbands' authority and protect male morale as heads of families, restrains women from protesting against marital hierarchy itself. The patriarchal beliefs in women's unconditional endurance in a marriage and sacrifice for the family also overwhelm some wives' perceived right to demand men's change in family work. With an awareness of the social stigma against female dominance and their husbands' insecure self-esteem, wives often apply the "politics of appeal" as a strategy to induce their husbands to participate in family work. This is a "patriarchal bargain," in which women maximize their power within patriarchy (Kandiyoti 1988; Kibria 1990).

The findings highlight the interplay of Korean immigrant wives' psychological resources, traditional patriarchal ideas, and immigrant family circumstances in affecting their challenge to gender inequality at home. However, it is important to recognize a difference in the effects of wives' economic resources and immigrant family circumstances on wives' challenges among Korean immigrant families. The effects are most salient among family business couples and nonprofessional wage-earner couples in this study. In these families, priority is still given to family survival, and being immigrants operates as an overriding status to legitimize their changes in the traditional marital roles. This is far less so among professional couples.

References

Berheide, Catherine W. 1984. Women's work in the home: Seems like old times. In *Women and the family: Two decades of change,* edited by Beth B. Hess and M. B. Sussman. New York: Haworth.

Berk, Sarah Fenstermaker. 1985. *The gender factory: The apportionment of work in American households.* New York and London: Plenum.

Blood, Robert O., and Donald M. Wolfe. 1960. *Husbands and wives.* New York: Free Press.

Blumberg, Rae Lesser, ed. 1991. *Gender, family, and economy: The triple overlap.* Newbury Park, CA: Sage.

Blumstein, Philip, and Pepper Schwartz. 1983. *American couples.* New York: William Morrow.

Bonacich, Edna, Mokerrom Houssain, and Jae-Hong Park. 1987. Korean immigrant working women in the early 1980s. In *Korean women in transition: At home and abroad,* edited by Eui-Yong Yu and Earl H. Phillips. Los Angeles: California State University Press.

Cho, Hae-Jung. 1988. *Women and men of Korea.* Seoul, Korea: Munhak and Gisung.

Collins, Patricia Hill. 1990. *Black feminist thought.* Boston: Unwin Hyman.

Ferree, Myra Marx. 1979. Employment without liberation: Cuban women in the United States. *Social Science Quarterly* 60:35–50.

Ferree, Myra Marx. 1984. The view from below: Women's employment and gender equality in working class families. In *Women and the family: Two decades of change,* edited by Beth B. Hess and M. B. Sussman. New York: Haworth.

Ferree, Myra Marx. 1987. The struggles of Superwoman. In *Hidden aspects of women's work,* edited by Christine Bose, Roslyn Feldberg, and Natalie Sokoloff. New York: Praeger.

Gilgun, Jane F., Kerry Daly, and Gerald Handel, eds. 1992. *Qualitative methods in family research.* Newbury Park, CA: Sage.

Glenn, Evelyn Nakano. 1983. Split household, small producer and dual wage earner: An analysis of Chinese-American family strategies. *Journal of Marriage and the Family,* 15:35–46.

Glenn, Evelyn Nakano. 1987. Racial ethnic women's labor: The intersection of race, gender, and class oppression. In *Hidden aspects of women's work,* edited by C. Bose, R. Feldberg, and N. Sokoloff. New York: Praeger.

Haas, Linda. 1987. Wives' orientation toward breadwinning: Sweden and the United States. *Journal of Family Issues* 7:358–81.

Hertz, R. 1986. *More equal than others: Men and women in dual-career marriages.* Berkeley: University of California Press.

Hochschild, Arlie, with Anne Machung. 1989. *The second shift.* New York: Avon Books.

Hondagneu-Sotelo, Pierrette. 1992. Overcoming patriarchal constraints: The reconstruction of gender relations among Mexican immigrant women and men. *Gender & Society* 6:393–415.

Hood, Jane C. 1983. *Becoming a two-job family.* New York: Praeger.

Hurh, Won Moo, and Kwang Chung Kim. 1984. *Korean immigrants in America: A structural analysis of ethnic confinement and adhesive adaptation.* Rutherford, NJ: Fairleigh Dickinson University Press.

Kandiyoti, Deniz. 1988. Bargaining with patriarchy. *Gender & Society* 2:274–90.

Kibria, Nazli. 1990. Power, patriarchy, and gender conflict in the Vietnamese immigrant community. *Gender & Society* 4:9–24.

Kim, Ill Soo. 1981. *New urban immigrants: The Korean community in New York.* Princeton, NJ: Princeton University Press.

Komter, Aafe. 1989. Hidden power in marriage. *Gender & Society* 3:187–216.

Korean Survey (Gallup) Polls Ltd. 1987. Life style and value system of housewives in Korea. Seoul, Korea.

Min, Pyong Gap. 1991. Cultural and economic boundaries of Korean ethnicity: A comparative analysis. *Ethnic and Racial Studies* 14:225–41.

Min, Pyong Gap. 1995. Korean Americans. In *Asian American: Contemporary trends and issues,* edited by Pyong Gap Min. Thousand Oaks, CA: Sage.

Pyke, Karen, D. 1994. Women's employment as a gift or burden?: Marital power across marriage, divorce, and remarriage. *Gender & Society* 8:73–91.

Scanzoni, John. 1979. Social process and power in families. In *Contemporary theories about the family,* edited by W. R. Burr, R. Hill, F. I. Nye, and I. L. Reiss. New York: Free Press.

Wallace, Ruth A., and Alison Wolf. 1991. *Contemporary sociological theory: Continuing the classical tradition.* Englewood Cliffs, NJ: Prentice Hall.

Zinn, Maxine Baca. 1990. Family, feminism and race in America. *Gender & Society* 4:68–82.

Zinn, Maxine Baca, Lyn Weber Cannon, Elizabeth Higginbotham, and Bonnie Thornton Dill. 1986. The costs of exclusionary practices in women's studies. *Signs: Journal of Women in Culture and Society* 11:290–303.

Questions for Thought

1. "Resource theory" identifies factors that determine the balance of power between a husband and a wife. What are the basic ideas of this theory? Assess how well the theory explains power in immigrant Korean working couples.

2. In addition to resource theory, what other factors must be taken into consideration to understand power and the division of family work (housework and child care) in immigrant Korean couples?

3. What are major sources of conflict in the marriages of these immigrant Korean working couples?

4. Based on this study, how have the attitudes of Korean-born husbands and wives changed as a result of immigrating to the United States? How has the wife's employment affected these attitudes?

5. What is the role of mothers and grandmothers in maintaining traditional family patterns in Korean immigrant couples?

6. Compare traditional Korean views of women's roles to traditional (prefeminist) American beliefs about women's roles.

7. Kim states, "As long as wives regard men's family work as a matter of help rather than a matter of responsibility, they cannot demand that their husbands help unless the men have extra time or energy." Explain this statement. Do you think it would apply to couples other than Korean immigrants? What would be required for couples to redefine family work as a responsibility shared by both spouses?

The Creation of Sexuality

Philip Blumstein

Pepper Schwartz

In this review paper, sociologists Blumstein and Schwartz criticize the "essentialist" view that human sexuality is biologically programmed and unchanging. Instead they argue that sexual behavior is created by the cultural context, including gender roles and the availability of opportunities for specific types of sexual behavior. In their view, human sexuality is flexible and can change over time. Blumstein and Schwartz illustrate their perspective with case studies and data from their large-scale survey of heterosexual, lesbian, and gay American couples.

The study of human sexuality has been dominated by the presumption that male and female behavior is biologically programmed, and much research has concerned itself with understanding what these programs are and to what extent biological predispositions are modified by social forces. Another prominent assumption posits that each individual has a *true* sexual core self that does not change. Some researchers emphasize that this self emerges over time, through a process of socialization, while others stress that desires are genetic and/or hormonal in origin, but both perspectives share a belief in the immutable core disposition.

The combined force of these two research traditions in the study of human sexuality has almost dismissed from serious scholarly discussion what we believe to be the true nature of human sexuality: that sexuality is situational and changeable,

Reprinted from D. P. McWhirter, S. A. Sanders, and J. M. Reinisch (Eds.) (1990), *Homosexuality/Heterosexuality: Concepts of Sexual Orientation* (pp. 307–320). New York: Oxford University Press. Copyright 1990 by The Kinsey Institute for Research in Sex, Gender, and Reproduction. Used by permission of Oxford University Press.

modified by day-to-day circumstances throughout the life course. In our perspective there are few absolute differences between male and female sexuality. What differences are observed are primarily the result of the different social organization of women's and men's lives in various cultural contexts. "Essentialist" theories, that is theories that assume immutable selves, ignore data that would disturb the assumption. One startling example of the field's willingness to be misled is the unfortunate interpretation of the ground-breaking Kinsey studies and the misuse of the Kinsey heterosexuality/homosexuality scale (Kinsey, Pomeroy, & Martin, 1948; Kinsey, Pomeroy, Martin, & Gebhard, 1953). We would like to reexamine the scale, using it to direct research away from essentialist reifications and more in the direction we believe Kinsey himself would have preferred: toward a kinetic model of sexual desire and away from a static and categorical model.

Unfortunately, when the Kinsey group constructed the scale of 0 to 6, they unintentionally endorsed and extended essentialist ways of thinking by establishing a typology allowing for seven kinds of sexual beings instead of only two. After Kinsey, there were such people as "Kinsey 4s" instead of simply heterosexuals and homosexuals. While the seven-point scale does enormously more justice to the range and subtlety of human sexuality, in its common usage it does not do justice to Kinsey's own belief in the changeability and plasticity of sexual behavior. As researchers have inevitably used Kinsey's scale as a shorthand system of sexual identification, they have reified the person as a sexual type. His or her "real" sexuality is discovered and seen as an essence that has been uncovered. It is the final summation of the person's sexual behavior and "psychic reactions."

Such essentialist thinking allows one to ignore concrete behaviors in assigning people to sexual categories. Even the verbal descriptions made by respondents and patients of their *own* behavior and feeling states may be swept aside in an essentialist judgment. As Katz (1975) has written on this general subject, "Persons conceive of essences as inherent qualities which may be manifested, reflected, indicated, or represented by, but do not exist in, conduct. . . . Essences exist independent of observable behavior" (p. 1371). Essentialism also allows one to capture the actor with one great biographical sweep, for example: "She is a homosexual" or "He is a bisexual." The Kinsey scale, as it is frequently used to aggregate behavior over a finite length of time or even over a lifetime, encourages the categorization of an actor's biography, for example: "She is a Kinsey 3."

The application of the Kinsey scale is hardly unique in this respect. Essentialism has dominated both lay and professional thinking about sexuality. Sexuality has been perceived as emanating from a core or innate *desire* that directs an individual's sex life. Before Kinsey, this desire had to be either homosexual or heterosexual; after Kinsey, this desire could be ambisexual. But in either case, it originated in constitutional factors or in the person's early experience and was a fixed part of the person. This desire has been seen as so powerful that even though behavior might vary over a lifetime, many psychotherapists and sex researchers have continued to believe in the existence of a basic predisposition reflecting the true nature of each individual's sexuality.

We do not deny that there are men and women who come to a therapist with unacted-upon homosexual desires that they believe reflect their true sexual selves. Nor do we deny that most Americans who call themselves heterosexual or homosexual feel strongly that their sexuality is highly channeled. They feel that they have only *categorical desire,* that is, desire for people of only one specific gender.[1] But the commonly held belief in the generality of this pattern has not been challenged to see if it reflects a truly universal experience. And indeed there is evidence to call that belief into question (e.g., Blumstein & Schwartz, 1976a, 1976b).

It is our position that it is not primarily categorical desire that determines whether people's sex patterns are male or female. Fundamental categorical desire may not even exist. Rather, it is culture that creates understandings about how people are sexual and thus determines whether people will be able to have only one sexual focus, to eroticize both sexes, or to experience categorical desire for one sex at one point in their lives and categorical desire for the other sex at another point in their lives (e.g., Herdt, 1981). In our society, because virtually everyone partakes of the dominant essentialist theory of sexuality, large numbers of people experience categorical sexual desire and see it as determining their sexual lives. But it is critical not to confuse this particular cultural pattern with scientific confirmation that there is a core sexual orientation within every human being. In our society there are also people whose fundamental sexual desire seems to be produced within the context of a relationship rather than by an abstract preference for women or men, or whose sense of sexual self never becomes consistently organized. The essentialist understanding of sexuality skirts questions of what experiences and understandings lead to the behaviors that create a sense of self. Essentialism ignores the *process* of the creation of a sense of self.[2]

But it is not only the essentialist nature of the Kinsey scale to which we object. The Kinsey scale, particularly as it is presently used in lax scientific discourse, is limited because it was based on a single cultural model of sexuality. The Kinsey group inadvertently took the dominant model of middle-class male sexuality as a guide for understanding human sexual behavior when other models, also cultural but perhaps ultimately more productive, could have been utilized. In the male model, behavior provides the critical data used to categorize core sexual selves. This is because in the modern Western world, men and their observers have used behavior as the indicator of internal psychic processes. This has been particularly true in the analysis of homosexuality because a homosexual behavior so violates cultural proscriptions that it has been assumed that such behavior must surely demonstrate an irrepressible core sexual self. Thus, once homosexual acts were discussed scientifically, the use of behavior as an indicator of an individual's true sexuality became more important.[3] Oddly enough, however, homosexual acts tend to be given greater weight than any heterosexual acts that the individual might also perform. In most cases, it is assumed that "psychic reaction" is the crucial factor to resolve any empirical oddities. If psychic arousal is more dramatic in homosexual relations, then a homosexual core self is adduced. How cross-situationally consistent such psychic arousal might be, however, is seldom contemplated.

The cross-cultural record amply suggests that the essentialist model of human sexuality has far from universal fit. Indeed one does not need a cross-cultural perspective; if one looks at the relatively ignored facts of modern Western female sexuality, the essentialist model's inadequacies become clear. As we have observed elsewhere

(Blumstein & Schwartz, 1976a, 1977), female sexuality in our culture does not justify an essentialist position. Women are less likely than men to view their sexual acts as a revelation of their "true sexual self," and female sexual choice seems to be based as much on situational constraints as on categorical desire. Desire seems to be aroused frequently by emotional intimacy rather than by abstract erotic taste.

Our sociological vision of sexuality is far different from the essentialist approach of many other sex researchers. Our thesis is simply that desire is created by its cultural context. Sexuality emerges from the circumstances and meanings available to individuals; it is a product of socialization, opportunity, and interpretation. For example, male sexuality in our cultural view is shaped by the scripts boys are offered almost from birth, by the cultural lessons they learn throughout the life course, among them, the belief in a sometimes overpowering male sex drive and the belief that men have immutable sexual needs that are manifested over and above individual attempts at repression.

Our approach leads to a different question than the one posed by essentialists. As sociologists, we do not wish to proliferate sexual categories but rather ask, "What circumstances create the possibility for sexual behavior—either homosexual or heterosexual?" This question cannot be approached fruitfully when one is relying on the seven-point Kinsey scale since concrete behaviors are lost in the data aggregation process used in applying the scale to people's lives.

Within a specific cultural setting there are many factors that facilitate or deter sexual behavior, both homosexual and heterosexual. The two key factors, which we will concentrate on in this chapter, are (1) the *gender roles* culturally available and (2) the *societal organization of opportunities*.

Biological sex is constrained and directed by the roles each society offers men and women. Expectations of role performance organize male and female sexuality. Thus, in order to understand human sexual behavior and the meaning of that behavior to people, it is crucial to know what members of each sex have learned is appropriate to feel and to do and what sanctions exist for inadequate or noncompliant role performance.

While there is still much to be understood about the subtle relationship between sexuality and gender, we are substantially more ignorant about the second factor, the social organization of opportunity. By this we mean how society does or does not offer circumstances that permit certain behaviors to occur. These circumstances may be as concrete as a woman's being unable to have heterosexual experience within an institution of chaperonage or as subtle as her being unable to have sexual relations outside of her marriage because she is a suburban housewife who, in the course of her typical day, never finds herself in the company of men. Even a wife who is propositioned may not have a real opportunity if the cost of giving in to temptation is ostracism from her community, expulsion from her marriage, and a future of being unacceptable to any other loving partner. Similarly, a boy who goes to all-male schools will have different sexual opportunities than one who is never in an all-male adolescent peer group, and a salesman who travels constantly is more likely to have extramarital temptations than a man who never leaves his small hometown.

Opportunity is also shaped in a less objective fashion by the meanings the culture makes available. A wife may not be able to be sexually responsive even if she is alone with a man other than her husband if she has learned that a healthy woman has little sexual appetite and that what appetite she has can only be aroused in the context of her role as wife and companion to her husband. A man may have difficulty experiencing homosexual desire in himself if he has been taught that such attractions do not exist in typical heterosexually active men.

From these examples it should be clear that we are not describing forces that affect individuals idiosyncratically, but rather we are focusing on the way society organizes social life. This does not mean that everyone acts according to a single cultural mandate. Sometimes social directives are in flux or they are actually in conflict with one another and leave room for individual choice. For example, when women in large numbers were first allowed college education, there was no deliberate social plan to make them men's equals or for them to have sexual appetites resembling men's. The same can be said of the development of safe and effective contraceptive technologies. The latent consequence of men and women having more similar lives, however, has been that attitudes and norms that had functioned well to maintain very different sex lives for women and men were no longer able to sustain their potency and legitimacy.

We would argue that understanding the dynamics of gender roles and social opportunities is a more fruitful approach to the question of why sexual behavior occurs and under what circumstances sexual identities are adopted than is the essentialist paradigm. We do not in this chapter perform the larger sociological task of developing a theory of how social opportunities arise in sexual life. Rather, we proceed from the idea that social opportunities exist and examine one type of opportunity structure in depth in order to show the utility of the concept. The source of opportunities we focus on here is intimate relationships, which we see as profoundly important in determining what behaviors will take place.

As an immediate caveat we must say that in our culture, this is truer for women than for men. If Kinsey had used female sexuality as a model, his scale might have been conceptualized not so much in terms of accumulated acts and psychic preoccupations but rather in terms of intensity and frequency of love relationships, some of which might have only incidental overt erotic components.

Women have been so effectively socialized to link love and attachment, love and sex, that eroticization is more often a consequence of emotional attraction than the trigger for the involvement. In cases where eroticization comes first, it is unlikely to continue without a relationship context; if the attraction is powerful, a relationship may have to be invented in order to sustain and justify continuing the liaison. Whether this attraction process is the result of women's relatively low position in the social structure (de Beauvoir, 1953), or whether it is a response to cultural themes governing female sexuality (Laws & Schwartz, 1977), or whether women's erotic cues are biologically different from men's (Symons, 1979; van den Berghe, 1979) is a large question, and we are unable to put it to rest in this chapter. We can, however, show that in our culture women's sexuality is organized by other than physical cues. For modern Western women, the recognition of love or admiration or the pleasure in companionship or deep friendship most often leads to erotic attraction and response. While women are not incapable of seeking sex for its own sake, this pattern of sexual behavior is relatively rare among them (Blumstein & Schwartz, 1983). Our research indicates that it is overwhelmingly more common for the relationship (or the desire for such a relationship) to establish itself first.

This pattern is less common among men in our culture. While homosexual and heterosexual erotic feelings can develop in an intimate relationship, it is much more common for a man to have sexual attractions (as early as adolescence) to a number of specific persons (some or all of whom may be total strangers), or to a generalized other, or to fantasized persons. If an opportunity exists and any personal or cultural interdictions can be overcome, he may seek to realize his erotic preferences in one or many concrete sexual contacts. An intimate or committed relationship is not necessary for excitation and in some cases may even be counterproductive to sexual arousal. Nonetheless, most men do form intimate relationships, and this leads us to ask, "What is the relevance of such relationships for their subsequent sexual behavior and self-identification?"

This is a complex question since in some cases the relationship, for example, marriage to a woman, seems to organize the man's sexual behavior and identity, while in other cases, such as the self-defined homosexual man who is married to a woman, it is less central. The husband who has sexual experiences with other men may feel torn, dishonest and fearful of exposure, but frequently he also feels a need to have a family and an approved social identity (Ross, 1971; Ross, 1983). He also finds the attraction of conventionality more compelling than the opportunity to have a less compromised homosexual sex life. A different but related example is a man with a previously exclusively homosexual life who decides that heterosexual marriage is important to him and that his homosexuality is too costly. We interviewed such a man, who decided to learn how, in his words, to "be heterosexual" in order to facilitate having children and, as he saw it, stability and respectability. While we cannot say that 20 years after this decision he would experience no residual homosexual desire, we can certainly claim that his attachment to a heterosexual relationship changed his behavior and, we believe, his self-identification.

How it is possible for men such as these to organize their lives in these ways is a question that needs and deserves further research. There is, however, some relevant information in the anthropological and historical records on the interaction of appetites, intimate relationships, and sexual self-identity. It is far from culturally universal to expect intimate relationships to be the major or sole outlet for the expression of sexual feelings or appetites. The modern Western desire for sexual, emotional, and life-style coherence is probably a rare accommodation. In the ancient world, for example, a gentleman was expected to marry and father children regardless of his attraction to males, and even in modern times, there are numerous examples of homosexual behavior occurring in the private lives of married men (e.g., Humphreys, 1970; Ross, 1971; Ross, 1983). This homosexual behavior has not exempted men from performing the male role of their time.

An interesting question is whether the separation of family and sexuality has been possible because of innate sexual flexibility or because of male socialization to be able to separate sexual, loving, and obligation impulses so that sex can be accomplished within whatever format is necessary. Or has this ability led to the existence of dual lives so that the appetite could be fulfilled without threatening home and family? Thus homosexual behavior could occur without homosexual self-identification, thereby inhibiting the development of an exclusively homosexual life-style.

An important question is why is there now such great emphasis on shaping one's life on the basis of one's intimate relationships. Perhaps the same social forces that helped create a bond between love and family and sex for women are starting to apply to men as well. Moreover, recent cultural themes of individual fulfillment and personal growth encourage and shape sexuality by giving people the impression that any disjunction between parts of the self is unhealthy and ultimately an inappropriate way to live. In addition, the ability to identify oneself as a homosexual man or lesbian and be viewed as gay by friends and acquaintances probably diminishes ability to identify with or practice heterosexual desire. The predominance of the essentialist paradigm leads men and women to create a coherent package of behavior, identity, and community, and they are thus more motivated to form same-sex relationships.

While sex role differences are a critical factor in understanding the impact of intimate relationships on sexuality, it is also important to consider the type of relationship. Sexuality is different in marriage as compared to heterosexual cohabitation, and opposite-sex relationships have a different sexual dynamic from same-sex relationships (Blumstein & Schwartz, 1983). An individual's sense of self is in part created by the relationship she or he is in, and most individuals find a transition that might occur—that is, from cohabitation to marriage or from an opposite-sex to a same-sex partner—has an enormous impact on their identity. For example, a man whom we interviewed had married his childhood sweetheart and had what he considered a happy, fulfilling, and monogamous marital sex life until unexpectedly his wife died. This man subsequently, in his words, "became in touch with" early homoerotic feelings and entered into a relationship with a man. He describes himself as having been "obsessed" with his new partner but also feels that he had been equally taken with his wife. While this man could be labeled as a Kinsey 3, or for that matter as a Kinsey 0 who changed to a Kinsey 6, we argue that it would be more fruitful to look at the circumstances that shaped his sexuality, courtship, marriage, and homosexual relationship. One might also want to know why this man, unlike most men in his society, was sexually galvanized by a tender relationship rather than by independent erotic desire.

Another example is the case of a woman, unhappily married for 23 years but feeling a profound absence of a real "soul mate." She met a woman at her son's college graduation ceremony, and over a long period of time, the two women gradually fell in love and left their husbands. Not only did the respondent's sense of self change but so did her sexual habits and desires. Again, instead of trying to determine who the "real person" is, we think it more productive to discover how changing relationships produced some new forms of behavior.

All of this would be theoretically trivial if we were only talking about individual histories. What makes these stories more compelling to a social scientist is that they are reflections of twentieth-century Western opportunities. The manner in which the intimate relationships are conducted is a cultural and historical phenomenon, which when studied in the aggregate can show us how sexuality is created.

The organization of opportunity in modern life is formed by the instability of marriage, a high remarriage rate, the ability to survive as an independent unmarried person, and the possibility of meeting eligible sex partners of either sex in institutions that have developed expressly for the purpose of bringing people together. The scenarios described in this chapter are uniquely twentieth-century stories and would not have been possible, for example, in nineteenth-century America. There would have been few opportunities for divorce, little ability to live a single or private life, and no conceptualization of the importance of sexual fulfillment or entry into a gay life-style. In fact "life-style" is a uniquely modern concept. Life-style incorporates the notion of sexual choice, and choice has simply not existed for most people in most historical periods. Furthermore, how people behaved within marriage or with a same-sex partner would have been entirely different from the way they would act today. A same-sex relationship in the nineteenth century would probably not be perceived as an appropriate public lifetime commitment.[4]

We are not historians and cannot do justice to the meanings and constructions of everyday sexuality in periods other than our own. We have, however, gathered data in the 1970s and 1980s that show how sexuality is shaped by the relationship scripts available. Our observations are based on two pieces of research: (1) the study of the antecedents of sexual identity and bisexuality, based on a sample of 150 interviews (Blumstein & Schwartz, 1976a, 1976b, 1977), and (2) the study of same-sex and opposite-sex couples, involving questionnaire, interview, and observational data, the overall sample representing approximately 1,000 male homosexual couples, 800 lesbian couples, 3,600 heterosexual marriages, and 650 heterosexual cohabitation relationships (Blumstein & Schwartz, 1983).

Two areas of couples' sexual lives—frequency of sexual activity and monogamy—are presented to illustrate the contention that intimate relationships shape sexuality.

Sexual Frequency

In all four groups of couples in our research, sexual frequency declines with the duration of the relationship (see Table 1). From this we infer that there is some habituation effect in all kinds of couples that serves to reduce sexual appetite.[5] Within heterosexual couples, this pattern varies by the simple fact of whether or not the pair

Table 1 ▧ Percentage of Couples Reporting Sex Three Times a Week or More

Years Living Together	Married Couples	Cohabiting Couples	Male Couples	Female Couples
2 or less	45% (344)	61% (349)	67% (309)	33% (357)
2–10	27% (1505)	38% (288)	32% (472)	7% (350)
10 or more	18% (1754)		11% (169)	1% (61)

Note: Numbers in parentheses are the numbers of couples on which the percentages are based. Very few of the cohabitors were together more than 10 years.

is legally married. People who live together without marriage are surely different from those who marry, and such differences may in some measure account for the differences in sexual frequency. But they probably do not account entirely for the differences. Rather, we suggest, it is the differences between marital and nonmarital heterosexual relationships themselves that create different opportunities and different motivations for sexual expression.

When we look at the three groups in our study that include women, we notice that those in relationships with men (both married and unmarried) have a greater sexual frequency than those in relationships with other women. We also note that the sexual frequencies in male homosexual relationships come closer to the heterosexual frequencies. The probable reason for these differences in sexual profiles is that men in our culture are allowed and encouraged to desire and demand more sex. They have fewer costs for experiencing or acting on sexual desires (i.e., no reduced marketability, no fear of becoming pregnant), and therefore they establish a fairly high sexual frequency in both heterosexual and homosexual relationships. We do not think women in heterosexual relationships have essentially different sexual appetites from women in lesbian relationships, since both groups of women have had similar sexual socialization and have learned similar inhibitions. If the heterosexual women in our study were suddenly put into a same-sex relationship, their sexual frequency would probably resemble lesbians' sexual frequency. The reduction in sexual frequency would occur because the norms of lesbian relationships are different from heterosexual relationships and because two women bring different cultural scripts to a sexual relationship than a man and a woman.[6]

In our study, men more often than women initiated opposite-sex relationships.[7] Men are assigned this role, and women in our society are taught to be receptive rather than aggressive in sexual matters.[8] It makes sense, then, that in lesbian couples, where both partners have experienced female sexual socialization, there would be a mutual reluctance to take the sexual lead. Such inheritance of social conditioning might contribute to lesbians having an overall lower initiation rate than other couples and hence a lower rate of sexual activity.

This reluctance to initiate, however, does not simply stem from the internalization of sexual prohibitions directed at women. Additionally, themes in some lesbian subcultures stigmatize sexual aggressiveness as "power plays" and male-type sexuality and place a lower premium on genital sexuality, with a corresponding emphasis on other forms of physical intimacy. Moreover, higher standards of relationship satisfaction are demanded in order to legitimate sexual intimacy. Relationship dynamics rather than essential core sexuality orient the individual's sexual frequency and sexual pattern.

The internal dynamics of the relationship can affect sexual experience in subtle ways. For example, among all four groups of couples in our study, the greater power one partner has, the more likely he or she is to refuse a sexual overture (Blumstein & Schwartz, 1983, pp. 219–221). And among the women in heterosexual couples, the more power they have, the less likely the couple's intercourse is to be restricted to the male-prone/female-supine position (Blumstein & Schwartz, 1983, pp. 229–230).

On the basis of these findings and with every indication that there will be greater equality between the sexes in the future, one might hypothesize that the sexual patterns of heterosexual couples will change in response to a more liberated female sexuality. In some couples frequency may increase and in others it may decrease, but in either event these changes will be responses to the structure of the relationship between the partners, not to some inherent capacity of women.

Monogamy

The rules of monogamous conduct provide insight into how male sexuality is affected by intimate relationships. With the exception of the male homosexual couples in our study, the majority of each group of couples feels that the rules of monogamous conduct are a cornerstone of the relationship and should not be broken.[9] Homosexual men, while presently intimidated by the risk of contracting AIDS, nonetheless have a long history of separating sexual desire from intimacy and love, and have evolved a norm of having relationships that allow either occasional or a great deal of sex with persons other than one's partner.

Heterosexual men, both married and cohabiting, have frequently mentioned in our interviews that they would like greater permission for "recreational" sex in their relationship, but the data show that they tend not to pursue it (see Table 2). If these men were in a same-sex relationship, they would have a higher rate of nonmonogamy because the rules of acceptability would be altered.[10] Thus an element of their sexuality is constructed by their female partner's wishes and by the norms that are shaped by the institution of marriage. Compliance to the norm is, of course, not perfect: many husbands do have extramarital sex, and sex outside their relationship is even more common among male cohabitors. The latter face less stringent guidelines within their relationship and are merely asked to comply with their partner's wishes rather than with the directives of marital vows. Looking at the difference between married men's and cohabiting men's extrarelationship sex tells us how much the norms of marriage organize sexuality.

This cursory look at sexual expression in intimate relationships is not intended

Table 2 ▪ **Percentage of Respondents Reporting at Least One Instance of Nonmonogamy in the Previous Year (couples living together between two and ten years)**

Husbands	11%	(1510)
Wives	9%	(1510)
Male cohabitors	25%	(288)
Female cohabitors	22%	(288)
Homosexual males	79%	(943)
Lesbians	19%	(706)

Note: Numbers in parentheses are the numbers of respondents on which the percentages are based.

as more than an illustration of the analytic mileage to be gained by conceptualizing sex within the context of social circumstances. Even by looking at relatively crude survey data we can see that sexual behavior is created by relationship expectations and traditions rather than by sexual essences. If we were to look more microscopically within relationships, we could see the subtle ways in which intimate interaction affects participants. We could see how friends, neighborhoods, community, law, and other constraints, affect sexual conduct. If research on sexuality were to proceed in this direction, if more attention were paid to opportunity structures—of which intimate relationships are but one—we would uncover the social construction of sexuality.

In sum, we look forward to research in which situational variables and cultural meanings are seen as the foundation of sexuality. But new research needs to avoid androcentrism so that opportunity structures are not chosen because of their relevance only to men's lives. A useful approach will take into account individual biography without producing a static and individualistic explanation of sexuality. Sexuality is best comprehended by noting and understanding the *processes* that encourage the occurrence of acts and the reason for their discontinuance. We should focus on the act, behaving not as accountants tabulating frequencies but as behavioral scientists looking at the meaning of the act for the actors. If we continue as we have in the past, focusing on the individual rather than on the social context that creates his or her behavior, we may end up with interesting biography but relatively little ability for further prediction or theory construction. We then run the risk of thinking we understand something merely because we have given it a number on a scale.

Notes

1. We would also argue that for most members of contemporary Western society, because of the hegemony of sexual essentialism, once an individual develops a sexual identity, it funnels much of his or her social experience into erotic and nonerotic circumstances that continually reinforce a subjective sense of categorical desire.

2. On the social construction of sexuality, see, among others, Gagnon and Simon (1973), McIntosh (1968), Plummer (1975), and Weinberg (1978, 1983).

3. The Kinsey scale was originally aimed at both behavior and "psychic reactions." The inclusion of the latter construct implicitly acknowledged ways in which purely behavioral tabulations could mislead. However, the conceptual and measurement problems associated with "psychic reactions" have remained largely unresolved.

4. It is important to note that homosexual behavior leads to the existence of gay male and lesbian couple relationships only under extremely rare historical and cultural circumstances. This means that most homosexuality occurs in very different contexts than much (we do not know how much) heterosexuality. This fact, as obvious as it is, has important implications. Most sensible researchers would be wary of equating heterosexual intercourse between two strangers (e.g., a man with a female prostitute) with that in a 25-year marriage. Neither situation reflects an "essence of heterosexuality." Researchers have been less sensitive in the case of homosexual behavior, as though the slogan were "Sodomy is sodomy is sodomy . . ." It is critical to see human sexual behavior as context embedded rather than as a simple expression of the underlying sexuality of the individual.

5. Two other interpretations of these data come immediately to mind. First is the argument that physical aging, which is correlated with relationship duration, is the real causal factor. Multivariate statistical analyses allowed an evaluation of the aging effects net of duration and the duration effects

net of aging. On the basis of these analyses, we concluded that both physical aging and habituation independently reduce sexual frequency. The other interpretation to consider is that couples with relatively low sexual frequency have greater likelihood of longevity. While we have no direct empirical test of this causal hypothesis, it seems implausible in light of substantial positive correlations between sexual frequency and sexual happiness and substantial negative correlations between sexual happiness and relationship durability.

6. Another way of looking at these data is to imagine a woman living in a heterosexual relationship for 10 years followed by a homosexual relationship of the same duration. In the typical case, the total number of sexual acts in the heterosexual relationship would be much greater than the total number of acts within the lesbian relationship. Ought we to label such a woman a Kinsey 3 because she was in two 10-year relationships? Or would she be a Kinsey 1 because her sexual activity was more frequent in the heterosexual union? Or would we label her a Kinsey 5 or 6 because of her most recent sexual life, especially if asserted that this relationship was permanent? These data suggest caution in the use of a scale that does not take into account the context and changing meaning of people's emotional and sexual lives.

7. Fifty-one percent of husbands say they initiate sex more than their wives as compared to 16% who say the reverse pattern holds true and the remainder who say initiation is equal ($N = 3,612$). While the wives are not in perfect agreement with their husbands, they are very close (48 percent and 12 percent, $N = 3,616$). Thirty-nine percent of male cohabitors say they initiate more, and 19% say their female partner initiates more ($N = 646$). The female percentages are 39% and 15% ($N = 648$).

8. Sociobiologists have argued that this difference is a reflection of the different reproductive strategies of men and women. Indeed Symons (1979) has applied this argument to the sexual behavior of lesbians. His discussion, however, does not adequately deal with the influence of cultural learning.

9. We asked respondents how important they felt it is that they themselves be monogamous. The percentages saying it is important are husbands, 75% ($N = 3,635$); wives, 84% ($N = 3,640$); male cohabitors, 62% ($N = 650$); female cohabitors, 70% ($N = 650$); lesbians, 71% ($N = 1,559$); and male homosexuals, 36% ($N = 1,924$).

10. It should be noted that the percentages in Table 2 are based on data gathered just before the AIDS crisis began to receive widespread attention in the gay community.

References

Blumstein, P., & Schwartz, P. (1976a). Bisexuality in women. *Archives of Sexual Behavior, 5,* 171–181.

Blumstein, P., & Schwartz, P. (1976b). Bisexuality in men. *Urban Life, 5,* 339–358.

Blumstein, P., & Schwartz, P. (1977). Bisexuality: Some social psychological issues. *Journal of Social Issues, 33*(2), 30–45.

Blumstein, P., & Schwartz, P. (1983). *American couples: Money, work, and sex.* New York: William Morrow.

de Beauvoir, S. (1953). *The second sex.* New York: Knopf.

Gagnon, J. H., & Simon, W. (1973). *Sexual conduct: The social sources of human sexuality.* Chicago: Aldine.

Herdt, G. H. (1981). *Guardians of the flutes: Idioms of masculinity.* New York: McGraw-Hill.

Humphreys, L. (1970). *Tearoom trade: Impersonal sex in public places.* Chicago: Aldine.

Katz, J. (1975). Essences as moral identities: Verifiability and responsibility in imputations of deviance and charisma. *American Journal of Sociology, 80,* 1369–1390.

Kinsey, A. C., Pomeroy, W. B., & Martin, C. E. (1948). *Sexual behavior in the human male.* Philadelphia: W. B. Saunders.

Kinsey, A. C., Pomeroy, W. B., Martin, C. E., & Gebhard, P. H. (1953). *Sexual behavior in the human female.* Philadelphia: W. B. Saunders.

Laws, J. L., & Schwartz, P. (1977). *Sexual scripts: The social construction of female sexuality.* Hinsdale, IL: Dryden Press.

McIntosh, M. (1968). The homosexual role. *Social Problems, 16,* 182–192.

Plummer, K. (1975). *Sexual stigma: An interactionist account.* London: Routledge & Kegan Paul.

Ross, H. L. (1971). Modes and adjustments of married homosexuals. *Social Problems, 18,* 385–393.

Ross, M. W. (1983). *The married homosexual man.* London: Routledge & Kegan Paul.

Symons, D. (1979). *The evolution of human sexuality.* New York: Oxford University Press.

van den Berghe, P. L. (1979). *Human family systems: An evolutionary view.* New York: Elsevier.

Weinberg, T. S. (1978). On "doing" and "being" gay: Sexual behavior and homosexual male self-identity. *Journal of Homosexuality, 4,* 143–156.

Weinberg, T. S. (1983). *Gay men, gay selves: The social construction of homosexual identities.* New York: Irvington.

Questions for Thought

1. Explain an "essentialist" perspective on human sexuality.

2. According to Blumstein and Schwartz, gender roles and social opportunities are the two key sociocultural factors that influence sexual behavior. Explain each of these factors.

3. In pioneering sex research in the 1940s and 1950s, Alfred Kinsey and his associates proposed replacing a simple dichotomy of heterosexuality versus homosexuality with a continuum. The seven-point "Kinsey scale" ranged from exclusive heterosexuality to exclusive homosexuality. According to Blumstein and Schwartz, what are the advantages and disadvantages of this scale?

4. Based on this article, summarize important male-female differences in sexuality.

5. Explain the distinction Blumstein and Schwartz make between homosexual behavior versus self-identification as gay, lesbian, or heterosexual.

6. Based on this article, analyze the factors that affect sexual frequency in heterosexual, lesbian, and gay male relationships.

7. In growing up we are exposed to cultural beliefs about sexuality from books, magazines, TV shows, movies, and the like. Select one type of medium and describe the messages conveyed about human sexuality. (For example, analyze six issues of a magazine for teenage girls or a popular advice book for teens.)

Sexual Practices of Heterosexual Asian American Young Adults

Susan D. Cochran

Vickie M. Mays

Laurie Leung

Traditional Asian cultures emphasize respect for parents and value family loyalty more highly than individualism. Does this cultural heritage translate into greater conservatism in the sexual activities of Asian American college students compared with students from other cultural backgrounds? To find out, Cochran and her colleagues administered questionnaires to a sample of young, unmarried, heterosexual Asian Americans. Consistent with the idea of sexual conservatism, Asian Americans were less likely than their White, Black, or Hispanic counterparts to have ever had sexual intercourse. Those Asian Americans who were sexually active, however, did not differ from other young adults in their sexual behaviors, including high rates of unprotected sex. Asian American men and women gave different reasons for not having sexual intercourse, but were fairly similar in their actual sexual behaviors.

Epidemiologic patterns of reported AIDS cases suggest that at present Asian Americans in the United States are an ethnic minority group at lower risk for human immunodeficiency virus (HIV) infection than Blacks, Hispanics, or Whites. Yet little is known empirically about the sexual behaviors of Asian Americans. The present study explores rates of sexual activity and patterns of sexual behavior in a sample of young, unmarried, heterosexual Asian Americans. Results suggest that previously reported sexual conservatism within this ethnic group may be limited to the initiation of sexual activity. Once sexually active, behaviors appear to be similar to their non-Asian counterparts and facilitative of HIV infection should the virus become widely distributed within the young, heterosexual population. This underscores the need for HIV prevention interventions directed toward this ethnic minority group despite current low rates of HIV infection.

Currently in the United States, Asian Americans represent an ethnic minority group at significantly lower risk than Blacks or Hispanics for infection with the Human Immunodeficiency Virus (HIV) (Centers for Disease Control, 1989), the presumed causal agent for the acquired immunodeficiency syndrome (AIDS) (Friedland and Klein, 1987). At present, the cumulative AIDS incidence rates for Blacks, Hispanics, and Whites are 83.8, 73.0, and 26.3 per 100,000 persons, respectively. In contrast, the Centers for Disease Control report that Asian/Pacific Islanders have a cumulative incidence rate of 13.9 per 100,000 persons. The reasons for this lower incidence may reflect a combination of a variety of factors including behavioral differences in intravenous drug use (Centers for Disease Control, 1989) and sexual behavior, current behavioral proximity to HIV (Cochran and Mays, 1988), and, possibly, under-identification of Asian cases (Aoki *et al.,* 1989).

Yet there is cause to be concerned about the future incidence of HIV infection in the Asian American communities. First, while current cases of AIDS are relatively low among Asians, there is an indication they are on the increase (Aoki *et al.,* 1989). In San Francisco, where Asian/Pacific Islanders comprise approximately one-third of the city's population, this group, in comparison to other ethnic groups, showed the largest percentage increase in reported AIDS cases (Mandel and Kitano, 1989). In other urban areas in the United States where Asians have immigrated and settled in large numbers, cases of HIV infection and AIDS have begun to appear, particularly among individuals who are of Filipino and Japanese descent (Aoki *et al.,* 1989).

Another reason for worry about future cases of HIV infection in Asian Americans lies in the difficulty of implementing AIDS education and prevention programs in an ethnic minority group in which over 32 distinct cultures, languages, customs, and religions can prevail (Aoki *et al.,* 1989). Each of these groups may differ in the outreach efforts necessary to protect them from HIV risk-related behaviors. These outreach efforts may be complicated by differing cultural mores that influence the delivery and receipt of sexually explicit information of at-risk behaviors. Indeed, a 1987 survey of high school students in the San Francisco Bay Area, an AIDS epicenter with established, widespread community AIDS education, revealed that Asian American students were significantly less knowledgeable about AIDS than their non-Asian counterparts (DiClemente *et al.,* 1987). An additional complication in educational efforts with the Asian American population is the lack of empirical information specific to this population on the prevalence of HIV-related risk behaviors.

Research on Asian American sexual behavior, while sparse, suggests cultural pressures may act to reduce behavioral risk for HIV. Christensen's (1973) study of students from nine distinct cultural groups found that Asians disapproved quite strongly of marital infidelity. In a more recent study, Erikson and Moore (1986) found that Asian Americans had a tendency for sexual conservatism. They also reported that Asian Americans were significantly less likely to talk about sex than Whites, Hispanics, or Blacks.

Several researchers posit that sexual conservatism among traditional Asians is a result of the familial dynamics of Asian cultures (Chun-Hoon, 1971; Connor, 1976; Hirayama and Hirayama, 1986). Within many traditional Asian cultures, social order and control of emotions and feelings are highly valued. An outward display of strong emotions is not viewed favorably (Hirayama and Hirayama, 1986). In contrast to the Western concept of individualism, Asian cultures stress group or family unity and cohesiveness. The children are taught to depend on the family and to have the utmost respect for their parents (filial piety). This restrictiveness may give the family a greater degree of control over their teenage and adult children. As a result, sexual expression and behavior of children may to a greater extent be influenced by familial values (Hirayama and Hirayama, 1986).

However, conservatism in the outward expression of one's sexuality should not be confused with the absence of HIV-related risk behavior. Indeed, in some traditional Asian cultures, such as Japan (Hirayama and Hirayama, 1986), China (Tsui, 1985), and the Philippines (Yap, 1986), sexuality, while constrained so as not to disrupt the social order, is viewed as a normal, private aspect of life. Thus the roots of sexual conservatism lie not in the Victorian influences noted in the West (D'Emilio and Freedman, 1988) but rather in traditional Asian values of familial unity.

The extent to which these cultural values impact Asian American young adults who are also exposed to values of the United States majority culture is relatively unknown. Sue (1982), for instance, reported in a survey of 36 Asian American college students who were enrolled in a human sexuality course that prevalence rates of the occurrence of premarital sexual behavior (80% of the sample) were no different from non-Asian students studied. These students were also no more likely to report sexual guilt feelings than non-Asian students.

The present study explores Asian American sexual behavior in young, unmarried heterosexual adults in an effort to determine the potential for HIV transmission should the virus become more widely dispersed in the United States heterosexual population.

Method

Questionnaires were completed by 153 individuals (64 men and 88 women) attending one of several Southern California universities. Approximately half were U.S. born; the remainder were immigrants from Korea ($n = 23$), Taiwan ($n = 16$), the Philippines ($n = 13$), Vietnam ($n = 7$), China ($n = 4$), Hong Kong ($n = 4$), Indonesia ($n = 2$), Thailand ($n = 1$), and other foreign countries ($n = 5$). Due to the small numbers of individuals from each foreign country, all the subgroups were analyzed together.

Subjects ranged from 18 to 25 years old (median age $= 19.0$). Consistent with inclusion criteria for the study, all were unmarried and self-defined as heterosexual. Most were from middle-class (33%) or upper-middle-class (53%) backgrounds, reflecting the student populations of the universities from which they were sampled. Native and foreign-born participants did not differ in terms of gender or age distributions.

Procedure

Questionnaires assessing prior dating and sexual experiences, among other topics, were administered to 665 college students recruited from Southern California university campuses. All were unmarried and between the ages of 18 and 25 years. Of these, 153 individuals were Asian American and constitute the sample of interest. All questionnaires were completed and constitute the sample of interest. All questionnaires were completed anonymously. Data for this sample were collected between November 1987 and July 1988.

The questionnaire was developed from previous surveys of sexual behavior in young adults (Cochran and Peplau, 1985, 1991; Cochran *et al.,* 1990; Mays, 1988). Additional questions addressing factors associated with delaying the onset of sexual behavior were developed using the focus group methodology with young adults. College students, ranging in age from 19 to 24 years and diverse in their ethnic backgrounds, met in a small research group composed of eight individuals, both male and female, for a series of 1-hr meetings over a period of 5 weeks. During this time, the participants generated a list of factors from their own personal experiences, those of their friends', and the literature on young adults' sexual behavior that they were reading. Items were discussed by the group to arrive at a consensus on factors that may be associated with choosing to become sexually active or not.

Results

Comparisons of Sexually Active and Sexually Inexperienced Participants

Overall, 44% of the men ($n = 28$) and 50% of the women ($n = 44$) had engaged in heterosexual sexual intercourse at least once in their lives (see Table 1). Men were no more likely to be sexually experienced than women, $\chi^2(1) = 0.35$, $p > 0.10$, nor were native-born participants more likely to be sexually active than foreign-born individuals, $\chi^2(1) = 0.24$, $p > 0.10$. In addition, those who were sexually active were not significantly older than those who were not, $F(1, 148) = 0.26$, $p > 0.10$. Instead, sexually active young adults, in contrast to those who were not, began dating at a significantly younger age, $F(1, 131) = 9.69$, $p < 0.01$, and had their first serious romantic attachment at a significantly younger age, $F(1, 89) = 10.08$, $p < 0.01$. Reflecting this latter finding, sexually active young adults reported that their longest romantic attachment had lasted on average approximately 8 months longer than the sexually inexperienced participants, $F(1, 88) = 8.72$, $p < 0.01$.

Sexual Experiences

Focusing on the sexually experienced individuals, there were few significant differences between men and women (Table 2). Average age at first occasion of sexual intercourse was between 16 and 17 years old (range = 13 to 21 years). On average, subjects reported a median of 2 previous sexual partners (range = 1 to 17 partners). However, women in the sample were at present significantly more sexually active

Table 1 ▦ Demographic Characteristics and Relationship Experiences of the Young Adult Asian American Sample[a]

| | Never engaged in sexual intercourse | | One or more instances of sexual intercourse | |
	Male (n = 36) Mean	Female (n = 44) Mean	Male (n = 28) Mean	Female (n = 44) Mean
Age in years	19.2	19.4	19.4	19.1
Age at first date	16.4	16.5	15.2	15.6[b]
Age of first serious relationship	17.4	18.0	16.6	16.6[b]
Months of longest serious relationship	12.6	10.0	17.8	18.4[b]
No. of relationships	1.6	1.9	2.2	2.0

[a] Statistical differences evaluated by 2 × 2 ANOVAs. There were no significant main effects of gender or interactions of gender and sexual experience.
[b] Significant main effects of sexual experience; $p < 0.05$.

Table 2 ▦ Behaviors of Sexually Experienced Young Adult Asian Americans

	Males (n = 28)	Female (n = 44)
Mean age in years at first sexual intercourse	16.8	17.4
Mean number of years sexually active	3.6	2.8
Median number of sexual partners—lifetime	2.0	2.0
Mean number of sexual partners—previous 6 months	0.7	1.3[a]
Mean frequency of sexual intercourse in past 6 months (3 = two to three times a month)	2.4	3.6[a]
% possibly exposed to sexually transmitted disease	14.3	18.2
% treated by physician for sexually transmitted disease	0.0	11.6
% who always use birth control	28.6	32.6
% who always use condoms	14.3	9.1
% who have suggested condom use to a partner	66.7	86.0
% whose partners have suggested condoms	63.0	86.4
% who have ever had a partner object to condom use	29.6	56.8[a]
Sexual practices ever engaged in (%)		
Vaginal intercourse without condom	92.9	93.2
Vaginal intercourse with condom	71.4	81.0
Fellatio	85.7	86.4
Cunnilingus	75.0	95.5[a]
Anal intercourse	14.3	15.9

[a] $p < 0.05$.

than men both in terms of number of partners in the previous 6 months, $t(60) =$ 2.03, $p < 0.05$, and sexual frequency in the previous month, $t(70) = 3.18, p < 0.01$.

As reported in other surveys of young adults' sexual behaviors (e.g., Kegeles *et al.,* 1988), few individuals reported consistent use of birth control or condoms. Only 31% reported that they always use birth control during sexual intercourse and only 11% use condoms every time they are sexually active. Two-thirds of men and 86% of women reported that they had at some point suggested the use of condoms to a sexual partner. Sixty-three percent of men and 86% of women also reported that a partner had suggested condom use at some point. Women were significantly more likely than men to report that a partner had expressed objections to using condoms, $\chi^2(1) = 4.18, p < 0.05$.

In terms of sexual behaviors, these young adults practice behaviors that will transmit HIV should it be present. Although 77% of the sample reported the experience of having used condoms for sexual intercourse at some point, 93% also practiced sexual intercourse without condoms and 15% had tried anal intercourse at least once. In fact, nearly 17% of the sample reported that they had been possibly exposed to a sexually transmitted disease (STD) at some point in the past and 12% of women surveyed had actually been treated for an STD. None of the men reported that they had received medical treatment for STD.

Comparisons of U.S.-born versus non-U.S.-born participants indicate few differences between the two groups except that those individuals born in the United States were significantly younger ($X = 16.6$ years) than the latter group ($X = 17.7$) when they first had sexual intercourse, $F(1, 52) = 6.11$, $p < 0.05$, and thus had been sexually active for a significantly longer duration when studied, $F(1, 52) = 4.13$, $p < 0.05$. However, there were no differences in self-reported sexual practices.

Reasons for Delaying Sexual Activity

For those who had not yet begun sexual activity, the questionnaire presented 10 possible reasons for this and asked participants to rate each as to how important it was in their not having had sexual intercourse. As can be seen in Table 3, participants' responses suggest that the double-standard for men and women in relationship to sexual activity remains. Women were significantly more likely than men to cite personal, religious, and familial beliefs against premarital sex as important reasons for not engaging in sexual behavior. They were also more likely to view sexual activity as interfering with attracting a desired marital partner. In contrast, men were somewhat more likely than women to report that an absence of opportunity for having sex was a more important factor in their not being sexually active.

In fact, men's and women's rankings from most to least important were not significantly correlated (Spearman's $\rho = 0.36$, $p > 0.10$). For men, the top five reasons given were worry about pregnancy, worry about getting AIDS, cause upset for family, against sex before marriage, and no opportunity. For women the top five reasons were against sex before marriage, cause upset for family, worry about pregnancy, religion is against it, and sex spoils chances for desired marriage partner.

There were no significant differences between native and foreign-born partici-

Table 3 ▨   **Reasons for Not Engaging in Sexual Intercourse Given by Sexually Inexperienced Young Asian American Adults**[a]

Reason	Male (n = 36) Mean	Female (n = 44) Mean	t
I'm worried about getting (her) pregnant	3.5	3.8	0.75
My family would be upset	2.8	4.0	3.01[c]
I am against sex before marriage	2.8	4.3	5.79[d]
I'm worried about getting AIDS	3.5	3.2	−0.95
My religion is against sex before marriage	2.4	3.7	3.61[d]
If you have sex now it may spoil your chances of getting the man (woman) that you really want later to marry you	2.3	3.4	2.52[c]
I haven't met a man (woman) who I wanted to have sex with	2.4	2.9	1.11
I have never had the opportunity to have sex	2.7	2.0	−1.92[b]
I'm still uncomfortable with the thought of having sex with a man (woman)	2.1	2.5	1.38
I'm not sure that I'm straight (heterosexual)	1.8	1.6	−0.77

[a] Items are listed in ranking order for total sample from most to least important. Responses given on 5-point scales from (1) *not important* to (5) *very important*. Statistical differences evaluated by *t* tests.
[b] $p = 0.06$.
[c] $p < 0.01$.
[d] $p < 0.001$.

pants in reasons for delaying sexual activity. Indeed, both groups tended to weigh the 10 possible factors equivalently (Spearman's $\rho = 0.84$, $p < 0.01$).

Discussion

While this study was unable to explore possible differences within cultural subgroupings of Asian Americans due to the small numbers from each group recruited, results, nonetheless, provide some preliminary information about the sexual behaviors of Asian American young adults. In the present sample of single, heterosexual, 18- to 25-year-old Asian Americans, 47% were sexually active, a rate significantly lower than among the other 480 White (72% sexually active), Black (84%), and Hispanic (59%) young adults we surveyed. The rate also appears lower than national estimates for White teenagers where somewhere between 54 and 57% of 19-year-olds are estimated to be sexually active (Kahn *et al.,* 1988). Among sexually active participants, those who were born in the United States, and thus may be influenced to a lesser extent by Asian-derived sexual norms, were significantly younger than their foreign-born counterparts when they initiated sexual activity. This supports the findings of previous studies (Erickson and Moore, 1986; Yap, 1986) reporting greater sexual conservatism among Asian Americans, at least in initiation of sexual activity.

For those Asian Americans in our study who were sexually active, behaviors were consistent with their non-Asian contemporaries. Like other young adults (Kegeles *et al.*, 1988), these individuals are practicing behaviors that are risky, including low rates of condom use and sexual behaviors that will transmit HIV if present. Indeed, the percentage of subjects in the current study who always used condoms (11%) does not differ significantly from the White (11%), Black (11%), or Hispanic (10%) students we surveyed. This underscores the importance of delineating the parameters of sexual conservatism among Asian Americans. That is, sexual conservatism may be expressed in some domains, such as delaying the onset of sexual activity, but in others, for example, types of behaviors practiced, there may be no difference between Asian Americans and their non-Asian counterparts. This has important implications for the transmission of HIV within the Asian American population.

Although determination of all the reasons responsible for delaying the onset of sexual activity were beyond the scope of the current study, we did find evidence of a continued gender difference in attitudes toward a double-standard for sexual behavior (Christensen, 1973). For women who were not sexually active, self-rated important factors focused on personal, familial, and religious proscriptions against premarital sexuality. In contrast, for men, most important were concerns about pregnancy, AIDS, familial and personal disapproval, and the lack of opportunity. These findings highlight the fact that young men and women may have very different motivations for engaging or not engaging in sexual activity. Efforts designed to influence sexual behaviors in young heterosexual ethnic minorities where sex-role influences are prevalent must take notice of these gender differences if the efforts are to be effective.

Asian Americans comprise diverse cultural and ethnic groups (Kitano and Chai, 1982; Patel, 1988), including those with immigrant roots from China, Japan, the Philippines, Korea, Vietnam, Cambodia, Laos, Thailand, Malaysia, and India. This diversity is also reflected in reported AIDS cases. For example, in San Francisco, 47% of cases in Asian Americans have involved Filipinos (Aoki *et al.*, 1989) although it was estimated that in 1980, Filipinos represented only 26% of San Francisco County's Asian American population. However, among Asian Americans, those of Japanese descent suffer the higher incidence of AIDS when adjusted for size of their community showing an incidence rate (per 1000) of 1.16 in contrast to American Filipinos (0.63), Vietnamese (0.37), and Chinese (0.13) (Ja and Ngin, 1987). Most probably these differences in AIDS incidence reflect AIDS-related behavioral diversity. As the epidemic spreads, both this behavioral diversity and behavioral proximity to HIV will shape the HIV infection pattern among Asian Americans. It is important in future research, when possible, that studies document and delineate the sexual behaviors of each of the distinct Asian/Pacific Island subpopulations.

In an era of increasing concern over the health and welfare of teens who in growing numbers are experiencing unwanted pregnancies and sexually transmitted diseases (Brooks-Gunn *et al.,* 1988), further research to determine the gender-based, cultural, and familial factors that lead to delayed initiation of sexual behavior is greatly needed. This is particularly important in the current era of the increasing incidence of AIDS in the heterosexual ethnic minority population (Cochran *et al.,* 1988). Sexually active individuals must possess the skills to determine low risk partners (Cochran and Mays, 1990), negotiate safer sex, master the correct use of condoms, and maintain a healthy outlook on sexual activity. This requires judgment, social maturity, and skills that develop as teenagers mature into young adults. Data from the current study offer some evidence for the importance of cultural and familial norms in potentially delaying young adults from possible exposure to HIV infection. Research exploring both the generalizability of these findings among specific subgroups of Asian Americans, as well as across other ethnic groups, would make a contribution to the fight against HIV infection in young heterosexual ethnic minorities. Data of this nature also provide those struggling to design effective prevention programs for ethnic minorities with an empirical base from which to work.

References

Aoki, B., Ngin, C. P. N., Mo, B., and Ja, D. Y. (1989). AIDS prevention models in the Asian American communities. In Mays, V. M., Albee, G. W., and Schneider S. F. (eds.), *Primary Prevention of AIDS: Psychological Approaches,* Sage, Newbury Park, CA, pp. 290–308.

Brooks-Gunn, J., Boyer, C. B., and Hein, K. (1988). Preventing HIV infection and AIDS in children and adolescents: Behavioral research and intervention strategies. *Am. Psychol.* 43: 958–965.

Centers for Disease Control (1989, May 12). AIDS and human immunodeficiency virus infection in the United States: 1988 update. *Morbid. Mortal. Week. Rep.* 38(S-4): 1–38.

Christensen, H. T. (1973). Attitudes toward marital infidelity: A nine-culture sampling of university student opinion. *J. Comp. Fam. Stud.* 4: 197–214.

Chun-Hoon, L. (1971). Jade Snow Wong and the fate of the Chinese-American identity. *Amerasia J.* 1: 52–63.

Cochran, S. D., Keidan, J., and Kalechstein, A. (1990). Sexually transmitted diseases and AIDS: Changes in risk reduction behaviors among young adults. *Sex. Transmit. Dis.* 17: 80–86.

Cochran, S. D., and Mays, V. M. (1988). Epidemiologic and sociocultural factors in the transmission of HIV infection in Black gay and bisexual men. In Shernoff, M., and Scott, W. (eds.), *A Sourcebook of Gay/Lesbian Health Care,* 2nd ed., National Gay and Lesbian Health Foundation, Washington, DC, pp. 202–211.

Cochran, S. D., and Mays, V. M. (1990). Sex, lies, and HIV. *New Engl. J. Med.* 322: 774–775.

Cochran, S. D., Mays, V. M., and Roberts, V. (1988). Ethnic minorities and AIDS. In Lewis, A. (ed.), *Nursing Care of the patient with AIDS/ARC.* Aspen Publications, Rockville, MD. pp. 17–24.

Cochran, S. D., and Peplau, L. A. (1985). Value orientations in heterosexual relationships. *Psych. Women Quart.* 9: 477–488.

Cochran, S. D., and Peplau, L. A. (1991). Sexual risk reduction behaviors in sexually active heterosexual young adults. *Soc. Sci. Med.* 33 (1), 25–36.

Connor, J. W. (1976). Family bonds, material closeness, and the suppression of sexuality in three generations of Japanese Americans. *Ethos* 4: 189–221.

D'Emilio, J., and Freedman, E. B. (1988). *Intimate Matters: A History of Sexuality in America,* Harper & Row, New York.

DiClemente, R. J., Zorn, J., and Temoshok, L. (1987). The association of gender, ethnicity, and length of residence in the Bay Area to adolescents' knowledge and attitudes about Acquired Immune Deficiency Syndrome. *J. Appl. Soc. Psychol.* 17: 216–230.

Erickson, P. I., and Moore, D. S. (1986). Sexual activity, birth control use, and attitudes among high school students from three minority groups. Paper presented at the meetings of the American Public Health Association, Las Vegas, NV.

Friedland, G. H., and Klein, R. S. (1987). Transmission of the human immunodeficiency virus. *New Eng. J. Med.* 317: 1125–1135.

Hirayama, H., and Hirayama, K. K. (1986). The sexuality of Japanese Americans. *J. Soc. Work Hum. Sex.* 4: 3, 81–98.

Ja, D. Y., and Ngin, P. (1987). AIDS in the Asian community: A review and analysis. Unpublished manuscript, Bay View Hunter's Point Foundation, Asian AIDS Project, San Francisco.

Kahn, J. R., Kalsbeek, W. D., and Hofferth, S. L. (1988). National estimates of teenage sexual activity: Evaluating the comparability of three national surveys. *Demography* 25: 189–204.

Kegeles, S. M., Adler, N. E., and Irwin, C. E. (1988). Sexually active adolescents and condoms: Changes over one year in knowledge, attitudes, and use. *Am. J. Public Health* 78: 460–461.

Kitano, H. H. L., and Chai, L. K. (1982). Korean interracial marriage. *Marr. Fam. Rev.* 5: 75–89.

Mandel, J. S., and Kitano, K. J. (1989). San Francisco looks at AIDS in Southeast Asia. *Multicult. Inquiry Res. AIDS Quart. Newsletter* 3: 1–2, 7.

Mays, V. M. (1988, August). Black women and AIDS: Is knowledge enough? Paper presented at the meetings of the American Psychological Association, Atlanta.

Patel, D. I. (1988). Asian Americans: A growing force. *J. State Gov.* 2: 71–76.

Sue, D. (1982). Sexual experience and attitudes for Asian-American students. *Psychol. Rep.* 51: 401–402.

Tsui, A. M. (1985). Psychotherapeutic considerations in sexual counseling for Asian immigrants. *Psychotherapy* 22: 357–362.

Yap, J. G. (1986). Philippine ethnoculture and human sexuality. *J. Soc. Work Hum. Sex.* 4: 121–134.

Questions for Thought

1. Compare the reasons given by Asian American men versus Asian American women for not engaging in sexual intercourse.

2. Are Asian American students more sexually conservative than students from other ethnic backgrounds? Based on this article, briefly summarize ways in which Asian Americans might be characterized as more sexually conservative. Then describe evidence that contradicts this characterization of Asian Americans as conservative.

3. These researchers found that sexually active Asian American men were no more sexually experienced than Asian American women. In fact, Asian American women had a greater number of sexual partners and had sexual intercourse more frequently in the past six months than did men. What reasons might explain these gender differences?

4. This research is based on a sample of middle-class to upper-middle-class Asian American students from southern California universities. Suggest at least two specific ways in which these results might not generalize to other Asian American young adults.

5. The authors report that the use of condoms to promote safer sex was the same—about 11%—among Asian American, White, Black, and Hispanic students. Suggest three factors that might account for this low rate of condom use among all four groups.

Working-Class Women, Middle-Class Women, and Models of Childbirth

Margaret K. Nelson

In this study of new mothers, Nelson demonstrates that working-class and middle-class women have different attitudes or "models" about pregnancy and childbirth. In general, middle-class women want to be actively involved in the birth process and prefer little medical intervention. In contrast, working-class women prefer more passive birth experiences with more medical intervention. Nelson examines the reasons for these social class differences and cautions against taking the middle-class model as a universal standard.

This paper suggests that middle-class feminists who have urged a new vision of childbirth are out of touch with the needs of working-class women. This conclusion is derived from a review of the childbirth literature and an analysis of data collected from 322 women who gave birth in a northern New England teaching hospital. The literature on childbirth—whether written from a feminist or non-feminist perspective—ignores the variable of social class. The data demonstrate, however, that working-class and middle-class women have different attitudes towards childbirth during pregnancy, different experiences during childbirth, and different post-partum evaluations of their childbirth experiences. A single set of prescriptions for childbirth may not, therefore, be appropriate for all women.

This paper began as an attempt to describe the class differences in childbirth procedures in a teaching hospital in New England. I assumed that I could show, as have others, that middle-class women received better medical services than working-class women, and that although the hospital had a long way to go before it provided

Reprinted from *Social Problems*, 1983, *30*(3), 284–297. Copyright 1983 by The Society for the Study of Social Problems. Used by permission of the University of California Press.

all women with an optimum birth experience, one's chances of reaching that goal were greatly enhanced if one entered as a middle-class client. This paper, then, began as a critique of birth practices in a modern hospital and the class biases implicit among medical personnel.

Responses to my questionnaires and interviews suggested that women could be divided along certain significant social dimensions which corresponded to kinds of birth experiences. One group of women experienced birth in a relatively active and involved way. Another group had more passive births, involving more monitoring, medication, transfers to the delivery room, and use of forceps.

I then went one step further: were the women within each of these groups having the kind of birth experience for which they had indicated preferences during the prenatal period? I hypothesized that middle-class women would be more likely to have their choices respected in the hospital than working-class women. I suspected that doctors would use low social status as a justification for disregarding client preferences, and select the procedures *they* deemed necessary for working-class women.

I was wrong on two counts. First, neither of the two groups of women that I studied received the precise treatment they wanted. Second, there were few differences between the two groups in the extent to which the women got what they wanted. What I found instead was that the middle-class women generally wanted active, involved births free from medical interventions; some of their requests were respected in the hospital. The working-class women wanted more passive birth experiences with more medical intervention; some of their requests also were met within the hospital.

The data thus suggested that within the hospital at least three different models of an appropriate childbirth were operating: two different client models and a medical model. My initial approach to this topic had overlooked the existence of more than one client model distinct from that of the doctors' model.

The literature on women's control over childbirth has highlighted the importance of this life event for women. It has also used a set of implicit assumptions: (1) women share a set of common desires and make choices about childbirth independent of their social backgrounds; and (2) women's desires are different from those of doctors. In short, the literature assumes that women all want (or will come to want) conscious control over a basically "natural" childbirth experience and that doctors have resisted these demands. However, my data suggest that these assumptions are not entirely accurate. There is clearly more than just one client model of childbirth: not all women want the same kind of birth experience. And doctors, in fact, appear to resist and reject aspects of *each* client model in favor of their own approach.

Social Class in Childbirth Research

Three traditions of research and theory on childbirth have, each for its own reason, ignored social class differences. These are: (1) the feminist literature; (2) the general medical sociology treatment; and (3) studies which focus on the effects of preparation for childbirth.

Middle-class feminists, eager to take childbirth out of the hands of male obstetricians, seem more intent on describing how childbirth has become distorted over the years than in examining whether the "warping" (Haire, 1978) has affected all groups in the same way. Numerous historical studies document how male physicians wrested control of childbirth from female midwives, and class biases in the way new technologies were distributed (Ehrenreich and English, 1973; Kobrin, 1966; Wertz and Wertz, 1977). They do not tell us whether women of different social classes felt the same way about the changes—or whether there are class differences in attitudes towards childbirth today. (For an exception see Hubert [1974] who explicitly notes the lack of homogeneity in attitudes about childbirth.)

Shaw (1974) found class differences in treatment during the prenatal and hospital periods: the medical staff were aware of the class origins of their clients and treated them according to preconceived notions of what was most appropriate for each group of women. However, the solutions Shaw offers at the end of her book suffer from the opposite type of discrimination and totally ignore social class differences. She assumed her solutions would be equally acceptable to all clients, but never asked how they—as individuals or as representatives of social categories—would like childbirth to proceed.

The heavy emphasis on personal experience in much of the childbirth literature has resulted in the emergence of a single critique which presumes to speak for all women (e.g., Comaroff, 1977; Hart, 1977. Oakley, [1979:627] makes a similar point.). Most of those who write about childbirth are middle-class women. They are motivated by a feminist consciousness and possess the verbal ability which is part of class privilege. Thus, those who are most interested in women defining for themselves the nature and meaning of childbirth are, perhaps, guilty of prescribing a perfect birth for all women, regardless of individual needs or motivations.

The non-feminist literature has also ignored social class, albeit for different reasons. First, the ahistorical bias in much social science has inhibited attention to the social history of childbirth movements, a history which is important for understanding different class attitudes towards childbirth. Second, the use of some of the major sociological concepts might also inhibit a consideration of social class. For instance, although Stewart and Erickson (1977) attack mainstream sociology for failing to seriously consider childbirth, their own emphasis on "roles" as the best possible approach to understanding pregnancy and childbirth leads them to ignore social class. They note, for example, that "the manner in which women describe their labor and delivery varies by many factors including the setting, the difficulty of the labor, their definitions of themselves as sick or healthy, their expectations and how well these were met" (1977:41).

The view of childbirth expounded by middle-class feminists has been the best articulated and, therefore, frequently adopted by academic writers as the only view. Thus, as feminist critiques of contemporary obstetric care became more frequent and solidified, they were adopted by academic writers as representative of a single model or paradigm of childbirth which conflicted with that offered by the medical establishment. For example, Nash and Nash (1979:493) argue that "In American society at the present time there exist two primary interpretations of the meaning and practice of childbirth: the medical and the 'natural' view."

Oakley (1979) offers by far the most sophisticated exploration of competing childbirth paradigms. She notes the paucity of client-oriented studies and emphasizes the different models at work in medical science, clinical psychiatry and psychology, and academic psychology and sociology. Until recently the sociologist's contribution had not been "to investigate the women's experience but to extend the limits of the medical model and propose a more elastic conception of the variables which can be seen to influence the biological outcome of maternity" (1979:624). However, Oakley emphasizes the "natural" model of childbirth as the principal one in conflict with the various medical models. Danziger (1978), in a paper on prenatal encounters between physicians and clients, also assumes that there is only one *client* paradigm.

Some research on childbirth has ignored social class by matching or controlling independent variables too rigorously. Studies on preparation for birth clearly fall within this category. Most research shows that preparation for childbirth has both physiological and psychological effects on the birth process (Doering *et al.*, 1980; Norr *et al.*, 1977), though some studies indicate little or no effect (Zax *et al.*, 1975). Motivation to learn about birth does not appear to be the key factor at work here: studies which compared women who wanted to take classes in childbirth preparation but could not, with women who did take classes (or were randomly assigned to classes) found that preparation was the critical variable (Enkin *et al.*, 1972; Huttel *et al.*, 1972). To test whether preparation is a significant factor in the birth process, researchers have been careful to control for socio-economic status and education in experimental and control groups. For example, Doering and Entwisle's (1975) work on the effects of preparation on the ability to cope with labor and delivery dismisses social class after noting that there were no significant social differences between trained and untrained subjects, even though only 18 percent of the total number of subjects were working-class women. Gaziano's (1979) work only looked at working-class women who used a clinic, and therefore could not compare clients at different levels of income or education. Other researchers who compared the effects of different kinds of preparation for childbirth also controlled for the class origins of the client groups (e.g., Zimmerman-Tansella *et al.*, 1979). Researchers have given only cursory attention to the issue of who chooses to attend childbirth classes and why.

Much of this research assumes that the outcomes of preparation—knowledge, control, cooperation, and an avoidance of medication—are definite, clearcut, and desirable. That is, the studies assume that everyone wants an identical birth. Yet not all women, and particularly working-class women, may perceive the outcome of preparation as a "benefit." In fact, the data I collected for this paper suggest otherwise, and I am no longer willing to assume that all women want the same kind of birth.

Method

Background

In response to the declining U.S. birth rate, the movement for home birth, and the criticisms of women committed to hospital birth without extensive intervention, the Department of Gynecology and Obstetrics of the Medical Center Hospital of Vermont

(MCHV) in Burlington, Vermont, decided in 1979 to revamp its maternity services. It hired certified nurse-midwives to work with clients (both alone, for low-risk clients, and in conjunction with obstetricians for all other clients), opened a labor lounge, altered labor rooms to do double duty as delivery rooms, and stated that clients could choose their own birth style. It immediately hired two social scientists to evaluate whether these changes were satisfying the demands of knowledgeable, consumer-conscious, low-risk clients. I was one of those hired. We thus collected the data on which this paper is based within the context of a specific mandate. The sponsors of the project were not interested in the particular issues underlying my present concern.

The Data

We collected data in three stages from all clients who were served by a private group of obstetricians in MCHV; this group accounted for 80 percent of all births in the hospital during a six-month period in the winter of 1979–80. During the ninth month of their pregnancy we gave the women questionnaires about their previous birth experiences, their feelings about pregnancy and childbirth, and their choices for childbirth procedures. Three or four days after the women gave birth we interviewed them in the hospital, asking them about the birth itself. When the women returned to the doctor for a post-partum check-up (generally six weeks after birth) we gave them a second questionnaire, which asked for their feelings about the birth. A total of 322 women completed the first questionnaire (94 percent of those asked to participate in the evaluation study); 273 were interviewed in the hospital; and 226 completed the second questionnaire. The attrition rate of 30 percent was the result of a number of factors, including early hospital discharges and client failure to keep scheduled appointments. Equal numbers of working-class and middle-class women were lost in this process.

Independent Variables

There are three independent variables in this study: social class, preparation, and parity. The first of these is the most important.

(1) *Social Class:* Since I suspected that social class affected choices about childbirth, I sought a way to distinguish class position among the clients. I chose education as the best indicator: women with no more than a high school diploma were categorized as working class; those with at least four years of college were categorized as middle class. Women with some college education or vocational training beyond high school were assigned to a category on the basis of the type of job they held at the time of participation in the evaluation study, or their prior work experience. These procedures resulted in a total of 127 working-class women and 124 middle-class women included in the analysis.

Information on client income was not available. In any case, the fact that my sample includes a small proportion of "voluntary poor"—highly educated women who chose subsistence farming or craft work as a way of life—made income a poor indicator. Nor could occupation alone be used. I found that differences in education made a significant difference in the kind of occupations the women held, either at the time of the study or prior to it, and the pattern of their work involvement. However, not all the women were working or reported ever holding jobs. Occupations of the husbands was also inappropriate, because I wanted a variable which would reflect the background experiences of the women themselves. Furthermore, whether a woman had a college education made a difference along a range of other experiences, such as whether she was a native of Vermont, her religion, and her age at the birth of her first child. I wanted to investigate whether education also made a difference in women's attitudes towards, and experiences during, childbirth. If it did, I could at least argue that childbirth, for these women, was experienced through a set of social mechanisms. I use the notions of middle class and working class to denote the two groups in my sample, although I am aware of the weakness of my indicator for examining social class.

(2) *Preparation for childbirth:* There is a strong relationship between social class and formal preparation for childbirth. Seventy-nine percent of the middle-class women in my sample took childbirth classes, compared with 50 percent of the working-class women. The middle-class women also read an average of three books about pregnancy and childbirth, compared with an average of one for working-class women. These two kinds of preparation were themselves related: women who took childbirth classes were more likely to read about pregnancy and childbirth than women who didn't. This naturally raises the question of whether I'm not, in fact, examining differences in knowledge rather than social class differences. My data do not support this conclusion. Among middle-class women, preparation for childbirth made little difference in the kinds of attitudes I am studying in this paper. Among working-class women, however, preparation for childbirth was extremely important: the attitudes of working-class women who were prepared for childbirth—whether through classes, reading, or a combination of both—were close to those I defined as "middle-class" than the attitudes of their unprepared peers. Had I examined the unprepared women in each social class I would have found even greater differences between the two groups than I did when I combined the prepared and unprepared women. Therefore, preparation is not relevant to the issue of attitude, except insofar as the findings about class differences in preparation reinforce my fundamental conclusions. When preparation is relevant to my analysis, I mention it below.

(3) *Parity:* One would expect women who have given birth before (multiparas) to have different attitudes about childbirth, compared to women who have never given birth (primiparas). Surprisingly, this was not the case. There were relatively few instances where multiparas and primiparas had different attitudes during the prenatal period about what they wanted, although parity was an important determinant of what actually happened once a woman entered the hospital: multiparous women were less likely to have births marked by extensive medical intervention. In those cases where parity was important, it had the same effects among middle-class women as it did among working-class women. Therefore, since parity—like preparation—is not crucial to most of the issues under consideration, I will discuss it only when it can help clarify my findings.

Attitudes Towards Childbirth

The middle-class and working-class women I studied had different attitudes towards childbirth during pregnancy, different experiences during childbirth, and different post-partum evaluations of their experiences.

Attitudes During Pregnancy

Working-class women were more likely than middle-class women to have negative feelings about pregnancy. They were less likely to say they felt good about the way they looked or felt and they did not feel they received sufficient consideration from others. Pregnancy was not an unambivalently positive state for working-class women. There were obvious material causes for this attitude: working-class women were more likely to become pregnant by accident (39 percent) than middle-class women (22 percent) and less likely to have the resources with which to find space to rest and relax. Ideological issues may also have been at the root of these differences. Middle-class women felt that pregnancy, labor, delivery and the post-partum presence of a baby were interrelated pleasures, and this was true regardless of either their preparation for childbirth or parity. Working-class women made a greater distinction between the stages that led to birth and the presence of the baby itself: the former was not necessarily desirable, though the latter was. As with middle-class women, these attitudes were unaffected by parity and preparation.

Furthermore, during pregnancy working-class women were more apprehensive than middle-class women about labor and delivery. They worried about their own knowledge and competence; they worried that they wouldn't know when they were actually in labor; they worried that they didn't know what would happen in the hospital. Clearly, the context in which birth occurred was somewhat threatening. In addition, working-class women were more worried than middle-class women about the discomfort of labor and delivery, and whether or not their personal physician would be present for the birth.[1] On the other hand, working-class and middle-class women had almost identical attitudes toward one birth issue and one issue pertaining to the baby itself: they all expressed strong concern about whether the birth would proceed according to personal desire, and they all felt certain that they would love the baby once it was born.

Among both groups, parity was relevant for all issues except concern about whether the baby would be healthy, and whether the mother would love it; those who had given birth before were less anxious. Yet among the primiparas within each social class the differences between the two social groups remain. Moreover, preparation for childbirth was related to concern about two issues: bearing the discomfort and having the birth as planned. However, in both groups those with more preparation were *more* concerned about these issues than were those with less preparation.

---

[1]This is not related to the fact that more working-class women than middle-class women see doctors in a clinic rather than in a private office, since clinic patients, like private patients, are assigned a regular doctor whom they see at each prenatal visit. In fact, no client in the group practice was promised that her personal doctor would be present at the birth.

Different levels of preparation do not account for the differences between the two groups.

Two additional questions in the questionnaire I gave to women in their ninth month of pregnancy were designed to elicit their *general* attitudes towards childbirth. The first of these asked clients whether they agreed with the statement: "I feel that the birth experience can affect the quality of the parent's relationship with the baby." Seventy-eight percent of middle-class women agreed with this statement, compared with 48 percent of working-class women. This indicates that middle-class women place more emphasis on the birth experience itself as a critical stage in becoming a parent. In response to a second question, 69 percent of middle-class women and 54 percent of working-class women agreed with the statement: "I feel that a natural childbirth will be best for my baby." This suggests that, not only do middle-class women think that the birth experience is significant in and of itself, but they have a *specific* idea about what kind of experience will be most appropriate.

Parity was not relevant to either of these attitudes. Among working-class women, preparation altered both attitudes; among middle-class women, only the feeling about a natural childbirth was affected by preparation. The class differences remained when I compared prepared women in each group (Nelson, 1982).

Similar differences between the middle-class and working-class women emerged when the multiparas within each group commented during pregnancy about how they would like the impending birth to differ from past ones. Middle-class women and working-class women shared a desire to have a spouse or partner present during the birth if he was not present before. Women in both groups complained about the treatment they received, but the content of their complaints was not the same. Middle-class women complained in detail about personality conflicts with their doctors, mismanagement (by the staff) of various aspects of labor, and the fact that medication was offered too frequently. Working-class women complained mostly about the lack of information offered to them during labor and delivery.

There were other differences as well. Working-class women often mentioned medical complications and the discomfort of labor and delivery. They expressed a wish that the next birth be faster and easier—if necessary, through the use of more intensive medication. Two comments were typical: "I would have liked to have been put to sleep—it was a long and painful labor"; and "Next time I want a quicker labor—my first was only eight hours but the pains were hard and came every two minutes." Middle-class women rarely mentioned either the intensity of pain or the length of labor. They stressed instead obstacles to a pleasurable experience: "I did not see my baby being born"; and "I would have wanted a more creative delivery."

Both working-class and middle-class clients felt they had a right to evaluate the past performance of medical personnel: if any of the women felt constrained by the professionalism of the staff, the constraint did not totally inhibit subsequent evaluation. Women in both groups felt the medical structure could be modified. However, there were significant differences between the groups. Working-class women felt that the responsibility for providing information rested with the doctor. In addition, they wanted to reduce the length of labor and avoid medical complications. They wanted

Table 1 ▮ **Client Attitudes Towards Pregnancy, Labor, and Delivery During the Ninth Month of Pregnancy**

Statements	Percentage of Working Class (N = 127)	Percentage of Middle Class (N = 124)
Attitudes Towards Pregnancy: [a]		
When I'm pregnant people don't take my feelings seriously.	25	14
I like the way I look when I'm pregnant.	27	40
When I'm pregnant I feel well most of the time.	67	77
When I'm pregnant I feel depressed a lot of the time.	35	17
Concerns About Labor and Delivery: [b]		
I worry that I won't know when I'm in real labor.	50	30
I worry that I won't be able to bear the discomfort.	43	33
I worry that I don't know what is going to happen to me in the hospital.	36	25
I worry that I don't know enough about the process of childbirth.	32	17
I worry that my doctor won't be there for the birth of my baby.	49	31
I worry that the birth of my baby won't be the way I want it to be.	52	58
I worry that there will be something wrong with my baby.	49	31
I worry that I won't love the baby.	7	6
General Attitudes Towards Childbirth: [a]		
I feel that the birth experience can affect the quality of the parent's relationship with the baby.	48	78
I feel that a natural childbirth will be best for my baby.	54	69

Notes: a. Five response options were offered for these statements: "Strongly Agree," "Agree," "Neither Agree Nor Disagree," "Disagree," and "Strongly Disagree." Percentages include those who gave either the "Agree" or "Strongly Agree" responses. b. Four response options to indicate the importance of each of these concerns were offered for these statements: "Very Important," "Pretty Important," "Not Too Important," and "Not Important At All." Percentages include those who gave either the "Very Important" or the "Pretty Important" responses.

a birth marked by less pain. In contrast, middle-class women were looking for a pleasurable, and often "natural," experience, and a more cooperative—rather than instructional—relationship with the doctor.

Two issues must be considered in evaluating the women's response to concrete questions about what they had wanted to happen when they entered the hospital to give birth: (1) whether the women even thought about the birth experience in detail during their ninth month of pregnancy; and (2) if so, what they wanted to have happen to them.

(1) With respect to the first issue, we can clearly divide the women into two

groups: those who knew about and had already considered the different aspects of the birth process and those who had not. In fact, more middle-class women than working-class women considered the procedures surrounding birth: with the exception of the delivery site, less than 90 percent of the working-class women considered any of the procedures; over 95 percent of the middle-class women considered each of the procedures except artificial rupture of membranes, fetal monitoring, and position at birth. However, these differences between the groups were not found for those procedures directly related to family formation: having the husband present, watching the birth, and holding the baby after it is born. Over 90 percent of the women in *both* groups considered each of these procedures. Middle-class women as a group thus considered each step of the birth process; a substantial minority of working-class women focused only on the final stage—the creation of a new family.

Parity was not relevant here, with the exception that those who had given birth before (in both groups) were less likely to say that they wanted medication during labor than those who had never before given birth. Preparation for childbirth was important here but, as indicated above, preparation changed the attitudes of working-class women but not the attitudes of middle-class women. Most of the unprepared working-class women had not thought about the issues; those who had, wanted medical intervention (Nelson, 1982).

(2) Among the women who actually thought about what they wanted to happen, there were differences in the content of their choices—differences which again corresponded to class. Working-class women selected medication during labor and delivery, artificial rupture of membranes, delivery room births, and fetal monitoring more often than middle-class women. The differences between the two groups on these issues ranged from 35 percent for delivery room births and fetal monitoring to 55 percent for the artificial rupture of membranes. Differences between the two groups with respect to the "social" aspects of birth were never more than 7 percent. Over 90 percent of both the middle-class and the working-class women chose to have the birth become an event in which they could participate by having a partner present during labor and delivery, watching the birth, and holding the baby as soon as it was born.

The working-class women seemed to be striving for speed (enema, episiotomy, artificial rupture of membranes), less pain (medication) and technological safety (delivery room birth, monitoring). They favored intervention because they thought it could bring the product easily, quickly, and safely. The middle-class women favored a process which entailed safety (as they defined it) and personal participation, but excluded medical intervention in a "natural" process.

In sum, the content of middle-class choices was "non-intervention." When middle-class women did not make choices, it was often because they wanted to leave control in the hands of the physicians or were unwilling to commit themselves in advance—not because they had not thought about the issues. "I'll let the doctor decide" was often how they responded to questions about their attitudes to specific procedures. Middle-class women selected this opinion more frequently than working-class women. In contrast, when working-class women made choices they favored

Table 2 ■ Prenatal Planning for Childbirth: Choices About Procedures and Hospital Events

Procedures	Percentage of Clients Who Had Thought About the Procedures		Percentage Who Wanted Each Procedure[a]		Hospital Events: Percentages of Clients Who Had Each Procedure		
	Working Class (N = 127)	Middle Class (N = 124)	Working Class	Middle Class	All Clients (N = 203)	Working Class (N = 105)	Middle Class (N = 98)
Shave	85	97	20 (47)	20 (67)	65	61	67
Enema	85	98	42 (55)	46 (68)	49	54	47
Labor Medication	81	98	57 (51)	11 (55)	44	50	35
Delivery Medication	84	96	58 (55)	17 (64)	41	52	30
Artificial Rupture of Membranes	44	68	59 (17)	4 (25)	70	69	75
Episiotomy	64	95	64 (14)	62 (37)	85	83	88
Fetal Monitoring	53	86	90 (31)	55 (44)	85	87	80
Lithotomy Position	64	77	—	—	75	84	67
Delivery Room Birth	90	95	80 (89)	45 (76)	87	96	82
IV Attached During Labor	—b	—	—	—	85	91	74
Forceps or Vacuum Suction	—	—	—	—	20	24	13
Support Person Present During Labor	96	100	88 (116)	98 (107)	94	96	98
Support Person Present During Delivery	93	100	83 (112)	96 (108)	87	83	94
Watch the Birth	91	92	89 (112)	93 (99)	45	44	46
Hold Baby at Birth	94	99	92 (106)	97 (111)	85	81	88

Notes: a. Based on the number of clients, in parentheses, who made a choice—positive or negative—with respect to the procedure.
b. Items for which there is no data, as indicated by a dash, were not asked on the pregnancy questionnaire or, in the case of the lithotomy position, did not have simple response options.

intervention; when they didn't make choices it was more often because they had not thought about the issues.

Among working-class women there was a tension between not thinking about the impending event and preparing for it by making decisions, between avoidance and self-determination. For the middle-class women the tension was between self-determination and reliance on professional expertise. Moreover, the goals of self-determination were also different for the two groups. Among middle-class women the goal was a definition of childbirth free from the prevailing medical and technological model embodied in the authority of the male physician. Working-class women sought freedom from the birth process itself through the use of strategies which would reduce pain and effort. Working-class women were not trying to give the experience a unique definition. They were trying to survive it with a minimum of embarrassment, discomfort, and isolation. There were exceptions to all of these generalizations. We can begin to speak about models only in the most general terms.

Experiences During Childbirth

Not only did working-class and middle-class women have different ideas about what they wanted to happen during childbirth, they also had different experiences during the actual birth. Working-class clients had births marked by more medical intervention and less client participation than middle-class women. To a certain extent these features are interrelated: the use of medication during labor and delivery makes it more likely that the delivery will take place in the delivery room and that forceps (or vacuum suction) will be required; the use of forceps ensures that an episiotomy will be necessary and that the client will have to be in a prone rather than sitting or semi-sitting position. And the more intervention, the less likely the woman is to be able to respond to the baby immediately.

Many middle-class women also had a great deal of intervention during labor and delivery: over 70 percent of them experienced an artificial rupture of membranes, an episiotomy, fetal monitoring, a delivery room birth, and forceps or vacuum suction. The proportion of middle-class women who had such intervention was less than for working-class women by more than 10 percent for the issues of labor and delivery medications, lithotomy position, delivery room birth, IV attached during labor, and forceps or vacuum suction. The middle-class women were more able to be active participants in the birth: they controlled the contractions with breathing techniques, pushed the baby out themselves, and held the baby as soon as it was born. Ninety-eight percent of them had a partner during labor and 94 percent had a partner present at the birth.

Parity was relevant to the birth experience in the same way within each group: primipara women had births which involved more extensive medical intervention. Preparation for childbirth influenced only the use of medication and the presence of a support person—and these only among working-class women. Therefore, preparation cannot explain the class differences (Nelson, 1982).

The difference between the births of middle-class and working-class clients

Table 3 ■ **Discrepancy Between Choice and Event: Percentage of Clients Who Got What They Wanted**

Procedure	Working Class		Middle Class		Percentage Difference: Working Class v. Middle Class
	Percentage	Number	Percentage	Number	
Shave	65	(34)	56	(52)	9
Enema	50	(38)	65	(51)	−15
Labor Medication	59	(37)	59	(37)	0
Delivery Medication	53	(51)	78	(60)	−15
Artificial Rupture of Membranes	50	(20)	38	(13)	12
Episiotomy	67	(9)	61	(28)	6
Fetal Monitoring	87	(23)	58	(31)	29
Delivery Site	86	(66)	70	(60)	16
Support Person Present During Labor	86	(85)	98	(87)	−12
Support Person Present During Delivery	79	(84)	95	(87)	−16
Watch the Birth	48	(84)	44	(73)	−4
Hold Baby at Birth	83	(76)	84	(81)	−1

corresponded roughly to what the women actually selected during pregnancy—although not, perhaps, to the motives behind the choices, in the case of working-class women. Working-class women wanted speedy access to the product. They didn't necessarily get speed, nor did they get the baby immediately. The middle-class concern with the entire process might have ensured a speedier labor and delivery and more immediate access to the baby (Doering *et al.,* 1980; Huttel *et al.,* 1972; Zax *et al.,* 1975).

Neither working-class nor middle-class women had all their choices met during labor and delivery. The extent to which client choices about shaves, labor medication, episiotomies, watching the birth, and holding the baby were respected was about the same for both groups. But the two groups differed in the extent to which other choices were respected. More middle-class women than working-class women had their wishes met with respect to enemas, delivery medications, and the presence of a support person during labor and delivery. More working-class women had their way with respect to fetal monitoring, artificial rupture of membranes, and the delivery site. The data do not indicate that doctors impose their will on working-class clients more frequently than they do on middle-class clients; nor do the data indicate that working-class clients are less effective in stating what they want than are middle-class clients. Both working-class and middle-class models of birth conflict with hospital protocol. Women in neither group were entirely successful in getting their way.

Post-Partum Evaluations

In the second questionnaire after birth, I asked a final question about their impressions of the experience: "If you were to tell a woman who had never given birth what it was like, what would you say?" Both working-class and middle-class women indicated that birth was worthwhile. But working-class women said that it was worthwhile in spite of the pain because you have a baby at the end: "I think it's worth it, a day of pain for all this." At the same time, many working-class women said that they forgot about the pain quickly. They said they wouldn't frighten other women, the way they had been frightened, with predictions of pain, and that women shouldn't believe all the terrible things they heard about giving birth.

Middle-class women had a very different set of ideas about what was appropriate to tell a woman who had never before given birth. First, they would focus on the process as an experience itself: "a high and painful experience"; "a fantastic experience." Second, they would talk about the work involved: "It's hard work; preparation is important"; and "Now I know why it is called labor. You really have to work." Third, they would be more likely to give details. Indirectly, they suggested that they had been told positive things about birth by their peers.: "It's as good an experience as I had been told it was"; "It was even better than my friends said it would be."

These responses reveal a further basic difference between the two groups of women. The working-class women did not value the process of birth itself. They almost never used the word "experience." They focused, instead, on the product—the baby. Labor and delivery were something to be endured to get the product. Middle-class women valued the process as well as the product. They felt fortunate to be able to enjoy the experience of birth en route to motherhood.

Discussion

There are at least two possible explanations for the different attitudes of middle-class and working-class women towards birth, and for their different experiences during the birth process.

One possibility is that working-class women are simply more inhibited by the context in which birth occurs. They don't become interested in the birth process because they don't think that they can determine what is going to happen to them. Caught between medical experts and nature, they see little room for individual initiative. This is clearly an element of working-class disaffection with birth. But working-class feelings of impotence cannot entirely explain the particular nature of the choices that some working-class women make, particularly since these choices are *not* congruent with those of the professionals who manage their care.

A second possibility is that the greater interest of middle-class women in childbirth issues derives from greater knowledge. Not only are middle-class women more

---

[2]Working-class women were far more likely than middle-class women to say that they relied on mothers and other relatives to provide them with information about childbirth. The middle-class rejection of their mothers as a source of information about childbirth suggests that they were aware that the ideology about childbirth has changed since they themselves were born and that their mothers' retell-

likely to prepare themselves for childbirth through reading and attending classes, but they draw on different kinds of information.[2] But these facts cannot entirely explain different attitudes either: the middle-class women hold their attitudes regardless of whether they have educated themselves about childbirth; the same is not true among working-class women: those who are prepared frequently hold different attitudes from those who are not. In any case, the search for information is probably the result—not the cause—of interest in childbirth.

Why, then, do working-class women remain uninterested in learning about childbirth? Why do they reject the middle-class ideology which not only stresses the value of information but holds as its goal a client-structured, "natural" childbirth? The answer lies in the contexts in which each group of women gives birth and in the fact that the movements that have created the middle-class model of the birth experience do not speak to both contexts equally.

The working-class women in our study started their families at a younger age, and at every subsequent age level had more children living in the home than did the middle-class women. The working-class women were more likely to have accidental pregnancies. Furthermore, when they chose to become pregnant, a small number of factors were taken into account, and these factors concerned only the family structure. Middle-class women were more likely to plan their pregnancies, and the total number of children they want to have. As with working-class women, the ideal family structure was central to their thinking, but this factor was diluted by self concerns (work and career, child care facilities) and world concerns (overpopulation). Working-class women, then, had their children earlier, had more of them, and frequently had them without planning. They also had fewer material resources with which to raise these children.

The movements that created the "middle-class" model of birth experience do not clearly address the working-class context of childbirth. In the early 1960s, middle-class women were not very interested in childbirth; in the early 1970s only elite portions of the middle-class took childbirth classes or attempted to define birth independently of the prevailing, high-technology, medical model. The change came with the convergence of (and occasional tension among) four social movements: (1) the natural childbirth movement; (2) feminism; (3) consumerism; and (4) "back to nature" romanticism.

Advocates of natural childbirth initially glorified it as a step toward motherhood. The movement appealed largely to middle-class women who were eager to be more active participants in this important event but who continued to accept professional (as distinct from technological) control over it. The feminist movement, on the other hand, told many of these same women that it was time to reject the authority of men in specifically female experiences, in order to gain personal control of their lives and their bodies. Feminists also rejected the notion that childbirth was primarily important as a step towards motherhood. Consumerism advocated questioning attitudes towards any and all prevalent medical practices. And the "back to nature" movement

---

ing of a painful—but ultimately anesthetized—birth offered nothing to them. Working-class women felt that more information could be obtained from their mothers, indicating that they had not recognized the changes that have occurred since the time when they were born.

advocated rejecting modern technology and returning to great-grandmother's way. None of these movements speaks to working-class women.

Natural childbirth preparation requires time, money, and a willing alliance with professionals. Within the feminist movement, the focus on middle-class concerns of access to professional jobs and consciousness-raising has alienated many working-class women who face employment problems of a very different cast and who are less able to live independent of their husbands' paycheck. Moreover, an "educated" contempt for professionals is easier for those who live among them than it is for those who may have to submit to experts in a wider range of life experiences. The failure of middle-class feminists to make contact with working-class concerns has been noted frequently: this analysis merely points to an additional consequence of this failure.

Consumerism depends on a steady income, mobility, and time. Middle-class women can afford to shop around for goods and services. But working-class women pay more out of necessity, not out of choice (Caplovitz, 1967); clinic clients see the doctor assigned to them. And a rejection of technology is the luxury of those who have already benefitted from it. That class of women who have always had access to the most sophisticated medical technology may make the decision to reject some aspects of that class privilege; those who have not yet consistently received these benefits may not be ready to abandon them.

In sum, I argue that the middle-class model of childbirth has its roots in social movements which do not have immediate relevance for working-class women. The model is also predicated on the idea of choice, the idea that one can take control of one's life and one's body (e.g., Boston Women's Health Book Collective, 1976). Working-class women have fewer opportunities for making choices; even pregnancy often appears to be outside their control.

The emerging model of hospital birth is, in fact, closer to the middle-class model than it is to the working-class model. Doctors have been greatly influenced by the criticisms of their most vocal clients and, in "progressive" hospitals, are making a conscious effort to "humanize" birth. Some of these changes may converge with working-class goals. But reducing the frequency with which medication is administered is foreign to working-class concerns and may seem like a threat to a woman (of any social class) who is unprepared to do without medication. In fact, doctors may use the middle-class model to force working-class compliance: one woman we interviewed said she was told by a doctor that if she "didn't stop yelling he would make [her] go natural."

Each of the two models of childbirth makes sense within the context of the lives its adopters lead. Each model confers benefits on the women who adhere to it. Each model may also have drawbacks. The middle-class model mystifies childbirth. Accepting it produces a sense of guilt and personal failure in women whose births fail to conform to its high standards. The working-class model engenders a dependence on potentially harmful medication and creates an anxiety which can prolong and complicate labor.

This kind of evaluation brings me back onto thin ice. My reading and research suggest that a single model of childbirth has too often been held up for all women. Initially, doctors defined the experience for all women. Then one group of women began speaking for all women. But women are not a single, undifferentiated category. Childbirth is a biological experience mediated by class position. We have to learn more about what women at different locations in the social structure want for themselves rather than pass judgment on what they do. If changes are to come in either working-class or middle-class birth styles, they must come from the women themselves—not from one group of women speaking for another, or from doctors dictating to all of them.

References

Boston Women's Health Book Collective. 1976. *Our Bodies, Ourselves.* New York: Simon and Schuster.

Caplovitz, David. 1967. *The Poor Pay More.* New York: The Free Press.

Comaroff, Jean. 1977. "Conflicting paradigms of pregnancy: Managing ambiguity in antenatal encounters." Pp. 115–134 in Alan Davis and Gordon Horobin (eds.), *Medical Encounters: The Experience of Illness and Treatment.* London: Croom, Helm Ltd.

Danziger, Sandra Klein. 1978. "The uses of expertise in doctor-patient encounters during pregnancy." *Social Science and Medicine* 12(5A):359–367.

Doering, Susan G., and Doris R. Entwisle. 1975. "Preparation during pregnancy and ability to cope with labor and delivery." *American Journal of Orthopsychiatry* 45(5):825–837.

Doering, Susan G., Doris R. Entwisle, and Daniel Quinlan. 1980. "Modeling the quality of women's birth experience." *Journal of Health and Social Behavior* 21(1):12–21.

Ehrenreich, Barbara, and Deidre English. 1973. *Witches, Midwives and Nurses.* Old Westbury, N.Y.: Feminist Press.

Enkin, N. W., S. L. Smith, S. W. Dermer, and J. D. Emmett. 1972. "An adequately controlled study of the effectiveness of PPM training." Pp. 62–67 in Norman Morris (ed.), *Psychosomatic Medicine in Obstetrics and Gynecology.* New York: S. Karger.

Gaziano, Emanuel P., Marlene Garvis, and Elaine Levine. 1979. "An evaluation of childbirth education for the clinic patient." *Birth and the Family Journal* 6 (Summer):89–94.

Haire, Doris. 1978. "The cultural warping of childbirth." Pp. 185–201 in John Ehrenreich (ed.), *The Cultural Crisis of Modern Medicine.* New York: The Monthly Review Press.

Hart, Nicky. 1977. "Parenthood and patienthood." Pp. 98–114 in Alan Davis and Gordon Horobin (eds.), *Medical Encounters: The Experience of Illness and Treatment.* London: Croom, Helm Ltd.

Hubert, Jane. 1974. "Beliefs and reality: Social factors in pregnancy and childbirth." Pp. 37–51 in Martin Richards (ed.), *The Integration of a Child Into a Social World.* New York: Cambridge University Press.

Huttel, F. A., I. Mitchell, W. M. Fischer, and A. E. Meyer. 1972. "A quantitative evaluation of psychoprophylaxis in childbirth." *Journal of Psychosomatic Research* 16(2):81–92.

Kobrin, Frances E. 1966. "The American midwife controversy: A crisis of professionalization." *Bulletin of the History of Medicine* 40 (July–August):350–363.

Nash, Anedith, and Jeffrey E. Nash. 1979. "Conflicting interpretations of childbirth: The medical and natural perspectives." *Urban Life* 7(4):493–511.

Nelson, Margaret K. 1982. "The impact of childbirth classes on women of different social classes." *Journal of Health and Social Behavior* 23(4):339–352.

Norr, Kathleen L., Carolyn R. Block, Allan Charles, Suzanne Meyering, and Ellen Meyers. 1977. "Explaining pain and enjoyment in childbirth." *Journal of Health and Social Behavior* 18 (September):260–275.

Oakley, Ann. 1979. "A case of maternity: Paradigms of women as maternity cases." *Signs: A Journal of Women in Culture and Society* 4(4):607–631.

Shaw, Nancy Stoller. 1974. *Forced Labor.* New York: Pergamon Press.

Stewart, Mary, and Pat Erickson. 1977. "The sociology of birth: A critical assessment of theory and research." *Social Sciences Journal* 14 (April):33–47.

Wertz, Richard W., and Dorothy C. Wertz. 1977. *Lying-In: A History of Childbirth in America*. New York: Schocken Books.

Zax, Melvin, Arnold J. Sameroff, and Janet E. Farnum. 1975. "Childbirth education, maternal attitudes, and delivery." *American Journal of Obstetrics and Gynecology* 123(2):185–190.

Zimmerman-Tansella, Ch., G. Dolcetta, V. Assini, G. Zacche, P. Bertagni, R. Siani, and M. Tansella. 1979. "Preparation courses for childbirth in Primipara: A comparison." *Journal of Psychosomatic Research* 23(4):227–233.

Questions for Thought

1. Compare and contrast the attitudes of working-class and middle-class women about pregnancy and childbirth.

2. How did Nelson measure "social class"? Evaluate the adequacy of her measurement.

3. Nelson suggests that middle-class women generally wanted active, involved births free of medical intervention; working-class women generally wanted more passive births with more medical intervention. Summarize the evidence she presents to support this assertion.

4. In this study working-class and middle-class women had different attitudes about childbirth and different experiences with labor and delivery. What factors may explain these differences?

5. Based on this article, what is "natural childbirth"? Why might this approach appeal more to middle-class women than to working-class women?

6. At a local bookstore or library, look at two or more books about childbirth written for expectant mothers. Analyze the model(s) of childbirth presented in these books.

19 Fraternities and Collegiate Rape Culture

Why Are Some Fraternities More Dangerous Places for Women?

A. Ayres Boswell

Joan Z. Spade

"Rape culture" refers to a set of values and beliefs that create an environment conducive to rape. In this study Boswell and Spade use the concept of culture to understand why some college fraternities are relatively dangerous places for women, and other fraternities are relatively safer places where rape is less likely to occur. Based on information from 40 college women, the researchers identified four "high-risk" and four "low-risk" fraternities at a private university. Through a combination of firsthand observations at fraternities and local bars, casual conversations, and formal interviews, Boswell and Spade analyzed how safer environments differed from more dangerous locales. This research demonstrates important ways in which the norms and attitudes of a small group such as a fraternity can influence individual behavior and contribute to the high incidence of acquaintance rape on campus.

Social interactions at fraternities that undergraduate women identified as places where there is a high risk of rape are compared to those at fraternities identified as low risk as well as two local bars. Factors that contribute to rape are common on this campus; however, both men and women behaved differently in different settings. Implications of these findings are considered.

Date rape and acquaintance rape on college campuses are topics of concern to both researchers and college administrators. Some estimate that 60 to 80 percent of rapes are date or acquaintance rape (Koss, Dinero, Seibel, and Cox 1988). Further, 1 out of 4 college women say they were raped or experienced an attempted rape, and

Reprinted from *Gender & Society*, 1996, *10*(2), 133–147. Copyright 1996 by Sociologists for Women in Society. Used by permission of Sage Publications.

1 out of 12 college men say they forced a woman to have sexual intercourse against her will (Koss, Gidycz, and Wisniewski 1985).

Although considerable attention focuses on the incidence of rape, we know relatively little about the context or the *rape culture* surrounding date and acquaintance rape. Rape culture is a set of values and beliefs that provide an environment conducive to rape (Buchwald, Fletcher, & Roth 1993; Herman 1984). The term applies to a generic culture surrounding and promoting rape, not the specific settings in which rape is likely to occur. We believe that the specific settings also are important in defining relationships between men and women.

Some have argued that fraternities are places where rape is likely to occur on college campuses (Martin and Hummer 1989; O'Sullivan 1993; Sanday 1990) and that the students most likely to accept rape myths and be more sexually aggressive are more likely to live in fraternities and sororities, consume higher doses of alcohol and drugs, and place a higher value on social life at college (Gwartney-Gibbs and Stockard 1989; Kalof and Cargill 1991). Others suggest that sexual aggression is learned in settings such as fraternities and is not part of predispositions or preexisting attitudes (Boeringer, Shehan, and Akers 1991). To prevent further incidences of rape on college campuses, we need to understand what it is about fraternities in particular and college life in general that may contribute to the maintenance of a rape culture on college campuses.

Our approach is to identify the social contexts that link fraternities to campus rape and promote a rape culture. Instead of assuming that all fraternities provide an environment conducive to rape, we compare the interactions of men and women at fraternities identified on campus as being especially *dangerous* places for women, where the likelihood of rape is high, to those seen as *safer* places, where the perceived probability of rape occurring is lower. Prior to collecting data for our study, we found that most women students identified some fraternities as having more sexually aggressive members and a higher probability of rape. These women also considered other fraternities as relatively safe houses, where a woman could go and get drunk if she wanted to and feel secure that the fraternity men would not take advantage of her. We compared parties at houses identified as high-risk and low-risk houses as well as at two local bars frequented by college students. Our analysis provides an opportunity to examine situations and contexts that hinder or facilitate positive social relations between undergraduate men and women.

The abusive attitudes toward women that some fraternities perpetuate exist within a general culture where rape is intertwined in traditional gender scripts. Men are viewed as initiators of sex and women as either passive partners or active resisters, preventing men from touching their bodies (LaPlante, McCormick, and Brannigan 1980). Rape culture is based on the assumptions that men are aggressive and dominant whereas women are passive and acquiescent (Buchwald et al. 1993; Herman 1984). What occurs on college campuses is an extension of the portrayal of domination and aggression of men over women that exemplifies the double standard of sexual behavior in U.S. society (Barthel 1988; Kimmel 1993).

Sexually active men are positively reinforced by being referred to as "studs," whereas women who are sexually active or report enjoying sex are derogatorily labeled as "sluts" (Herman 1984; O'Sullivan 1993). These gender scripts are embodied in rape myths and stereotypes such as "She really wanted it; she just said no because she didn't want me to think she was a bad girl" (Burke, Stets, and Pirog-Good 1989; Jenkins and Dambrot 1987; Lisak and Roth 1988; Malamuth 1986; Muehlenhard and Linton 1987; Peterson and Franzese 1987). Because men's sexuality is seen as more natural, acceptable, and uncontrollable than women's sexuality, many men and women excuse acquaintance rape by affirming that men cannot control their natural urges (Miller and Marshall 1987).

Whereas some researchers explain these attitudes toward sexuality and rape using an individual or a psychological interpretation, we argue that rape has a social basis, one in which both men and women create and recreate masculine and feminine identities and relations. Based on the assumption that rape is part of the social construction of gender, we examine how men and women "do gender" on a college campus (West and Zimmerman 1987). We focus on fraternities because they have been identified as settings that encourage rape (Sanday 1990). By comparing fraternities that are viewed by women as places where there is a high risk of rape to those where women believe there is a low risk of rape as well as two local commercial bars, we seek to identify characteristics that make some social settings more likely places for the occurrence of rape.

Method

We observed social interactions between men and women at a private coeducational school in which a high percentage (49.4 percent) of students affiliate with Greek organizations. The university has an undergraduate population of approximately 4,500 students, just more than one third of whom are women; the students are primarily from upper-middle-class families. The school, which admitted only men until 1971, is highly competitive academically.

We used a variety of data collection approaches: observations of interactions between men and women at fraternity parties and bars, formal interviews, and informal conversations. The first author, a former undergraduate at this school and a graduate student at the time of the study, collected the data. She knew about the social life at the school and had established rapport and trust between herself and undergraduate students as a teaching assistant in a human sexuality course.

The process of identifying high- and low-risk fraternity houses followed Hunter's (1953) reputational approach. In our study, 40 women students identified fraternities that they considered to be high risk, or to have more sexually aggressive members and higher incidence of rape, as well as fraternities that they considered to be safe houses. The women represented all four years of undergraduate college and different living groups (sororities, residence halls, and off-campus housing). Observations focused on the four fraternities named most often by these women as high-risk houses and the four identified as low-risk houses.

Throughout the spring semester, the first author observed at two fraternity parties each weekend at two different houses (fraternities could have parties only on weekends at this campus). She also observed students' interactions in two popular university bars on weeknights to provide a comparison of students' behavior in non-Greek settings. The first local bar at which she observed was popular with seniors and older students; the second bar was popular with first-, second-, and third-year undergraduates because the management did not strictly enforce drinking age laws in this bar.

The observer focused on the social context as well as interaction among participants at each setting. In terms of social context, she observed the following: ratio of men to women, physical setting such as the party decor and theme, use and control of alcohol and level of intoxication, and explicit and implicit norms. She noted interactions between men and women (i.e., physical contact, conversational style, use of jokes) and the relations among men (i.e., their treatment of pledges and other men at fraternity parties). Other than the observer, no one knew the identity of the high- or low-risk fraternities. Although this may have introduced bias into the data collection, students on this campus who read this article before it was submitted for publication commented on how accurately the social scene is described.

In addition, 50 individuals were interviewed including men from the selected fraternities, women who attended those parties, men not affiliated with fraternities, and self-identified rape victims known to the first author. The first author approached men and women by telephone or on campus and asked them to participate in interviews. The interviews included open-ended questions about gender relations on campus, attitudes about date rape, and their own experiences on campus.

To assess whether self-selection was a factor in determining the classification of the fraternity, we compared high-risk houses to low-risk houses on several characteristics. In terms of status on campus, the high- and low-risk houses we studied attracted about the same number of pledges; however, many of the high-risk houses had more members. There was no difference in grade point averages for the two types of houses. In fact, the highest and lowest grade point averages were found in the high-risk category. Although both high- and low-risk fraternities participated in sports, brothers in the low-risk houses tended to play intramural sports whereas brothers in the high-risk houses were more likely to be varsity athletes. The high-risk houses may be more aggressive, as they had a slightly larger number of disciplinary incidents and their reports were more severe, often with physical harm to others and damage to property. Further, in year-end reports, there was more property damage in the high-risk houses. Last, more of the low-risk houses participated in a campus rape-prevention program. In summary, both high- and low-risk fraternities seem to be equally attractive to freshmen men on this campus, and differences between the eight fraternities we studied were not great; however, the high-risk houses had a slightly larger number of reports of aggression and physical destruction in the houses and the low-risk houses were more likely to participate in a rape prevention program.

Results

The Settings

Fraternity Parties   We observed several differences in the quality of the interaction of men and women at parties at high-risk fraternities compared to those at low-risk houses. A typical party at a low-risk house included an equal number of women and men. The social atmosphere was friendly, with considerable interaction between women and men. Men and women danced in groups and in couples, with many of the couples kissing and displaying affection toward each other. Brothers explained that, because many of the men in these houses had girlfriends, it was normal to see couples kissing on the dance floor. Coed groups engaged in conversations at many of these houses, with women and men engaging in friendly exchanges, giving the impression that they knew each other well. Almost no cursing and yelling was observed at parties in low-risk houses; when pushing occurred, the participants apologized. Respect for women extended to the women's bathrooms, which were clean and well supplied.

At high-risk houses, parties typically had skewed gender ratios, sometimes involving more men and other times involving more women. Gender segregation also was evident at these parties, with the men on one side of a room or in the bar drinking while women gathered in another area. Men treated women differently in the high-risk houses. The women's bathrooms in the high-risk houses were filthy, including clogged toilets and vomit in the sinks. When a brother was told of the mess in the bathroom at a high-risk house, he replied, "Good, maybe some of these beer wenches will leave so there will be more beer for us."

Men attending parties at high-risk houses treated women less respectfully, engaging in jokes, conversations, and behaviors that degraded women. Men made a display of assessing women's bodies and rated them with thumbs up or thumbs down for the other men in the sight of the women. One man attending a party at a high-risk fraternity said to another, "Did you know that this week is Women's Awareness Week? I guess that means we get to abuse them more this week." Men behaved more crudely at parties at high-risk houses. At one party, a brother dropped his pants, including his underwear, while dancing in front of several women. Another brother slid across the dance floor completely naked.

The atmosphere at parties in high-risk fraternities was less friendly overall. With the exception of greetings, men and women rarely smiled or laughed and spoke to each other less often than was the case at parties in low-risk houses. The few one-on-one conversations between women and men appeared to be strictly flirtatious (lots of eye contact, touching, and very close talking). It was rare to see a group of men and women together talking. Men were openly hostile, which made the high-risk parties seem almost threatening at times. For example, there was a lot of touching, pushing, profanity, and name calling, some done by women.

Students at parties at the high-risk houses seemed self-conscious and aware of the presence of members of the opposite sex, an awareness that was sexually charged. Dancing early in the evening was usually between women. Close to midnight, the sex ratio began to balance out with the arrival of more men or more women. Couples began to dance together but in a sexual way (close dancing with lots of pelvic thrusts). Men tried to pick up women using lines such as "Want to see my fish tank?" and "Let's go upstairs so that we can talk; I can't hear what you're saying in here."

Although many of the same people who attended high-risk parties also attended low-risk parties, their behavior changed as they moved from setting to setting. Group norms differed across contexts as well. At a party that was held jointly at a low-risk house with a high-risk fraternity, the ambience was that of a party at a high-risk fraternity with heavier drinking, less dancing, and fewer conversations between women and men. The men from both high- and low-risk fraternities were very aggressive; a fight broke out, and there was pushing and shoving on the dance floor and in general.

As others have found, fraternity brothers at high-risk houses on this campus told about routinely discussing their sexual exploits at breakfast the morning after parties and sometimes at house meetings (cf. Martin and Hummer 1989; O'Sullivan 1993; Sanday 1990). During these sessions, the brothers we interviewed said that men bragged about what they did the night before with stories of sexual conquests often told by the same men, usually sophomores. The women involved in these exploits were women they did not know or knew but did not respect, or *faceless victims*. Men usually treated girlfriends with respect and did not talk about them in these story-telling sessions. Men from low-risk houses, however, did not describe similar sessions in their houses.

The Bar Scene   The bar atmosphere and social context differed from those of fraternity parties. The music was not as loud, and both bars had places to sit and have conversations. At all fraternity parties, it was difficult to maintain conversations with loud music playing and no place to sit. The volume of music at parties at high-risk fraternities was even louder than it was at low-risk houses, making it virtually impossible to have conversations. In general, students in the local bars behaved in the same way that students did at parties in low-risk houses with conversations typical, most occurring between men and women.

The first bar, frequented by older students, had live entertainment every night of the week. Some nights were more crowded than others, and the atmosphere was friendly, relaxed, and conducive to conversation. People laughed and smiled and behaved politely toward each other. The ratio of men to women was fairly equal, with students congregating in mostly coed groups. Conversation flowed freely and people listened to each other.

Although the women and men at the first bar also were at parties at low- and high-risk fraternities, their behavior at the bar included none of the blatant sexual or intoxicated behaviors observed at some of these parties. As the evenings wore on, the number of one-on-one conversations between men and women increased and conversations shifted from small talk to topics such as war and AIDS. Conversations did not revolve around picking up another person, and most people left the bar with same-sex friends or in coed groups.

The second bar was less popular with older students. Younger students, often under the legal drinking age, went there to drink, sometimes after leaving campus parties. This bar was much smaller and usually not as crowded as the first bar. The atmosphere was more mellow and relaxed than it was at the fraternity parties. People went there to hang out and talk to each other.

On a couple of occasions, however, the atmosphere at the second bar became similar to that of a party at a high-risk fraternity. As the number of people in the bar increased, they removed chairs and tables, leaving no place to sit and talk. The music also was turned up louder, drowning out conversation. With no place to dance or sit, most people stood around but could not maintain conversations because of the noise and crowds. Interactions between women and men consisted mostly of flirting. Alcohol consumption also was greater than it was on the less crowded nights, and the number of visibly drunk people increased. The more people drank, the more conversation and socializing broke down. The only differences between this setting and that of a party at a high-risk house were that brothers no longer controlled the territory and bedrooms were not available upstairs.

Gender Relations

Relations between women and men are shaped by the contexts in which they meet and interact. As is the case on other college campuses, *hooking up* has replaced dating on this campus, and fraternities are places where many students hook up. Hooking up is a loosely applied term on college campuses that had different meanings for men and women on this campus.

Most men defined hooking up similarly. One man said it was something that happens

> when you are really drunk and meet up with a woman you sort of know, or possibly don't know at all and don't care about. You go home with her with the intention of getting as much sexual, physical pleasure as she'll give you, which can range anywhere from kissing to intercourse, without any strings attached.

The exception to this rule is when men hook up with women they admire. Men said they are less likely to press for sexual activity with someone they know and like because they want the relationship to continue and be based on respect.

Women's version of hooking up differed. Women said they hook up only with men they cared about and described hooking up as kissing and petting but not sexual intercourse. Many women said that hooking up was disappointing because they wanted longer-term relationships. First-year women students realized quickly that hook-ups were usually one-night stands with no strings attached, but many continued to hook up because they had few opportunities to develop relationships with men on campus. One first-year woman said that "70 percent of hook-ups never talk again and try to avoid one another; 26 percent may actually hear from them or talk to them again, and 4 percent may actually go on a date, which can lead to a relationship." Another first-year woman said, "It was fun in the beginning. You get a lot of attention and kiss a lot of boys and think this is what college is about, but it gets tiresome fast."

Whereas first-year women get tired of the hook-up scene early on, many men do not become bored with it until their junior or senior year. As one upperclassman said, "The whole game of hooking up became really meaningless and tiresome for me during my second semester of my sophomore year, but most of my friends didn't get bored with it until the following year."

In contrast to hooking up, students also described monogamous relationships with steady partners. Some type of commitment was expected, but most people did not anticipate marriage. The term *seeing each other* was applied when people were sexually involved but free to date other people. This type of relationship involved less commitment than did one of boyfriend/girlfriend but was not considered to be a hook-up.

The general consensus of women and men interviewed on this campus was that the Greek system, called "the hill," set the scene for gender relations. The predominance of Greek membership and subsequent living arrangements segregated men and women. During the week, little interaction occurred between women and men after their first year in college because students in fraternities or sororities live and dine in separate quarters. In addition, many non-Greek upper-class students move off campus into apartments. Therefore, students see each other in classes or in the library, but there is no place where students can just hang out together.

Both men and women said that fraternities dominate campus social life, a situation that everyone felt limited opportunities for meaningful interactions. One senior Greek man said,

> This environment is horrible and so unhealthy for good male and female relationships and interactions to occur. It is so segregated and male dominated. . . . It is our party, with our rules and our beer. We are allowing these women and other men to come to our party. Men can feel superior in their domain.

Comments from a senior woman reinforced his views: "Men are dominant; they are the kings of the campus. It is their environment that they allow us to enter; therefore, we have to abide by their rules." A junior woman described fraternity parties as

> good for meeting acquaintances but almost impossible to really get to know anyone. The environment is so superficial, probably because there are so many social cliques due to the Greek system. Also, the music is too loud and the people are too drunk to attempt to have a real conversation, anyway.

Some students claim that fraternities even control the dating relationships of their members. One senior woman said, "Guys dictate how dating occurs on this campus, whether it's cool, who it's with, how much time can be spent with the girlfriend and with the brothers." Couples either left campus for an evening or hung out separately with their own same-gender friends at fraternity parties, finally getting together with each other at about 2 a.m. Couples rarely went together to fraternity parties. Some men felt that a girlfriend was just a replacement for a hook-up. According to one junior man, "Basically a girlfriend is someone you go to at 2 a.m. after you've hung out with the guys. She is the sexual outlet that the guys can't provide you with."

Some fraternity brothers pressure each other to limit their time with and commitment to their girlfriends. One senior man said, "The hill [fraternities] and girlfriends don't mix." A brother described a constant battle between girlfriends and brothers over who the guy is going out with for the night, with the brothers usually winning. Brothers teased men with girlfriends with remarks such as "whipped" or "where's the ball and chain?" A brother from a high-risk house said that few brothers at his house had girlfriends; some did, but it was uncommon. One man said that from the minute he was a pledge he knew he would probably never have a girlfriend on this campus because "it was just not the norm in my house. No one has girlfriends; the guys have too much fun with [each other]."

The pressure on men to limit their commitment to girlfriends, however, was not true of all fraternities or of all men on campus. Couples attended low-risk fraternity parties together, and men in the low-risk houses went out on dates more often. A man in one low-risk house said that about 70 percent of the members of his house were involved in relationships with women, including the pledges (who were sophomores).

Treatment of Women

Not all men held negative attitudes toward women that are typical of a rape culture, and not all social contexts promoted the negative treatment of women. When men were asked whether they treated the women on campus with respect, the most common response was "On an individual basis, yes, but when you have a group of men together, no." Men said that, when together in groups with other men, they sensed a pressure to be disrespectful toward women. A first-year man's perception of the treatment of women was that "they are treated with more respect to their faces, but behind closed doors, with a group of men present, respect for women is not an issue." One senior man stated, "In general, college-aged men don't treat women their age with respect because 90 percent of them think of women as merely a means to sex." Women reinforced this perception. A first-year woman stated, "Men here are more interested in hooking up and drinking beer than they are in getting to know women as real people." Another woman said, "Men here use and abuse women."

Characteristic of rape culture, a double standard of sexual behavior for men versus women was prevalent on this campus. As one Greek senior man stated, "Women who sleep around are sluts and get bad reputations; men who do are champions and get a pat on the back from their brothers." Women also supported a double standard for sexual behavior by criticizing sexually active women. A first-year woman spoke out against women who are sexually active: "I think some girls here make it difficult for the men to respect women as a whole."

One concrete example of demeaning sexually active women on this campus is the "walk of shame." Fraternity brothers come out on the porches of their houses the night after parties and heckle women walking by. It is assumed that these women spent the night at fraternity houses and that the men they were with did not care enough about them to drive them home. Although sororities now reside in former fraternity houses, this practice continues and sometimes the victims of hecklings are sorority women on their way to study in the library.

A junior man in a high-risk fraternity described another ritual of disrespect toward women called "chatter." When an unknown woman sleeps over at the house, the brothers yell degrading remarks out the window at her as she leaves the next morning such as "Fuck that bitch" and "Who is that slut?" He said that sometimes brothers harass the brothers whose girlfriends stay over instead of heckling those women.

Fraternity men most often mistreated women they did not know personally. Men and women alike reported incidents in which brothers observed other brothers having sex with unknown women or women they knew only casually. A sophomore woman's experience exemplifies this anonymous state: "I don't mind if 10 guys were watching or it was videotaped. That's expected on this campus. It's the fact that he didn't apologize or even offer to drive me home that really upset me." Descriptions of sexual encounters involved the satisfaction of men by nameless women. A brother in a high-risk fraternity described a similar occurrence:

> A brother of mine was hooking up upstairs with an unattractive woman who had been pursuing him all night. He told some brothers to go outside the window and watch. Well, one thing led to another and they were almost completely naked when the woman noticed the brothers outside. She was then unwilling to go any further, so the brother went outside and yelled at the other brothers and then closed the shades. I don't know if he scored or not, because the woman was pretty upset. But he did win the award for hooking up with the ugliest chick that weekend.

Attitudes Toward Rape

The sexually charged environment of college campuses raises many questions about cultures that facilitate the rape of women. How women and men define their sexual behavior is important legally as well as interpersonally. We asked students how they defined rape and had them compare it to the following legal definition: the perpetration of an act of sexual intercourse with a female against her will and consent, whether her will is overcome by force or fear resulting from the threat of force, or by drugs or intoxicants; or when, because of mental deficiency, she is incapable of exercising rational judgment. (Brownmiller 1975, 368)

When presented with this legal definition, most women interviewed recognized it as well as the complexities involved in applying it. A first-year woman said, "If a girl is drunk and the guy knows it and the girl says, 'Yes, I want to have sex,' and they do, that is still rape because the girl can't make a conscious, rational decision under the influence of alcohol." Some women disagreed. Another first-year woman stated, "I don't think it is fair that the guy gets blamed when both people involved are drunk."

The typical definition men gave for rape was "when a guy jumps out of the bushes and forces himself sexually onto a girl." When asked what date rape was, the most common answer was "when one person has sex with another person who did not consent." Many men said, however, that "date rape is when a woman wakes up the next morning and regrets having sex." Some men said that date rape was too gray an area to define. "Consent is a fine line," said a Greek senior man student. For the most part, the men we spoke with argued that rape did not occur on this campus. One Greek sophomore man said, "I think it is ridiculous that someone here would rape someone." A first-year man stated, "I have a problem with the word rape. It sounds so criminal, and we are not criminals; we are sane people."

Whether aware of the legal definitions of rape, most men resisted the idea that a woman who is intoxicated is unable to consent to sex. A Greek junior man said, "Men should not be responsible for women's drunkenness." One first-year man said, "If that is the legal definition of rape, then it happens all the time on this campus." A senior man said, "I don't care whether alcohol is involved or not; that is not rape. Rapists are people that have something seriously wrong with them." A first-year man even claimed that when women get drunk, they invite sex. He said, "Girls get so drunk here and then come on to us. What are we supposed to do? We are only human."

Discussion and Conclusion

These findings describe the physical and normative aspects of one college campus as they relate to attitudes about and relations between men and women. Our findings suggest that an explanation emphasizing rape culture also must focus on those characteristics of the social setting that play a role in defining heterosexual relationships on college campuses (Kalof and Cargill 1991). The degradation of women as portrayed in rape culture was not found in all fraternities on this campus. Both group norms and individual behavior changed as students went from one place to another. Although individual men are the ones who rape, we found that some settings are more likely places for rape than are others. Our findings suggest that rape cannot be seen only as an isolated act and blamed on individual behavior and proclivities, whether it be alcohol consumption or attitudes. We also must consider characteristics of the settings that promote the behaviors that reinforce a rape culture.

Relations between women and men at parties in low-risk fraternities varied considerably from those in high-risk houses. Peer pressure and situational norms influenced women as well as men. Although many men in high- and low-risk houses shared similar views and attitudes about the Greek system, women on this campus, and date rape, their behaviors at fraternity parties were quite different.

Women who are at highest risk of rape are women whom fraternity brothers did not know. These women are faceless victims, nameless acquaintances—not friends. Men said their responsibility to such persons and the level of guilt they feel later if the hook-ups end in sexual intercourse are much lower if they hook up with women they do not know. In high-risk houses, brothers treated women as subordinates and kept them at a distance. Men in high-risk houses actively discouraged ongoing heterosexual relationships, routinely degraded women, and participated more fully in the hook-up scene; thus, the probability that women would become faceless victims was higher in these houses. The flirtatious nature of the parties indicated that women go to these parties looking for available men, but finding boyfriends or relationships was difficult at parties in high-risk houses. However, in the low-risk houses, where more men had long-term relationships, the women were not strangers and were less likely to become faceless victims.

The social scene on this campus, and on most others, offers women and men few other options to socialize. Although there may be no such thing as a completely safe fraternity party for women, parties at low-risk houses and commercial bars encouraged men and women to get know each other better and decreased the probability that women would become faceless victims. Although both men and women found the social scene on this campus demeaning, neither demanded different settings for socializing, and attendance at fraternity parties is a common form of entertainment.

These findings suggest that a more conducive environment for conversation can promote more positive interactions between men and women. Simple changes would provide the opportunity for men and women to interact in meaningful ways such as adding places to sit and lowering the volume of music at fraternity parties or having parties in neutral locations, where men are not in control. The typical party room in fraternity houses includes a place to dance but not to sit and talk. The music often is loud, making it difficult, if not impossible, to carry on conversations; however, there were more conversations at the low-risk parties, where there also was more respect shown toward women. Although the number of brothers who had steady girlfriends in the low-risk houses as compared to those in the high-risk houses may explain the differences, we found that commercial bars also provided a context for interaction between men and women. At the bars, students sat and talked and conversations between men and women flowed freely, resulting in deep discussions and fewer hook-ups.

Alcohol consumption was a major focus of social events here and intensified attitudes and orientations of a rape culture. Although pressure to drink was evident at all fraternity parties and at both bars, drinking dominated high-risk fraternity parties, at which nonalcoholic beverages usually were not available and people chugged beers and became visibly drunk. A rape culture is strengthened by rules that permit alcohol only at fraternity parties. Under this system, men control the parties and dominate the men as well as the women who attend. As college administrators crack down on fraternities and alcohol on campus, however, the same behaviors and norms may transfer to other places such as parties in apartments or private homes where administrators have much less control. At commercial bars, interaction and socialization with others were as important as drinking, with the exception of the nights when the bar frequented by under-class students became crowded. Although one solution is to offer nonalcoholic social activities, such events receive little support on this campus. Either these alternative events lacked the prestige of the fraternity parties or the alcohol was seen as necessary to unwind, or both.

In many ways, the fraternities on this campus determined the settings in which men and women interacted. As others before us have found, pressures for conformity to the norms and values exist at both high-risk and low-risk houses (Kalof and Cargill 1991; Martin and Hummer 1989; Sanday 1990). The desire to be accepted is not unique to this campus or the Greek system (Holland and Eisenhart 1990; Horowitz 1988; Moffat 1989). The degree of conformity required by Greeks may be greater than that required in most social groups, with considerable pressure to adopt and maintain the image of their houses. The fraternity system intensifies the "groupthink syndrome" (Janis 1972) by solidifying the identity of the in-group and creating an us/them atmosphere. Within the fraternity culture, brothers are highly regarded and women are viewed as outsiders. For men in high-risk fraternities, women threatened their brotherhood; therefore, brothers discouraged relationships and harassed those who treated women as equals or with respect. The pressure to be one of the guys and hang out with the guys strengthens a rape culture on college campus by demeaning women and encouraging the segregation of men and women.

Students on this campus were aware of the contexts in which they operated and the choices available to them. They recognized that, in their interactions, they created differences between men and women that are not natural, essential, or biological (West and Zimmerman 1987). Not all men and women accepted the demeaning treatment of women, but they continued to participate in behaviors that supported aspects of a rape culture. Many women participated in the hook-up scene even after they had been humiliated and hurt because they had few other means of initiating contact with men on campus. Men and women alike played out this scene, recognizing its injustices in many cases but being unable to change the course of their behaviors.

Although this research provides some clues to gender relations on college campuses, it raises many questions. Why do men and women participate in activities that support a rape culture when they see its injustices? What would happen if alcohol were not controlled by groups of men who admit that they disrespect women when they get together? What can be done to give men and women on college campuses more opportunities to interact responsibly and get to know each other better? These questions should be studied on other campuses with a focus on the social settings in which the incidence of rape and the attitudes that support a rape culture exist. Fraternities are social contexts that may or may not foster a rape culture.

Our findings indicate that a rape culture exists in some fraternities, especially those we identified as high-risk houses. College administrators are responding to this situation by providing counseling and educational programs that increase awareness of date rape including campaigns such as "No means no." These strategies are important in changing attitudes, values, and behaviors; however, changing individuals is not enough. The structure of campus life and the impact of that structure on gender relations on campus are highly determinative. To eliminate campus rape culture, student leaders and administrators must examine the situations in which women and men meet and restructure these settings to provide opportunities for respectful interaction. Change may not require abolishing fraternities; rather, it may require promoting settings that facilitate positive gender relations.

References

Barthel, D. 1988. *Putting on appearances: Gender and advertising.* Philadelphia: Temple University Press.

Boeringer, S. B., C. L. Shehan, and R. L. Akers. 1991. Social contexts and social learning in sexual coercion and aggression: Assessing the contribution of fraternity membership. *Family Relations* 40: 58–64.

Brownmiller, S. 1975. *Against our will: Men, women and rape.* New York: Simon & Schuster.

Buchwald, E., P. R. Fletcher, and M. Roth, eds. 1993. *Transforming a rape culture.* Minneapolis, MN: Milkweed Editions.

Burke, P., J. E. Stets, and M. A. Pirog-Good. 1989. Gender identity, self-esteem, physical abuse and sexual abuse in dating relationships. In *Violence in dating relationships: Emerging social issues,* edited by M. A. Pirog-Good and J. E. Stets. New York: Praeger.

Gwartney-Gibbs, P., and J. Stockard. 1989. Courtship aggression and mixed-sex peer groups. In *Violence in dating relationships: Emerging social issues,* edited by M. A. Pirog-Good and J. E. Stets. New York: Praeger.

Herman, D. 1984. The rape culture. In *Women: A feminist perspective,* edited by J. Freeman. Mountain View, CA: Mayfield.

Holland, D. C., and M. A. Eisenhart. 1990. *Educated in romance: Women, achievement, and college culture.* Chicago: University of Chicago Press.

Horowitz, H. L. 1988. *Campus life: Undergraduate cultures from the end of the 18th century to the present.* Chicago: University of Chicago Press.

Hunter, F. 1953. *Community power structure.* Chapel Hill: University of North Carolina Press.

Jenkins, M. J., and F. H. Dambrot. 1987. The attribution of date rape: Observer's attitudes and sexual experiences and the dating situation. *Journal of Applied Social Psychology* 17:875–95.

Janis, I. L. 1972. *Victims of groupthink.* Boston: Houghton Mifflin.

Kalof, L., and T. Cargill. 1991. Fraternity and sorority membership and gender dominance attitudes. *Sex Roles* 25:417–23.

Kimmel, M. S. 1993. Clarence, William, Iron Mike, Tailhook, Senator Packwood, Spur Posse, Magic . . . and us. In *Transforming a rape culture,* edited by E. Buchwald, P. R. Fletcher, and M. Roth. Minneapolis, MN: Milkweed Editions.

Koss, M. P., T. E. Dinero, C. A. Seibel, and S. L. Cox. 1988. Stranger and acquaintance rape: Are there differences in the victim's experience? *Psychology of Women Quarterly* 12:1–24.

Koss, M. P., C. A. Gidycz, and N. Wisniewski. 1985. The scope of rape: Incidence and prevalence of sexual aggression and victimization in a national sample of higher education students. *Journal of Consulting and Clinical Psychology* 55:162–70.

LaPlante, M. N., N. McCormick, and G. G. Brannigan. 1980. Living the sexual script: College students' views of influence in sexual encounters. *Journal of Sex Research* 16:338–55.

Lisak, D., and S. Roth. 1988. Motivational factors in nonincarcerated sexually aggressive men. *Journal of Personality and Social Psychology* 55:795–802.

Malamuth, N. 1986. Predictors of naturalistic sexual aggression. *Journal of Personality and Social Psychology* 50:953–62.

Martin, P. Y., and R. Hummer. 1989. Fraternities and rape on campus. *Gender & Society* 3:457–73.

Miller, B., and J. C. Marshall. 1987. Coercive sex on the university campus. *Journal of College Student Personnel* 28:38–47.

Moffat, M. 1989. *Coming of age in New Jersey: College life in American culture.* New Brunswick, NJ: Rutgers University Press.

Muehlenhard, C. L., and M. A. Linton. 1987. Date rape and sexual aggression in dating situations: Incidence and risk factors. *Journal of Counseling Psychology* 34:186–96.

O'Sullivan, C. 1993. Fraternities and the rape culture. In *Transforming a rape culture,* edited by E. Buchwald, P. R. Fletcher, and M. Roth. Minneapolis, MN: Milkweed Editions.

Peterson, S. A., and B. Franzese. 1987. Correlates of college men's sexual abuse of women. *Journal of College Student Personnel* 28:223–28.

Sanday, P. R. 1990. *Fraternity gang rape: Sex, brotherhood, and privilege on campus.* New York: New York University Press.

West, C., and D. Zimmerman. 1987. Doing gender. *Gender & Society* 1:125–51.

Questions for Thought

1. Boswell and Spade describe the concepts of "hooking up" and "seeing each other." Compare and contrast these two concepts. Are these terms relevant to social interactions at your school?

2. Based on this article, compare and contrast the attitudes, norms, and behaviors found at high-risk fraternity parties, low-risk fraternity parties, and commercial bars.

3. Boswell and Spade suggest that college women often know which fraternities are safer and which more dangerous. Why might a woman decide to go to a party at a high-risk fraternity?

4. Based on this article, discuss three specific strategies that college administrators might use to reduce the incidence of date rape on campus.

5. According to Boswell and Spade, both women and men behaved differently when they attended high-risk versus low-risk fraternity parties. In other words, their behavior changed because of the social setting. Explain why individuals might behave differently in these two cultural environments.

6. Identify two situations in which your own behavior was quite different, for instance, at your grandmother's birthday party versus a holiday party with friends your own age. Describe how your behavior differed. Analyze the factors that influenced your behavior, such as the social norms (rules) in the situation, the values of the other people present, or your own personality.

20 Women, Men, and Aggression in an Egalitarian Society

Maria Lepowsky

In most cultures men are more likely than women to engage in physical aggression. Is this pattern of greater male violence an inevitable aspect of human nature? Research by anthropologist Maria Lepowsky suggests that it is not. Among the Vanatinai of New Guinea, violence among family, friends, neighbors, and other community members (intragroup aggression) is rare. Why? Vanatinai society is "egalitarian" in two ways. First, men and women are relatively equal in assertiveness and personal rights. Second, in this small island culture there is no formal social hierarchy, no system of royalty or social class to confer greater status or privileges on some group members. Lepowsky argues that this egalitarianism reduces both general levels of aggression and male violence against women.

> Vanatinai, a small island society off New Guinea, is egalitarian, with no indigenous formal systems of rank or authority. Assertiveness and autonomy are highly valued as personal qualities and equivalent for males and females. Overt aggression is condemned and violence is rare. Women were the aggressors in four out of five incidents over ten years. Sexual jealousy was the dominant motif in all five cases. . . . The Vanatinai case is evidence that the rarity of intragroup violence, especially of attacks by men on women, is a characteristic of egalitarian societies.

Vanatinai is a small and remote island in the South Pacific, where women still wear coconut leaf skirts, and where men and women alike sail outrigger canoes to distant islands, seeking the shell-disc necklaces and axe blades of polished greenstone exchanged in feasts honoring the dead. Part of the independent nation of Papua New

Guinea, the island, which lies about 200 miles southeast of the New Guinea mainland, is also a striking contrast to Western societies because of the absence of any indigenous ideologies of male superiority or of any formal authority of men over women.

Except through colonial legal systems and, since 1975, national law, sporadically enforced by outsiders such as government officers, nobody on Vanatinai has a recognized right to tell another adult what to do. Both girls and boys are socialized to be confident and assertive. Unmarried young people have equal rights to control their own sexual behavior. Women choose their own marriage partners and can divorce at will. Women and men have equivalent control of their own persons. Women are central to the island's matrilineal kinship system and are considered to be the "owners of the gardens," controlling the distribution of most staple foods. As adults, both sexes can, if they want to, accumulate ceremonial valuables from exchange partners and then host lavish feasts. By giving away enormous quantities of food and valuables they earn the gender-blind title of *gia,* literally, "giver," or big woman/big man. The same personal qualities of strength, wisdom, and generosity are admired in both women and men. . . .

In a culture with prevailing ideologies of gender equality, no indigenous system of formal authority, and a high value on assertiveness and personal autonomy for both sexes, do concepts of female and male personal power differ? What happens when these strong-willed, autonomous people have conflicts?

I focus here on gendered constructions of the person and personal power as revealed by physical aggression. . . . The example of Vanatinai in the late twentieth century generally supports the position that overt anger—and the physical aggression with which it is often associated—are less prevalent in egalitarian societies (see Burbank, 1994; Myers, 1988). . . .

Overt physical aggression by either men or women is extremely rare on Vanatinai. Since 1943, in a population of about 2000, there has been one murder by a Vanatinai person: in the 1950s a man hit his wife in a jealous rage and killed her, then tried to weight her body in the lagoon. Also in the 1950s an Australian trader went berserk and killed two island men with a shotgun. Both killers were reported to Australian colonial authorities, charged with murder, and sentenced to prison. I have never observed or heard about two men engaged in a physical fight. Nor have I heard of or seen two children, of either sex, in a physical fight. These are significant negative instances, compared to any representative eighteen months of residence in a North American or European community, that suggest the distinct absence of any "culture of violence" on Vanatinai. A tolerance for overt interpersonal violence seems to correlate cross-culturally with a widespread prevalence of violence against women (Levinson, 1989, 40–45, 84; Mitchell, 1992, 90; Tracy and Crawford, 1992, 30).

On Vanatinai physical abuse of a woman by any man, including her husband, is very unusual, and it is abhorred. Levinson (1989, 84), based on a cross-cultural study of ninety small-scale and peasant societies, concludes that "gender-based economic inequality," along with a general propensity toward "violent conflict resolution," are the key contextual factors in societal patterns of widespread violence against wives. The rarity or absence of violence against women has in itself been suggested as a significant index cross-culturally of high female autonomy or the absence of a male supremacist complex (Schlegel, 1972; Divale and Harris, 1976; Sanday, 1981; cf. Lepowsky, 1990).

In more than a decade since my first field research, I have only heard about five acts of violence. While others may well have occurred, it seems to be highly unusual behavior. Of these five incidents, four of the aggressors were women, two attacking other women and two their husbands. The fifth was a man who hit his wife. In four of the cases, the aggressors felt the strong social disapproval of neighbors and the shame of their own kinspeople, and they feared retaliation through supernatural attack by the victim's kin. I explain the reasons for the one exception below. The government Officer-in-Charge, in each case a man from another part of Papua New Guinea residing at the government station twenty miles away, never heard about any of these acts of violence, all of them crimes under the legal code inherited from Australian colonial administration at independence.

The motif of sexual jealousy runs through all of these incidents. This is congruent with the finding in Victoria Burbank's (1987) cross-cultural study of female aggression that female "rivals in sex and marriage are the most common victims" (cf. Kerns, 1992, 128) and that husbands are the most common male targets of female attacks. Male sexual jealousy, and male accusations of female adultery or sexual infractions, are among the most common precursors of acts of violence against women in all human societies (Daly and Wilson, 1988, 200; Levinson, 1989, 34, 84; Brown, 1992, 3–4, 8; Campbell, 1992, 235, 245).

The first violent incident I heard about on Vanatinai occurred after I had lived on the island for some months. A woman I knew, in her early twenties—call her Urupo (all names in this article have been changed)—had been having an adulterous intrigue. Women, and men, often use their friends as third parties to arrange rendez-vous, and I had heard Urupo discussing details with a mutual woman friend, who was reluctant to get involved because she liked Urupo's husband. I had also seen Urupo meet another lover a month earlier one night when we were at a feast in another hamlet and all sleeping in the same house. One morning, her husband came into the house where I lived with a local family with his wrist broken and an ugly, infected burn on his chest. The night before, Urupo had flown into a jealous rage, accusing her husband of meeting a lover, which he repeatedly denied. Finally she seized a burning brand from the fire, struck him hard on the wrist, and then lunged forward and burned him.

The neighbors were appalled, and her kinfolk were ashamed. Public opinion held that the husband was innocent and that Urupo, in fact, was the adulterer, who suspected him of her own wrongdoing, an indigenous model of projection. Her kin and friends were also afraid, not of physical retaliation but of the supernatural retaliation of his mother's witchcraft on the violent and adulterous wife, whom the mother had never liked. The couple divorced the following year.

Unmarried people are expected to have many lovers, but married people have exclusive sexual rights over one another. Many marriages, especially those of people in their twenties, break up because one or the other spouse cannot make this transition and continues to seduce others or respond to their invitations. Both women and men make sexual propositions.

Success in love is believed due to the practice of love magic, by either sex, that makes a person dazzlingly attractive and renders others *negenege,* or dizzy with desire, and helpless to defend themselves against the will of the seducer. Human powers in all types of magic, sorcery, and witchcraft flow primarily from a person's secret knowledge of how to gain the assistance of male and female ancestor spirits or place spirits (see Lepowsky, 1993).

The principle of seduction also operates in the magic of ceremonial exchange. Vanatinai and neighboring islands are part of a regional, interisland system of ritual exchange linking people speaking a dozen different languages. They travel by sailing or canoe in quest of ceremonial valuables such as shell-disc necklaces and greenstone axe blades as well as pigs, baskets of yams, clay pots, and other household goods. This exchange network was made famous in anthropology by the pioneering work of Bronislaw Malinowski (1922) in 1915–1918 in the Trobriand Islands, 300 miles northwest of Vanatinai, where it is known as *kula.* On Vanatinai, exchange visitors, male and female, beautify themselves and use magic, based on the power of ancestor and other spirits, to render the host and exchange partner of either sex *negenege* and eager to part with a prized valuable, metaphorically the genitals of a seduced lover....

A second incident, again of a woman striking her husband, is the exception I mentioned to the pattern of shame and disgust with violent behavior felt by kinspeople and neighbors. In this case, a middle-aged man, well known throughout the region for his success in ceremonial exchange, announced to his wife of twenty years that he planned to take a second wife, a slightly younger widow with whom he had been having an affair. Polygyny is permissible on Vanatinai, but it is rare, and the man must have his wife's consent to take a co-wife. As in this instance, the permission is not always forthcoming. Furious, the wife hit her husband once with her hand, without injuring him, and told him that he was welcome to take another wife, but that if he did, she was leaving him. The man never did take a second wife, and in fact he ended his affair. This story was told to me by a witness, a young kinswoman of the wife, who recounted it in tones of admiration (with a tinge of amusement) for a woman who asserted herself. If the wife had actually injured her husband, I think her kinspeople would have been ashamed of her behavior, even though they believed she acted with provocation.

Neither of the Vanatinai cases of violence against a husband occurred in the context of a "mutually violent relationship or in self-defense" as postulated by Campbell (1992, 230–32) and Levinson (1989) based upon comparisons of human societies cross-culturally. Violence against husbands may well be related to, or triggered by, wife abuse where there is a well-developed "culture of violence" and where spouse abuse is more common and more tolerated, but it was not in these two rare incidents, both triggered by female sexual jealousy, on Vanatinai.

In the only incident of male violence against a woman, a man accused his wife of adultery and then punched her once in the jaw, loosening her teeth. Again, as in the first case of the violent wife, public opinion held that the violent spouse, the husband, was the adulterous one and the victim was innocent. (I myself saw the husband slip away into the darkness with a young widow during the midnight dancing at a feast a few months earlier.)

The final two incidents of violence involved women who attacked "the other woman." In one, a wife physically attacked a young widow with whom her husband had been having an affair. The attack (not the adulterous affair) scandalized the community and, her neighbors believed, later led to retaliatory witchcraft attacks against the violent woman and her child. In the last incident, a middle-aged widow attacked a younger widow with whom her live-in lover had been dallying, injuring and disfiguring her rival's ear. The brutality of the attack caused her kinspeople great shame, and her neighbors condemned and avoided the aggressor for months afterward. . . .

In Vanatinai constructions of the gendered person, males and females experience equally strong emotions of envy, jealousy, frustrated desire, and rage. There is no perception that a man's feelings of anger are any stronger than a woman's. But both men and women, unlike small children, should learn to control not the internal experience of anger but its public expression in angry words or violent behavior (cf. Briggs, 1970). The very word for anger, *gaizi,* also means war.

Even angry words are dangerous, for they signal the desire to commit violence through supernatural attack. They will trigger the anger of their hearer, who is likely to seek revenge or compensation for his or her rage or humiliation through sorcery or witchcraft. The option of supernatural violence, available to both men and women on Vanatinai, is a way of sublimating public anger and avoiding open interpersonal violence.[1]

A distinctive characteristic of Vanatinai understandings of the person is the notion that it is impossible to know what another is thinking. It is therefore impossible to explain overt behavior by reference to someone else's private thoughts. Both men and women are assumed to experience strong emotions of anger and desire, but this is their business, "something of theirs," as people say. And both sexes act on these emotions at times through covert use of love or exchange magic that subverts the will of another or through acts of sorcery and witchcraft. This channeling of anger and frustration into supernatural acts of aggression, and the strong fear of supernatural attacks by others, are Vanatinai people's explanations for why there is so little physical aggression on the island.

In spite of the historical particulars of the Vanatinai case, and its distinctively Melanesian cultural flavor, the example of Vanatinai offers evidence that the rarity of intragroup violence, especially of attacks by men on women, is a characteristic of egalitarian societies.

References

Briggs, J. (1970). *Never in anger: Portrait of an Eskimo family.* Cambridge, MA: Harvard University Press.

Brown, J. (1992). Introduction: Definitions, assumptions, themes, and issues. In D. Counts, J. Brown, & J. Campbell (Eds.), *Sanctions and sanctuary: Cultural perspectives on the beating of wives.* Boulder, CO: Westview Press.

---

[1] The incidence of violence against women is also reported as low in four other small-scale societies where the possibility of supernatural attack is a culturally validated option for both sexes: the Garífuna of Belize (Kerns, 1992, 127, 131, 133), the islanders of Mayotte, in the Western Indian Ocean (Lambek, 1992, 159–60), the islanders of Ujelang, in Micronesia (Carucci, 1992, 113, 119–20), and the Wape of New Guinea (Mitchell, 1992, 92–93).

Burbank, V. (1987). Female aggression in cross-cultural perspective. *Behavior Science Research 21,* 70–100.

Burbank, V. (1994). Cross-cultural perspectives on aggression in women and girls: An introduction. *Sex Roles, 30,* 169–176.

Campbell, J. (1992). Wife-battering: Cultural contexts versus Western social science. In D. Counts, J. Brown, & J. Campbell (Eds.), *Sanctions and sanctuary: Cultural perspectives on the beating of wives.* Boulder, CO: Westview Press.

Carucci, L. (1992). Nudging her harshly and killing him softly: Displays of disenfranchisement on Ujelang atoll. In D. Counts, J. Brown, & J. Campbell (Eds.), *Sanctions and sanctuary: Cultural perspectives on the beating of wives.* Boulder, CO: Westview Press.

Daly, M., & Wilson, M. (1988). *Homicide.* New York: Aldine de Gruyter.

Divale, W., & Harris, M. (1976). Population, warfare, and the male supremacist complex. *American Anthropologist, 78,* 521–538.

Kerns, V. (1992). Preventing violence against women: A Central American case. In D. Counts, J. Brown, & J. Campbell (Eds.), *Sanctions and sanctuary: Cultural perspectives of the beating of wives.* Boulder, CO: Westview Press.

Lambek, M. (1992). Like tooth biting tongue: The proscription and practice of spouse abuse in Mayotte. In D. Counts, J. Brown, & J. Campbell (Eds.), *Sanctions and sanctuary: Cultural perspectives on the beating of wives.* Boulder, CO: Westview Press.

Lepowsky, M. (1990). Gender in an egalitarian society: Lessons from a Coral Sea island. In P. Sanday & R. Goodenough (Eds.), *Beyond the second sex: New directions in the anthropology of gender.* Philadelphia: University of Pennsylvania Press.

Lepowsky, M. (1993). *Fruit of the motherland: Gender in an egalitarian society.* New York: Columbia University Press.

Levinson, D. (1989). *Family violence in cross-cultural perspective.* Newbury Park, CA: Sage Publications.

Malinowski, B. (1922). *Argonauts of the Western Pacific.* New York: E. P. Dutton.

Malinowski, B. (1935). *Coral gardens and their magic* (Two volumes). New York: American Book Company.

Mitchell, W. (1992). Why Wape men don't beat their wives: Constraints toward domestic tranquility in a New Guinea society. In D. Counts, J. Brown, & J. Campbell (Eds.), *Sanctions and sanctuary: Cultural perspectives on the beating of wives.* Boulder, CO: Westview Press.

Myers, F. (1988). The logic and meaning of anger among Pintupi Aborigines. *Man, 23,* 589–610.

Sanday, P. (1981). *Female power and male dominance: On the origins of sexual inequality.* Cambridge: Cambridge University Press.

Schlegel, A. (1972). *Male dominance and female autonomy: Domestic authority in matrilineal societies.* New Haven, CT: HRAF Press.

Strathern, M. (1988). *The gender of the gift: Problems with women and problems with society in Melanesia.* Berkeley: University of California Press.

Tracy, K., & Crawford, C. (1992). Wife abuse: Does it have an evolutionary origin? In D. Counts, J. Brown, & J. Campbell (Eds.), *Sanctions and sanctuary: Cultural perspectives on the beating of wives.* Boulder, CO: Westview Press.

Questions for Thought

1. What evidence does Lepowsky provide to demonstrate that aggression is uncommon among the Vanatinai?

2. The author reports several specific incidents of violence. Describe who initiated each act of violence and the apparent reasons for the violence.

3. What is the social reaction to violence among the Vanatinai? Support your position with specific examples.

4. Compare and contrast the extent of male-female equality and of social equality in the United States and in Vanatinai society.

5. Male aggression is rare among the Vanatinai but relatively common in industrialized societies. What aspects of Vanatinai culture may reduce the general level of verbal and physical violence among boys and men?

6. Male violence toward women is unusual among the Vanatinai. Indeed, Lepowsky describes more incidents in which women are the aggressors against men. What factors may minimize male violence toward women?

7. What lessons might we learn from the Vanatinai about how to reduce aggression in our society? What might be the problems of trying to "import" social practices from Vanatinai culture into our own?

The Triple Threat
A Discussion of Gender, Class, and Race Differences in Weight

Deborah J. Bowen

Naomi Tomoyasu

Ana Mari Cauce

Many American women are concerned about their weight, but as this review documents, the issues facing women differ depending on their social class and ethnic or racial background. For example, whereas some middle-class and upper-class White women struggle to achieve an unhealthy standard of thinness, poor women more often confront the health risks of being overweight. Cultural differences in attitudes about weight and food are also important.

ABSTRACT. Gender, poverty and race, the "triple threat" referred to in the title, are three major risk factors that contribute to the high prevalence of weight-related problems in this country. Current psychological literature on weight management has generally ignored the effects of these variables and their implications for developing interventions for underserved populations which include women, minorities and poor people. The present paper discusses the literature on the effects of gender, race, and class on weight levels and associated psychosocial variables. Conclusions drawn illustrate that weight is a major issue for women, and that race and class also have effects on weight levels which can affect health status. Areas of further exploration and of action are identified to address problems that women face regarding weight.

When I go to work in the upper-east side (of Manhattan) from my home (in Brooklyn), I feel like I've gained 10 to 20 pounds!

—*27 year old Latina*

Reprinted from *Women & Health*, 1991, 17(4), 123–143. Copyright 1991 by Haworth Press, Inc. Used by permission.

At work, where there are only a few of us Black women, I feel pretty fat. At home, with my friends, I don't think about it hardly at all. I guess it's because I'm closer to the middle (of my Black friends' weight range).

—34 year old Black woman

I weigh myself everyday; I watch everything that goes into my mouth; I do aerobics 3 times a week. If I don't stick to it, I know I'm going to blimp out.

—A White woman—5'6", 110 lbs.

I'd kill to be a size 6.

—A size 8 White woman

Gender, poverty and race, the "triple threat" referred to in the title, are three major risk factors that contribute to the high prevalence of weight-related problems in this country. Current psychological literature on weight management has generally ignored the effects of these variables and their implications for developing interventions for underserved populations which include women, minorities and poor people.

The interactive effects of gender, race[1] and class as risk factors for weight problems are social phenomena which become readily apparent from casual observations of women of color in real life or as depicted in television shows and advertising (cf. "Aunt Jemima"). Indeed, whereas the common stereotype of women of color as both nurturing (especially of white children or audiences) and obviously well-nurtured is more a reflection of racism than of reality, it does contain a kernel of truth (as is often the case with stereotypes). That is, women of color, in particular poor Black and Latina women, are more apt to be overweight than White middle-class women, or Black and Latino men (Stern, Pugh, Gaskill, & Hazuda, 1982; Stunkard, 1980; Stunkard, d'Aquili, Fox & Filion, 1972; National Center for Health Statistics, 1987).

Research suggesting race and class play powerful, but often neglected, roles in women's weight and in the perceptions and attitudes that accompany it has been available for over twenty years. An early article by Goldblatt, Moore, and Stunkard, (1965) depicts an inverse association between both original and current socioeconomic status and prevalence of obesity. Obesity occurred six times more frequently among poor women than among more affluent women. Since race was not a focus of this study, the interactive effects of the race, class and gender cannot be determined. Current psychological literature on weight management has also generally ignored the effects of race, gender, and class and their implications for developing interventions for minority and poor women with weight problems. For example, a review paper on women and weight by Rodin, Silberstein, and Striegel-Moore (1985) presents a cogent and vivid account of the problems experienced by women (many of whom are within the average weight range) striving to maintain unrealistic images of feminine beauty. This otherwise excellent review does not address the issue of weight-related racial/cultural or class differences among women. Although an entire section of the paper is entitled "Cultural Attitudes," the ensuing discussion focuses exclusively on those attitudes most prevalent among the White middle to upper classes.

This paper addresses how race, class and gender separately affect attitudes about weight and body image and the experience of poor women of color with obesity. The behavioral focus of this paper is on eating. Exercise, a behavior that plays a role in weight levels, is mentioned where appropriate.

Prevalence of Overweight and Underweight

Obesity, or excessive body fat, is an important and pervasive problem in the United States (Grunberg, 1982; Powers, 1980; Stunkard, 1980; Bray, 1980). Obesity is associated, either directly or indirectly, with a variety of diseases, including diabetes, hypertension, menstrual and reproductive abnormalities, arthritis, gout, atherosclerosis, abnormal heart size and function, and gallbladder disease (Rimm & White, 1980), health problems that are more prevalent in communities of color. In addition, the psychological problems that may result from obesity are numerous: anxiety, negative self-perception, disturbed body image, and discrimination in the job market. Although a recent National Institutes of Health Consensus Conference illustrated the controversy that currently exists as to the exact level of obesity at which health risks appear, most scholars agree that, in general, moderate obesity poses health risks for an individual (National Institutes of Health, 1985). Therefore, a woman who becomes obese faces a range of psychological and physiological health hazards.

Table 1 presents data from the second National Health and Nutritional Examination Survey (NHANES II) (National Center for Health Statistics, 1987) which found that approximately one-fourth of U.S. adults are overweight and that this prevalence is not evenly distributed by race, sex and social class. The incidence of overweight is higher for women than for men and higher for Blacks than for Whites. However, among Black and Latina women, there is an even more striking disproportionality in the obesity rate. The prevalence of overweight for Black women is higher than for either Black men or White women and tends to increase with age. Within the 45 to 75 year age range, as many as 60% of all Black women are overweight. Among Latinos, epidemiological research suggests that the incidence of obesity may be approximately 4 to 6 times that of the rest of the U.S. population and that nearly half of the adult Mexican American population may be obese (Stern et al., 1982).

At the other end of the body weight continuum, the prevalence of excess underweight is high among White women of middle- and upper-middle-class groups. The high prevalence of underweight is, in large part, due to the intense preoccupation that women in this society have with weight loss and dieting. This strong preference for a lean look is so pervasive that it has become "normal" for individuals in this society to express concern about weight and to control weight through periodic dieting (Polivy & Herman, 1987). In essence, dieting rather than nondieting, has become the normative behavior. It is not surprising that some researchers claim that the incidence of eating disorders in this country has increased over the last two decades (Garfinkel & Garner, 1982) given the extreme cultural pressures for some women to stay thin.

Table 1   ▦   **Percent of Overweight Persons 20–74 Years of Age, by Race, Sex, and Age: United States, 1976–80**

Sex and Age	White	Black	All other races
Both sexes			
20–74 years	24.8	35.7	25.7
20–24 years	11.2	15.3	11.7
25–34 years	19.4	26.3	20.2
35–44 years	26.4	40.8	27.9
45–54 years	30.2	52.1	31.7
55–64 years	31.9	44.2	32.8
65–74 years	31.9	46.0	32.7
Men			
20–74 years	24.4	25.7	24.2
20–24 years	12.7	5.5	12.1
25–34 years	20.9	17.5	20.4
35–44 years	28.2	40.9	28.9
45–54 years	30.5	41.4	31.0
55–64 years	28.6	26.0	28.1
65–74 years	25.8	26.4	25.2
Women			
20–74 years	25.1	43.8	27.1
20–24 years	9.6	23.7	11.4
25–34 years	17.9	33.5	20.0
35–44 years	24.8	40.8	27.0
45–54 years	29.9	61.2	32.5
55–64 years	34.8	59.4	37.0
65–74 years	36.5	60.8	38.5

Note. Overweight is defined as a sex-specific body mass index (kilograms divided by height in meters squared) equal to or higher than the 85th percentile for examinees 20–29 years of age.

Gender Influences on Weight

Gender plays an important role in the development of a variety of weight-related problems (Rodin et al., 1985; Forster & Jeffrey, 1986). Over the past 15 years, researchers have investigated the social underpinnings of gender and how they influence weight-related variables. Reported differences between desirable body images of women and men support the notion that societal pressures to be thin are different for males and females. College women reported that their current figure was heavier than the "most attractive" figure, which was heavier than the "ideal" figure (Fallon & Rozin, 1985). College men's current, attractive, and ideal figures were nearly identical. These results were basically replicated with adolescent boys and girls (Cohn, Adler, Irwin, Millstein, Kegeles & Stone, 1987). Both overweight and even normal-weight women, but not thin women, are less satisfied with their weight than are normal and overweight men (Mintz & Betz, 1986). Taken together, these studies show that women are more dissatisfied with their bodies than are men, a difference that, for women, may be related to disordered eating patterns and attitudes about weight and appearance.

In current U.S. society there is a focus on female appearance and beauty and particularly, on thinness. For example, Silverstein and colleagues have documented the high prevalence of both underweight actresses and normal-to overweight actors appearing on prime time television program (Silverstein, Perdue, Peterson & Kelly, 1985). Garner, Garfinkel, Schwartz, and Thompson (1980) have documented the increasing thinness of women presented as role models for physical beauty in events such as Miss America Pageants and photographs in Playboy magazine centerfolds. Eighty-five percent of college-age women reported that they wished to weigh less, compared with 40 percent of same-aged men (Drewnowski & Yee, 1987). A recent review concluded that women are more stigmatized than are men for obesity, and experience discontent and dissatisfaction because of sex-specific pressures to be thin and to obtain a desirable body image (Rodin et al., 1985). Chronic dieting and restraint have become normative aspects of women's lives, because of the intense pressure to mold themselves into a societally-constructed image of excessive thinness for women (Polivy & Herman, 1987; Streigel-Moore, Silberstein, & Rodin, 1986).

Not all women in this culture, however, possess attitudes that focus on thinness. Among low socioeconomic (SES) groups, it appears that gender interacts with class to produce higher rates of overweight (Ross & Mirowsky, 1983). The "normal" lifestyle of poor women does not include chronic dieting and exercise as it does with middle-class women. Poor women more often encounter the stigma that is associated with being overweight (Sobal & Stunkard, 1989). They experience not only physical degradation but also character assassinations in a society that believes so naively that weight loss could be achieved if fat women were simply more "weight-conscious and responsible" (Crandall & Biernat, 1990).

Social Class Factors in Weight

Social class also contributes to the prevalence of obesity and underweight. The earliest data come from the Midtown Manhattan study (Goldblatt et al., 1965) which showed a strong negative relationship between social class and weight. More recent research has similarly supported the earlier findings of a greater prevalence of obesity among lower SES than among higher SES groups (Golden, Saltzer, Depaul-Snyder, & Reiff, 1983; Sobal & Stunkard, 1989). This relationship between class and weight was particularly strong for women (Goldblatt et al., 1965; Garn et al., 1977; Ross & Mirowsky, 1983).

The reasons for the greater prevalence of obesity among lower SES groups have been discussed in a recent review (Sobal & Stunkard, 1989). The authors identified four mediating variables that could explain the inverse relationship between SES and weight in women's varying attitudes toward obesity: differing levels of dietary restraint, differing physical activity levels, and inheritance, both genetic and social. Of these, the authors speculate that differences in restrained eating are probably the most powerful in affecting attitudes about weight. Restrained eating is defined as the cognitive control of eating behavior (Ruderman, 1986). The authors discuss the consistent finding that women of higher SES categories show more restrained eating, defined as consciously holding back from eating everything desired, than do women of low SES. Reasons for this class difference, however, are still unclear.

There are a number of other factors that may contribute to the higher obesity rate among the lower social classes in the United States. Poor people may be constrained by economic pressures to buy less expensive foods which tend to be calorie-rich and high in fats and sugars (Furukawa & Harris, 1986; Stern et al., 1982; Cozens, 1982). In addition to budgetary constraints, there is a great deal of pressure from certain industries who spend considerable sums a year in advertisements to promote cheap high-fat foods to the poor. Fast food restaurants not so coincidentally occur in areas where low SES and ethnic minorities are concentrated (Freedman, 1990).

Another explanation for the higher frequency of overweight among low SES groups may be due, in part, to lack of adequate nutritional knowledge. Golden et al. (1983) found that low income groups, who had a higher incidence of being overweight, had less information about nutritional needs compared to higher SES groups. However, other researchers have concluded that the greater obesity rates of the poor may not be necessarily due to lack of nutritional knowledge, but rather may reflect economic limitations (Dewalt & Pelto, 1976; Calloway & Gibbs, 1976) which lead to a greater consumption of cheaper, high-fat foods.

The greater incidence of obesity among the low SES also may be due to an external loss of control. A number of researchers have shown that poor people perceive themselves to be unable to control their environment and their lives as a whole (Vomoto, 1986; Smith, 1985). This psychological style may well reflect the reality of living in a social situation that allows certain groups of people to have limited or no control over life choices and opportunities. Consequently, their appraisal of their ability to control their life situation may be reflected in other areas of their lives, such as their nutritional and weight status. Stern et al. (1982) found that lower SES Mexican American women felt more than upper SES Anglo women that they could not do much about their weight. Likewise in a study examining obesity in low income mothers and children, it was shown that lower SES mothers, compared to higher SES mothers, were not only significantly heavier, but also perceived themselves to be less in control of their own weight as well as their children's weight (Golden et al., 1983).

It can be concluded that several variables associated with low SES may combine and unfortunately perpetuate obesity. One frustration with the literature on SES and obesity is that it is primarily descriptive and not focused on testing hypotheses about why socioeconomic factors influence weight levels. For example, the specific elements of SES that influence weight are unknown. Actual family income during childhood may contribute less than familial expectations of success in the world of the dominant culture, or increased education without increased income may be more influential in determining weight levels than making a stable, plentiful salary in a working class occupation. Future research should explore these and other elements of the effects of socioeconomic factors on women's weight.

Racial/Cultural Factors in Weight

The racial and cultural factors that help to determine weight have been much less well studied than those of SES or gender. However, there have been a few studies that have attempted to examine racial influences independent of SES and these studies have found that obesity rates are higher among certain ethnic minorities. In the San Antonio Heart Study (Stern et al., 1982) for example, Mexican Americans were found to be heavier than their Anglo counterparts even when socioeconomic factors were controlled, thus supporting a role for culture in weight determination independent of economic factors. Perhaps one of the most striking findings of the San Antonio study was the difference in cultural attitudes regarding ideal norms of leanness. Mexican Americans of both sexes, even when SES effects were removed, believed that Anglos were overly concerned about weight and body image. This skepticism about the desirability of being thin was, in turn, reflected in their dieting attitudes and behaviors. Mexican Americans scored lower on dieting behavior and sugar avoidance scales compared to Anglos. Their skepticism about leanness, in part, may have reflected cultural differences in attitude about weight and provided strong evidence that they had not yet fully accepted the mainstream ideals of leanness. Massara (1980) has suggested that in certain cultures, obesity may arise either from a residual fear of hunger when food was not available in the past, or from the cultural belief that fatness is a sign of health, wealth and psychological well-being. This perspective on weight may thus explain the greater prevalence of obesity in Hispanics, as well as other ethnic groups in spite of strong pressures for leaner weights and body images.

Cultural differences in attitudes regarding weight and food may also contribute to the higher obesity rate among Blacks. In a study of high school students in Berkeley, California, Blacks not only had higher preferred weights and greater body image satisfaction, but they were also less likely to perceive themselves as fat and were less inclined to initiate weight control compared to Whites (Huenemann et al., 1966). Among similarly "heavy" Black and White adolescents, Black girls perceived themselves as less heavy compared with White girls (Desmond, Price, Hallinan, & Smith, 1989). In addition, Blacks show a greater preference for sweet foods (Huenemann et al., 1966; Desor, Greene, & Miller, 1975), and consume more calories in general than Whites. These Black-White differences are particularly apparent among females. In a study among women in Philadelphia, for example, Black women made up only 6 percent, while White women made up as much as 94 percent of all "diet conscious dieters" who preferred low-calorie items (Fetzer, Solt, & McKinney, 1985). This difference in consumption rate may be explained by the lower degree of restrained eating among Black women and their lower inclination to accept reductions in dietary fat as potential strategies for weight management more so than White females

(Huenemann et al., 1966). Taken together, the cultural differences in food preferences, overall calorie intake, lower degree of restrained eating, and a more relaxed attitude about weight may all contribute to the higher incidence of obesity among Blacks in this country.

Currently, ethnic minorities deal more often with issues of overweight than underweight. However, as they become more acculturated, they adopt the majority belief that leanness, not overweight is a sign of health and subjective well-being. For example, Hazuda, Haffner, Stern, and Eifler (1988) found that as Mexican Americans acculturate more to majority group norms, they become less obese. This acculturation process may or may not have covaried with economic standing. Other data suggest that as Black women become more integrated into mainstream culture, they become similar to White women in terms of their attitudes about weight. Kumanyaka et al., (1985) reported that 50 percent of Black women ranging from 20–50 years of age, considered themselves overweight. This is comparable to the 54 percent of women in the general population who consider themselves overweight (Stephenson, Levy, Sass, & McGarvey, 1987). However, this trend towards greater similarity between Black and White women may also lead to a greater degree of disordered eating. Anderson and Hay (1985) showed that as Black women acculturate economically and socially, they, like middle- and upper-class White women, also face strong cultural pressures to diet and to be lean. Attitudes about weight and body image undergo changes most readily since physical appearance is one of the most visible evidences of acculturation. For Black women, adoption of majority group standards for weight may be one avenue in which cultural acceptance and social and economic success may be achieved.

While data on weight and attitudes about weight among Hispanics and Blacks are scanty, there is even less data for other minority groups, such as Asian and Native Americans. According to a study by Nevo (1985) examining the prevalence of bulimic symptoms among college females, Asian American women had fewer concerns about binge-eating, dieting and weight in relation to White women. A few studies, however, suggest a greater degree of overweight as a whole among Native Americans. Garb and Stunkard (1975), for example, have shown that among acculturated Navaho Indian children, the incidence of obesity is alarmingly high. This higher rate may be due to not only cultural factors, but also SES factors. Economic limitations may restrict American Indians to consume primarily high fat diets and to live in environments that predispose them to obesity and its physical complications, which include diabetes, cardiovascular diseases and hypertension (Grunberg, 1982). Clearly, further examination is needed in investigating the factors that contribute to the high morbidity rate among American Indians in this country.

It appears that race and class can exert independent effects on obesity levels for women in this country. The question of *why* both non-White and non-affluent women should develop higher levels of obesity than their White and/or more well-off sisters has not been empirically addressed. One commonality that these two groups of women share is being excluded from the dominant culture. The particular experience must be examined with regards to issues of body image and obesity. Again, as with SES, the question of why a woman of color is at a higher risk for obesity has not been empirically determined and deserves more focused research attention.

Another issue that must be addressed in order to understand ethnic influences on eating and obesity and to design successful interventions is the cultural meanings of food and eating. Nutritionists agree that ethnic cultures develop and maintain dietary practices that hold meaning within the cultures (Kittler & Sucher, 1989). Some of these practices are healthful and some directly contribute to obesity and subsequent health problems. How to maintain cultural integrity while modifying culturally meaningful behavior is an issue that needs further attention.

Obesity and Poor Women of Color

The effects of gender, race and social class on weight have been separately discussed in previous sections. Each variable alone affects the chances of weight-related problems. However, poor women of color, who experience the combined effects of all three factors are particularly vulnerable to weight problems, and specifically to being overweight.

The high prevalence of obesity among minority women, to a large extent, can be linked to the growing rate of poverty in this country. Nearly two-thirds of people over 17 years of age who are living below the poverty line are women. Women earn about three-fifths of what men earn and minority women earn even less. Among Black women, three out of five employed Black women earn incomes below the poverty line (Woody & Malson, 1984). These economic constraints probably influence low SES minority women, who often also are single parents, to buy cheap, high fat foods for themselves and their children (Caster, 1980). In addition, poor women have little access to physical exercise for weight control given the social and physical environments in which they live. Inner city Blacks and Latinos are concentrated in apartments which frequently have no backyard play areas or park facilities. Diet centers and health clubs that are more economically accessible to middle- and upper-income groups, are virtually nonexistent for poor women (Simms & Malveaux, 1986). To further exacerbate the already constrained situation, the high crime rate in low SES areas could literally be scaring poor women from outdoor physical activities. They are frightened even to jog in the streets for fear of muggings and rapes; this fear, unfortunately, is justified and all too real.

Poor women of color face major difficulties if they identify their obesity as a problem and seek assistance for it. Limited access to medical care among poor people and people of color is a chronic problem in the United States (Cooper, et al. 1981). While improving this may not solve all issues of obesity for these women, it could mean the dissemination of more knowledge about nutrition and dietary habits and better treatment of obesity-related problems (Cope, 1985). Equally important, successful health promotion and disease prevention efforts that target minority and poor communities are rare. As researchers and clinicians acknowledge the difficulty in treating established obesity (Jeffrey, 1987), prevention offers must be given more attention.

In addition to the realities of economic and environmental constraints, women of color also must face yet another obstacle, and that is the common stereotype of minority women as being nurturing, well-nurtured and overweight. As mentioned earlier, societal discrimination and negative judgments accompany obesity in the dominant culture. When negative assessments of abilities and character due to obesity are coupled with the effects of racism and oppression that poor women of color face daily, the results are devastating. Given the judgments of mainstream ideology that regards obesity as an example of personal lack of willpower, strength, or value, it is no wonder that the higher prevalence of obesity in minority and poor women reinforces existing race and class oppression. White, middle-class women also suffer from this ideology at the thinner end of the continuum, as discussed previously. These stereotypes also promote and maintain damaging and unhealthy images of poor women of color which unfortunately feed back on their self-esteem and self-worth, and cause further problems.

Pregnancy and Excess Weight Gain

Because of the higher prevalence of obesity poor women of color are at greater risk for weight gains during certain critical periods. One example of a more vulnerable period is during pregnancy, as some women gain excess weight during their pregnancies (Niswander & Gordon, 1972; Hytten, 1981). Poor women, in particular, show the greatest weight gain during pregnancy (Newcombe, 1982) in addition to showing the highest obesity rates. The excess weight gain before and during pregnancy places these women in more vulnerable positions in terms of nutritional health and higher probabilities of weight-related complications such as toxemia, diabetes and hypertension (Naeye, 1979; Woods, Dewar, Malan, Heese, & Rush, 1980). Thus, a further examination of factors that underlie the differences between poor minorities and middle-class White women in the amount of weight gained during pregnancy is warranted since excess weight has significant consequences during pregnancy.

Although very few studies have examined the influence of race and gender on obesity and weight gains during pregnancy, data from two studies of taste preference during pregnancy (Bowen, in press) could shed some light in this area. The first study (Bowen, in press) was conducted with upper-middle-class White women in a wealthy suburb of a large East Coast metropolis. Subjects from the second study were recruited from a small relatively isolated city in the Southwest. Subjects in the second study were 67% Latina and were poor (average annual family income was less than $10,000 for three fourths of subjects). In both studies, women in the second trimester consumed significantly more sweet food, but not salty or bland food, as compared with women at any other point in pregnancy. Yet subjects from the two studies differed on the amount of weight gained at the time of the laboratory measurement. Very few middle-class White women (6 of 50) had gained excess weight at the time of the laboratory visit. However, 69% of Latinas in the second study were gaining excess weight for their particular time in pregnancy. White middle-class subjects consistently reported higher levels of restrained eating as compared with poor Latinas. The higher levels of restrained eating may have accounted for the lower weight gains among White women. These studies suggest that both pregnancy-related biological changes and psychosocial variables, like restrained eating and cultural pressures, control food preferences, eating, and weight gains in pregnancy. Restrained eating is one possible individual mechanism to explain both cultural and class differences in obesity.

There is yet another consequence of the excess weight gain among women of color both during and after pregnancy, and that is the effect of excess weight on the children of poor women of color (Huenemann, 1974). A number of studies have found that maternal weight or excess weight during pregnancy increases the probability that the child will also be overweight. Childhood obesity is a major problem in this country and the prognosis is less than optimistic since approximately 85% of children who are obese after age 2 remain so throughout adulthood (Abraham & Nordsieck, 1970). In addition, obesity may be propagated intergenerationally due to genetic as well as cultural and social class factors that are resistant to change over time (Woody & Constanzo, 1984). Thus, from the viewpoint of treatment and particularly prevention of childhood obesity, further examination of factors that underlie obesity during pregnancy and development is warranted.

Discussion

Weight is a major issue for women. For some women, there are major pressures to be thin and to conform to a mainstream or illusory idea of beauty that demands an unhealthy thinness. For others, obesity takes its toll on health. The determinants of weight problems for women are imbedded within the social values and expectations of this society. These expectations have placed women on a continuum of problems from too thin to too fat. At one end, the thinness and chronic dieting behavior found within relatively affluent and White women can be traced to the conditions that surround their lives. These conditions include pressure to succeed specifically in areas that focus on appearance and beauty, both traditionally feminine channels. Women's struggles for equality in the past 20 years have been accompanied by a toll on their bodies and minds, in terms of disordered eating and chronic restrained eating behavior.

On the other end of the continuum, we find women who are not striving to be thin, who in general do not chronically diet, but who are obese. This description is particularly accurate for women of color and for poor women. Because of financial and social limitations such as ethnic roles surrounding weight and poverty, these women become obese and suffer the consequences of being overweight. Obese minority and low SES women show higher incidences of hypertension, weight-related diabetes and cardiovascular illnesses. Additionally, they experience unfair and incorrect attributions regarding the morality of their character and soundness of mind because of the stigma attached to being overweight in this society. The higher incidence of obesity among women does not stem from any inherent flaws in character, but more accurately reflects the cultural differences in attitude about weight and the realistic economic constraints that force poor women to buy primarily high-calorie, high-fat foods because that is simply all that they can afford.

Perhaps it is time to reevaluate the direction of the women's movement to ensure that we play a minimal role in the development of these problems and that we actively struggle to eliminate societal pressures and restrictions on women's weight and health issues. Women and men have argued that the damaging stereotype and cultural pressures for women to be thin should be removed. The economic pressures and cultural biases that affect women of color and poor women must also be addressed by feminists and by all progressive people.

The previous discussion raises some questions that challenge health care providers, psychologists, and the general community. If the health care system is expected to prevent illness and maintain health, then when is the preventative measure more problematic than the original problem? The current social focus on thinness is brought on, in part, by an unhealthy emphasis on thinness for women. This culturally-induced emphasis on being in shape and thin has probably played a role in the development of chronic dieting and disordered eating in women from certain race and class backgrounds. Perhaps the prevention of illness via weight loss is a desirable goal for obese individuals, but such a preventative effort should not be used to perpetuate or justify a fanatical emphasis on thinness and beauty, especially for women.

Psychology as well can play a role in the appropriate emphasis on healthy, not skinny, ideal body image. There has been a large and lucrative emphasis on research and treatment of obesity as a health-impairing condition. Why have we not developed thinness prevention projects to counter exiting health-impairing disordered eating and to maintain appropriate body images for girls and women? Also, why have obesity prevention programs not been directly targeting women of color and poor women? Most of the women who attended organized groups to reduce weight are White and middle class. Much of the research presented in this paper has come from community and sociological studies. Other scientists with interests in women's health must become aware of the influences of race and class on health outcomes, both mental and physical. As socially responsible researchers and clinicians, we must use our skills to investigate and treat these excluded populations, while ensuring that we not exploit the anxieties of those who can afford treatment.

A major question, of course, is how to address the weight concerns of all women. Given that the problems for women around the issues of eating and weight exist on a community level, changing the societal demands, expectations, and values may also be done on the community, rather than the individual level. Using the framework of community psychology, with the dual goals of empowerment and prevention, changes in social norms regarding eating and weight would be important issues for psychologists to target. It would also be a necessary goal considering the prevalence of health hazards that obesity poses to women of color and poor women and that thinness poses for White women of middle and upper classes. Prevention strategies could include mass media interventions to promote the idea of healthful eating and weight levels as positive goals. In Cuba, for example, recent public health campaigns extolled the virtues of eating yogurt in a culture which has traditionally favored high fat and starchy foods. Another strategy is to develop counteradvertising to demythologize the connection between thinness and happiness or associate eating more healthful diets with well-being. Public service announcements, for example, could promote healthful eating and more realistic weight levels as promoting a more appealing image or desirable qualities.

Exercise may be another strategy for weight maintenance that would not carry a focus on eating. Programs exist that were designed to increase exercise in low-income Black women (Baranowski, Simons-Morton, Hooks, & Henske, 1990; Sullivan, 1985); these programs could be adapted for other groups of women. If kept to a reasonable, healthful level, regular exercise could be used to maintain healthy weight levels, as well as improve mental health (Biddle & Fox, 1989).

Programs and policies that empower and enable women to take control of their lives and of their health will probably do more toward eliminating weight problems in the long run than will offering weight loss and exercise classes or distributing nutrition information. An example of a successful health promotion program for poor women of color is the Black Women's Health Project currently ongoing in Atlanta, Georgia. In this program, focused on poor Black women living in housing projects, women come together in small consciousness-raising groups to discuss common health issues and potential solutions. By sharing experiences and generating plans and strategies for dealing with them, women who previously were unable to change health impairing behaviors are taking control of their lives in many different realms. More attention to the data and lessons of programs like this one will guide us in our efforts to promote health for all women.

Note

1. Race here refers to the current major racial groups of the U.S., including Black, Hispanic, Asian, Native Indian, and White.

References

Abraham, S., & Nordsieck, M. (1970). Relationship of excess weight in children and adults. *Public Health Report, 75,* 263–273.

Anderson, A. E., & Hay, A. (1985). Racial and socioeconomic influences in anorexia nervosa and bulimia. *International Journal of Eating Disorders, 4,* 479–487.

Baranowski, T., Simons-Morton, B., Hooks, P., & Henske, J. (1990). A center-based program for exercise change among Black-American families. *Health Education Quarterly, 17,* 179–196.

Biddle, S. J. H., & Fox, K. R. (1989). Exercise and health psychology: emerging relationships. *British Journal of Medical Psychology, 62,* 205–216.

Bowen, D. J. (in press). Taste and pregnancy: A possible explanation for excess weight gains. *Appetite.*

Bray, G. A. (Ed.). (1980). *Obesity in America.* USDHEW (PHS) NIH.

Calloway, D. H. & Gibbs, J. C. (1976). Food patterns and food assistance programs in the Cocopah Indian community. *Ecology of Food Nutrition, 5,* 183–196.

Caster, W. O. (1980). The core diet of lower-economic class women in Georgia. *Ecology of Food and Nutrition, 9,* 241–260.

Cohn, L. D., Adler, N. E., Irwin, C. E., Millstein, S. G., Kegeles, S. M., & Stone, G. (1987). Body-figure preferences in male and female adolescents. *Journal of Abnormal Psychology, 96,* 276–279.

Cooper, R., Steinhaur, M., Miller, W. et al. (1981). Racism, society and disease. *International Journal of Health Services, 11*(3), 39–41.

Cope, N. R. (Fall, 1985). The health status of Black women in the U.S.: Implications for health psychology and behavioral medicine. *Sage: A Scholarly Journal on Black Women, 2,* 20–24.

Cozens, R. E. (1982). Obesity in the aged—not just a case of overeating. *Nursing Clinics of North America, 17,* 227–354.

Crandall, C., & Biernat, M. (1990). The ideology of anti-fat attitudes. *Journal of Applied Social Psychology, 20,* 227–243.

Desmond, S. M., Price, J. H., Hallinan, C. & Smith, D. (1989). Black and white adolescents' perceptions of their weight. *Journal of School Health, 59,* 353–358.

Desor, J. A., Greene, L. S., & Miller, O. (1975). Preferences for sweet and salt in 9 to 15 year old and adult humans. *Science, 190,* 686–687.

DeWalt, K. M., & Pelto, G. H. (1976). Food use and household ecology in a Mexican community. In T. Fitzgerald (Ed.), *Nutrition and Anthropology in Action.*

Drewnowski, A., & Yee, D. K. (1987). Men and body image: Are males satisfied with their body weight? *Psychosomatic Medicine, 49,* 626–634.

Fallon, A. E. & Rozin, P. (1985). Sex differences in perceptions of desirable body shape. *Journal of Abnormal Psychology, 94,* 102–105.

Fetzer, J. N., Solt, P. F., McKinney, S. (1985). Typology of food preferences identified by Nutri-Food sort. *Journal of the American Dietetic Association,* 85(8):961–965.

Forster, J. L. & Jeffery, R. W. (1986). Gender differences related to weight history, eating patterns, efficacy expectations, self-esteem, and weight loss among participants in a weight reduction program. *Addictive Behaviors, 11,* 141–147.

Freedman, A. M. (1990). New York Times, Vol. CXXIII, No. 121.

Furukawa, C. & Harris, M. (1986). Some correlates of obesity in the elderly: Hereditary and environmental factors. *The Journal of Obesity and Weight Regulation, 5,* 55–76.

Garfinkel, P. E. & Garner, D. M. (1982). *Anorexia nervosa: A multidimensional perspective.* New York: Brunner/Mazd.

Garb, J. L., & Stunkard, A. J. Social factors and obesity in Navaho Indian Children. In A. Howard (Ed.). *Recent Advances in Obesity Research.* London: Newman (1975).

Garn, S. M., et al. (1977). Level of education, level of income, and level of fatness in adults. *American Journal of Clinical Nutrition, 30,* 721–725.

Garner, D. M., Garfinkel, P. E., Schwartz, D., & Thompson, M. (1980). Cultural expectations of thinness in women. *Psychological Reports, 47,* 483–491.

Goldblatt, J. T., Moore, M. E., & Stunkard, A. J. (1965). Social factors in obesity. *Journal of the American Medical Association, 192,* 1039–1044.

Golden, M. P., Saltzer, E. B., Depaul-Snyder, S., & Reiff, M. I. (1983). Obesity and socioeconomic class in children and their mothers. *Journal of Developmental and Behavioral Pediatrics, 4,* 113–118.

Grunberg, N. E. (1982). Obesity: etiology, hazards, and treatment. In R. Gatchel, A. Baum, & J. E. Singer (Eds.). *Handbook of Psychology and Health, Vol. I, Clinical Psychology and Behavioral Medicine: Overlapping Disciplines.* Hillsdale: NJ: Laurence Erlbaum.

Hazuda, H. P., Haffner, S. M., Stern, M. P., & Eifler, C. W. (1988). Effects of acculturation and socioeconomic status on obesity and diabetes in Mexican-Americans—The San Antonio Heart Study. *American Journal Epidemiology,* 128(6):1289–1301.

Huenemann, R. L., et al. (1966). A longitudinal study of gross body composition and body conformations and their association with food and activity in a teenage population: View of teenage subjects on body conformation, food, and activity. *American Journal of Clinical Nutrition, 18,* 325–338.

Huenemann, R. L. (1974). Environmental factors associated with pre-school obesity. *International Journal of the American Dietetic Association, 64,* 480–487.

Hytten, F. E. (1981). Weight gain and pregnancy—30 years of research. *South Africa Mediese Tydskrif,* 15–19.

Jeffery, R. W. (1987). Behavioral Treatment of Obesity. *Annals of Behavioral Medicine, 9,* 20–24.

Kittler, P. G. & Sucher, K. (1989). *Food and Culture in America: A Nutrition Handbook.* New York: Van Nostrand Reinhold.

Kumanyka, S. K., Savage, D. D., & Beu, D., et al. (1985). Awareness of risk factors for coronary heart disease and high blood pressure in a random sample of urban Black and Hispanic adults: Findings of a March 1985 telephone survey in Chicago, IL., *Urban Health, 14,* 11–14.

Massara, E. B. (1980). Obesity and cultural weight valuations: A Puerto Rican case. *Appetite, 1,* 291–298.

Mintz, L. B., & Betz, N. E. (1986). Sex differences in the nature, realism, and correlates of body image. *Sex Roles, 15,* 185–195.

Naeye, R. L. (1979). Weight gain and the outcome of pregnancy. *American Journal of Obstetrics and Gynecology, 135,* 5–9.

National Center for Health Statistics. (1987). *Anthropometric Reference Data and Prevalence of Over-weight, United States, 1976–80* (Vital and Health Statistics, Series 11, No. 238) (DHHS Pub. No. (PHS) 87-1688). Washington, D.C.: U.S. Government Printing Office.

National Institutes of Health. (1985). *Health Consequences of Obesity,* Conference proceedings, NIH.

Nevo, S. (1985). Bulimic symptoms—prevalence and ethnic differences among college women. *International Journal of Eating Disorders,* 4(2): 151–168.

Newcombe, R. G. (1982). Development of obesity in parous women. *Journal of Epidemiology & Community Medicine, 36,* 306–309.

Niswander, E. L. & Gordon, J. J. (1972). *The Women and their Pregnancies.* Philadelphia: W. B. Saunders.

Polivy, J., & Herman, C. P. (1987). Diagnosis and treatment of normal eating. *Journal of Consulting and Clinical Psychology, 55,* 635–644.

Powers, P. S. (1980). *Obesity, the Regulation of Weight.* Baltimore, MD: Williams and Wilkins.

Rimm, A. A., & White, P. L. (1980). Obesity: Its risks and hazards. In A. G. Bray, (Ed.). *Obesity in America,* USDHEW (PHS) NIH.

Rodin, J., Silberstein, L., & Striegel-Moore, R. (1985). Women and weight: A normative discontent. In T. B. Sonderegger (Ed.), *Nebraska Symposium on Motivation, Vol. 32.* Psychology and Gender (pp. 267–307). Lincoln: University of Nebraska Press.

Ross, C. E., & Mirowsky, J. (1983). Social epidemiology of overweight: A substantive and methodological investigation. *Journal of Health and Social Behavior, 24,* 288–298.

Ruderman, A. J. (1986). Dietary restraint: A theoretical and empirical review. *Psychological Bulletin, 99,* 247–262.

Simms, M. C., & Malveaux, J. M. (1986). *Slipping through the cracks.* Transaction Books: New Brunswick, N.J.

Silverstein, B., Perdue, L., Peterson, B., & Kelly, E. (1986). The role of the mass-media in promoting a thin standard of bodily attractiveness for women. *Sex Roles,* 14(9–10): 519–532.

Smith, E. M. (1985). Ethnic minorities: Life stress, social support, and mental issues. *Counseling Psychologist, 13,* 537–579.

Sobal, J. & Stunkard, A. J. (1989). Socioeconomic status and obesity: A review of the literature. *Psychological Bulletin, 105,* 260–275.

Stephenson, M. G., Levy, A. S., Sass, N. L., & McGarvey, W. E. (1987). 1985 NHIS findings: Nutrition knowledge and baseline data for the weight-loss objectives. *Public Health Reports, 102,* 61–67.

Stern, M. P., Pugh, J. A., Gaskill, S. P., & Hazuda, H. P. (1982). Knowledge, attitudes, and behavior related to obesity and dieting in Mexican Americans and Anglos: The San Antonio heart study. *American Journal of Epidemiology, 115,* 917–927.

Striegel-Moore, R. H., Silberstein, L. R., & Rodin, J. (1986). Toward an understanding of risk factors for bulimia. *American Psychologist, 41,* 246–263.

Stunkard, A. J. (Ed.). (1980). *Obesity.* Philadelphia: W. B. Saunders.

Stunkard, A. J. (1980). The social environment and the control of obesity. In A. Stunkard (Ed.). *Obesity* (pp. 438–462). Philadelphia, PA: W. B. Saunders Company.

Stunkard, A. J., d'Aquili, E., Fox, S., & Filion, R. D. L. (1972). Influence of social class on obesity and thinness in children. *Journal of the American Medical Association, 221,* 579–584.

Vomoto, J. M. (1986). Examination of psychological distress in ethnic minorities from a learned helplessness framework. *Professional Psychology Research and Practice, 17,* 448–453.

Woods, D. L., Dewar, R., Malan, A. F., Heese, H. V., & Rush, R. W. (1980). Maternal post-delivery weight in the assessment of obesity. *South African Mediese Tydskrif,* 500–501.

Woody, E. Z., & Constanzo, P. R. (1984). Parental perspectives on obesity in children: the importance of sex differences. *Journal of Social Clinical Psychology,* 2(4): 305–313.

Woody, B., & Malson, M. (1984). In crises: Low-income Black employed women in the U.S. workplace (working paper #131). Wellesley, MA: Wellesley College Center for Research on Women.

Questions for Thought

1. Compare the rates of being overweight for White, Black, and Latina women.

2. How does social class affect women's weight? Discuss several reasons for the association between social class/income and being overweight.

3. Discuss at least three ways in which cultural factors or the process of acculturation may influence women's weight.

4. Discuss the meaning of being "overweight" versus "underweight." How might medical experts create an objective standard of healthy versus unhealthy weight? How do cultures define who is too heavy versus too thin?

5. Consider the images of overweight people on TV or in the movies. Try to identify at least two men and two women who are overweight. Describe their age, ethnicity, and social class. How would you characterize their personalities and social lives?

Gender and Health on the Kibbutz

Ofra Anson

Arieh Levenson

Dan Y. Bonneh

*In the United States, there are consistent sex differences in health and longevity. On aver-
age, American women live seven years longer than men, a substantial difference in mortality. Yet women have greater morbidity than men, meaning that they suffer from more
chronic and acute illnesses and health problems. Further, American women use health services more often than men and are more likely to restrict their activities for health reasons.
A common explanation for these differences is that they result from traditional gender roles
and social attitudes about the sexes. To test this explanation, Anson and her colleagues
studied women and men who live in communal agricultural settlements (kibbutzim) in
Israel. Kibbutz culture encourages an ideology of gender equality, and women participate
fully in the labor force. Do these relatively egalitarian social conditions reduce gender differences in health? As predicted, women and men on the kibbutz were similar in health
and exhibited similar illness behavior. This finding suggests that cultural attitudes may
be an important source of male-female differences in health and illness.*

Gender differences in health status and illness behavior have been explained in
terms of sex roles and gender-related personality traits. It may be hypothesized
that in a community that is committed to gender-negating ideology, where men
and women alike participate in public life, and housework and child care are largely
collectivized, gender health differences will disappear. The kibbutz movement is
committed to the ideology of the emancipation of women: women fully participate
in the labor force and decision making. Nonetheless, women on the kibbutz are

Adapted from *Sex Roles*, 1990, 22, 213–233. Copyright 1990 by Plenum Publishing Corporation. Used
by permission.

responsible for the housework and are concentrated in feminine occupations. The kibbutz, then, allows us to test the relationship between gender ideology and participation in public life vs. gender roles and tasks, and health. The health behavior, health status, and illness behavior of 230 members of two kibbutzim, one religious and one secular, were studied. Men and women report similar health status and illness behavior; parental status is not related to health; and marital status is related to psychological distress only. Similar patterns were observed for the secular kibbutz and the religious one despite the more traditional division of labor in the latter.

Sex differences in health status and illness behavior have been well documented (Nathanson, 1975, 1977; Waldron, 1982, 1983; Wingrad, 1984; Verbrugge, 1985, 1986a). Except for fatal chronic conditions, the rates of acute and chronic health problems are higher at all ages among women than among men (Verbrugge, 1985). Women are also more frequently involved in all types of illness behavior, such as days of restricted activity and bed disability days, and use health services and medications more often than men (Caffereta, Kasper, & Bernstein, 1983; Rossiter, 1983; Meininger, 1986).

The attempt to understand the sex differences in mortality, morbidity, and illness behavior has yielded several explanations (Waldron, 1976, 1983; Nathanson, 1975, 1977; for a detailed summary see Verbrugge, 1985; Veevers & Gee, 1986). All but one of these (biogenetic predispositions) refer to women's social roles and socially attributed personality traits as the source of sex differences in morbidity and mortality. Thus, their excess morbidity and illness behavior have been explained in terms of the psychological and infectious risks that women are exposed to as housekeepers and caretakers. It has been suggested that women's responsibility for reproduction and the health of their family increases their sensitivity to an awareness of bodily and physical symptoms. It has also been argued that women's personality traits (such as being legitimately weak, dependent, and in need of help) are compatible with the sick role, and that the higher morbidity rates reported by women are a product of differential interviewing behavior, in which women tend to recall and report symptoms and disease more readily. The male/female differences in morbidity have thus been attributed, in part, to a differential socialization process, with its obverse in women's greater longevity. By this argument, men tend to die younger because of a male role that encourages them to take on "risky" behavior, in contrast to a female role in which women take on health-maintaining and -promoting behavior.

Through each of these hypotheses, sex differences in mortality, morbidity, and illness behavior illustrate gender, rather than sex, differences. They offer an explanation in terms of psychological, social, and cultural frame concepts, rather than sheer biological predispositions. The major purpose of this paper is to study gender differences in health behavior, health status, and illness behavior of kibbutz (communal agricultural settlement) members, who are ideologically committed to the emancipation of the woman, and thus negate gender differences (Antonovsky & Antonovsky, 1974; Tiger & Shepher, 1975).

The ideology of gender emancipation combined with the ideology of the commune has indeed led the founders of the kibbutz to establish a structural organization that enables women to be liberated from some gender tasks and roles carried by women in industrial societies. Some of these were preserved, and survived the changes undergone by the kibbutz during the last four decades (Talmon-Garber, 1970; Tiger & Shepher, 1975; Spiro, 1983). First, all the major housework tasks are collectivized. There is hardly any shopping for food, meals are served collectively, dishes are washed and clothes are laundered on a collective basis. Furthermore, many of these tasks are performed by men and women alike on a rotating basis. Nowadays, some families tend to perform some of these, such as the evening meal, on a household basis, but the collective option still exists and is normative (Ben-Rafael, 1983).

Second, health services are equally accessible to both men and women, provided by the collective. Third, the social status of men and women alike is independent of their marital, legal, and economic status. This is not to say that marriage and parenthood are not important in the kibbutz. On the contrary, the family has become dominant in the kibbutz social life (Cohen, 1983), as indicated by the high birth rates of the kibbutz movement (*Statistical Abstract,* 1988), and by the increased investment in children (Shepher & Tiger, 1983). Nonetheless, the formal responsibility for health and child care remains in the hands of the collective, and the rates of single (both never- and formerly-married) parents on the kibbutz is somewhat higher than in the towns (Shepher & Tiger, 1983).

Fourth, all men and women on the kibbutz work, and are economically committed to and dependent on the collective but not on their partners (Leviatan & Cohen, 1985). Thus, not only are there no housewives, but there are no socially defined principal or secondary breadwinners. Finally, men and women alike participate in the public life and in decision making. Major decisions are taken in the General Assembly of the kibbutz, which is open to all members, and men and women serve equally on specialized standing and ad hoc committees.

At the same time, social stratification exists on the kibbutz (Ben-Rafael, 1983), and some gender differences, comparable to those found in industrial societies (Chafetz-Saltman, 1988), persist. Similar to the traditional division of labor, the women on the kibbutz maintain primary responsibility for household tasks, minimal as they are. Moreover, the accelerating importance of the nuclear family has led most kibbutzim to move to family living arrangements, although children still spend the entire day in nurseries. The new living arrangements, in turn, have increased the volume of traditional feminine tasks: there is more child care and housework to be done, and more involvement in children's education and health care.

Furthermore, the routinization processes of Israeli society and the kibbutz movement, and the transition from the revolutionary stage to normalization, have led to occupational gender segregation. Women's work is largely the extension of familial roles, and women are concentrated in female traditional jobs, such as education and services (Talmon-Garber, 1970). Similarly, men are clustered in traditional breadwinning jobs, such as agriculture and industry (Tiger & Shepher, 1975).

These characteristics of the kibbutz lead to contradictory hypotheses. Some properties of the kibbutz, in particular the ideology of gender equality and the ideological commitment to the emancipation of the woman, led us to hypothesize that women's health behavior, health status, and illness behavior will be similar to that of men. Ideologies, according to Durkheim (1895), are "social fact(s)" which "constitute a reality in their own right . . . ," although "None of these can be found entirely reproduced in the applications made of them by individuals, since they can exist even without being actually applied" (p. 7). This ideological commitment, moreover, expresses itself in women's full participation in the labor force and in public life. The beneficial effect of employment on women's physical and mental health and illness behavior has been consistently documented (Gove & Geerken, 1977; Waldron, 1980; Anson & Anson, 1987). Sharing social responsibilities and political decision making should further reduce gender health differences. On a practical plane, the sharing of child care, and the community-organized professional health care, even under familial living arrangements, should decrease health care risks (Bernard, 1976; Hare-Mustin, 1987); and the intensive formal and informal networks of social support, combined with the formal irrelevance of marriage and motherhood for women's social and economic status, all lead to the hypothesis that marital and parental statuses will not affect the health of kibbutz members in the way they do in other industrial societies (Gove & Geerken, 1977; Verbrugge, 1979, 1986b; Anson, 1989).

This line of argument, then, leads us to predict that gender, marital, and parental status will not be related to the health behavior, health status, and the illness behavior of kibbutz members. No less cogently, however, we may hypothesize that gender health differences on the kibbutz will resemble those found in industrial societies. There is a wide gap between the ideology of equality and its application; and in particular, women on the kibbutz are responsible for the housework, and are concentrated in housework-like occupations similar to those of women in urban industrial societies. In Merton's (1957) terms, the clash between the ideology of equal participation in public life on one hand, and the reality of daily life on the other, may be described as anomie. Anomie, "an acute disjunction between the cultural norms and goals and the socially structured capacities of members of the group to act in accord with them . . . ," "'exerts pressure' for deviant behavior . . . " (pp. 162, 176), and as Parsons argued (1960, 1964a,b, 1972), social deviance can take on the form of ill-health and illness behavior. Moreover, with the transition to familial living arrangements, women reassume some of the traditional mother's role, and thus the health risks associated with caring for children. Thus, according to this line of argument it might be expected that women on the kibbutz will take on more health-promoting behaviors, will be in poorer health status, and will present more illness behavior than men; the married will be in better health status and will report less illness behavior than the unmarried; and that mothers of preschool children will be in poorer health status and will report more illness behavior.

The purpose of this study is to test these contradictory hypotheses, which are derived from two distinct and contrasting theoretical frameworks (Hilbert, 1989), by studying two kibbutzim, one religious and one secular, which share gender ideology but differ in the discrepancy between ideology and its accomplishment. Similar to the secular kibbutz movements, the Religious Kibbutz Federation is committed to socialist collectivity, to communal life of cooperation and equality (Fishman, 1983). Its founders have challenged the insensitivity of Orthodox Jewry to the needs of a modern community life, and aimed at integrating national and socialist orientations with religious laws. Moreover, the ideological commitment of the Religious Kibbutz Federation to socialist collectivity stems from its religious interpretation: communality and quality are conceived as the realization of the intended organization of economic and interpersonal relationship. Yet although the Religious Kibbutz Federation is committed to gender equality and has adopted the organizational structure of the nonreligious kibbutz movement, its commitment to religion has led to a more traditional gender relationship and division of labor than in the secular kibbutz. The religious kibbutzim have higher fertility rates, which escalate not only feminine tasks, but also occupational segregation (Adar & Louis, 1988). If we consider the active participation of women in key roles in the kibbutz on the national level, we find that the average number of women holding such roles in the Religious Kibbutz Federation is much lower (10.1 per kibbutz) than in the nonreligious kibbutzim (18.9 per kibbutz) (Adar & Louis, 1988). The differences are even sharper when we look at the type of key roles held by these active women. In the Religious Kibbutz Federation only 8.1% of the active women hold important executive positions, such as general secretary, treasurer, and management of the productive sectors, compared with 20.4% in the secular kibbutzim. Similarly, almost half (42.3%) of the women in key roles in the religious kibbutzim are in services, compared with less than a quarter (22.3%) of the women in key roles in the secular kibbutzim. Thus, looking at both types of kibbutzim is fruitful to test the role of ideology vs. the role of daily reality in explaining gender health differences: the two kibbutzim share egalitarian gender ideology, but the discrepancy between ideology and its accomplishment is sharper in the religious kibbutz. Based on Merton's conceptualization of anomie (1957) and the effect of gender roles and tasks in men/women health differences, gender differences in health behavior, health status, and illness behavior should be more obvious in the religious kibbutz.

Yet previous research lends some support to the hypotheses based on the Durkheimian thought. A study of gender differences in mortality among kibbutz members (Leviatan & Cohen, 1985) has shown that the gap between the life expectancy of men and women is smaller among kibbutz members than the gap found in 73 developed countries. They conclude that kibbutz men are the "bigger winners" (Leviatan & Cohen, 1985, p. 549), relieved from the stressors shared by breadwinners elsewhere in the industrial world. Nonetheless, as mentioned, male/female mortality differences are also explained largely by gender, rather than sex, differences (Waldron, 1976, 1988; Veevers & Gee, 1986). Are women, the unmarried, and parents on the kibbutz "winners" too? If they are, it may be hypothesized that

I. there will be no differences in the health behavior, health status, and the illness behavior of men and women on the kibbutz;

II. marital status will not be related to the health behavior, health status, and the illness behavior of kibbutz members; and

III. parental status will not be related to the health behavior, health status, and the illness behavior of men and women on a kibbutz.

Method

The Settings

Two kibbutzim located in the same region in Israel and similar in their sociodemographic characteristics were chosen for the present study. Three criteria were used in choosing the kibbutzim: geographical proximity, to control for ecological variation; similar size (the religious kibbutz has 370 members aged 21+, and the secular kibbutz has 430 members of the same age); and well-established kibbutzim to avoid differences that might reflect the enthusiasm on one hand and the social disorganization on the other, peculiar to new communities (the religious kibbutz was established in 1947 and the secular kibbutz in 1946).

The Sample

Structured questionnaires were distributed to randomly selected samples of adults (members aged 21 years or older) in the two kibbutzim. The questionnaires were anonymously returned to a designated mailbox. A sample of 300 kibbutz members was chosen from the kibbutzim. Of these, 230 full questionnaires were returned, by 111 men and 119 women (77% response rate). The response rate in the secular kibbutz was higher than that of the religious kibbutz (83% and 75%, respectively) as a result of a better follow-up procedure in the secular kibbutz. In both kibbutzim the questionnaires were distributed by a physician member of the kibbutz, but while in the secular kibbutz members (not sample in particular) were reminded, on several public occasions, to return the questionnaires, no such procedure was taken in the religious kibbutz.

There are almost no significant differences in the demographic characteristics of the two samples (Table 1). Although the respondents of the religious kibbutz are slightly older, and more men than women volunteered to fill the questionnaire than in the secular kibbutz, the differences are not statistically significant. Moreover, both samples represent the age and sex distributions of their respective kibbutzim.

A similar proportion of the respondents in the two kibbutzim was born in Israel and on a kibbutz. Respondents from the religious kibbutz who are not native born immigrated to Israel significantly earlier than respondents from the secular kibbutz. Similarly, religious kibbutz respondents not born on a kibbutz have been significantly longer on the kibbutz. Nonetheless, the mean years since immigration and the mean years on the kibbutz indicate that respondents of both kibbutzim have spent most of their lives in Israel, and on the kibbutz.

As might be expected, significantly more of the adult members of the religious kibbutz are married and have significantly more children. The mean number of youngsters (under the age of 6), however, is similar in the two kibbutzim.

Health Measures

Health Behavior   The Breslow Health Behavior Scale was used to assess health behavior. All seven items, which cover daily health practices such as diet, sleep, smok-

Table 1 ▓ **Sociodemographic Background—The Two Samples**

	Secular kibbutz (n = 125)	Religious kibbutz (n = 105)	p
Age			
Sample (mean)	42.9 (13.1)	46.2 (14.2)	ns
Population (mean)[a]	41.5 (13.8)	42.6 (15.1)	ns
Sex			
Sample (% male)	43.2	54.3	ns
Population (% male)	48.4	48.5	ns
Place of birth[b]			
Israel (%)	70.5	65.4	
Europe-America	22.1	32.7	
Asia-Africa	7.4	1.9	ns
Born on a kibbutz (%)	27.0	30.0	ns
Years since immigration[c] (mean)	35.3 (12.1)	48.5 (18.1)	.05
Years on the kibbutz[d] (mean)	29.5 (15.6)	37.1 (22.1)	.05
Familial status[b]			
Married (%)	75.2	88.6	.01
Number of children (mean)	2.7 (1.3)	3.8 (1.7)	.001
Children under 6 (mean)	0.6 (0.9)	0.7 (1.1)	ns

[a] Obtained from the secretarial of each kibbutz.
[b] Standard deviations are given in parenthesis.
[c] For respondents not born in Israel.
[d] For respondents not born on a kibbutz.

ing, and exercise, were included in the questionnaire. These practices have been shown to predict longevity (Belloc & Breslow, 1972; Belloc, 1973; Berkman & Breslow, 1983) and seem appropriate for assessing health promoting behavior. Scores from 0 to 7 were assigned, using the number of health practices reported.

Health Status   One measure of mental well-being and four measures of physical health were used. Psychological well-being was measured by the Scale of Psychological Distress (SPD; Ben-Sira, 1982), a six-item scale in which the respondent is asked to report the frequency of psychophysiological symptoms. The possible range of scores is from 6 (*most distressed person*) to 24 (*least distressed*).

Physical Health   Physical Health was measured by the following:

- subjective evaluation of health—the subjects were asked to evaluate their own health on a 5 point scale, from (5) *excellent* to (1) *poor;*

- reported frequency of having any of 14 symptoms, adapted for the present study from the much more elaborate Quality of Well-Being Scale (Bush, 1984), during the previous month, the possible range being 14 (*often experienced all symptoms*) to 56 (*did not experience any of the symptoms during the past month*);

- reported disability—the respondents were asked the extent to which their health limits their daily activity (1) *very much* to (4) *not at all;* and

- reported number of chronic conditions.

Illness Behavior   Three measures of illness behavior were used:

- The reported number of restricted activity days during the year before the interview;

- the number of doctor visits during the past month and the past year; and

- the reported number of medications taken regularly.

In analyzing illness behavior, health status (particularly the number of chronic conditions) will be controlled for.

Mode of Analysis

To test the hypotheses presented, multiple regression analyses were performed. The dependent variables were health behavior, each of the five health status measures, and each of the four illness behaviors. In each analysis, variables relevant to health behavior, health status, and illness behavior were controlled for. Thus, age and kibbutz type (1 = religious, 0 = secular) were entered into all the equations. Kibbutz type was controlled for for three reasons. First, religious rules regulate health-related behavior, such as diet, fertility, smoking, and the consumption of alcohol (Troyer, 1988); second, in numerous studies, religiosity was found associated with health status and well-being (Witter et al., 1985; Levin & Schiller, 1987; Levin & Vanderpool, 1987); finally, to control for norms of illness behavior that might be kibbutz specific. The number of chronic conditions, which by definition increase the utilization of health services, medication, and days of restricted activity, were controlled for in the analysis of illness behavior.

The hypothesis regarding gender differences was tested in two steps. First, gender and the control variables were entered into the equations. Then, to explore the possibility that in the more traditionally oriented kibbutz gender health differences will resemble the patterns of the larger society, an interaction term (Sex·Kibbutz), designed to examine the health of women in the religious kibbutz, was entered into the equation.

The same procedure was followed to test the hypotheses about marital and parental status on the kibbutz. First, marital status (1 = married, 0 = unmarried) and parenthood (the number of children and the number of preschool children) were entered into the equations, together with the control variables and gender. Then the interaction between gender (women) and each of these were added.

The distribution of two of the health measures, the number of chronic conditions, and the number of medications regularly taken, was skewed. For these two variables, logistic regression, following the same procedure, was calculated.

Findings

Bivariate analysis (Pearson correlation) between the dependent variables and the independent and control variables was performed on the total sample and for each kibbutz separately (Table 2). This analysis shows first, that gender, marital status, and the number of children are not *systematically* associated with health behavior, health status, and illness behavior. That is, while sex is significantly and positively associated with self-rated health and less disability, it is almost as strongly but negatively associated with psychological distress, and not associated with the other two health status measures. Marital status is positively associated with two of the health status measures, but not with any of the other three, and the association between marital status and illness behavior is inconsistent.

Second, the bivariate analysis clearly shows that when a significant association between a dependent and an independent variable is observed, there is also a significant association between that particular dependent variable and at least one of the control variables. Women rate their own health better than men, and are less disabled by their health, yet both are significantly correlated with age, which is also correlated with sex ($r = -.12$, $p < .05$). The married score better on psychological distress, symptoms experiences, and use fewer medications, yet these could be an artifact of the kibbutz type and of age, both of which are significantly correlated with marital status. The number of preschool children, which is strongly associated with age ($r = -.48$, $p < .001$), is the only independent variable consistently related to better health status and less illness behavior. Finally, looking at the same correlation matrix for each kibbutz, we find a few inconsistencies, but no *systematic* differences between the two kibbutzim.

In general, the bivariate and the multivariate analyses support the first hypothesis. Kibbutz women benefit from the egalitarian gender ideology, and from playing their part in the labor force and in the social and political activity of the kibbutz. These seem to affect women's health much more than the actual tasks associated with gender division of labor. Thus, on none of the nine health status and illness behavior measures did women's scores differ significantly from the men's scores. When the interaction between gender and type of kibbutz is considered, to study the additional effect of being a woman in a traditionally oriented kibbutz, neither the male–female difference nor the interaction term are statistically significant.

Kibbutz type significantly predicts health behavior, three of the health status measures, and days of restricted activity. These findings are in line with the literature that focuses on religion and health (Witter et al., 1985; Levin & Schiller, 1987; Levin & Vanderpool, 1987; Troyer, 1988). Nonetheless, no gender differences in health status and illness behavior were detected when each kibbutz was analyzed separately.

Table 2   ▪   Bivariate Analysis of the Dependent, Independent, and Control Variables (Pearson Correlation Coefficients[a])

The whole sample (N = 230)

	Kibbutz (religious)	Age	Sex (women)	Married	No. of children	Pre-school
Health behavior	.30[d]	.08	.09	.08	.10	.08
Psychological distress	.12[b]	.01	−.10	.18[c]	.03	.13[b]
Self-rated health	.13[b]	−.26[d]	.12[b]	−.00	−.07	.13[b]
Symptoms	.23[d]	−.14[b]	−.01	.14[b]	.06	.22[d]
Disability	.03	−.43[d]	.14[b]	.04	−.12[b]	.30[d]
Chronic conditions	.09	.32[d]	.02	.08	−.05	.11[b]
Restricted activity days	−.26[d]	−.03	.01	.05	.00	.00
Doctor visits (last month)	−.08	.20[d]	−.03	.10	−.01	−.12[b]
Doctor visits (last year)	−.10	.17[c]	−.02	.02	.00	−.13[b]
Medications	−.09	.41[d]	.02	−.12[b]	.05	−.12[b]

The secular subsample (N = 125)

	Age	Sex (women)	Married	No. of children	Pre-school
Health behavior	.13	.19[b]	.12	.11	.01
Psychological distress	−.05	−.01	.21[c]	.09	.14
Self-rated health	−.24[c]	.13	.06	.14	.05
Symptoms	−.24[c]	.00	.21[c]	.02	.25[c]
Disability	−.38[d]	.07	.04	.13	.23[c]
Chronic conditions	−.36[d]	−.04	.07	−.08	.08
Restricted activity days	−.02	−.01	.06	.03	.00
Doctor visits (last month)	.24[c]	.02	−.14	−.05	−.09
Doctor visits (last year)	.22[c]	−.02	.01	.02	−.11
Medications	.47[d]	−.01	−.08	.10	−.01

The health behavior of men and women differs significantly, however, and women score significantly higher on the Breslow Health Behavior Scale. This finding could be interpreted in terms of traditional gender roles (Verbrugge, 1985; Waldron, 1988), but could also be spurious. First, in both bivariate and multivariate analyses, gender differences in health behavior were observed for the secular kibbutz only, where the sample included more women. Second, this is the only variable for which gender differences are observed.

The multivariate analysis supports the hypothesis regarding marital status (Hypothesis II). Married members of the kibbutz do not differ significantly from the

Table 2 ■ (*Continued*)

The religious subsample (N = 105)

	Age	Sex (women)	Married	No. of children	Pre-school
Health behavior	−.04	.06	.12	−.10	.11
Psychological distress	.01	−.08	.19[b]	−.10	.10
Self-rated health	−.33[d]	.15	.05	−.11	.20[b]
Symptoms	−.09[d]	.04	.07	−.05	.14
Disability	−.50[d]	.21[b]	−.04	−.15	.35[d]
Chronic conditions	−.34[d]	.06	−.06	−.12	.14
Restricted activity days	.03	−.04	−.19[b]	.20[b]	.04
Doctor visits (last month)	.19[b]	−.15	−.01	.12	−.18[b]
Doctor visits (last year)	.13	−.05	.02	.07	−.15
Medications	.37[d]	.04	.14	.08	−.27[b]

[a] For health measures, a high score indicates more health behavior, better health status, and more illness behavior.
[b] $p < .05$.
[c] $p < .01$.
[d] $p < .001$.

unmarried members on health behavior, illness behavior, and for the most part, on health status. Only on the Scale of Psychological Distress do unmarried members of the kibbutz score more poorly. Unlike the health behavior of women, this single finding does not seem spurious: it is consistently observed in both bi- and multivariate analyses, and in each kibbutz. In none of the analyses were the two-way interactions between gender, kibbutz type, and marital status statistically significant, and these were therefore omitted from the final analyses. With two exceptions (symptoms experienced in the secular kibbutz and the number of restricted activity days in the religious one), these findings persisted when the two kibbutzim were analyzed separately.

The effect of the number of children and the number of preschool children on the health behavior, health status, and the illness behavior of kibbutz members is not clear-cut. In general, the data support the hypothesis that predicted that parental status will not be related to health behavior, health status, and illness behavior of kibbutz members. The number of children is not associated significantly with any of the 11 measures. The interaction between gender and the number of children, designed to detect the excess health consequences that parenthood might have on mothers, was also not related to any of the health behavior, health status, or the illness behaviors studied (and was omitted from the analyses).

The pattern found for the effect of preschool children on the health status of their parents is inconsistent, but it generally supports the hypothesis. Parents of preschool children do report significantly fewer symptoms, but also more chronic conditions; when each kibbutz was analyzed separately these significant associations disappeared; and interaction between gender and the number of preschool children was, again, not statistically significant (and therefore omitted).

Summary and Discussion

The consistent finding that men are healthier than women, although women enjoy greater longevity, is often explained in terms of differential gender roles and traits. The kibbutz, which is ideologically committed to socialist collectivity and the emancipation of the woman, where women fully participate in public life, and where health and child care are a communal responsibility, gives us the opportunity to test this line of explanation. In this paper, gender differences in the health behavior, health status, and the illness behavior of 230 kibbutz members were studied.

The negation of gender on the ideological level and the full participation of women in public life in the kibbutz led us to expect no gender differences in health behavior, health status, and illness behavior. Other ideological characteristics, such as the formal irrelevance of marital and parental statuses to one's social status on the kibbutz, led us to expect that familial status will not be related to the health behavior, health status, and the illness behavior of men and women on the kibbutz.

However, the incomplete application of values in everyday reality led to the opposite hypotheses. The pattern of household division of labor, and the concentration of women on the kibbutz in service occupations, resemble the housework division of labor and the occupational segregation of women in industrial societies. Thus, it might be expected that gender differences in health behavior, health status, and illness behavior on the kibbutz will also resemble those found in other Western cultures.

To test these hypotheses, data were collected from two kibbutzim, similar in their ecology and sociodemography, but belonging to two different kibbutz movements. One is a secular kibbutz, the other is religious, and although equally committed to socialist collectivity and gender equality, represents a more traditional perspective and gender division of labor, and a larger discrepancy between gender ideology and its application. A sample of 111 men and 119 women kibbutz members volunteered to answer a self-administered anonymous questionnaire, which was used in this analysis.

The data in general support the hypotheses that predicted that gender, marital, and parental statuses will not affect the health behavior, health status, and the illness behavior of kibbutz members. In our study, the well-documented positive association between marital status and health is apparent only with regard to psychological distress. Parental status (measured by the number of children) is not related to the health behavior, health status, or the illness behavior of kibbutz members, and the effect for preschool children on the health of their parents is not clear-cut. Parents of preschool children experience fewer symptoms but they also report significantly more chronic conditions. This inconsistency, however, is not unique to our study, and has been reported in previous studies (Welch & Booth, 1977; Arber, Gilbert, & Dale, 1985; Muller, 1986).

Yet the purpose of our study was to focus on gender differences. Our findings clearly indicate that women and men on the kibbutz are in similar health status and manifest similar illness behavior. Men and women do not differ significantly on any of the five health status measures studied, or on any of the four illness behavior indices used. Moreover, where marital and parental statuses did affect health status, men and women alike were affected: in none of the analyses did the interaction between gender and these statuses reach the level of statistical significance.

Nonetheless, women score significantly better on the Breslow Health Behavior Scale. It is to be noted that gender differences in health behavior cannot be explained by gender occupational segregation, which concentrates women in the center of the kibbutz and thus provides women with more opportunities for regular meals, rest, and exercise. Men and women alike work regular hours, regular meals are collectively prepared and sent out to the periphery for field workers.

In sum, the ideological commitment to the emancipation of the woman and women's participation in public life cancels out gender health status and illness behavior differences. Our findings, combined with those reported by Leviatan and Cohen (1985), support the suggestion that male/female morbidity and mortality differences reflect gender rather than sex differences. Men on the kibbutz, although largely assigned to breadwinning occupations, are relieved from their traditional gender roles, the responsibility to provide for their dependents being one example. As a result their life expectancy becomes more similar to that of women than the life expectancy of men in other developed countries. Women, although concentrated in traditional female occupations and responsible for housework and child care, limited as they are, fully participate in the labor force and in the communal decision-making process. As a result their health status and illness behavior are similar to that of men. Our findings are also consistent with two of Durkheim's major contributions (1895, 1897): almost a century ago he observed that the origin of women's (health) disadvantage is rooted in their insufficient participation in social, public life, and that "social facts," such as a gender-negating ideology, do have an impact even when not fully applied in daily reality. Thus, although the religious kibbutz has been less successful in applying the gender equality ideology, women still benefit from taking part in public life, and their health status and illness behavior are similar to those of men.

References

Adar, G., & Louis, H. (1988). *(Women) Members in the Kibbutz* (Hebrew). Efal: Yad-Tabenkin, Israel.

Anson, O. (1989). Marital status and women's health revisited: The importance of a proximate adult. *Journal of Marriage and the Family, 51*, 185–194.

Anson, O., & Anson, J. (1987). Women's health and labor force status: An inquiry using a multipoint measure of labor force status. *Social Science & Medicine, 25*, 57–63.

Antonovsky, H. F., & Antonovsky, A. (1974). Commitment in an Israeli kibbutz. *Human Relations, 27*, 303–319.

Arber, S., Gilbert, G. L., & Dale, A. (1985). Paid employment and women's health: A benefit or a source of role strain? *Sociology of Health & Illness, 7*, 375–400.

Belloc, N. B. (1973). Relationship of health practices and mortality. *Preventive Medicine, 2*, 67–81.

Belloc, N. B., & Breslow, L. (1972). The relation of physical health status and health practice. *Preventive Medicine, 1,* 409–421.

Ben-Sira, Z. (1982). The Scale of Psychological Distress (SPD). *Research Communications in Psychology, Psychiatry and Behavior, 7,* 329–346.

Ben-Rafael, E. (1983). Dynamics of social stratification in kibbutzim. In E. Krausz (Ed.), *The sociology of the kibbutz.* New Brunswick, NJ: Transaction Books.

Berkman, L. F., & Breslow, L. (1983). *Health and ways of living: The Alameda county study.* New York: Oxford.

Bernard, J. (1976). The mother role. In J. Freeman (Ed.), *Women: A feminist perspective.* Palo Alto, CA: Mayfield Publishing Company.

Bush, J. W. (1984). General health policy model: The Quality of Well-Being (QWB) Scale. In N. K. Wenger, M. E. Matson, C. O. Furberg, & J. Elinson (Eds.), *Assessment of quality of life.* New York: LeJacq.

Caffereta, G. L., Kasper, J. A., & Bernstein, A. (1983). Family roles, structure, and stressors in relation to sex differences in obtaining psychotropic drugs. *Journal of Health and Social Behavior, 24,* 132–143.

Chafetz-Saltman, J. (1988). The gender division of labor and the reproduction of female disadvantage. *Journal of Family Issues, 9,* 108–131.

Cohen, E. (1983). The structural transformation of the kibbutz. In E. Krausz (Ed.), *The sociology of the kibbutz.* New Brunswick, NJ: Transaction Books.

Durkheim, E. (1895). *The rules of sociological method.* New York: Free Press.

Durkheim, E. (1897). *Suicide.* London: Routledge & Kegan Paul.

Fishman, A. (1983). The religious kibbutz: Religion, nationalism, and socialism in communal framework. In E. Krausz (Ed.), *The sociology of the kibbutz.* New Brunswick, NJ: Transaction Books.

Gove, W. R., & Geerken, M. R. (1977). The effect of children and employment on the mental health of men and women. *Social Forces, 56,* 66–76.

Hare-Mustin, R. T. (1987). The problem of gender in family therapy theory. *Family Process, 26,* 15–27.

Hilbert, R. A. (1989). Durkheim and Merton on anomie: An unexplored contrast and its derivatives. *Social Problems, 36,* 242–249.

Leviatan, U., & Cohen, J. (1985). Gender differences in life expectancy among kibbutz members. *Social Science & Medicine, 21,* 545–551.

Levin, J. S., & Schiller, P. L. (1987). Is there a religious factor in health? *Journal of Religion and Health, 26,* 9–36.

Levin, J. S., & Vanderpool, H. Y. (1987). Is frequent religious attendance really conducive to better health: Toward an epidemiology of religion. *Social Science & Medicine, 24,* 589–600.

Meininger, J. C. (1986). Sex differences in factors associated with use of medical care and alternative illness behaviors. *Social Science & Medicine, 22,* 285–292.

Merton, R. K. (1957). *Social theory and social structure.* Glencoe, IL: Free Press, chaps. 4 and 5.

Muller, C. (1986). Health and health care of employed women and homemakers: Family factors. *Women & Health, 11,* 47–54.

Nathanson, C. A. (1975). Illness and the feminine role: A theoretical review. *Social Science & Medicine, 9,* 57–62.

Nathanson, C. A. (1977). Sex, illness, and medical care: A review of data, theory, and method. *Social Science & Medicine, 11,* 13–25.

Parsons, T. (1960). *Structure and process in modern societies.* New York: Free Press.

Parsons, T. (1964a). *Social structure and personality.* London: Free Press, chap. 12.

Parsons, T. (1964b). *The social system.* New York: Free Press.

Parsons, T. (1972). Definitions of health illness in the light of American values and social structure. In E. G. Jaco (Ed.), *Patients, physicians and illness.* New York: Free Press.

Rossiter, L. F. (1983). Prescribed medicines: Findings from the National Care Expenditure Survey. *American Journal of Public Health, 73,* 1312–1315.

Shepher, J., & Tiger, L. (1983). Kibbutz and parental investment. In E. Krausz (Ed.), *The sociology of the kibbutz.* New Brunswick, NJ: Transaction Books.

Spiro, M. E. (1983). Introduction: Thirty years of kibbutz research. In E. Krausz (Ed.), *The sociology of the kibbutz*. New Brunswick, NJ: Transaction Books.

Statistical Abstract of Israel (1988). No. 39, Central Bureau of Statistics.

Talmon-Garber, Y. (1970). *The kibbutz: Sociological studies*. Jerusalem: The Magnes Press.

Tiger, L., & Shepher, J. (1975). *Women in the kibbutz*. New York: Harcourt Brace Jovanovich.

Troyer, H. (1988). Review of cancer among 4 religious sects: Evidence that life-styles are distinctive sets of risk factors. *Social Science & Medicine, 26,* 1007–1017.

Veevers, J. E., & Gee, E. M. (1986). Playing it safe: Accident mortality and gender roles. *Sociological Focus, 19,* 349–359.

Verbrugge, L. M. (1979). Marital status and health. *Journal of Marriage and the Family, 41,* 267–285.

Verbrugge, L. M. (1985). Gender and health: An update of hypotheses and evidence. *Journal of Health and Social Behavior, 26,* 156–182.

Verbrugge, L. M. (1986a). From sneezes to adieux: Stages of health for American men and women. *Social Science & Medicine, 22,* 1195–1212.

Verbrugge, L. M. (1986b). Role burdens and physical health of women and men. *Women & Health, 11,* 47–77.

Waldron, I. (1976). Why do women live longer than men? *Social Science & Medicine, 10,* 349–362.

Waldron, I. (1980). Employment and women's health: An analysis of causal relationship. *International Journal of Health Services, 10,* 435–454.

Waldron, I. (1982). An analysis of causes of sex differences in mortality and morbidity. In W. R. Gove & G. R. Carpenter (Eds.), *The fundamental connection between nature and nurture*. Lexington Books, Washington, D.C.

Waldron, I. (1983). Sex differences in illness incidence, prognosis, and mortality: Issues and evidence. *Social Science & Medicine, 17,* 1107–1123.

Waldron, I. (1988). Gender and health related behavior. In D. S. Gochman (Ed.), *Health Behavior: Emerging research perspectives*. New York: Plenum Press.

Welch, S., & Booth, A. (1977). Employment and health among married women with children. *Sex Roles, 3,* 385–397.

Wingrad, D. L. (1984). The sex differential in morbidity, mortality and life style. In L. Breslow, J. E. Fielding, & L. B. Lave (Eds.), *Annual review of public health* (Vol. 5). Palo Alto, CA.

Witter, R. A., Stock, W. A., Okun, M. A., & Harting, M. J. (1985). Religion and subjective well-being in adulthood: A quantitative synthesis. *Review of Religious Research, 26,* 332–342.

Questions for Thought

1. In what ways may the traditional male role be harmful to American men's health?

2. Anson and her associates identify four features of kibbutz life that liberate women from many of the "feminine" tasks and roles performed by women in industrial societies. Describe these four features.

3. The researchers presented two contradictory hypotheses about whether they would or would not find sex differences in health and illness among kibbutz members. What factors led them to expect sex differences? What factors led them to expect no sex differences?

4. The researchers collected data from people living on two different kibbutzim. Compare and contrast these two kibbutzim. Explain why Anson and her associates selected these two and what they expected to find.

5. Based on this research, what might we predict about the health and illness of American women who are employed full-time versus those who are full-time homemakers? Explain your answer.

6. Although the life of the kibbutz does much to promote gender equality, men are still relatively uninvolved in housework and child care. What do you think are the major barriers to men's equal participation in these traditionally "feminine" aspects of daily life?

Feminist Therapy With Mainland Puerto Rican Women

Lillian Comas-Diaz

Effective psychotherapy must consider not only the personal problems of the individuals seeking help, but also the broader cultural context of their lives. Comas-Diaz discusses key elements of Puerto Rican culture that affect women's experiences and identifies many ways in which feminist therapy can empower women.

This article discusses the use of feminist therapy with mainland Puerto Rican women. Sociocultural factors such as the experience of cross-cultural translocation, the process of transculturation, and the colonial background of Puerto Rico with its deleterious effects are examined. Special emphasis is given to Puerto Rican sex roles, the paradoxical condition of power and powerlessness, and Puertorriqueñas' complex sense of identity. These issues are illustrated with a clinical population, and as such, may represent an extreme position within the range of reactions to these sociocultural variables. Clinical vignettes present the use of feminist therapy with this client population. Feminism—with its emphasis on empowerment, adaptation and flexibility in role relationships, promotion of competence, and commitment to social change—is particularly relevant for Puerto Rican women. However, in order for feminist therapy to be effective with this population, it must be embedded in a sociocultural context.

The integration of feminist principles into theory, practice and ethical standards of traditional psychotherapies offers a potentially relevant approach to addressing the mental health concerns of Hispanic women. Societal developments such as the

Reprinted from *Psychology of Women Quarterly*, 1987, *11*, 461–474. Copyright 1987 by Division 35 of the American Psychological Association, Inc. Used by permission of Cambridge University Press.

U.N. Decade for Women (1976–1985), the international women's movement, and the presence of women in the labor force, have contributed to a growing awareness of the gender roles of men and women in the Third World (Sundal-Hansen, 1985). For instance, there has been an increase in feminist awareness and questioning of traditional gender roles among Latin American women (Costello, 1977). Increasingly, women have been well represented as participants in the struggles of Latin American countries (Miranda-King, 1974; Nieto, 1974). Defined as a set of political and social values that support the equalization of power between the sexes, feminism becomes relevant to all women, although it acquires a different form in the specific Hispanic reality, and it depends on the socioeconomic, political and acculturative/transculturative contexts. This article examines the application of feminist therapy to a specific Hispanic group: mainland Puerto Rican females.

Gender-role issues have received special attention in psychotherapy (Kaplan, 1979). These issues take on added significance in psychotherapy with ethnic minority women, since the interaction of gender and ethnicity can complicate, if not actually hinder, the process and outcome of psychotherapy. In fact, Wilkinson (1980) asserted that the risk of miscommunication is highest when the client is an ethnic minority female and the therapist is an Anglo male. Thus, understanding the ethnicity/gender interaction in psychotherapy with ethnic minorities is crucial. Most research on ethnicity and psychotherapy has not been gender-specific, leading Wilkinson to call for systematic studies that consider the clinical significance of the sex and race/ethnicity of both clients and therapists. Feminist therapy can provide an effective forum for the examination of these issues.

In their examination of the relevance of feminist therapy for Black and Hispanic populations, Mays and Comas-Diaz (in press) stated that the concerns regarding its applicability emerge out of two beliefs held by some feminists: (a) women's oppression is the most fundamental oppression; and (b) sisterhood postulates that a woman has most in common with another woman regardless of ethnic, racial, or socioeconomic group. These beliefs do not sufficiently recognize the central role that ethnicity, culture, race and class play in the lives of ethnic minority group members, and the potential conflict of values feminism might pose for ethnic minority women. Nonetheless, current feminist theorizing does advocate pluralism, integration, and a dialectical relationship between theory and practice. This orientation encourages understanding of the intricate and complex sociocultural realities of ethnic minority populations and the effect of economic, environmental, political, and biological systems in their lives. Clearly, this model increases the relevance of feminist therapy as a treatment modality for Puerto Rican women.

Sociocultural Issues

Sex Roles

Feminism recognizes the process whereby the socialization of women differs from that of men, and that sex-role stereotyping is destructive and oppressive to women. With this premise in mind, let us examine its application to Puerto Rican women.

Within the traditional Puerto Rican culture, sex roles have been rigidly defined and demarcated. Sex roles are encouraged early in the socialization process, when boys and girls are taught two very different codes of behavior. Boys are given greater freedom of movement, are encouraged to be sexually aggressive, and are not expected to share in domestic or household responsibilities. On the other hand, girls are expected to be passive, obedient, and homebound. Furthermore, males are considered strong by nature, not needing the protection required by females, who are perceived as weak by nature and vulnerable to the sexual advances of males (Nieves-Falcón, 1972). This rigid demarcation of sex roles encourages a double moral standard for the sexes and is epitomized in the syndromes of *machismo* and *marianismo*. Literally, the word *machismo* means maleness or virility. Culturally, the code of *machismo* mandates the male as the provider and the one responsible for the welfare and honor of the family. It stipulates that by virtue of gender, males are in a privileged position and are to be treated as authority figures. In its extreme form, *machismo* tends to be manifested in a male's sexual freedom, affective detachment, physical dominance over females, and at times, excessive alcohol consumption (Giraldo, 1972). Although it has been argued that *machismo* is more prevalent among lower socioeconomic classes (Kinzer, 1973), it is nevertheless believed to have influenced behavior in all strata of Latin American society (Giraldo, 1972). An early systematic exploration conducted in Puerto Rico revealed a positive correlation between *machismo* and the double sexual standard (Stycos, 1952). That investigation found that men high in *machismo* placed more importance on fathering a child immediately after marriage, preferred sons over daughters, and participated in extramarital affairs more frequently than men who scored low in *machismo*. It would be interesting to replicate that research in contemporary Puerto Rican society.

The cultural counterpart of *machismo* is *marianismo*. Based on the Catholic worship of Mother Mary, who is both a virgin and a madonna, the concept underlying *marianismo* is that women are spiritually superior to men, and therefore capable of enduring all suffering inflicted by men (Stevens, 1973). Similarly, a martyr complex among traditional Puerto Rican women dictates that the female must accept and adjust to her partner's *macho* behavior. In addition, she is self-sacrificing in favor of the children and family. Puerto Rican society attributes high esteem to motherhood. Traditionally, when Puertorriqueñas have faced a conflict in roles, they have usually opted for their roles as mothers (Christensen, 1975).

On the surface, these traditional sexual codes seem to condone the oppression of one group (female) by another (male), coinciding with the feminist precept that sex-role stereotyping is destructive and oppressive to women. However, the dynamics involved in the male-female relationships are intricate and complex, and power relationships between the sexes are not straightforward. For example, Stevens (1973) asserted that the *marianista* code rewards women who adhere to it. Due to the sacredness of motherhood, women who bear children enjoy a certain degree of power despite the outward submissiveness of their behavior. She further posited that as women grow older, they attain a semi-divine status, in which adult offspring revere them. Frequently adult offspring ally with their mothers' struggles, especially against their fathers. Hence, power is achieved through passivity and conforming to the *marianista* role.

Contemporary Puerto Rican women have begun to explore alternative roles. *Hembrismo,* which literally means femaleness, is one such attempt. The concept of *hembrismo* acknowledges the powerful aspects of women's position in the Puerto Rican culture. *Hembrismo* has historical roots, in that the Taíno Indians, the indigenous Puerto Ricans, were a matriarchal society. Borinquén (Puerto Rico's Indian name) was ruled by the "earth mother," imbuing the female political influence with spiritual power (Fernández-Méndez, 1972). In addition, the advent of Black slavery on the island contributed to a basis for *hembrismo* in that the Black women, doubly oppressed by gender and race, needed to develop strength for survival and flexibility for adaptation. Thus, *hembrismo* connotes strength, perseverance, flexibility, and an ability for survival. Mainland Puerto Rican women may adhere to the *hembrista* norm as a means of preserving their identity and cultural beliefs while simultaneously creating a more flexible role for themselves in American society (Comas-Diaz, in press).

Many Puertorriqueñas are successfully integrating the traditional sex roles with the new emerging ones. They have been described as persevering, achieving, ambitious, and determined (Christensen, 1975). Similarly, mainland Puertorriqueñas have emerged as vibrant, providing emotional and financial support to their families (Sanchez-Korrol, 1980) as well as to their communities. However, why do some Puerto Rican women develop psychological distress while others are able to mobilize resources and adapt to stressful conditions? Garrison (1978) attempted to examine this issue by analyzing social networks and support systems among Puertorriqueñas. She studied functional and dysfunctional migrant Puerto Rican women in reference to their support systems. Her findings indicate that there were seven patterns of social support with associated family and emotional status.

For functional women, the categories were: (a) a network of many relationships of both intimate and non-intimate nature; (b) a network of kin and friends with a focus on several good friends; (c) sectarian with an emphasis on church friends; (d) grouping with non-kin group; and (e) cultic with major relationships with spiritualists/mediums. In contrast, dysfunctional women had (a) one friend only; and (b) no support system.

Thus, functional Puerto Rican females seem to have a support system whereas dysfunctional women have minimal or no support. These social support patterns present a helpful framework for assessing resilience and vulnerability in addition to offering a tool for psychotherapeutic interventions with mainland Puertorriqueñas.

Power and Oppression

Historically, women in most cultures have resorted to healing and magic as a means of empowerment (Bourguignon, 1979). Similarly, the Puerto Rican culture assigns the healing role to women: Most espiritistas are female. Espin's (1984) research on Hispanic female healers in the United States found that the role of healers was associated with power and status. She asserted that Hispanic female healers were transformed, by virtue of their healing powers, from powerless members in the family (due to cultural sex-role expectations) to the most powerful ones. Moreover, these women obtained control over their lives, performing behaviors usually associated with women who espouse feminist values. These behaviors include leaving their family in order to pursue their healing "careers," and consequently achieving social mobility, financial independence, and community prestige. Furthermore, Comas-Diaz (in press) asserted that within Puerto Rican culture, some females may enjoy a culturally powerful albeit passive position, in that the task of communicating with the spirits is still a predominantly female one. Thus, being a medium symbolizes the paradox of being powerful, but in a passive, receptive, mediative mode.

Belief in *espiritismo* can be perceived as a response to political oppression which reinforces an external locus of control characteristic of oppressed people. Wittkover (1970) stated that the spirit possession flourishes among descendants of African slaves who have been subjected to oppression. Due to the colonial relationship between Puerto Rico and the United States, Puerto Ricans have experienced political oppression. As a nation, Puerto Rico has always borne a colonial status, first as a Spanish colony and now as an American territory.

Political oppression has been perceived as a possible causative factor of the so-called *Puerto Rican Syndrome* (Comas-Diaz, 1977). The term was coined by Anglo psychiatrists who observed that Puerto Rican soldiers in military settings behaved in a "peculiar" way when anxious in situations such as combat, handling dangerous weapons, and when criticized by superiors (Ramirez de Arrellano, 1956). The Puerto Rican soldiers exhibited an attack characterized by mutism, hyperventilation, bizarreness, hyperkinesis, uncommunicativeness, and violence (Rothenberg, 1964). Because of these symptoms, the disorder has also been called *ataque, mal de pelea,* or hyperkinetic seizure. The *ataque* has also been observed in non-military settings, among both males and females.

On some occasions, the *ataque* is socially expected and even culturally reinforced. For instance, when a beloved dies, an *ataque* denotes profound sorrow (Fernández-Marina, 1961). In the Pentecostal church ceremony, *ataque* symbolizes the welcoming of the Holy Spirit into the body. Finally, in an *espiritista* session, the *ataque* implies the desired ability to become a medium.

Bird (1982) illustrated how individual self-definition, self-esteem, and dependency have been negatively affected in Puerto Rico by the colonial experience. Within this context, outright rebellion is seen as impractical, which leads to passive aggressiveness. Thus, the so-called Puerto Rican syndrome is a "safe" aggressive reaction within the Puerto Rican society. To illustrate this, Ramirez de Arrellano (1956) conducted an empirical study of the syndrome. This study examined the medical, social and psychological characteristics of persons suffering from the *ataque*. Among other things, the investigation indicated that one of the precipitating events for the disorder was evident in the clients' reply: "I could not stand so much authority." Rothenberg (1964) argued that Puerto Ricans have difficulty dealing with aggressive and angry feelings, which he perceived to be the main cause of the syndrome. These difficulties are connected with childrearing, where inconsistent messages about aggression are given.

Like Anglo women, Puerto Rican females receive multiple cultural messages prohibiting their expression of anger. In the marital relationship, the Puertorriqueña's expected role is to accept any extramarital affair her partner may have in order to preserve his macho role; therefore, she develops a martyr complex that maintains her docile, dependent position. Ramos-McKay and her associates (Ramos-McKay,

Comas-Diaz, & Rivera, in press) suggested that the so-called Puerto Rican syndrome in women is analogous to the symptoms observed in the 19th century American women who experienced hysterical "fits." Smith-Rosenberg (1973) described the role of women of that period as one that lent itself to inconsistency and ambiguity. On one hand, the female was expected to be soft, yielding, and submissive, not allowed to display "masculine" behavior such as aggressiveness, assertiveness, and independence. However, on the other hand, she had to fulfill a strong maternal role in which she had to be self-reliant, protective, and a good manager at home. This contradiction created confusion, frustration, and anger within some women, who found themselves unable to express their anger. Such women "suffered" from the malady of the time—hysteria—which provided a passive, more acceptable way to discharge their aggression. Similarly, Rothenberg (1964) asserted that Puerto Ricans suppress and repress aggressiveness and assertiveness in order to behave according to their cultural values, but at the expense of psychological needs.

Feminist theorizing, which encourages examination of political, economic, and social roles, can be useful in the assessment of Puerto Rican women. Such variables as feelings of inferiority, premature marriages, and early childbearing among Hispanic women have been related to their traditional female roles (Canino, 1982a). Moreover, López-Garrida (1978) described Puerto Rican women's use of manipulation strategies in order to exert power in a culturally acceptable manner. She suggested that these strategies are characteristic of oppressed people of both sexes and ethnicities.

Transculturation

Another process that the feminist therapist needs to understand while working with the Puerto Rican population is transculturation, which is the process whereby a distinct culture emerges from a conflict in opposing cultural values (de Granda, 1968). It differs from acculturation in that a new culture emerges. Although the Puerto Rican diaspora in the United States is an entity unto itself, it maintains close contact with the island Puerto Rican community by migration and reverse migration. The constant flow between the island and the mainland and the reverse migration yield a unique Puerto Rican transculturation involving an adaptive and readaptive process. However, this process can engender a collective identity crisis among Puerto Ricans, manifested in their inability to self-identify as Puerto Ricans, Americans, or Ricans (second and third generation Puerto Ricans on the mainland). For Puertorriqueñas the identity problem is further complicated. Confronted with multifaceted identities comprised of ethnic, gender, and racial aspects which are potentially conflictive, they struggle with culturally imposed behaviors, while attempting to develop alternative ones. As women, they cope with gender discrimination and oppression, and as Puerto Ricans they cope with an ethnic identity crisis. Many Puerto Rican women defend and perpetuate *machismo* as a way of coping with the oppression that ethnic minorities face in the United States. For instance, Steiner (1974) described Puerto Rican women defending machismo as a response to socioeconomic deprivations as well as racism; men take their frustrations out on women because they are oppressed.

The diverse degrees of transculturation exhibited by Puerto Ricans in the United States are related to gender roles. Traditional sex roles are changing among mainland Puerto Ricans. The *machismo/marianismo* codes are not reinforced by the American culture, which itself has been more influenced by the women's movement. As an illustration, Torres-Matrullo (1980) found a significant relationship between level of acculturation, level of education, and family and sex-role attitudes among mainland Puertorriqueñas. Traditional conceptions of womanhood appeared to be changing toward a more egalitarian model due to increased education and exposure to American society, but the sacredness of motherhood remained as a cultural value.

Cultural transition itself often presents Puerto Rican men and women with a sex-role reversal in terms of public interactions. For example, studies of immigrant families reveal that the family member who most often deals with the dominant culture assumes the instrumental role, thus becoming autonomous and more acculturated; while the one who assumes the affective role becomes increasingly isolated (Sluzki, 1979). In many instances, the instrumental role is filled by the male and the affective one by the female. However, among Hispanics, instrumental/affective role taking is not always respectively male/female (Canino, 1982b), as is evident among many Puerto Ricans. The pressures of economic survival in the United States, as well as the types of skills that are in demand, have contributed to the expansion of Puerto Rican women's roles into traditionally male domains. Since it is often easier for low income Puerto Rican females to obtain employment in the United States than it is for males, this expansion may occur at the time when males are unable to fulfill the traditional expectations of the provider role. Male resentment, hostility and rejection may result. According to Rosario (1982), Puertorriqueñas' participation in the work force is perceived as a threat to the male role as provider and to the sacredness of motherhood. She suggested that when both partners work, there is a tendency toward more financial independence for women and egalitarianism in the familial decision-making process. As a result, Puerto Rican women may present to therapy their struggles with the consequences of violating traditional sex-role expectations. In this situation, feminism—with its emphasis on the empowerment of women, adaptation and flexibility in role relationships, the promotion of competence and autonomy, and a commitment to social change—provides important analytical tools for interpreting and addressing central therapeutic issues.

In therapy, the degree of transculturation needs to be carefully monitored and intergenerational differences recognized. In addition, regardless of transculturation, gender roles should be assessed and the socioeconomic context considered. For instance, it is common to see a middle-class first-generation Puerto Rican woman professing progressive and even feminist views regarding education and employment of women, while holding traditional values on marital relationships.

Application of Feminist Therapy to Puertorriqueñas

Hispanic populations do not differentiate physical from mental health in the same way as Anglos (Padilla & Ruiz, 1973). This has clear implications for their help-seeking behavior, clinical presentations, and attitudes and expectations of mental health care. For example, some authors have indicated that Hispanic women tend to report somatic complaints as a means of expressing their needs and thereby obtaining support from significant others (Espin, 1985; Hynes & Werbin, 1977).

Successful feminist therapy with Puertorriqueñas needs to integrate a socio-cultural perspective. For example, all-female groups have been used successfully with Hispanic women, due to the cultural tendency to confide personal problems to other women (Hynes & Werbin, 1977). In a similar vein, assertiveness training has been effectively used with Puerto Rican women, when a cultural component has been incorporated into the training in order to culturally "translate" the concept of Puerto Rican women (Comas-Diaz & Duncan, 1985).

As indicated earlier, feminist therapy requires recognition of the cultural context if it is to be successfully applied to Puerto Rican women. The author's conceptualization of feminist therapy is not restricted by any particular theoretical orientation. It is a perspective that integrates feminism into theory, practice and ethical standards of traditional psychotherapies (Douglas & Walker, in press). As an interactive process, feminist therapy allows for the accommodation of the ethno-sociocultural world and inner reality, and their consequent impact on the etiology, presentation, expectations, and approach to the treatment of ethnic minority group members (Mays & Comas-Diaz, in press). As a dialectical process, feminist therapy encourages mutual accountability between theory and practice.

Feminist therapy also entails a commitment to social change. When working with Puerto Rican women, as well as with other ethnic minorities, social change becomes a crucial issue. The translation of feminist theory into attitudes, values, and behaviors, calls for proactive stances. Delivering services to Puerto Rican women requires an understanding of the socio-political forces that shape their lives, and demands an active involvement of these issues in treatment (avoiding the "blaming the victim" attitude). Such a perspective examines the unique experiences of Puerto Rican women, acknowledging the influence that the environment has on them. In sum, feminist therapy is conceptualized as a pluralistic, integrative, and dialectical perspective that has the potential to accommodate the complex, unique, and changing needs of Puerto Rican women.

In the author's clinical experience, using feminist therapy with Puerto Rican women results in a greater awareness and understanding of the oppressive effects of traditional sex roles and of ethnic minority group membership while functioning within the Anglo society. This approach also helps in the adaptation to cultural change, and offers a more functional coping style. Women become more aware of their oppressive situations and are able to make informed decisions. For instance, regarding their expression of needs and feelings, Puertorriqueñas become more culturally congruent by being more assertive and less covertly manipulative and dysfunctional.

In general, the use of feminist therapy can empower Puerto Rican women. Mays and Comas-Diaz (in press) described the concept of empowerment for ethnic minority women within the feminist psychotherapeutic context as helping them to: (a) acknowledge the deleterious effects of sexism and racism, (b) deal with feelings of anger and self-degradation imposed by their status of ethnic minorities, (c) perceive themselves as causal agents in achieving solutions to their problems, (d) understand the interplay between the external environment and their inner reality, and (e) perceive opportunities to change the responses from the wider society. In addition, feminist therapy can empower Puerto Rican women to: (a) cope with cultural change and shape the transculturation process, and (b) integrate ethnic, gender, and racial components into their identity.

Case Vignettes

Following are two case vignettes in which the author utilized a feminist perspective with Puertorriqueñas with varying degrees of success. Clients' identifying data have been altered to preserve confidentiality.

Olga, a 28-year-old first generation Puertorriqueña, attended therapy after being referred by her son's school social worker. She complained of headaches, sleeping and eating disturbances, "nerves," and *coraje* (anger). At the time of referral, Olga was working in a governmental agency as a case manager. The client was living with her 34-year-old boyfriend and her eight-year-old son (from a previous marriage). The assessment revealed that Olga's depressive picture began the previous month when a junior Anglo female co-worker was promoted instead of her. Olga, a non-White Puertorriqueña, complained that she was not promoted due to racial reasons. Further exploration revealed that the client was experiencing a role conflict in that she wanted to return to school, but feared that this action would impede her parenting. Olga had no previous history of mental health problems. A psychiatric consultation showed no underlying physical component to Olga's complaints.

Relaxation techniques were utilized for alleviating Olga's headaches. This intervention was successful and cemented the therapeutic alliance. A feminist orientation was used in interpreting the client's problems. A discussion of racism within the mainstream society helped Olga to stop personalizing what she labelled "her failure at work." Assertiveness training was also used to help her properly express her needs and rights in the employment setting. In order to address the client's role conflict, the therapist utilized the feminist premise that oppression can result from stereotyped sex roles. She openly discussed with Olga the oppressive effects of traditional Puerto Rican sex-role socialization. Olga's situation was presented as an illustration. At this point, she was able to intellectually understand her situation, but affectively she was still experiencing role conflict.

Olga's major problem was her belief that returning to school was equated with being a "bad mother." Cognitive restructuring within a feminist framework was used to address this issue. Olga was made aware of the relationship between taking care of her own needs (in this case, returning to school) and being able to better take care of her son later. The client was very receptive to this approach and began to discuss her relationship with her lover Carlos, who she believed would be unsupportive of her decision to return to school. Carlos, also a first generation Puerto Rican, was invited to attend couples' sessions. It was clear that Carlos was not opposed to Olga's returning to school, and instead, was invested in examining his changing role within the relationship. A feminist perspective encouraging more flexibility in gender roles was utilized to help them deal with Carlos' changing role within the relationship. With the aid of therapy, Olga was able to reassess her own expectations as well as those of her partner. Through a decision analysis emphasizing the feminist premise of power-balanced relationships, Olga was able to work through her role inconsistencies and develop plans to attend college. Therapy was terminated when Olga's presenting complaints disappeared. A three month follow-up session indicated that Olga had enrolled in college on a part-time basis and was not experiencing dysfunction problems.

The use of feminist therapy was successful partly because Olga's support system was available to her during her role conflict examination. She was able to make choices that were meaningful for her and did not disrupt her support system. The following vignette presents a case where the supportive network was not available, and indeed, was threatened by the client's potential assertion of choices.

Hilda, a 30-year-old, second generation Puertorriqueña, was referred to therapy by her internist. She expressed somatic concerns (backaches and dizzy spells) without an underlying physical cause. Hilda, a successful professional woman, appeared to have balanced a career and family. She was married to a first generation Puerto Rican professional man and had two daughters aged 3 and 5.

During evaluation, Hilda presented herself as a well educated, bright woman. She stated that her problems stemmed from her marital relationship. Exploration revealed that she identified her marital problem as wanting to have a son because her husband was tired of being a *chancletero* (a man who only fathers females; *chancleta* is a slipper, something without value). Although Hilda was able to verbalize that she did not particularly care about the sex of her offspring, she stated that she needed to have a son or she would "be considered a failure."

Feminist orientation was utilized in helping Hilda assess her dilemma. Therapy was used as a forum for examining Hilda's conflicted female identity: successful as a career woman, and failure as a wife. Her husband Miguel agreed to attend therapy. At that time, Miguel indicated that he wanted to have another child, and that although he "preferred a son, it really did not matter." His mixed message was pointed out, but he persisted in his position, refusing to accept the therapeutic confrontation. A couples' session revealed that Miguel had begun to exert pressure about having a son soon after Hilda was promoted at work to a supervisory position. Furthermore, it was revealed that Miguel was threatened by Hilda's career success and was "asserting" his role as husband in order to regain power over the relationship. Given the expression of this dynamic, he refused to continue attending therapy, but "gave his permission for Hilda's continued attendance."

Hilda attended therapy on an individual basis and during this period admitted that she did not want another child. She stated that having another child would negatively affect her work performance and hinder her opportunity for future promotions. Hilda further explored the effect of her success on her marital power balance. She identified this problem as "the marital Catch-22" or her conflict of being successful in her career while exhibiting a traditional response to her husband's *macho* demands. She complained of being alone in her predicament because her family (especially her mother) believed that she should have a son. Hilda was very afraid of upsetting her mother because she suffered from *ataques,* particularly when she was confronted by a "strong emotion." She feared that talking with her about her dilemma would precipitate her mother to have an *ataque.* The client also expressed conflict within her multiple roles: daughter, wife, mother, and professional woman. Hilda suddenly stopped treatment when she became pregnant.

Feminist therapy had a limited success in Hilda's treatment. Her consciousness was raised *vis-à-vis* the detrimental effects of traditional Puerto Rican sex roles. However, treatment was abruptly terminated. As Christensen (1975) indicated, when Puerto Rican women face a conflict in their diverse roles, they usually opt for their roles as mothers. If Hilda had openly refused to have another child, it would have meant her questioning the high value that the Puerto Rican culture attributes to motherhood. Furthermore, the therapist failed to properly assess Hilda's support system for changing her role identity as a wife. The strong influence of Hilda's mother including the power of her *ataques,* was not further explored in treatment. Consequently, the mother was not invited to attend therapy. Reaching out to the mother could have potentially helped Hilda to make better use of the mother-daughter bond prevalent among Puerto Ricans. It is believed that having her mother understand the negative effects that Hilda's role conflict was creating for her would have helped the mother to re-examine her own role as a mother (not as a mother in-law), relieving some of the pressure that Hilda was experiencing. Notwithstanding these limitations, the use of feminist therapy helped Hilda to understand her dilemma better and to examine her options as well as their consequences. In other words, she was empowered to make an informed decision.

Conclusions

Feminist therapy is potentially beneficial to Puerto Rican women. With its precepts of empowering the client, feminist therapy can help Puertorriqueñas to better identify and utilize their resources and support systems that are available within the Puerto Rican culture. As illustrated, the extended family can be a source of both frustration and support. Feminist therapy, with its emphasis on the collective, can help individuals negotiate this complex network. Furthermore, feminist therapy allows Puertorriqueñas to examine their ethnocultural identity in the treatment process. Moreover, the conceptualization of feminist therapy as a dialectical process enables Puertorriqueñas to address the dynamic and evolving process of transculturation and its subsequent impact on identity. Many Puertorriqueñas have a bicultural identity with multiple roles, which at times may be conflictive. Feminist therapy can also help them to negotiate these conflicting demands and achieve meaning through an awareness of increased choices.

References

Bird, H. R. (1982). The cultural dichotomy of colonial people. *Journal of the American Academy of Psychoanalysis, 10,* 195–209.

Bourguignon, E. (1979). *A world of women: Anthropological studies of women in the societies of the world.* New York: Praeger.

Canino, G. (1982a). The Hispanic women: Sociocultural influences on diagnoses and treatment. In

R. Becerra, M. Karno, & J. Escobar (Eds.), *Mental health and Hispanic Americans* (pp. 117–138). New York: Grune & Stratton.

Canino, G. (1982b). Transactional family patterns: A preliminary exploration of Puerto Rican female adolescents. In R. E. Zambrana (Ed.), *Work, family and health: Latina women in transition* (pp. 27–36). New York: Hispanic Research Center, Fordham University.

Christensen, E. (1975, March). The Puerto Rican woman: The challenge of a changing society. *Character Potential*, pp. 89–96.

Comas-Diaz, L. (1977). *Puerto Rican espiritismo: A model of diagnosis and treatment for Puerto Rican communities.* Unpublished manuscript. Psychology Department, University of Massachusetts, Amherst.

Comas-Diaz, L. (in press). Mainland Puerto Rican women: A sociocultural approach. *Journal of Community Psychology.*

Comas-Diaz, L., & Duncan, J. W. (1985). The cultural context: A factor in assertiveness training with mainland Puerto Rican women. *Psychology of Women Quarterly, 9,* 463–475.

Costello, R. (1977). "Chicana liberation" and the Mexican American marriage. *Psychiatric Annals, 7*(12), 52–63.

de Granda, G. (1968). *Transculturación e interferencia lingüística en el Puerto Rico contemporáneo.* (Transculturation and linguistic interference in the contemporary Puerto Rico). Bogotá, Colombia: Ediciones Bogotá.

Douglas, M. A., & Walker, L. (Eds.). (in press). *Feminist psychotherapies: Integration of therapeutic and feminist systems.* New York: Ablex.

Espin, O. M. (1984, August). *Selection of Hispanic female healers in urban U.S. communities.* Paper presented at the American Psychological Association Meeting, Toronto.

Espin, O. M. (1985). Psychotherapy with Hispanic women: Some considerations. In P. Pedersen (Ed.), *Handbook of cross-cultural counseling and therapy* (pp. 165–171). Westport, CT: Greenwood Press.

Fernández-Marina, R. (1961). The Puerto Rican syndrome: Its dynamics and cultural determinants. *Psychiatry, 24,* 79–82.

Fernández-Méndez, E. (1972). *Art and mythology of the Taíno Indians of the Greater West Indies.* San Juan: Ediciones El Cemí.

Garrison, V. (1978). Support systems of schizophrenic and nonschizophrenic Puerto Rican migrant women in New York City. *Schizophrenia Bulletin, 4,* 561–596.

Giraldo, D. (1972). El machismo como fenómeno psicocultural. (Machismo as a psychocultural phenomenon). *Revista Latino-Americana del Psicología, 4,* 295–309.

Hynes, K. & Werbin, J. (1977). Group psychotherapy for Spanish-speaking women. *Psychiatric Annals, 7,* 52–63.

Kaplan, A. G. (1979). Toward an analysis of sex-role related issues in the therapeutic relationship. *Psychiatry, 42,* 112–120.

Kinzer, N. (1973). Women in Latin America: Priests, machos, and babies, or Latin American women and the Manichean heresy. *Journal of Marriage and the Family, 35,* 299–312.

López-Garrida, M. (1978). Estrategias de autoafirmación en mujeres puertorriqueñas (Strategies of self-affirmation among Puerto Rican women). *Revista de Ciencias Sociales, 20,* 259–267.

Mays, V., & Comas-Diaz, L. (in press). Feminist therapy with ethnic minority populations: A closer look at Blacks and Hispanics. In M. A. Douglas & L. E. Walker (Eds.), *Feminist psychotherapies: Integration of therapeutic and feminist systems.* New York: Ablex.

Miranda-King, L. (1974). Puertorriqueñas in the United States: The impact of double discrimination. *Civil Rights Digest, 6*(3), 20–27.

Nieto, C. (1974). Chicanas and the Women's Rights Movement. *Civil Rights Digest, 6*(3), 36–42.

Nieves-Falcón, L. (1972). *Diagnóstico de Puerto Rico* (Puerto Rico's diagnosis). Río Piedras, Puerto Rico: Editorial Edil.

Padilla, A. M., & Ruiz, R. (1973). *Latino mental health: A review of literature.* Rockville, MD: National Institute of Mental Health.

Ramirez de Arrellano, M. (1956). *"Ataques" hyperkinetic type: The so-called Puerto Rican syndrome. Its medical, psychological and social implications.* San Juan: Veterans Administration Report.

Ramos-McKay, J., Comas-Diaz, L., & Rivera, L. (in press). Puerto Ricans. In L. Comas-Diaz & E. E. H. Griffith (Eds.), *Clinical guidelines in cross-cultural mental health.* New York: Wiley.

Rosario, L. (1982). The self-perception of Puerto Rican women toward their societal roles. In R. E. Zambrana (Ed.), *Work, family and health: Latina women in transition* (pp. 11–16). New York: Hispanic Research Center, Fordham University.

Rothenberg, A. (1964). Puerto Rico and aggression. *American Journal of Psychiatry, 120,* 962–970.

Sanchez-Korrol, V. (1980). Survival of Puerto Rican women in New York before World War II. In C. Rodriguez, V. Sanchez-Korrol, & J. Alers (Eds.), *The Puerto Rican struggle: Essays in survival in the U.S.* New York: Puerto Rican Migration Consortium, Inc.

Sluzki, C. E. (1979). Migration and family conflict. *Family Process, 18,* 379–403.

Smith-Rosenberg, C. (1973). The hysterical woman: Sex roles and role conflict in 19th century America. *Journal of Social Research, 3,* 653–678.

Steiner, S. (1974). *The islands: The worlds of the Puerto Ricans.* New York: Harper Calophon Books.

Stevens, E. (1973). Machismo and marianismo. *Transaction–Society, 10*(6), 57–63.

Stycos, M. (1952). Family and fertility in Puerto Rico. *American Sociological Review, 17,* 572–580.

Sundal-Hansen, L. S. (1985). Sex-role issues in counselling women and men. In Pedersen (Ed.), *Handbook of cross-cultural counseling and therapy* (pp. 213–222). Westport, CT: Greenwood Press.

Torres-Matrullo, C. (1976). Acculturation and psychopathology among Puerto Rican women in mainland United States. *American Journal of Orthopsychiatry, 46,* 710–719.

Torres-Matrullo, C. (1980). Acculturation, sex-role values and mental health among Puerto Ricans in mainland United States. In A. M. Padilla (Ed.), *Acculturation: Theory, models and some new findings* (pp. 120–132). Boulder: Westview Press.

Wilkinson, D. Y. (1980). Minority women: Socio-cultural issues. In A. Brodsky & R. Hare-Mustin (Eds.), *Women and psychotherapy* (pp. 285–304). New York: Guilford Press.

Wittkover, E. (1970). Trance and possession states. *International Journal of Social Psychiatry, 16,* 153–190.

Questions for Thought

1. Compare and contrast the concepts of *marianismo* and *hembrista*.

2. Based on this article, describe women's role as healers (*espiritistas*) in Puerto Rican culture.

3. Describe the cultural conflicts that may be experienced by Puerto Rican women who live on the U.S. mainland.

4. According to this article, what are seven ways in which feminist therapy can empower Puerto Rican women? Use the case histories of Olga and Hilda to illustrate some of these points.

5. As noted by Comas-Diaz, the risk of miscommunication and cultural insensitivity may be especially great in therapy when the client is an ethnic minority woman and the therapist is an Anglo man. What are three important lessons that male therapists working with ethnic minority women might learn from this article?

6. If your family recently immigrated to the United States, describe some of the experiences that women and men in your family had in adjusting to this culture.

7. If you are not Puerto Rican, imagine that you need to move to Puerto Rico because of your employment. Discuss three issues that you might face in adjusting to this new culture.

Poor Women in Psychological Research
Shut Up and Shut Out

Pamela Trotman Reid

The ability to engage in constructive self-criticism is a sign of growing maturity. In this article Reid criticizes psychological researchers and feminist scholars for ignoring crucial differences among women and for neglecting the experiences of poor women. In addition to documenting this problem, Reid analyzes the reasons for the exclusion of poor women from psychological research. These include the acceptance of the White middle class as a norm or standard, the tendency for middle-class researchers to study people like themselves, the difficulties encountered in studying low-income populations, and the lack of adequate professional training. Reid emphasizes the importance of understanding the social context of women's lives.

For the most part, theory and empirical study in the psychology of women have failed to recognize many distinctions among women. Indeed, the focus of feminist theory and research has been directed to the explication of women's essential experience of gender, as if this could be separated from the confounds of class and race. This presentation raises the issue of the diversity among poor women, the need to disentangle ethnicity and class, and the limitation of adopting a middle-class White perspective. In addition to racism, other possible causes of exclusion are explored. Silencing of poor women is also discussed in terms of causes and impact on the discipline of psychology. We have not provided sufficient mechanisms to allow diverse groups of women to tell their own stories; instead, we have felt comfortable in making assumptions and drawing parallels that may be inappropriate and incorrect. Suggestions for achieving feminist goals are provided.

The inspiration for my title came from a quote of Simone de Beauvoir in which she described the difficulty women have dealing with the simultaneous limitations and variety of our roles. She said that women were "shut up in our world" (cited in Bernard, 1981, p. 20). She referred to social limitations and exclusions based on gender. I want to extend de Beauvoir's words to women who experience the world of poverty and low economic status. I plan to consider how women with few resources have been poorly served by psychological researchers, including researchers who focus on the psychology of women. My title is intended to convey that low-income women have been silenced through a lack of attention and have been excluded from participation in the process of defining their life experiences by our methodological strategies and our theoretical formulations.

In the psychology of women, we often claim to study women *qua* women. As Elizabeth Spelman (1988) and others have suggested, this claim appears false, or at least misleading. For the most part, theory and empirical study in the psychology of women have failed to recognize many distinctions among women. Indeed, the focus of feminist theory and research has been directed to the explication of women's essential experience of gender, as if this could be separated from the confounds of class and race. The traditional and simplistic notions of our discipline continue to lead us to search for the atoms of experience, although human behavior would be better represented by a more complex model. The persistent belief has been advanced that we can distil segments of personal experience and then add these segments together for an accurate characterization and understanding of reality. The strategy of "add social class and mix" or "add race and mix" has not worked. Thus, we should feel compelled to ask, "What do we need to know, and what should we do, to understand and explain the true diversity of women?"

Purpose of Study

I have chosen to focus on poor women because the work and attitudes toward them may best represent how psychology remains both egocentric and introspective. Too often we have taken the easy road, examining our own middle-class educated thoughts and our own middle-class educated experiences and using them as criteria against which we measure others. Feminist psychology does not differ greatly in this respect from traditional psychology. Indeed, poor women are virtually unnamed in feminist work. In research and practice, poor women are underrepresented as participants for observation and clients for intervention. Even though some of us may have originated in low-income families, these past experiences are now filtered through our current perspectives. I am reminded of how my own experiences and views differ from those of my grandmother, who emigrated as a teenager from Trinidad to work in a New York garment factory shortly before the 1920s.

Just as the perspectives of women of color have been ignored by White American women in the psychological literature (Reid, 1988), so too have the perspectives of poor women been ignored by the middle class. I want to underscore that the omission of these perspectives is not exclusively an oversight of one race or another. I believe that the reduction of poor women's perspectives to a coinciding version of the middle-class view occurs repeatedly, both implicitly and explicitly, in our thinking and writing.

To examine this phenomenon, we should recognize that the majority of professional women, psychologists among them, come from well-educated middle-class homes, from families that, if not exactly middle class in income, are middle class in values, that is, who have placed a high value on education and who subscribe to middle-class beliefs. There was support for this contention in a survey of African-American women and men with doctorates. The African-American women with doctorates came from families that could be described as middle class more frequently than did African-American men with doctorates (Reid & Robinson, 1985).

Certainly not all middle-class female psychologists are removed from close associations with poor women and working-class women; however, many have few daily connections with economically deprived people. Whether or not we have these connections, we can recognize that there have been few discussions within our discipline that offer insight or understanding of lives different from our own. There appears instead an implicit assumption that only quantitative differences separate women's experiences, that is, there is a belief that all women undergo, more or less, the same socialization and oppression. It seems easier for us to accept that poor White women may experience more oppression than do middle-class White women but not that they experience different forms of oppression. Similarly, poor women of color are seen as enduring more racism and sexism but not anything fundamentally different from what middle-class women of color endure. The egocentricity of this belief has allowed us to accept a psychology of women that treats the middle-class experience as totally representative, if not the totality, of women's worlds.

Diversity Among "Poor" Women

If we are to challenge this basic notion, perhaps we need first to examine who are the poor women. Of course, the largest numbers of poor women, men, and children do not live in the United States, but considering the limitations of space and expertise, I will focus on low-income populations in this country. According to the U.S. Bureau of the Census (1991b), in 1990 over 33 million people in the U.S. (more than 15% of the total population) lived below the poverty level. This group included more women and girls than men and boys overall, and at every specific age group.

Smith (1984) explained that the growth of women's poverty in the U.S. was largely because more women than ever before must support themselves through income or welfare, more women are working, fewer women are marrying, and most new jobs offer little opportunity for self-sufficiency or escape from poverty. D'Ercole (1988) concurred in this analysis. Her review of factors that impact the lives of poor women indicated that increased education and labor force participation have not really changed the economic status of women. The earnings of women still fall far below that of men, and the number of women who are considered below the poverty line is increasing. Smith credited (or blamed) the growth of the low-paid service sector, which includes retail work, as the major factor in poverty in the U.S. Also contributing to poverty is the assumption that women are in a position to accept less than full-time work or temporary positions that do not carry health and retirement benefits.

The U.S. Bureau of the Census (1991a) also noted that the strongest predictor of poverty is being a female householder with no spouse. Single-parent female house-holders constituted almost half of all poor households in the U.S. Although poor families with children were only about 20% of all families with children, female-headed families represented more than 50% of this group. In addition to being poor in their own households, women are also poor in male-headed households as wives and daughters. Other poor women live alone.

Poor women are elderly with inadequate medical care and emotional support. Poor women are teenage mothers and high-school dropouts. They are welfare re-cipients and underpaid employees. They are clerical workers, receptionists, sales clerks, waitresses, babysitters, hotel maintenance staff, and domestic workers. Thus, even when women are in the labor market, they earn less than men (Taeuber & Valdisera, 1986).

Increasingly, poor women are among the homeless. They are disproportionately, but not exclusively, ethnic minorities, African Americans, and Latinas. They live in the crowded urban areas of our country such as Baltimore, Chicago, Newark, San Francisco, Seattle, and the nation's capital. They also live in the rural areas of our country such as Hope, AK; Polk County, TN; rural New Mexico and Oklahoma; in the villages of Puerto Rico; and in the remote towns of Alaska. Poor women are im-migrants from China, Ecuador, Guiana, Ghana, Mexico, and Vietnam.

In short, poor women, just as any other group of people, may not be represented in simple terms. They have a diversity of backgrounds. They live different daily exis-tences that depend on their particular family responsibilities, their local region, and the composition and expectations of their communities. Their languages, religious practices, personal beliefs, educational experiences, and aspirations may also vary greatly. From our research, we know little about such women. They do appear to share the distinction of being largely ignored in psychological research. (This exclu-sion may be somewhat greater in psychology than in any other of the social sciences because our discipline demands that we seek universal explanations for individual behavior.)

Although we may look at the government thresholds to provide some indication of who is seriously financially deprived, economic status cannot be accepted as the sole criterion for the classification of working class or poor. Although I refer in part to the economic conditions that limit and define the lives of many women, I am also inferring the state of mind that this condition engenders. Being poor, like being middle class or Black or Jewish and maybe even like being too fat or too short, is more than a quantitative difference. It is a condition that affects how we look at our-selves and how others look at us.

Being poor carries a set of expectations, a way of living, a way of thinking about the world. Instead of merely another variable to be added to or subtracted from our investigations, being poor may set the context for many other dimensions of daily existence. Although little psychological data exist, there are indications that class differences influence aspirations, parenting styles, language, social perception, and many other behaviors.

Poor Women Shut Out

The exclusion of poor women is not limited to the psychology of women or any one subarea of psychology. Mulvey (1988) decried the paucity of diverse populations in community psychology, Spencer (1990) and McLoyd (1990a, 1990b) pointed to the lack of diversity in developmental psychology, and Graham (1992) documented the limited attention to ethnic populations in mainstream psychology journals. Most relevant for us, however, is Laura Brown's (1990) argument that White populations and Eurocentric attitudes are the sole basis of the development of feminist theories and therapies. I must agree that in spite of the prodding of many scholars, empirical and theoretical psychology has remained as insensitive to the complexities of race and social class as any other institution in this society.

Riger (1992) suggested that the bias demonstrated in research on psychology of women results from the lack of attention to social context. Like Brown (1990), she pointed out that although feminists maintain the importance of context, the research and theory demonstrate an ignorance of the variety of contexts that are possible. I find it rather difficult to believe that there really is an ignorance of social context among scholars who so often and so elegantly articulate the perspective of social construction. Indeed, recognition of the importance of context has been a legacy of feminist research dating back to the work of Carolyn Sherif (cited in Frieze, Sales, & Smith, 1991). Yet, Frieze et al. (1991) pointed out that the contexts that have typically been investigated are limited by the convenience of our participant populations. They asserted that we have been particularly constrained when using traditional White college students. Their analysis suggests caution when interpreting results from samples controlled for age, race, class status, and so on. In practice, few investigators appear circumspect in discussing the results of their efforts. Instead, studies project conclusions that encompass all women and men, while the severe limitations of the sample are forgotten.

Is it really "forgetting," as Brown (1990) suggested, that leads us to equate the socialization of a 20-year-old White middle-class Jewish woman with that of a 35-year-old middle-class African-American Southern Baptist woman or that of a 16-year-old Latina who is middle class and Catholic? I cannot easily discard the notion that the framing of questions from the perspective of the dominant group and the perpetual oversight of ethnic and class issues represent anything other than elements of racism and incipient class bias. The suggestion that racism, classism, and ethnic stratification are inherent in the traditional research enterprise has been strongly intimated by Landrine, Klonoff, and Brown-Collins (1992). They described the difficulty of disembedding the culture of the investigator from the entire process of investigating. Furthermore, through an empirical example, they attempted to demonstrate that equivalent behavior does not convey similar meanings when cultural contexts are understood and appropriately considered.

The difficulty of contextual and cultural variability was made most dramatically at the American Psychological Association (APA) convention of 1991 in the speech given by an American Indian woman (the designation she gave herself). Robbie Ferron (1991) stunned our pro-choice feminist sensibilities when she presented a perspective on reproductive problems from a culture that was focused on group survival rather than on individual rights. We were prepared to hear a different version of our same story, not a different story. Her message about the fear of cultural extinction raised issues that members of a majority group need never seriously consider. At the same time, she inadvertently challenged the willingness of feminists to accept legitimate, but contradictory, views. As many have indicated, race and class bias play an important role in the inability to accept divergence from a set world view. However, bias alone is too simplistic to serve as a complete explanation for the apparent unwillingness to change from a unidimensional view in research on women. Other factors must play a role in this process.

If the exclusion or shutting out of poor people in general and poor women in particular in psychological research has resulted from factors other than racism and class bias, central among them must be the widespread acceptance of the White middle class as the norm group for every behavior. Feminists have worked insistently to overturn the use of the male norm. Unfortunately, the acceptance of both race and class standards has remained virtually untouched. As White middle-class men were treated as the standard for people, White middle-class women are now treated as the standard of appropriate female behavior (Brown, 1990; Denny, 1986; Espin, 1991; Lorde, 1984). Women in low socioeconomic groups are often held to middle-class White standards, and feminist research offers little or no recognition of the realities and disparities of their lives.

A library computer search provided a gross assessment of the degree of attention given to women in lower socioeconomic groups. Using the data base for the years 1984–1991, I found that the word "woman" accessed 14,517 abstracts; "poverty" produced 556. The combination of "woman" and "poverty" provided only 86 abstracts. "Woman" and "working class" resulted in 82 citations; "woman" and "low income," 99. This represented little more than 0.5% of the abstracts that contained the word "woman." Considering that a sizable proportion of the abstracts were not empirical and that others offered only demographic information and not psychological analysis, the findings were fairly disappointing. Even more devastating was the combination of "feminist" and "poverty," which produced only seven abstracts, or "feminist" and "working class," which resulted in five.

As a discipline, psychology seems to cast ethnic minorities of both genders and working-class people of all colors into marginal roles. If recent histories of the discipline are used to indicate the place of social status and ethnicity, these issues are low in importance. Two special journal issues are illustrative: the *American Psychologist's* Special Issue on the History of Psychology (Benjamin, 1992) and the 50th anniversary issue of the *Journal of Social Issues* (Levinger, 1986). Neither issue dealt directly with social class, ethnicity, or race.

The Need to Disentangle Ethnicity and Class

The issue of how to deal with ethnicity and class has in recent years had a somewhat superficial solution. Now, more than in the past, researchers are likely to be meticulous in providing demographic information about populations they have studied. However, this effort is not sufficient. Although the race and social class of participants are included as descriptors, they are typically not evaluated as factors that affect the experience of the participants. For example, in research on college students, we see little or no recognition that there is privilege associated with being White, middle class, and well educated. Questions about the impact of race remain reserved for people of color, and queries on social class are saved for working-class and poor people.

There appears to be a type of segregation in the topics selected for feminist research. Brown (1990, p. 7) called it "word ghettos." The manifestation of this grouping is seen in many forums. For example, only middle-class White women are studied when there are issues of body image, eating disorders, professional work issues, and sexual harassment. Middle-class White women are sought for illustrations of theoretical assumptions and for scale or measurement development. And middle-class White women are used for basic studies of developmental, social, and personal functioning. Low-income and working-class women, when investigated, have been isolated from mainstream academic psychology. Research on such real-world groups is typically considered applied, so that there is a stratification or dichotomy of populations, with the higher ones being theoretical research on middle-class populations.

This separation of theoretical middle-class populations from applied lower-income populations is not admitted but is regularly accepted. As feminists, we regularly discuss issues of violence, intimacy, and deprivation, yet apparently we still feel uncomfortable in discussing the stigmatization of racism or the impact of class bias. In the literature on homelessness, for example, there has been obvious resistance to considering racism as a component of the experience of economic deprivation among minority groups (Milburn & D'Ercole, 1991). Study after study has failed to make explicit the recognition that much of the hostility and anger against the homeless and poor in our society is the result of their depiction as ethnic minorities and foreign born (e.g., Bassuk, 1990; Belle, 1990; Masten, 1992). Indeed, few empirical investigations examine these complex phenomena.

Reviews of studies of poor women of color suggest that research may have produced commonly held views that are distortions of reality. For example, many investigations of women of color have focused on their childbearing behavior, often to the exclusion of other life experiences. Amaro (1988) found this to be the case for Mexican-American women. In her interviews with these women, she found greater heterogeneity than previous studies suggested, even among those who were low income and relatively unacculturated. Similarly, Wyatt and Lyons-Rowe's (1990) interviews with low-income African-American women revealed complexities in their sexual attitudes and sexual behavior not suggested in earlier investigations of similar populations.

The insistence that "women" are not only White but middle class has undoubtedly assisted in the creation of a counterimage of poor women. This stereotype, which is depicted nightly by the media, holds that poor women are best represented as African American and Latina. The acceptance of these characteristics are also obvious in the review of studies of teenage and single mothers (Goodman, 1987; Panzarine, 1989; Pillary, 1987), homeless women (Bassuk, 1990), and welfare recipients (Glassman, 1970). In these studies, where women are presented as aberrant, disturbed, abnormal, and needy, minority women are treated as the appropriate norm group.

This skewed image of ethnic minority women is, as most distortions, only a partial misrepresentation. Ethnic minority women are overrepresented among the poor. Almost 80% of all U.S. women are White, 12% Black, and 8% Hispanic (as designated by the government). However, the U.S. Bureau of the Census (1991b) reported that 35% of all Black women are poor (6 million) and 30% of Hispanic women live in poverty (3 million). Only 12% of all White women are poor. However, this 12% represents two thirds of all poor women, that is, 13 million poor women are White (U.S. Bureau of the Census, 1991b). Thus, the images created serve to facilitate the distancing that occurs from women in poverty and to limit the sampling of their experiences to those society has already defined as aberrant.

Feminist psychologists apparently have accepted and reified these media and social stereotypes in our research populations. In feminist books and journal articles, "women" typically refers to middle-class White women, unless otherwise indicated (Reid, 1988). Measure of attitudes toward women and other feminist scales have already been created using middle-class White women as the norm group. Brown (1990), myself (Reid, 1988), and others have cited feminist authors from de Beauvoir to Gilligan who have developed entire arguments without mention of women of color, differences in economic conditions, or the relevance of sexual orientation. Thus, we are left, as Diane Harriford (1991, p. 3) suggested, "to refute the reality created by others."

Causes of Exclusion

Although acceptance of the White middle-class norm is of paramount significance, there are several other factors that also contribute to the exclusion of poor women in psychological research. Some of these factors are strongly influenced by practicality and professional expectations. These factors include personal affiliation, effort maximization, and investigator training.

I have defined *personal affiliation* as a combination of access and interest. Psychologists tend to study people who are close at hand, that is, our children, our friends, our clients, and, most of all, our students. Data indicate that much of the research in psychology of women has been conducted on populations of convenience, that is, those to whom easy access is possible. For many academic researchers, this has meant an unusually strong reliance on students. Confirmation of our dependence on student participants was revealed by the number of *PsycLIT* data base citations that included both "woman" and "students." There were close to 2,500 citations, that is, 17% of all abstracts. The Division 35 journal, *Psychology of Women Quarterly,* has recently responded to this challenge of bias by changing its editorial policy. It will no longer accept college students as representative of all women but will limit articles on students to research about students.

Personal affiliation also leads psychologists to investigate populations that are like them. Male psychologists have been more likely to study men, female psychologists to study women, and ethnic minorities to study ethnic minorities. Contributing to the likelihood that we study people like us may be what Bem and Bem (1970) called a nonconscious ideology. They suggested that it never occurred to men to study women because at some level they already "knew" about women's behavior. There may well be an analogous nonconscious ideology for middle-class feminists who appear to believe that low-income and working-class women are like them or not like them in ways that need not be articulated. Indeed, many White feminists feel that all female experience can be subsumed under a single feminist perspective. Similarly, there are some feminists of color who believe that regardless of social status, the ethnic experience is a unified one. Diane Harriford, an African-American woman who conducted a study of 600 working-class female labor union members, challenged the belief that women's experiences may be reduced to a single dimension (1991). Although she shared "skin color and the experience of racial oppression," "familiarity with the lives of Black women, ability to see and value their standpoint," and "willingness to rearticulate their reality" (p. 10), as a university-educated woman she was not defined by the union women as a member of their group. She did not find an African-American style of knowledge; instead she found that women, regardless of race, who shared the routine of a dreary work-a-day world defined their own group based on a similarity of economic and political realities.

A second factor identified as leading to the exclusion of poor women from research is *effort maximization*. Effort maximization may be defined as a concern for getting the most benefit for your work. Dealing with working-class and poor populations in either research or practice typically means greater effort. Working-class and poor populations may live in different communities, speak a different language, and hold attitudes that make them less willing to cooperate in research. Research may be delayed as investigators attempt to establish rapport and obtain consent. In work with poor and working-class women, not only may different research strategies be necessary, but often new research measures must be developed. Many of the existing measures and assessment techniques have not been normed or used with poor populations of any ethnicity or for any ethnic groups. More time and effort to obtain access makes the research more expensive to conduct and more time consuming to complete. Many psychologists are led to conclude that the cost-benefit ratio for working with poor populations is low.

An additional disincentive is the fact that it is not easy to publish nontraditional research in the traditional psychology journals. Publications in less traditional journals lack the prestige or the benefit to the researcher. Therefore, it appears that the lack of incentives in environments that stress the need to produce inhibits the desire to examine certain populations. This inability to maximize one's benefit for one's effort is both perceived and real and may well be viewed as an impediment to research that addresses issues of diversity.

A third factor that I have identified as a barrier to research on diverse populations is *investigator training*. Along with the overall higher level of difficulty of conducting research among nontraditional populations, most psychologists are not trained to work with diverse populations. The lack of strong data or a well-developed theoretical base makes it difficult for an investigator to prepare herself. The lack of training with and exposure to low-income populations, particularly ethnic populations, also raises legitimate concerns about the researcher's ability to assess behavior and interpret results. As are many of my colleagues, I am concerned about healthcare providers and professors who hold stereotyped, and at times pernicious, views of the clients and students they allegedly serve. Herein lies the circularity and the dilemma: there are few data, curricula, or sources of information with which to prepare psychologists, yet we need majority as well as minority faculty, researchers, and practitioners to concern themselves with poor and ethnically diverse populations.

Although the causes of exclusions are not trivial, none of them are insurmountable barriers to research with low-income women. Yet, barriers do exist, together with what Graham (1992) and Scarr (1988) have referred to as a fear associated with conducting socially sensitive research. The factors of exclusion do impede the progress of our science, the development of theory, and the delivery of appropriate services. Additionally, the impact of the exclusion of a wider variety of women in our research serves to solidify the narrowness of the discipline and to maintain its gatekeeping functions.

Poor Women Shut Up

If a woman cries out in the forest and no one listens, does she make a sound? Women who have had the experience of their words being literally ignored in meetings understand the fleeting bewilderment and remember thinking, "Didn't I just say something?" The experience of being silenced is more than a symbolic gagging; it is also a literal restraint of the ability to voice one's perspective. Lois Gould (1974) presented this dialogue between two women in her book *Final Analysis* (p. 52):

> "Why the hell don't women ever make a scene? Men are always making scenes, yelling in the halls. Why can't you yell in the halls?" "Because," she sighed, "women don't get away with yelling in the halls. They call you a hysterical bitch if you yell in the halls." "Also," Sophy noted wryly, "they fire you. It's their halls."

Being silenced means having no access to dialogue and decision making. It means that others will set policies and define rules. In psychological research, poor women have been shut out and also shut up, that is, effectively silenced. When we accept middle-class standards without evaluating what the implications are, we ignore the experiences of large numbers of women whom we purport to represent. The result is that we begin to believe that poor women need us (psychologists) to define their problems and articulate their needs. Indeed, there is ample evidence that low-income women are aware of the issues and problems they face. They have voices, but if no one listens. . . .

Causes of Silencing

The silencing of poor women in psychological research has resulted in large part from psychology's reliance on *expert testimony,* that is, a reliance on our own interpretations of the experiences of others. We have not provided sufficient mechanisms to allow diverse groups of women to tell their own stories; instead, we have felt comfortable in making assumptions and drawing parallels, which may be inappropriate and incorrect. Even when researchers purport to study working-class women, middle-class values are frequently imposed into the investigation. For example, Luttrell (1989) interviewed 30 African-American and White American working-class women to describe their "ways of knowing." She argued that the knowledge base held by these women was "embedded in community, family, and work relationships and could not be judged by dominant academic standards" (p. 33). Ironically, the women she interviewed were all enrolled in adult basic education classes and sought (in her words) "to change their lives through education" (p. 34). Implicit in her selection of participants, and undoubtedly transparent at some level to them, was the author's agreement and approval of their attempts to further their education. In effect, she selected participants who had adopted her values. In fairness to Luttrell, she acknowledged the danger of interpreting the experiences of those who have different backgrounds, and in her analysis she included selected quotes from the women themselves. Nevertheless, the unavoidable impact of the status differential between her and her participants (she was formerly a teacher in the program) was never addressed.

In addition to the silencing that occurs due to the gatekeeping of expert witnesses, Mulvey (1988) observed an aloofness, which she described as "professionalism." She suggested that the sense of aloofness allows psychologists to maintain a distance from the general population of women. She further contended that the use of global theories (macro level) rather than specific models has encouraged this distancing on the part of both academics and healthcare providers. Gardner, Dean, and McKaig (1989) also identified distancing as a problem. They suggested that the glorification of objective knowledge has led to discounting experiential knowledge. The current movement to increase the acceptability of qualitative data and innovative research is a direct response to this charge. However, the distancing that feminist psychology appears to practice may be more than an attempt to maintain an appropriate stance or the reaction developed through traditional techniques; instead, the distancing may be a form of denial on the part of middle-class women of their elevated and privileged status. Such elevation and privilege is, on the one hand, antithetical to the principles of feminism and is, on the other hand, consistent with being middle class. Middle-class feminists may not want to be reminded of the distinctions that appear to exist among groups of women.

Reviews of research reveal that although a number of investigators have confirmed that distinctions exist between working-class and middle-class women (Ferree, 1984; Luttrell, 1989; Nelson, 1983; Unger, Draper, & Pendergrass, 1986), there are often contradictory findings. Some studies indicate that members of the middle class are less stereotyped; others indicate that it is the lower class who hold more egalitarian views. For example, Romer and Cherry (1980) demonstrated that middle-class children's self-descriptions were more blended across genders than were those of working-class children. However, it has also been suggested that women with lower incomes hold strongly feminist views. For example, Faludi (1991) cited a 1986 Gallup poll that found that significantly more upper-income women than lower-income women disavowed the label "feminist." Anyon (1984) also found that lower-income girls held stronger feminist aspirations. The unexpected direction of some studies reinforces the suggestion that distancing may signal a desire to deny the impact of class and other differences among women.

A second factor contributing to the silencing of low-income women is the establishment of a feminist hierarchy. Silencing of women in society was originally achieved by men. However, so-called "high status" women now appear to participate in the silencing of poor women through the control of what is accepted as feminist knowledge. In an analysis of a psychology of women class, Gardner et al. (1989) found that when differences in knowledge, class, or sexuality arose, a hierarchical mode of conceptualizing and responding to differences typically resulted. They observed that the women who held the identity of feminist for the longest time and those who were most familiar with feminist concepts and assumptions appropriated positions of dominance over those women who were newly considering feminism. Similar contests involving who is more feminist have occurred among psychologists. In part, this competition results because feminists have posed questions of hierarchy almost exclusively in terms of gender. As long as we accept the arrogation that gender is more important than any other status characteristic, we appear to diminish unrealistically the potency of those other characteristics.

Much of the psychological research on women reifies positions of privilege by neglecting to address other life situations or by implicitly suggesting that middle-class values, behavior, and ethics are the standards by which all women should be evaluated. However, analysis of Black and White working-class women strongly challenges claims for a single or universal mode of knowing among women (Luttrell, 1989). When we listen to working-class women, we learn about the complex gender, race, and class relations of power that shape how women think and the paradoxical situations to which they must respond. The privilege of middle-class women appears to render them unaware of this complexity. In Espin's words (1991), they have an "impairment"; she suggested that they cannot see what they cannot see, or to maintain my metaphor, they cannot hear what they cannot hear. For the advancement of our theory and practice, we cannot afford to let an "impairment" force us into a defensive attitude with respect to women from low-income groups. Neither can we abrogate our individual responsibility by failing to correct the existing discrepancy between "what is" and "what should be" in feminist research.

Need to Include Social Class and Ethnicity

Although I often assume that the need for including class and ethnic issues is obvious, on occasion I have encountered colleagues who question this assumption. For some researchers, the training they received represents the way to truth, and that truth does not include references to groups considered outside the traditional spheres of attention. Indeed, one social psychologist explained to me that his attraction was to psychology as a science devoted to seeking and identifying general principles and universal laws. He implied that I was subverting this goal by insisting on addressing specific populations. He did not seem disturbed by a sense of inconsistency. For example, it was acceptable that studies of White middle-class people could represent universals and studies of Asian working-class populations could not. Perhaps the explanation lies in what McPherson (1992) referred to as "the subordination of subject matter to method" (p. 334). He suggested that psychologists appear more concerned with data than with real life.

When we consider real life demographic data, the pressing need for feminist psychology to concern itself with poor and working-class women, men, and children is apparent. Our theories must become more representative of the world around us. Many believe that psychology is in a state of turmoil and transition (Spence, 1987), that we face not only a breakup of discipline loyalty but also an erosion of credibility with the public we purport to serve. Our need to address the diversity of real life comes at a time when people are more aware of what science and healthcare services are supposed to accomplish. People are not afraid to be critical of professionals. The science of psychology has been demystified; the practice of psychology is grist for television comedies.

In these times of reformation, the call for increased diversity is not a new alert for the psychological community. Almost every year, voices are raised to express dismay about the lack of attention to these issues. For example in 1986, Denny warned that we must be aware of the dysfunctional areas in feminist therapy, particularly those that have served to create new biases and stereotypes that continue to exclude some groups. She advised that if "feminist therapy is to serve the lower classes, it must be cognizant of the peculiarities of sex role socializations as they relate to socialization into a socioeconomic class within a stratified social system" (p. 62). Mulvey (1988) claimed that although diversity is valued by the women's movement, we have failed to achieve our goals by focusing too narrowly and maintaining nonrepresentative perspectives. Russo (1990) identified poverty as one of the major areas in need of more research for women. Herek, Kimmel, Amaro, and Melton (1991) discussed bias in research on gay and lesbian populations and called into question the representativeness of samples with respect to age, ethnicity, and social class. It is now time to move beyond the rhetoric to an action agenda.

Strategies to Reach Feminist Goals

I offer suggestions for concrete commitments that we must make for psychology in general and feminist psychology in particular to progress according to our publicly espoused goals and principles. Although there are many needs and many strategies, I propose only two.

The first is directed primarily at the research community. As we recognize that women's economic status is interwoven with factors such as political clout, educational achievement, and occupational roles, we must seek to analyze women in multiple contexts. The contexts that are particularly in need of study include those of poor and working-class women. We must attempt to move our science beyond the realms of convenience. As feminists, we have demanded that investigators eschew studies of males only, except when it is theoretically reasonable; we should similarly refrain from conducting studies that unnecessarily focus on a single social class or on a single race. It is no longer acceptable to offer a weak disclaimer. To tell the consumers of our research that the participants were 95% White or that they were largely from middle-class backgrounds tells them nothing useful.

Our goal must be to conduct research that provides a meaningful analysis of gender as it is experienced in many different contexts. We can no longer pretend that we can ignore context and still understand gender. Given the inattention and dearth of psychological research on working-class women, on poor women, and on ethnic women, we must accept the call to develop a sound data base that can lead us to meaningful theory about the many spheres inhabited by women. The accomplishment of this goal will necessitate collaborative efforts of middle-class psychologists with women from different communities. To gain access, we must share our expertise while learning from those who already are skilled in those communities. (Those skilled may include our students, colleagues, and people outside the psychological community.)

The second goal applies to everyone: researchers, practitioners, professors, consultants. As we recognize the limitations inherent in our own training, in the classes we teach, and in the services we offer, we must make the commitment to expand our own knowledge and then to assist in extending the knowledge of our students and colleagues. At universities, at mental health centers, and in private practices across the country, psychologists should be leading the efforts to address issues of social class and ethnicity. There is an increasing number of workshops, books, and articles that attempt to meet this objective. However, these attempts are inadequate. The need is so great that each one of us must make the commitment to include these issues in every forum, to reach out for assistance to community resources, and to develop a sense of respect for the values of communities and their various perspectives. We should also consider seriously the consequences if we maintain a collective unwillingness to do so.

The poet Audre Lorde (1984), who described herself as a Black lesbian warrior, noted that we cannot create bonds of sisterhood among women by pretending that everyone is alike. Her message is well taken. As feminists, we must admit our differences if we are to respect each other's perspectives. As psychologists, we must create forums to discuss and examine these differences and the relationship they have to the way we construct our world.

References

Amaro, H. (1988). Women in the Mexican-American community: Religion, culture, and reproductive attitudes and experiences. *Journal of Community Psychology, 16,* 6–20.

Anyon, J. (1984). Intersections of gender and class: Accommodation and resistance by working-class and affluent females to contradictory sex role ideologies. *Journal of Education, 166,* 25–48.

Bassuk, E. L. (1990). Who are the homeless families? Characteristics of sheltered mothers and children. *Community Health Journal, 26,* 425–434.

Beal, F. M. (1969). Double jeopardy: To be Black and female. In R. Morgan (Ed.), *Sisterhood is powerful* (pp. 340–353). New York: Random House.

Belle, D. (1990). Poverty and women's mental health. *American Psychologist, 45,* 385–389.

Bem, S. L., & Bem, D. J. (1970). Training the woman to know her place: The power of nonconscious ideology. In D. J. Bem (Ed.), *Beliefs, attitudes, and human affairs.* Belmont, CA: Brooks/Cole.

Benjamin, L. T. (1992). Special issue: The history of American psychology. *American Psychologist, 47,* 109–335.

Bernard, J. (1981). *The female world.* New York: Free Press.

Brown, L. S. (1990). The meaning of a multicultural perspective for theory-building in feminist therapy. *Women and Therapy, 9,* 1–21.

Denny, P. A. (1986). Women and poverty: A challenge to the intellectual and therapeutic integrity of feminist therapy. *Women and Therapy, 5,* 51–63.

D'Ercole, A. (1988). Single mothers: Stress, coping and social support. *Journal of Community Psychology, 16,* 41–54.

Espin, O. M. (1991, August). *Ethnicity, race and class and the future of feminist psychology.* Invited address presented at the ninety-ninth annual convention of the American Psychological Association, San Francisco, CA.

Faludi, S. (1991). *Backlash: The undeclared war against American women.* New York: Crown.

Ferree, M. M. (1984). Class, housework, and happiness: Women's work and life satisfaction. *Sex Roles, 11,* 1057–1074.

Ferron, R. (1991). *Current issues in the lives of American Indian women.* Unpublished manuscript, University of Washington, Seattle.

Frieze, I. H., Sales, E., & Smith, C. (1991). Considering the social context in gender research: The impact of college students' life stage. *Psychology of Women Quarterly, 15,* 371–392.

Gardner, S., Dean, C., & McKaig, D. (1989). Responding to differences in the classroom: The politics of knowledge, class, and sexuality. *Sociology of Education, 62,* 64–74.

Glassman, C. (1970). Women and the welfare system. In R. Morgan (Ed.), *Sisterhood is powerful* (pp. 102–115). New York: Random House.

Goodman, S. H. (1987). Emory University project on children of disturbed parents. *Schizophrenia Bulletin, 13,* 411–423.

Gould, L. (1974). *Final analysis.* New York: Random House.

Graham, S. (1992). "Most of the subjects were White and middle class": Trends in published research on African Americans in selected APA journals, 1970–1989. *American Psychologist, 47,* 629–639.

Harriford, D. (1991). *The occlusion of class in and by Black feminist thought.* Unpublished manuscript, Vassar College, Poughkeepsie, NY.

Herek, G. M., Kimmel, D. C., Amaro, H., & Melton, G. B. (1991). Avoiding heterosexist bias in psychological research. *American Psychologist, 46,* 957–963.

Landrine, H., Klonoff, E. A., & Brown-Collins, A. (1992). Cultural diversity and methodology in feminist psychology: Critique, proposal, empirical example. *Psychology of Women Quarterly, 16,* 145–164.

Levinger, G. (Ed.). (1986). SPSSI at 50: Historical accounts and selected appraisals [Special issue]. *Journal of Social Issues, 42*(4).

Lorde, A. (1984). *Sister outsider.* Trumansburg, NY: Crossing Press.

Luttrell, W. (1989). Working-class women's ways of knowing: Effects of gender, race, and class. *Sociology of Education, 62,* 33–46.

Masten, A. S. (1992). Homeless children in the United States: Mark of a nation at risk. *Current Directions in Psychological Science, 1,* 41–44.

McLoyd, V. C. (1990a). Minority children: Introduction to the special issue. *Child Development, 61,* 267–269.

McLoyd, V. C. (1990b). The impact of economic hardship on Black families and children: Psychosocial distress, parenting and socioemotional development. *Child Development, 61,* 311–346.

McPherson, M. W. (1992). Is psychology the science of behavior? *American Psychologist, 47,* 329–335.

Milburn, N., & D'Ercole, A. (1991). Homeless women: Moving toward a comprehensive model. *American Psychologist, 46,* 1161–1169.

Mulvey, A. (1988). Community psychology and feminism: Tensions and commonalities. *Journal of Community Psychology, 16,* 70–84.

Nelson, M. K. (1983). Working class women, middle class women, and models of childbirth. *Social Problems, 30,* 284–297.

Panzarine, S. (1989). Interpersonal problem solving and its relation to adolescent mothering behaviors. *Journal of Adolescent Research, 4,* 63–74.

Pillary, A. L. (1987). Psychological disturbances in children of single parents. *Psychological Reports, 61,* 803–806.

Reid, P. T. (1988). Racism and sexism: Comparisons and conflicts. In P. A. Katz & D. A. Taylor (Eds.), *Eliminating racism* (pp. 203–221). New York: Plenum.

Reid, P. T., & Robinson, W. L. (1985). Professional Black men and women: Attainment of terminal degrees. *Psychological Reports, 56,* 547–555.

Riger, S. (1992). Epistemological debates, feminist voices: Science, social values, and the study of women. *American Psychologist, 47,* 730–740.

Romer, N., & Cherry, D. (1980). Ethnic and social class differences in children's sex-role concepts. *Sex Roles, 6,* 245–263.

Russo, N. F. (1990). Overview: Forging research priorities for women's mental health. *American Psychologist, 45,* 366–373.

Scarr, S. (1988). Race and gender as psychological variables: Social and ethical issues. *American Psychologist, 43,* 56–59.

Smith, J. (1984). The paradox of women's poverty: Wage-earning women and economic transformation. *Signs, 10,* 291–310.

Spelman, E. V. (1988). *Inessential woman: Problems of exclusion in feminist thought.* Boston, MA: Beacon Press.

Spence, J. T. (1987). Centrifugal versus centripetal tendencies in psychology: Will the center hold? *American Psychologist, 42,* 1052–1054.

Spencer, M. B. (1990). Development of minority children: An introduction. *Child Development, 61,* 267–269.

Taeuber, C. M., & Valdisera, V. (1986). *Women in the American economy* (U.S. Bureau of the Census, Current Population Reports, Series P-23, No. 146). Washington, DC: U.S. Government Printing Office.

Unger, R. K., Draper, R. D., & Pendergrass, M. L. (1986). Personal epistemology and personal experience. *Journal of Social Issues, 42,* 67–79.

U.S. Bureau of the Census. (1991a). *Population profile of the United States: 1991* (Current Population Reports, Series P-23, No. 173). Washington, DC: U.S. Government Printing Office.

U.S. Bureau of the Census. (1991b). *Poverty in the United States: 1990* (Current Population Reports, Series P-60, No. 175). Washington, DC: U.S. Government Printing Office.

Wyatt, G., & Lyons-Rowe, S. (1990). African American women's sexual satisfaction as a dimension of their sex roles. *Sex Roles, 22,* 509–524.

Questions for Thought

1. Reid suggests that researchers often study different topics among White middle-class women versus low-income and working-class women. Summarize the differences she outlines.

2. Reid describes three factors that contribute to the exclusion of poor women from psychological research: personal affiliation, effort maximization, and investigator training. Explain each concept and how it contributes to the exclusion of poor women from psychological research.

3. College students are frequently the participants in psychological research. Discuss three ways in which the experiences of a 21-year-old college student might differ from the experiences of a 21 year old who does not attend college.

4. According to Reid, the stereotype of poor women "which is depicted nightly by the media holds that poor women are best represented as African American and Latina." Do TV news programs typically focus on ethnic minorities when

discussing issues of poverty? Test this idea by watching several newscasts and taking systematic notes on what you observe. Discuss your findings.

5. Reid focuses on the exclusion of poor women from psychological research. It could be argued that the lives of the "rich and famous" are also underrepresented in research. Suggest three reasons why researchers seldom study the upper class. Do you think this is a serious problem for psychology? Why or why not?

6. Reid emphasizes important *differences* among women from different economic and ethnic backgrounds. Other feminists have emphasized the *commonalities* among women's experiences, regardless of social class or ethnicity. Discuss both perspectives. What do you personally conclude?

Race and Class Bias in Qualitative Research on Women

Lynn Weber

Elizabeth Higginbotham

Marianne L. A. Leung

In quantitative research, information about participants is coded into numerical categories that can be analyzed using statistics. In contrast, qualitative methods try to capture the richness of human experience, using more descriptive approaches such as in-depth life history interviews. Some feminist scholars have suggested that qualitative research should be used to overcome the shortcomings of traditional quantitative research. In this study Weber and her colleagues clearly demonstrate that qualitative methods do not provide a panacea, but rather have their own biases and limitations. Based on their experiences recruiting Black and White women for a study of women professionals, the authors conclude that ignoring race and class can lead to false inferences about research findings. The issues raised in this article are not unique to research on women workers, but can readily be applied to qualitative studies of other topics.

Exploratory studies employing volunteer subjects are especially vulnerable to race and class bias. This article illustrates how inattention to race and class as critical dimensions in women's lives can produce biased research samples and lead to false conclusions. It analyzes the race and class background of women who volunteered to participate in an in-depth study of Black and White professional, managerial, and administrative women. Despite a multiplicity of methods used to solicit subjects, White women raised in middle-class families who worked in male-dominated occupations were the most likely to volunteer, and White women were

Adapted from *Gender & Society*, 1988, 2(4), 449–462. Copyright 1988 by Sociologists for Women in Society. Used by permission of Sage Publications.

more than twice as likely to respond to media solicitations or letters. To recruit most Black subjects and address their concerns about participation required more labor-intensive strategies involving personal contact. The article discusses reasons for differential volunteering and ways to integrate race and class into qualitative research on women.

Feminist research has relied heavily on qualitative methodologies (Cook and Fonow 1986; Grant, Ward, and Rong 1987; Roberts 1981; Stacey and Thorne 1985; Ward and Grant 1985). In-depth qualitative studies can reveal much about social processes that women experience, but like all research methods, they have limitations. Prominent among them are the relatively small and homogeneous samples that constitute the subjects of each study. While in-depth analysis of small homogeneous samples is key to discovering the unique quality of subjects' lives, if this approach is used repeatedly on the same population, it can block discovery of the diversity of human experience. Although qualitative research on women has accumulated useful data in many substantive areas, too often the emergent body of knowledge excludes women of color and working-class women (Zinn, Cannon, Higginbotham, and Dill 1986).

Correcting this imbalance in feminist scholarship requires theoretical conceptualizations that include all dimensions of inequality, more complex research designs, and strategies that confront the obstacles to the incorporation of diverse groups of women. This article discusses the obstacles to integrating race and class into qualitative research on women and offers some solutions to the problem. It reports the sampling strategy for an in-depth study of Black and White professional, managerial, and administrative women, and the obstacles to achieving a sample balanced by the race and class background of the subjects and the gender composition of their occupations.

We found that White women working in male-dominated occupations who were raised in middle-class families volunteered more often than any other group. We suggest that this difference is due to the higher concentration of White women of middle-class origins in the population of middle-class women and to fewer obstacles to their participation in research projects. In order to get Black women to participate, we had to use more labor-intensive recruitment strategies, such as verbal contact, usually face-to-face, with Black women researchers or other Black women working with the research team. Interviews also took more time to complete because of interruptions and canceled appointments. When Black women felt assured that the research was worthwhile, they were eager to participate.

This article discusses the sample selection for a study designed to control race and class background. The subjects were women employed full-time as professionals, managers, and administrators; the methodology used in-depth interviews. We report here the problems we faced in subject recruitment and the strategies we used to produce a heterogeneous sample. Our study suggests that researchers who are committed to incorporating subjects of different races and classes in their qualitative research designs must be prepared to allow more time and money for subject recruitment and data collection.

The Study

The study explores the relationship of race, class, and gender inequality to the general well-being and mental health of full-time employed professional, managerial, and administrative women in the United States. Data were collected with face-to-face, focused, life-history interviews, lasting 2 to 3 hours each.

We wanted a sample of 200 Black and White professionals, managers, and administrators from the Memphis, Tennessee, metropolitan area. As is the case with many studies of women, there was no way to randomly sample the specific population of concern. We employed a quota sample structured by three dimensions of inequality: race and class background of the respondent and the gender composition of her occupation. We dichotomized the three dimensions, creating an eight-cell, $2 \times 2 \times 2$ design. Each cell contained 25 cases, a sample size large enough to allow statistical estimates of the relationships of the three major independent variables with other variables in the study.

Study Parameters We restricted the study to women born between 1945 and 1960 who were 25–40 years old at the time of the interview, because their formal education took place at a time when greater funds and opportunities were available for working-class and Black women to attend college. Seeking to examine institutional supports for upward mobility through college attendance (e.g., the role of high school counselors and teachers), we restricted the study to full-time employed college graduates who had gone to college immediately or within two years of finishing high school. Because we wanted to compare Black and White women raised in middle-class and working-class families, we excluded nurses (a popular occupation for mobile working-class women but rarely the choice of women from middle-class families) and physicians (few working-class women can secure funds needed to cover years of medical education). Because many White teachers but few Black teachers in the area are employed in the private sector, we limited the sample of primary and secondary school teachers to those employed in the public schools.

Our interest in investigating how class background manifests itself in the lives of middle-class women required that our sample include women in the full range of middle-class positions (e.g., professionals, managers, and administrators). The sample included women in each of three primary relations of control over the working class: political (supervision), economic (ownership), and ideological (mental labor), in order to shed light on issues such as the nature of social interactions across class lines (Braverman 1974; Ehrenreich and Ehrenreich 1979; Poulantzas 1974; Vanneman and Cannon 1987). The study also examines how women of different races, from different class backgrounds, and with different support networks manage these across-class contacts.

Since professional networks tend to be homogeneous and insular, we set quotas for the proportions of professionals, managers, and administrators, and within each of those broad categories, for specific occupations. To match regional representation, the design called for 60 percent professionals and 40 percent managers and administrators in the male-dominated occupations, and 76 percent professionals and 24 percent managers and administrators in the female-dominated occupations.

Within each gender-composition category, we selected particular occupations for inclusion in the sample, based on their regional proportions among professionals, managers, and administrators.

Finally, subjects were selected to minimize confounding race or class background with their occupations. A growing body of evidence indicates that in addition to gender segregation in the labor force, substantial race segregation occurs as well (National Committee on Pay Equity 1987). Given the structural relations among race, class, and occupation, we could easily draw a sample of upwardly mobile working-class or Black women who are concentrated in the specific occupations that are more open to them (e.g., public school teaching, social work). To avoid the confounding of race, class background, and occupation, we selected subjects so that each race and class-background category contained women from the same or closely related occupations. For example, in the category of male-dominated professionals, the sample includes equal numbers of Black and White lawyers raised in working-class and middle-class families. Subjects were also classified into three age groupings defined by birth cohort (1956–1960, 1951–1955, and 1945–1950) to prevent overrepresentation of any age group in a race, class background, or specific occupational category.

Every few weeks, volunteers who met all study parameters were sorted according to all of the stratifying variables (race, class, gender composition of occupation, professional versus managers and administrators, specific occupation, and age category). We then randomly selected subjects to interview from each pool.

Recruitment of Subjects

Less Labor-Intensive Outreach Strategies

The first subject recruitment strategies we employed were less labor intensive. These strategies, quite common in sociological and psychological research, consisted mainly of letters to organizations and individuals known to fit the study criteria, and announcements in the local media (radio programs, daily newspaper, a business daily magazine, and so on) describing the study and asking for volunteers.

All 46 women's organizations that were listed in the public library's most recent list and were likely to include members eligible for the study received letters. This included both professional organizations such as the American Society of Certified Public Accountants and social organizations such as the National Council of Negro Women. The letters asked that organizations inform their members of the study and offered to send study team members to speak to their groups if they so desired. Individuals interested in participating in the study received a personal letter containing a general description of the study and describing the criteria for inclusion in it (i.e., age 25–40; direct route to college degree; full-time employed professional, manager, or administrator). Regarding the three major independent variables in the study, the letter indicated our interest in studying the life histories of Black and White women in male- and female-dominated occupations. The letter did not mention social class.

Volunteers completed a one-page information form and returned it to the au-

Table 1 ■ **Success of Recruitment by Race and Class Origins**

	Black Participants			White Participants		
Type of Strategy	Working Class 62.7% (N = 84)	Middle Class 37.3% (N = 50)	Total Black 100% (N = 134)	Working Class 32.3% (N = 86)	Middle Class 67.7% (N = 180)	Total White 100% (N = 266)
Less labor intensive						
mass media	6.0 (5)	—	3.7 (5)	27.9 (24)	20.6 (37)	22.9 (61)
occupational mailing lists	14.2 (12)	12.0 (6)	13.4 (18)	23.2 (20)	35.0 (63)	31.2 (83)
other mailings	20.2 (17)	24.0 (12)	21.7 (29)	18.6 (16)	20.6 (37)	20.0 (53)
Subtotal	40.4 (34)	36.0 (18)	38.8 (52)	69.7 (60)	76.1 (137)	74.1 (197)
More labor intensive						
organizational presentations	6.0 (5)	4.0 (2)	5.2 (7)	4.7 (4)	2.2 (4)	3.0 (8)
snowball technique	53.6 (45)	60.0 (30)	56.0 (75)	25.6 (22)	21.6 (39)	22.9 (61)
Subtotal	59.6 (50)	64.0 (32)	61.2 (82)	30.3 (26)	23.8 (43)	25.9 (69)

Note: For each item, the top row of figures represents percentages; the numbers in parentheses indicate the number of participants.

thors' university. Since the women knew the eligibility criteria, the sampling frame included almost all of the volunteers.

Less labor-intensive strategies reached more White than Black subjects. As Table 1 reveals, we recruited 22.9 percent of the Whites but only 3.7 percent of the Blacks through the media (see columns 3 and 6). Letters to occupational groups garnered 31.2 percent of the Whites and 13.4 percent of the Blacks. In all, these strategies reached 74.1 percent of the White but only 38.8 percent of the Black women volunteers.

More Labor-Intensive Outreach Strategies

After tracking the characteristics of the women who responded to letters and media solicitations, we started using more labor-intensive strategies to recruit other categories of women. Those strategies included personal presentations to women's organizations' meetings, snowball techniques of calling individuals to recommend others for the study, and identifying special newsletters to receive advertisements.

Most Black women (61.2 percent) were recruited through labor-intensive strategies such as presentations at meetings and, most often, through word-of-mouth snowball techniques. We recruited over half (56 percent) of the Black volunteers through direct contact by project staff or by other Black women professionals who either participated in the study themselves and recommended other names to their interviewer or worked with the project staff from the beginning of the study to recruit volunteers.

Class Background and Outreach Strategies

Despite a strong race effect, class background did not influence the success of the recruitment strategies (see Table 1, columns 1, 2, 4, and 5). Within each race, every recruitment strategy was about equally likely to reach subjects from working- and middle-class backgrounds. The one exception is the 11.8 percent greater likelihood of reaching White middle-class as opposed to White working-class volunteers through occupational mailing lists. Such a difference may have resulted from greater concentrations of women of middle-class origins in the particular occupations for which we had mailing lists.

Race and Class Background of the Volunteers

After nine months of subject recruitment, 400 women employed as professionals, managers, and administrators had volunteered to participate in the study. Of the total, 134 or 33.5 percent were Black, and 266 or 66.5 percent were White. According to the 1980 census, Black women constituted 25.3 percent of the women employed as professionals, managers, or administrators in the Memphis Standard Metropolitan Statistical Area (U.S. Bureau of the Census 1983). Since Black women's concentration in the middle class had not greatly increased during the period from 1980 to 1985 (Higginbotham 1987), we felt that Black women had volunteered at a rate consistent with—and perhaps slightly higher than—their representation in the population under study. However, we used different recruitment strategies to achieve these roughly equivalent rates of volunteering among Black and White women. Had we not employed different strategies, our sample would have been disproportionately White.

There were 170 volunteers with working-class origins, and 230 with middle-class origins. The class origins of these professional and managerial women differed significantly for Blacks and Whites. Of the 400 volunteers, 180 (45.0 percent) were Whites raised middle class, 86 (21.5 percent) were Whites raised working class, 84 (21.0 percent) were Blacks raised working class, and 50 (12.5 percent) were Blacks raised middle class.

Although our data do not permit a thorough examination of the issue, two factors seem likely to have produced a pool of volunteers that was heavily weighted to White women who had come from and stayed in the middle class, and among Black women, to the upwardly mobile. These factors are the race and class background of the population of middle-class women employed full-time and the structural and social psychological factors restricting Black women's participation in this kind of research.

Population Parameters

Our sample was not random; so we cannot infer directly from these data that two-thirds of the Black middle-class women were upwardly mobile while two-thirds of White middle-class women were born into the middle class. However, these proportions are plausible, since the extent of intraclass mobility from the working class to the professional-managerial class in the United States has never been high (Coleman and Rainwater 1978; Ryan and Sackrey 1984; Vanneman and Cannon 1987).

At first glance, a sample with one-third of its Whites upwardly mobile might seem to overrepresent that group. But the post-World War II era (especially between the late 1950s and the early 1970s) brought the greatest increase in the size of the professional-managerial class (Vanneman and Cannon 1987). In addition, the economic boom of the 1960s and early 1970s, coupled with the breakdown of racial barriers, nearly doubled the size of the Black middle-class population, a larger increase than for Whites (Cannon 1984). Consequently, after World War II and for the first time in American history, the Black class structure began to approximate the White class structure (Vanneman and Cannon 1987; Wilson 1978).

It was the "baby-boom" generation educated in the 1960s and 1970s, who benefited most from post-World War II changes and who are the subjects of our study. They reached college age just as the civil rights movement brought down legal segregation and a strong economy provided the financial support for college attendance among large numbers of Black and working-class youth. Thus we feel confident the proportions of upwardly mobile volunteers in our sample approximate their prevalence in the population.

Obstacles to Participation

Some social psychological and structural factors militated against Black women's participation. These factors were skepticism about the purpose of the research, worries about protection of anonymity, and structural obstacles such as less free time. Dominant-group women have less reason than minority-group women to suspect that they or members of their group will be exploited in research (Zinn 1979). As a result, White women in this study were more than twice as likely to respond to letters or media solicitations, but personal contact was usually required to recruit Black subjects. The contact enabled Black women to gain the assurances they needed that neither they nor others would be exploited by the research process or its products.

We expected that the Black women might also be apprehensive about participating, since the request came from researchers at a predominantly White educational institution. Anticipating many of these concerns, we devised research strategies to minimize their impact. For example, we made explicit in every communication about the study that the coprincipal investigators for the study were a Black and a White woman, that the research team was biracial, and that we sought both Black and White subjects. We also sent Black members of the research team to speak to exclusively Black groups, White members to speak to exclusively White groups, and a biracial team to speak to every group that had both Black and White women. Only Black interviewers interviewed Black subjects, and White interviewers interviewed White subjects.

Despite the above precautions, more Black than White women required additional assurance, especially about guarantees of anonymity. Many Black middle-class subjects were highly visible in the community as, for example, the only or one of a few bank vice presidents, newscasters, university administrators, library branch directors, or judges. White women in similar positions were more numerous, if not in a single firm, at least throughout the city. The Black women were more likely to ask for specific details, for example, about how we would refer to them in any future reports, before they felt comfortable about the protection of their anonymity.

In addition, it became clear that these Black middle-class women had less free time than the White middle-class women to devote to activities like participation in social research. Even though there were no racial differences in marital status in the final sample, 65 percent of the Black women had children, and 65 percent of the White had no children. It was more difficult to schedule and complete interviews with Black volunteers. They had less free time to devote to the project, were often unable to complete the interview in one sitting, and were more likely to cancel scheduled interviews because of unforeseen circumstances. We did not interpret these actions as reflecting resistance to the project or the interview because these women continued to express an interest in participation, and almost all did in fact complete the interview.

Female-Dominated Occupations

Although we cannot be sure of the population distribution across class origins of the middle-class women, census data do indicate the gender-composition of the female middle-class labor force. In the Memphis SMSA, 55 percent of the women professionals, managers, and administrators worked in female-dominated occupations. The volunteers for our study, however, came mainly from male-dominated occupations—57 percent of the Black (N = 76) and 56 percent (N = 148) of the White women volunteers.

Many women in female-dominated occupations also appeared to have less control over their time and less free time. Scheduling and completing interviews with women teachers, for example, was more difficult than with lawyers or administrators who could block out time during the work day while secretaries held their calls. Thus in the cases of both Black women and women in female-dominated occupations, greater persistence was required to recruit subjects, to schedule, and to complete interviews. These structural realities meant that the White interviewers completed their interviews sooner than the Black interviewers. White interviewers were then able to facilitate the work of Black project team members by assisting with transcriptions, coding, and other activities.

Biased Samples—Biased Results

Although we have only begun to analyze the data from the study, we have already identified several areas in which we would have made false inferences had we not attended to the race and class background of the middle-class women. For example, we investigated the level of social supports that women received in making the transition from high school to college (Cannon, Higginbotham, and Leung 1987; Newsome 1986). The working-class women received far less financial support and information from family. Since the typical Black woman volunteer for our study was raised in a working-class family, while the typical White volunteer was raised in a middle-class family, had we not attended to the class background of the women as well as their race, we would have concluded that these Black women had received far less family support than White women. Such a conclusion could easily have fueled a "cultural deficit" interpretation. Had we not interviewed Black women raised in middle-class families and White women from the working-class, we would have neglected a small but theoretically significant segment of professional and managerial women. Failing to recognize their experiences could greatly distort our conclusions about how they had reached their current occupations and class position.

Conclusions

Since qualitative research frequently involves face-to-face contact between researcher and subject, open-ended rather than closed-ended questions, unstructured rather than structured interview schedules, samples are typically small. To generate theory, it is much more useful if the small samples under study are relatively homogeneous, since extreme diversity makes the task of identifying common patterns almost impossible. Unfortunately, as a result, much of the newly emerging scholarship on women excludes women of color and working-class women of all races. For example, in her review of research on women's occupational experiences, Harkess (1985) reports that the most commonly studied group of women workers is still white-collar workers, and that even among them, women working in male-dominated spheres receive the most attention, despite the fact that the majority of women still work in female-dominated occupations (Dill, Cannon, and Vanneman 1987; Reskin 1984).

Feminist research in sociology and psychology is replete with caveats like that reported in a study that samples White undergraduate students at a private university to identify "generational differences in women's attitudes toward the female role in society." The authors, Slevin and Wingrove (1983) state, "Selection of subjects this way avoided the complexities of analysis which would have been introduced by racial and regional differences" (p. 611). Chodorow's (1978) study, *The Reproduction of Mothering,* drew criticism for "trying to explain the perpetuation of a certain kind of mothering—middle class, psychologically oriented, and achievement oriented (husbands and sons toward careers, mothers and daughters toward perfect children)—in short, the hothouse tending of two or three offspring in an isolated nuclear family" (Lorber 1981, p. 485).

For some researchers, issues of race or class never surface until the research is completed. Hertz (1986) stated in her recent book, *More Equal Than Others: Women and Men in Dual-Career Marriages,* "Although this was not a deliberate sampling strategy, all respondents were Caucasian" (p. 217). However, the exclusion of other groups frequently takes place despite feminist researchers' awareness of the importance of the many dimensions of inequality.

In some cases, feminist researchers make politically motivated decisions to exclude particular groups from research. In her powerful study, *Father-Daughter Incest,* Herman (1981) took account of dominant-culture views of minority families and the potential for misuse of results in her decision to exclude minority women:

> All of the informants [40 women] were white. We made the decision to restrict the interviewing to white women in order to avoid even the possibility that the information gathered might be used to fuel idle speculation about racial differences. (p. 68)

While such deliberate exclusion might be protective, the pervasiveness of exclusionary practices produces a cumulative impact on the empirical generalizations that constitute the elements of feminist theory. As a result, the prevailing literature, which seems to identify particular "social realities," merely represents White and middle-class experiences. The social realities of other groups, such as minorities and the working classes, become relegated to side issues in the field (Zinn et al. 1986).

References

Braverman, H. 1974. *Labor and Monopoly Capital.* New York: Monthly Review Press.

Cannon, L. Weber. 1984. "Trends in Class Identification Among Blacks from 1952 to 1978." *Social Science Quarterly* 65:112–26.

————, E. Higginbotham, and M. L. A. Leung. 1987. "Race and Class Bias in Research on Women: A Methodological Note." Working Paper 5. Center for Research on Women, Memphis State University, Memphis, TN.

Chodorow, N. 1978. *The Reproduction of Mothering.* Berkeley: University of California Press.

Coleman, R. P. and L. Rainwater. 1978. *Social Standing in America: New Dimensions of Class.* New York: Basic Books.

Cook, J. A. and M. M. Fonow. 1986. "Knowledge and Women's Interests: Issues of Feminist Epistemology and Methodology in Feminist Sociological Research." *Sociological Inquiry* 56:2–29.

Dill, B. Thornton, L. Weber Cannon, and R. Vanneman. 1987. "Race and Gender in Occupational Segregation." Pp. 13–70 in *Pay Equity: An Issue of Race, Ethnicity, and Sex.* Washington, DC: National Committee on Pay Equity.

Ehrenreich, B. and J. Ehrenreich. 1979. "The Professional-Managerial Class." Pp. 5–45 in *Between Labor and Capital,* edited by P. Walker. Boston: South End Press.

Grant, L., K. B. Ward, and X. L. Rong. 1987. "Is There an Association Between Gender and Methods in Sociological Research?" *American Sociological Review* 52:856–62.

Harkess, S. 1985. "Women's Occupational Experience in the 1970's: Sociology and Economics." *Signs: Journal of Women in Culture and Society* 10:495–516.

Herman, J. 1981. *Father-Daughter Incest.* Cambridge: MA: Harvard University Press.

Hertz, R. 1986. *More Equal Than Others: Women and Men in Dual-Career Marriages.* Berkeley: University of California Press.

Higginbotham, E. 1987. "Employment for Professional Black Women in the Twentieth Century." Pp. 73–91 in *Ingredients for Women's Employment Policy,* edited by C. Bose and G. Spitze. Albany: SUNY Press.

Lorber, J. 1981. "On *The Reproduction of Mothering:* A Debate." *Signs: Journal of Women in Culture and Society* 6:482–86.

National Committee on Pay Equity. 1987. *Pay Equity: An Issue of Race, Ethnicity and Sex.* Washington, DC: National Committee on Pay Equity.

Poulantzas, N. 1974. *Classes in Contemporary Capitalism.* London: New Left Books.

Roberts, H. 1981. *Doing Feminist Research.* Boston: Routledge & Kegan Paul.

Ryan, J. and C. Sackrey. 1984. *Strangers in Paradise: Academics from the Working Class.* Boston: South End Press.

Slevin, K. F. and C. R. Wingrove. 1983. "Similarities and Differences Among Three Generations of Women in Attitudes Toward the Female Role in Contemporary Society." *Sex Roles* 9:609–24.

Stacey, J. and B. Thorne. 1985. "The Missing Feminist Revolution in Sociology." *Social Problems* 32: 301–16.

U.S. Bureau of the Census. 1983. "Detailed Population Characteristics: Tennessee." *U.S. Census of the Population, 1980.* Washington, DC: U.S. Government Printing Office.

Vanneman, R. and L. Weber Cannon. 1987. *The American Perception of Class.* Philadelphia: Temple University Press.

Ward, K. B. and L. Grant. 1985. "The Feminist Critique and a Decade of Published Research in Sociology Journals." *Sociological Quarterly* 26:139–57.

Wilson, W. J. 1978. *The Declining Significance of Race.* Chicago: University of Chicago Press.

Zinn, M. Baca. 1979. "Field Research in Minority Communities: Ethical, Methodological, and Political Observations by an Insider." *Social Problems* 27:209–19.

———, L. W. Cannon, E. Higginbotham, and B. Dill. 1986. "The Cost of Exclusionary Practices in Women's Studies." *Signs: Journal of Women and Culture in Society* 11:290–303.

Questions for Thought

1. Compare and contrast the specific "less labor intensive" and "more labor intensive" methods that Weber and her colleagues used to recruit participants.

2. Explain how race and social class affected the success of specific recruitment methods used in this study.

3. Black women were less likely than White women to volunteer for this study. Describe three important obstacles to participating in this research experienced by Black women.

4. Imagine a researcher who finds that Mexican American high school students receive less encouragement from their families to attend college than do their Anglo American high school classmates. The researcher concludes that Mexican American culture does not place a strong value on higher education. Based on what you've learned from this article, evaluate this research conclusion. What alternative interpretation should be considered?

5. A researcher wants to study young mothers who abandon their unwanted newborn babies. She decides to restrict her sample to White teenage girls. How might the researcher justify her decision to use an all-White sample? What problems or bias might this decision create?